LOCAL HISTORIES/GLOBAL DESIGNS

EDITORS

Sherry B. Ortner, Nicholas B. Dirks, Geoff Eley

A LIST OF TITLES

IN THIS SERIES APPEARS

AT THE BACK OF

THE BOOK

PRINCETON STUDIES IN
CULTURE / POWER / HISTORY

LOCAL HISTORIES/GLOBAL DESIGNS

COLONIALITY, SUBALTERN KNOWLEDGES, AND BORDER THINKING

Walter D. Mignolo

PRINCETON UNIVERSITY PRESS

PRINCETON, NEW JERSEY

Library of Congress Cataloging-in-Publication Data
Mignolo, Walter.
Local histories/global designs : coloniality, subaltern
knowledges, and border thinking / Walter D. Mignolo.
p. cm. — (Princeton studies in culture/power/history)
Includes bibliographical references and index.
ISBN 0-691-00139-1 (alk. paper). — ISBN 0-691-00140-5 (pb : alk. paper)
1. Colonies. 2. Postcolonialism. 3. Culture. 4. Knowledge.
Theory of—Political aspects. 5. Hermeneutics. I. Title. II. Series.
JV51.M54 1999
901—dc21 99-32342

This book has been composed in Berkeley Ten

The paper used in this publication meets the minimum requirements
of ANSI/NISO Z39.48-1992 (R1997) (*Permanence of Paper*)

http://pup.princeton.edu

7   9   10   8   6
Printed in the United States of America

ISBN-13: 978-0-691-00140-1 (pbk.)

ISBN-10: 0-691-00140-5 (pbk.)

To Andrea and Alexander

FOR ALL THE CONVERSATIONS BETWEEN

HIGH SCHOOL AND COLLEGE, MANY OF THEM RELATED TO THE TOPIC

OF THIS BOOK WHEN IT WAS STILL IN PROGRESS

To Anne

FOR MAKING THOSE CONVERSATIONS POSSIBLE, AND FOR HER

PATIENCE AND UNDERSTANDING

Contents

Preface and Acknowledgments

THE MAIN topic of this book is the colonial difference in the formation and transformation of the modern/colonial world system. Immanuel Wallerstein's (1974, 1980, 1989) seminal and controversial study is my starting point and the colonial difference my departing point. A corollary and consequence of it constitute the second topic, the emergence of the Americas and their historical location and transformation in the modern/colonial world order, from 1500 to the end of the twentieth century. The modern world system was described and theorized from inside itself, and the variety of colonial experiences and histories were attached to it and look at if from inside the system. However, it has an advantage over the chronology of the early modern, modern, and late modern periods I adopted in *The Darker Side of the Renaissance* (Mignolo 1995a, 2). And the advantage is the spatial dimension imbedded in the modern world system that is lacking in the linear conception of modern Western history. The spatial dimension of the system shows its external borders where the colonial difference was and still is played out. Until the middle of the twentieth century the colonial difference honored the classical distinction between centers and peripheries. In the second half of the twentieth century the emergence of global colonialism, managed by transnational corporations, erased the distinction that was valid for early forms of colonialism and the coloniality of power. Yesterday the colonial difference was out there, away from the center. Today it is all over, in the peripheries of the center and in the centers of the periphery.

The colonial difference is the space where coloniality of power is enacted. It is also the space where the restitution of subaltern knowledge is taking place and where border thinking is emerging. The colonial difference is the space where *local* histories inventing and implementing global designs meet *local* histories, the space in which global designs have to be adapted, adopted, rejected, integrated, or ignored. The colonial difference is, finally, the physical as well as imaginary location where the coloniality of power is at work in the confrontation of two kinds of local histories displayed in different spaces and times across the planet. If Western cosmology is the historically unavoidable reference point, the multiple confrontations of two kinds of local histories defy dichotomies. Christian and Native American cosmologies, Christian and Amerindian cosmologies, Christian and Islamic cosmologies, and Christian and Confucian cosmologies among others only enact dichotomies when you look at them one at a time, not when you compare them in the geohistorical confines of the modern/colonial world system. The colonial difference in/of the modern/colonial world is also the

place where "Occidentalism," as the overarching imaginary of the modern/
colonial world, was articulated. Orientalism later and area studies more recently are complementary aspects of such overarching imaginary. The end
of the cold war and, consequently, the demise of area studies correspond to
the moment in which a new form of colonialism, a global colonialism, keeps
on reproducing the colonial difference on a world scale, although without
being located in one particular nation-state. Global colonialism reveals the
colonial difference on a world scale when "Occidentalism" meets the East
that was precisely its very condition of possibility—in the same way that,
paradoxically, Occidentalism in the eighteenth and nineteenth centuries was
the condition of possibility of Orientalism.

Border thinking (or "border gnosis" as I explain soon) is a logical consequence of the colonial difference. It could be traced back to the initial moment of Spanish colonialism in the Andes and Mesoamerica. In the Andes,
the by now classic critical narrative in images by Amerindian Guaman Poma
(Waman Puma), *Nueva corónica y buen gobierno*, at the end of the sixteenth
and the beginning of the seventeenth century (Murra and Adorno 1980), is
an outstanding exemplar. As I already analyzed in *The Darker Side of the
Renaissance* (1995a, 247–56; 303–11), the fractured locus of enunciation
from a subaltern perspective defines border thinking as a response to the
colonial difference. "Nepantla," a word coined by Nahuatl speaker in the
second half of the sixteenth century, is another exemplar. "To be or feel in
between," as the word could be translated into English, was possible in the
mouth of an Amerindian, not of a Spaniard (see Mignolo 1995b). The colonial difference creates the conditions for dialogic situations in which a fractured enunciation is enacted from the subaltern perspective as a response to
the hegemonic discourse and perspective. Thus, border thinking is more
than a hybrid enunciation. It is a fractured enunciation in dialogic situations
with the territorial and hegemonic cosmology (e.g., ideology, perspective).
In the sixteenth century, border thinking remained under the control of
hegemonic colonial discourses. That is why Waman Puma's narrative remained unpublished until 1936 whereas hegemonic colonial discourses
(even when such discourses were critical of the Spanish hegemony, like Bar-
tolome de las Casas) were published, translated, and highly distributed, taking advantage of the emerging printing press. At the end of the twentieth
century, border thinking can no longer be controlled and it offers new critical horizons to the limitations of critical discourses within hegemonic cosmologies (such as Marxism, deconstruction, world system analysis, or postmodern theories).

The decision to frame my argument in the modern/colonial world model
rather than in the linear chronology ascending from the early modern to the
modern to the late modern was prompted by the need to think beyond the
linearity in the geohistorical mapping of Western modernity. The geohistori-

cal density of the modern/colonial world system, its interior (conflicts between empires) and exterior (conflicts between cosmologies) borders, cannot be perceived and theorized from a perspective inside modernity itself
(as is the case for world system analysis, deconstruction, and different postmodern perspectives). On the other hand, the current and available production under the name of "postcolonial" studies or theories or criticism starts
from the eighteenth century leaving aside a crucial and constitutive moment
of modernity/coloniality that was the sixteenth century.

The main research for this book consisted in conversations—conversations of several kinds, with students in and out of class, with colleagues
and students in Latin America and the United States, with undergraduate
students, with colleagues and graduate students at Duke and outside of
Duke, and with all sorts of people outside academia, from taxi drivers to
medical doctors, from female servants in Bolivia to small-industry executives, and all those who have something to say about their experiences of
local histories and their perception of global designs. These were not "interviews," just conversations, casual conversations. Although I did not plan it
as a book from the beginning, I did plan writing articles on a set of issues
that, as I have explained in the introduction, emerged around 1992. Conversation as research method was decided on during the spring semester of
1994. I had finished the manuscript of *The Darker Side of the Renaissance* in
the summer of 1993 and I was not ready to start another long and involved
research project, nor did I have a clear idea of what I wanted to do next.
Furthermore, I was appointed chair of Romance Studies, and we all know
that administrative duties are not conducive to research projects.

Thus, I decided that for the next three to four years I would devote myself
to conversations and writing about issues on coloniality and globalization,
projecting the sixteenth century, or the early global period, to the nineteenth
and the twentieth century. By conversations I do not mean statements that
can be recorded, transcribed, and used as documents. Most of the time the
most influential conversations were people's comments, in passing, about
an event, a book, an idea, a person. These are documents that cannot be
transcribed, knowledge that comes and goes, but remains with you and introduces changes in a given argument. Conversations allowed me to pursue
two parallel tasks: to entertain a dialogue with intellectuals in Latin America,
particularly in the Andes and Mexico; and to tie research agendas with teaching goals, since what you will read was previously delivered and discussed
in graduate seminars at Duke and in Latin America, and in undergraduate
seminars at Duke. The book is the journey of these conversations, and my
acknowledgment goes mainly to the people who guided my thinking with
their wisdom, although I cannot quote what they said, and perhaps they do
not even remember it. An anonymous rumor is what constitutes the "data"
of this book beyond, of course, the bibliography I cite at the end. But it is

also an indirect conversation with Immanuel Wallerstein and Samuel Huntington. In the first case, I deal with his concepts of modern world system (1974) and its geopolitics and geoculture (1991a), in the second case, with Samuel Huntington (1996) and his concepts of civilization, the clash of civilization (to which border thinking is a way out) and, above all, of "Latin American civilization." I contest on the bases of the spatial history of the modern/colonial world and of the Latin American/U.S. relations since 1848 and 1898. In short, my conversation with them is from the perspective of the humanities in dialogue with the social sciences. Indirectly, this book has been written under the conviction that the humanities lost their ground after World War II and did not respond to the increasing influence of the social and natural sciences. "Cultural studies" filled that gap dispersed in several posts and ethnic and gender studies. The "Sokal affair," in *Social Text*, was possible precisely because of the absence of a strong philosophy holding together the humanities in "confrontation" with the natural and the (hard) social sciences. If the Kantian university was based on *reason*, the Humboldtian university was based on *culture* and the neoliberal university on *excellence* and *expertise*, a future (or posthistorical; Readings 1996, 119–34) university shall be envisioned in which the humanities will be rearticulated on *a critique of knowledge and cultural practices*. It is from this perspective, from the perspective of the humanities, that I enter into indirect dialogue with the social sciences through Wallerstein and Huntington. But I am also pursuing this dialogue from the perspective of Latin American thought, as I introduce it here through Anibal Quijano, Enrique Dussel, Silvia Rivera-Cusicanqui, Salazar Bondy, Rodolfo Kusch, and Nelly Richard, among others. This dialogue also results last but not least, from the Latino/a/American contributions in the United States, such as those by Gloria Anzaldúa, Norma Alarcón, Frances Aparicio, José Saldívar, David Montejano, Rosaura Sánchez, José Limón, and Gustavo Pérez-Firmat, among others. It is finally from the double perspective of the structure of knowledge (humanities and social sciences) and of the sensibilities of particular geohistorical locations in the formation and transformation of the modern/colonial world that I engage (in) this dialogue.

The first experience in this direction was a two-week seminar I taught at the Institute for Social Research at the Universidad de Puebla, Mexico, in the summer of 1994. The topic was the "postcolonial reason," an embryo of what is now chapter 2. Raúl Dorra, Luisa Moreno, and Marisa Filinich, who were running a workshop within the Institute for Social Research, invited me. My first thanks go to them and to Alonso Vélez Pliego, director of the institute. Enrique Dussel gave one of the seminar lectures on colonization and the world system, one of the first versions of an article that has recently been published under the title "Beyond Eurocentrism: The World System and the Limits of Modernity" (Dussel 1998a). Not only have we remained in touch since that encounter but my own reflections—as the reader will soon see—became very much framed by Dussel's on the articulation of modernity, coloniality, and the world system.

The piece that initiated the mediations that ended up in this book was "The Postcolonial Reason: Colonial Legacies and Postcolonial Theories," first prepared for the conference on "Cultures and Globalization," organized by Fred Jameson, Masao Miyhosi, et al., which took place, at Duke University in November 1994. Rewritten in Spanish, the article was published in Brazil (Mignolo 1996a), in Germany (Mignolo 1997c), and in Venezuela (Mignolo 1998). I mention these reprints for one reason, which is related to the subalternization of knowledge. If you publish in English, there is less need for reprinting because of the wider circulation. If you publish in Spanish, normally publications do not go beyond the local circuit. Rewritten again in English, this piece became "The Post-Occidential Reason" and is now chapter 2 of this book.

The seminar in Puebla was the first of a long list of talks and seminars I gave in Latin America (Argentina, Brazil, Bolivia, Colombia). The list of people I should thank here is too large and I will limit myself to thank, first, the participants in all those seminars, graduate students and colleagues. Second, I would like to thank personally those who invited me and with whom I engaged in longer and more sustained conversations. In Argentina, Enrique Tandeter and Noé Jitrik, at the Universidad Nacional de Buenos Aires; Laura and Mónica Scarano and Lisa Bradford, at the Universidad de Mar del Plata; Mirta Antonelli, at the Universidad de Córdoba; and David Lagmanovich, and Carmen Pirilli, at the Universidad de Tucumán. In Bolivia, I am in great debt to Javier Sanjinés for introducing me to many great Bolivian thinkers for whom coloniality, far from being a question of the past, is alive and well in the Andes today. In Bolivia also Juan Carlos Mariacca and Ricardo Kaliman invited me to the first Jornadas de Literatura Latinoamericana (in 1993) and to lecture at the Facultad de Humanidades of the Universidad de San Andrés. This visit to La Paz indeed oriented a great deal of this book. In Colombia Carlos Rincón and Hugo Niño allowed me to have personal experiences and conversations with colleagues and graduate students in Bogotá and Cartagena de Indias. In Brazil I am in debt to Jorge Schwartz and Ligia Chiapini for inviting me on a couple of occasions to participate in workshops and lectures at the center Angel Rama and at the Institute for Advanced Studies, at the University of São Paolo; to Ana Lucia Gazolla, who organized a "tour" through Rio de Janeiro, Bahia, Minas Gerais, and São Paolo, in May 1995; to Juan Carlos Olea and to Rebecca Barriga for asking me to teach a seminar at El Colegio de México in May 1997.

From all these seminars with colleagues and graduate students I learned, first and foremost, to gauge local histories with global designs: to weigh local histories and interests in Latin America and the United States—to continue reflecting on my own personal location as a Latin American (Hispanic) and Latin Americanist in the United States (Mignolo 1991); to measure the extent to which the end of the cold war was transforming "Latin American Studies," a scholarly project engrained in global designs (e.g., area studies); to ponder how "Latin American thoughts" (a philosophical enterprise whose main concern was to define and relocate an identity that was being allocated by the new colonial empires, parallel to [Latin] American nation building) were also changing with the end of the cold war. Consequently, I also learned how the disciplines in the "human sciences" can no longer remain as the intellectual arbiter of global designs detached from local histories. And, finally, I learned how much globalization was creating the condition for building from knowledges suppressed from local histories; how much such building, facing the unavoidable spread of modern and Western epistemology, had to work on the border in order to be successful, since a divisive frontier and the affirmation of "authenticity" would contribute to the suppression of knowledge in the internal and external frontiers of the modern world system.

What I also learned through this experience was the suspicion, mainly in the Southern Cone and in Colombia, about coloniality and postcoloniality. The fact that the independence of most Latin American countries was achieved at the beginning of the nineteenth century meant that the focus of discussion became modernity, and not coloniality; postmodernity, and not postcoloniality. I make an effort, in the book, to understand why things are as they are and to distinguish the "colonial period" (an expression that refers to Spanish and Portuguese colonization, mainly) from the "coloniality of power" that is well and alive today in its new guise of "global coloniality." I also picked up the suspicion, in several places, that cultural studies and postcoloniality were imperial fashion being imported to Latin America. This suspicion talks directly to the question of Latin American studies and Latin American thoughts during the cold war that I just mentioned. What drew my attention, however, was that the suspicions were expressed by the same people, sometimes by their followers, who in the 1970s were the enthusiastic supporters and mediators in introducing Derrida, Lacan, Foucault, the Frankfurt School, Raymond Williams, et al. This seemed to me a very revealing case for understanding the coloniality of power and knowledge in Latin America, where Europe still holds its hegemonic epistemological position, while the United States, particularly since 1898, became more of the "imperial other." I was surprised again in Brazil, in contrast with my experience in Latin American countries, when I found a critical but also more generous propensity to receive and evaluate "foreign" theories, be they from Europe or from the United States. Perhaps the towering figure of Milton Santos had something to do with the kind of conversations I was engaged in. It was not by chance that the name of architect, environmentalist, and theoretician of globalization Milton Santos was brought to my attention in Bahia, after one of my lectures. His views as well as those of other participants in conferences and books edited by him have been influential in chapters 3 and 7.

At Duke, the main conversations that were decisive in shaping the book occurred around graduate and undergraduate seminars, and two international and interdisciplinary workshops, "Globalization and Culture" (November 1994) and "Relocation of Languages and Cultures" (May 1997). The workshop, organized by Fredric Jameson and Masao Miyoshi, with the collaboration of Ariel Dorfman, Alberto Moreiras, and myself, was very influential in the overall conception of the book. Chapter 7 is the version of a paper I read at that conference; and an early version of chapter 2 appeared in the "Workshop Reader," in a mimeograph version. The second workshop, organized by myself with the participation of a large steering committee composed of colleagues and graduate and undergraduate students, was equally important for all I have to say in this book, about language, transnationalism, and globalization (chapters 5, 6, and 7). The colleagues and graduate and undergraduate students with whom I discussed the issues related to the conference topics are Miriam Cooke, Leo Ching, Eric Zakim, Mohadev Apte, Catherine Ewin, Teresa Vilarós, Lynn James, Helmi Balig, Alejandra Vidal, Gregory P. Meyjes, Jean Jonassaint, Chris Chia, Ifeoma Nwankwo, Meredith Parker, Benjamin B. Au, and Roberto González. Chapter 5 is a developed version of an article I wrote before, which was the platform of the second workshop.

Two parallel teaching experiences occurred between the fall semester of 1994 and the spring semester of 1997. First, Bruce Lawrence, who was the director of "Globalization and Cultural Changes," one of the units of *Focus* (an interdisciplinary program for first-semester freshmen at Duke), passed the torch on to me. I directed and taught in the program from 1994 to 1997. Since each *Focus* unit is composed of four seminars, and therefore, four professors, a graduate student assistant, and a graduate student in charge of English composition, and since the program is built on a constant flow of interactive conversations between students and instructors, I have enormously benefited from this experience–not only because I gained more "knowledge" but mainly because it was a learning experience to discuss issues on globalization with students coming right from high school. My recognition and thanks then go to colleagues and graduate students participating in this experience: Bruce Lawrence, Marcy Little, Miriam Cooke, Bai Gao, Orin Starn, Michael Hardt, Sybille Fischer, Silvia Tendeciarz, Freya Schiwy, and Pramod Mishra.

In 1994, Miriam Cooke and I forged a three-year seminar on colonial legacies and postcolonial theorizing. Miriam was in charge mainly of North Africa and the Middle East and I was in charge of Latin America, including the Caribbean and the Latino/a question in the United States. Beyond that geohistorical configuration, we decided to focus the first seminar on language, the second on space, and the third on memory. Unfortunately, Miriam was on sabbatical and I had to teach the second seminar, on space, by myself. However, the experience of conceiving mentally the seminar and coteaching two of them, not only taught me a lot about areas of the world of which I knew little, but it established a fruitful dialogue whose consequences are evident throughout the book. I am indebted to Miriam Cooke again for organizing and inviting me to a workshop on Mediterranean studies, in Tunisia, where I had the chance, over three days, to listen to the presentations of Tunisian intellectuals and to converse with them outside the conference room.

After finishing the three-year seminar, I cotaught, in the fall semester of 1997 and the spring semester of 1998, an undergraduate and a graduate seminar with Irene Silverblatt on modernity, coloniality, and Latin America. Beyond all the beauties of these seminars, to which the students largely contributed, the most striking experience for me was the difference in how you address undergraduate (juniors and seniors, mainly) and graduate students on the same topic, because the seminar was exactly the same but at different levels. Both seminars, in addition, were part of the program in Latin American cultural studies.

Finally, in the spring semester of 1998, Enrique Dussel and I cotaught a seminar on alternative forms of rationality. This seminar, together with long conversations before classes and in different conversational settings, was indeed a crucial experience for the formulation of "border thinking" in this book, as well as for restating my previous debts and differences with Dussel's enormous intellectual contributions to several of the issues discussed in this book. This seminar was decisive for the changes I introduced in chapter 3, which had been previously published as an article (Mignolo 1995c). Elizabeth Mudimbe-Boyi (who unfortunately left Duke in the fall of 1994) and then Jean Jonassaint brought la Francophonie close to home and to my own interests. Jonassaint brought it literally close by bringing key figures from the Francophone and Caribbean intelligentsia to Duke over the past three years.

Through all these years, the active participation of graduate students was indeed as beneficial as the dialogue with my own colleagues. I cannot mention the names of all the graduate students taking these four seminars, but I would like to thank them collectively. I would like to mention, however, the names of those students whose dissertations were closely related to some of the issues discussed in this book and that have influenced my own perspectives. Chronologically, Juan Poblete showed me a new panorama on the politics of language and literature in nineteenth-century Chile. From Verónica Feliú I learned to further evaluate the difficulties in writing "from" here "about people" down there, particularly because Veronica, who *partici-*

pated in the political performance by women in Chile at the end of the 1980s, wrote a dissertation *about* it in the middle of the 1990s. José Muñoz, who was already at the end of his graduate student years when I came to Duke, brought to me a new perspective on identity politics with his reflections on ethnic and sexual disidentification. Ifeoma Nwankwo brought in her perspective as a Jamaican in the United States and taught me to think about the differences between Afro-Caribbeans and Afro-Americans. Chris Chia showed me how important Gloria Anzaldúa was for a Chinese graduate student who came to Duke in the early 1990s; and how to write about North American cultural history from an "outsider" perspective. From Zilkia Janer I learned to think in more detail about the national colonialism in Puerto Rico and from Lucía Suárez to conceive interlanguage connections among Caribbean women writers, in English, French, and Spanish. With Pramod Mishra I have entertained long conversations on his view on southern U.S. culture and literature mixed with his autobiographical stories from Nepal and India. I owe much to Shireen Lewis for writing a dissertation on "Negritude," "Antillanité," and "Creolité," which displayed a panorama of almost a century of Afro and Afro-Caribbean intellectual production, and so thanks are due for the conversations we had during the process. Fernando Gómez made me think about the difference between writing "utopias" in Europe and Franciscans "planning" utopias in the New World. Finally, I am thankful to Marc Brudzinski and Doris Garroway for organizing a wonderful conference on postcoloniality and the Caribbean. This conference showed in its own development that the Caribbean, far from being a repeating island, is a complex historical configuration of competing colonialisms in the movable structure of the modern/colonial world system.

Outside of Duke two conversational experiences were prominent in the final shape of the book. One entails the discussions within the Latin American Subaltern Studies Group, which I joined in February 1994. Chapter 4 is a direct illustration of my debt to the group. The second I owe to Kelvin Santiago and Agustin Lao for graciously inviting me to join the working group on the coloniality of power. Discussions and conversations with members of the group occurred in the past year, and have very much impinged on the final version of the manuscript. Regarding individuals outside of Duke, I continue to thank, for what they write and what they say, Norma Alarcón, Frances Aparicio, Fernando Coronil, and José Saldívar. I thank Roberto Fernández-Retamar first for his intellectual generosity; for being the only Spanish-American intellectual I know for whom the Haitian Revolution was a crucial event in the shaping of Caribbean and Latin American modernity/coloniality; also for making it possible for me to continue our conversations in Cuba, in January 1998; and for making it possible for me to entertain conversations with other Cuban intellectuals. My personal acquaintance with Michel-Rolph Trouillot came late, in March 1998, although his work on the Haitian Revolution was already part of my own reflections. However, I had three occasions of listening and talking to him since then and the final corrections of this manuscript. In these conversations I perceived connections between his project and mine that I was not aware of by just reading his work, chiefly his latest book, *Silencing the Past* (1995). I kept them constantly in mind while making the final corrections. Eduardo Mendieta and Santiago Castro-Gómez entered also in the domain of conversations in the past two years, but both have contributed with their training in philosophy to a discussion that was mainly—with the exception of Enrique Dussel—between literary and cultural critics, anthropologists, historians (including historians of religions), and sociologists. Ramón Grosfogel taught me how to look at dependency theory in the context of the world system and to rethink Puerto Rico in the colonial horizon of modernity.

Last but not least, I owe much also to colleagues and friends at Duke whom I have not mentioned yet: Ariel Dorfman for many reasons but mainly for writing *Heading South, Looking North* (1998) and for telling me, before it was finished, stories about his bilingual experience. My thanks go to Gustávo Pérez-Firmat for writing *Next Year in Cuba* (1995) and for constantly expressing his doubts about what I write about. In chapters 5 and 6 I deal, in argumentative style, with problems that Dorfman and Pérez-Firmat framed in seductive and powerful narratives. Discussions in the Marxist Working Group, lead by Fred Jameson and Michael Hardt, have also been instrumental to understand and to work out the question of Marxism in the Americas and the compatibilities and incompatibilities between North and South Marxism. In this book, I pursued this issue through José Arico's reflections on Marxism and Latin America.

I am also indebted to Gabriela Nouzeilles and Alberto Moreiras for our long and recursive conversations that, among other things, ended up in the publication project and soon to be published journal *Nepantla: Views from South*; to Teresa Vilarós for bringing a plurilingual and plurinational Spain to Duke; to Cathy Davidson for opening up the conversation between "(North) American" and "Latin American Studies"; to Karla Holloway and Rick Powell for opening up a new perspective on Afro-American issues in this country, and to Rick particularly for his effort to show the connections of black North American with black Latin American art; and to Andrea Giunta, in the same vein, for making me aware of the links between development ideologies, dependency theory, on the one hand, and art production, museums, and international exhibits sponsored by private institutions in Latin America after the 1960s, on the other. I also wish to thank Leo Ching, who guided me through some basic readings about colonialism and Japan's entry into contact with the modern/colonial world system; John Richards, for making me part of one of his obsessions, expressed through working and reading groups, on the current meaning and possibilities of world and/or universal history; Sucheta Mazundar, who brought China into contact with the Americas for me; Eric Zakim, who participated in one of the seminars I cotaught with Miriam Cooke and connected, in the seminar as well as in his published works, the Jewish with the (post) colonial question; and Jean Sullivan-Beals, for her support and for helping to put together the first draft of the manuscript, and Avital Rosenberg, for her patience in putting together the final version.

Pramod Mishra reappeared in the last stage of the book, reading the last version of the manuscript and contributing his expertise as a writer, his colonial experiences from Nepal, and his skill as instructor of English composition. Valentin Mudimbe and Nick Dirks were kind enough to make me believe that the manuscript was promising when they saw the first version. Finally my thanks go to Mary Murrell, at Princeton University Press, for her enthusiasm and professionalism.

LOCAL HISTORIES/GLOBAL DESIGNS

On Gnosis and the Imaginary of the Modern/Colonial World System

I

In the sixteenth century, Spanish missionaries judged and ranked human intelligence and civilization by whether the people were in possession of alphabetic writing. This was an initial moment in the configuration of the colonial difference and the building of the Atlantic imaginary, which will become the imaginary of the modern/colonial world. *Translation* was the special tool to absorb the colonial difference previously established. *Border thinking*, as we shall see, works toward the restitution of the colonial difference that colonial translation (unidirectional, as today's globalization) attempted to erase. In the sixteenth century, the colonial difference was located in space. Toward the end of the eighteenth and the beginning of the nineteenth century, the measuring stick was history and no longer writing. "People without history" were located in a time "before" the "present." People with history could write the history of those people without. At the beginning of the twentieth century, Max Weber transformed this lack (of alphabetic writing, of history) into a celebration of the possession of true knowledge, an Occidental achievement of universal value. I have had this overall picture in mind during the process of writing this book, as I was conceiving subaltern knowledges and border thinking as the response to Weber from the end of the twentieth century. Weber never mentioned colonialism, was unaware of the colonial difference and did not reflect on the fact that he was providing such a celebratory picture at the highest moment of European expansion and capital accumulation in the history of the modern/colonial world system. I would like to remind the reader of the initial sentences of the introduction to Weber's *Protestant Ethics and the Spirit of Capitalism* ([1904] 1992) that provoked the reflections evolving into the book the reader has in her hands:

> A product of modern European civilization, studying any problem of universal history, is bound to ask himself to what combination of circumstances the fact should be attributed that in Western civilization, and in Western civilization only, cultural phenomena have appeared which (as we like to think) lie in a line of development having *universal* significance and value.

Only in the West does science exist at a stage of development which we recognize to-day as valid. . . . In short, knowledge and observation of great refinement have existed elsewhere, above all in India, China, Babylonia, Egypt. But in Babylonia and elsewhere astronomy lacked—which makes its development all the more astounding—the mathematical foundation which it first received from the Greeks. The Indian geometry had no rational proof. . . . The Indian natural sciences . . . lacked the method of experiment. (Weber [1904] 1992, 13)

Weber was blind to the colonial difference and to the subalternization of knowledge built into it. It is difficult to imagine at the end of the twentieth century a book or a master thought that would continue the tradition of Spanish missionaries in the sixteenth century, French and German philosophers after the Enlightenment, and European social scientists at the beginning of the twentieth century. Sociologist and political scientist Samuel Huntington has recognized that people from "other" civilizations and with "other" forms of knowledge are claiming a *gnoseology* that they have been taught to despise (this is the particular topic of chapter 7). Weber provoked in me a reflection on coloniality and epistemology, although I had no intention, initially, of writing such a book as this on the topic. This book, however, is not just a collection of articles, even though part of the material in each chapter has already been published. Each chapter has been substantially rewritten in view of the overall argument. Looking back, the seed of the book was actually planted in a debate published by *Latin American Research Review* in 1993, on colonial discourse, postcoloniality, and Latin America, prompted by a review article authored by historian Patricia Seed (Seed 1991). I closed my response to the article with a long paragraph I would like to repeat here, this time in thematic parallel with Weber's assertion:

When Barbadian poet Edward Kamau Brathwaite recounts the story of his search for a rhythm that would match his living experience in the Caribbean, he highlights the moment when skipping a pebble on the ocean gave him a rhythm that he could not find by reading John Milton. Brathwaite also highlights a second and subsequent moment when he perceived the parallels between the skipping of the pebble and Calypso music, a rhythm that he could not find in listening to Beethoven.[1] If Brathwaite found a voice and a form of knowledge at the intersection of the classical models he learned in a colonial school with his life experience in the Caribbean and consciousness of African people's history, his poetry is less a discourse of resistance than a discourse claiming its centrality. Similar claims could be found indirectly in the writings of Jamaican novelist and essayist Michelle Cliff, who states that one effect of British West Indian colonial discourse is "that you believe absolutely in the hegemony of the King's

---

[1] I am referring here to Brathwaite (1992). His general position regarding poetic practices in colonial situations has been articulated in Brathwaite (1983, 1984).

English and the form in which it is meant to be expressed. Or else your writing is not literature; it is folklore and can never be art. . . . The anglican ideal— Milton, Wordsworth, Keats—was held before us with an assurance that we were unable, and would never be enabled, to compose a work of similar correctness. . . . No reggae spoken here" (Cliff 1985). While Thiong'o, Lamming, and Brathwaite simultaneously construct and theorize about alternative centers of enunciation in what have been considered the margins of colonial empires, Latinos and Black Americans in the United States are demonstrating that either the margins are also in the center or (as Thiong'o expresses it) that knowledge and aesthetic norms are not universally established by a transcendent subject but are universally established by historical subjects in diverse cultural centers. Chicano writer Gloria Anzaldúa, for instance, has articulated a powerful alternative aesthetic and political hermeneutic by placing herself at the cross-road of three traditions (Spanish-American, Nahuatl, and Anglo-American) and by creating a locus of enunciation where different ways of knowing and individual and collective expressions mingle (Anzaldúa 1987). . . . My concern is to underscore the point that "colonial and postcolonial discourse" is not just a new field of study or a gold mine for extracting new riches but the condition of possibility for constructing new loci of enunciation as well as for reflecting that academic "knowledge and understanding" should be complemented with "learning from" those who are living in and thinking from colonial and postcolonial legacies, from Rigoberta Menchú to Angel Rama. Otherwise, we run the risk of promoting mimicry, exportation of theories, and internal (cultural) colonialism rather than promoting new forms of cultural critique and intellectual and political emancipations—of making colonial and postcolonial studies a field of study instead of a liminal and critical locus of enunciation. The "native point of view" also includes intellectuals. In the apportionment of scientific labor since World War II, which has been described well by Carl Pletsch (1981), the Third World produces not only "cultures" to be studied by anthropologists and ethnohistorians but also intellectuals who generate theories and reflect on their own culture and history. (Mignolo 1993a, 129–31)

The situation is no different for natural scientists in Africa or Latin America, since intellectual achievements need material conditions, and satisfactory material conditions are related to the coloniality of power. "Thinking from" was an expression and an idea that kept on haunting me, and I discussed it in seminars and attempted to develop it in some of my published articles after that date (see, for instance, Mignolo 1994; 1996a). "Border thinking" was the second expression that began to gain a life of its own. Although "border" is an overused word (e.g., border writing, border culture, border matters), none of the discussions I read using the word dealt with knowledge and understanding, epistemology and hermeneutics, those two sides of the intellectual frontiers of European modernity. My own idea of "border thinking," which I modeled on the Chicano/a experience, also owes much to the idea of "African *gnosis*" as it has been introduced by Valentin Mudimbe in his study on the invention of Africa (Mudimbe 1988). Border thinking, as I conceive it here, is unthinkable without understanding the colonial difference. Furthermore, it is the recognition of the colonial difference from subaltern perspectives that demands border thinking.

But let me add a few additional elements to explain what I have in mind and what this book is all about. Compare my initial quotation from Weber with the following quotation by Tu Wei-ming [1985] 1996):

> Historically, the emergence of individualism as a motivating force in Western society may have been intertwined with highly particularized political, economic, ethical, and religious traditions. It seems reasonable that one can endorse an insight into the self as a basis for equality and liberty without accepting Locke's idea of private property, Adam Smith's and Hobbes' idea of private interest, John Stuart Mill's idea of privacy, Kierkegaard's idea of loneliness, or the early Sartre's idea of freedom. ([1985] 1996, 78)

Now, Tu Wei-ming's is not just another contribution along the lines of Fritjof Capra's *Tao of Physics* (1975). *Tao of Physics* was and still is an important argument to show that the differences between "modern physics" and "Eastern mysticism" are historical and "superficial" rather than ontological. Beyond both of them we find a human capacity for logical articulation and sophisticated thinking, which failed to underline the colonial difference implied in the very naming of them. "Modern physics" retained in Capra's book the hegemonic weight of Western sciences, whereas "Eastern mysticism" retained the exotic connotations constructed by several centuries of Occidentalism. Tu Wei-ming defines himself as a Confucian practitioner, while Capra is a believer in the universality (nonhistorical) of the Western concept of reason. And what Tu Wei-ming is contributing to it is precisely to redress the balance between equal epistemological potentials that have been subordinated to each other by the coloniality of power and the articulation of the colonial epistemic difference.

The two last sentences of Tu Wei-ming's introduction to his classic *Confucian Thoughts* (1985) reveal in an elegant way the epistemological limits of Western thought and its epistemological potential, as sustainable knowledge and not as a relic of the past to be "studied" and "fixed" from the perspective of Western disciplines. As sustainable knowledge, the epistemological potential of Confucian legacy dwells in the possibility of showing the limits of modern epistemology, in both its disciplinary and its area studies dimension. As such, there is no longer the possibility of looking at "translation" or "information" from "other cultures," by which it is implied that "other cultures" are not scientific and are knowable from the scientific approaches of Western epistemology. Tu Wei-ming is clear, in the preceding passage, in implying that a post-Occidental stage is being thought out and that such a stage is a point of no return and of the erasure of the colonial epistemic difference from the perspective of what has been a subaltern form of knowledge. On the other hand, Tu Wei-ming could be criticized from the perspective of Chinese leftist intellectuals for supporting the uses of Confucianism, in China, to counter the ideology of Western capitalism with an ideology of Eastern capitalism. Or he could also be criticized for using Weber's own logic to criticize Protestant ethics from the perspective of a Confucian ethics (Wang 1997, 64–78). Both cases, however, enter a new player into the game, albeit not the ideal player for all the coaches involved. We could imagine similar scenarios, in the future, in which subaltern religions will take the place left empty by the historical collapse of socialism. And that they could be used to justify capitalist expansion beyond the West and to counter Christianity and the Protestant ethics upon which Western capitalism built its imaginary and its ideological force. This possibility does not prevent Confucianism and other forms of subaltern knowledge from being enacted with different purposes. Once "authenticities" are no longer an issue, what remains are the marks left by the colonial difference and the coloniality of power articulating both, the struggle for new forms of domination (e.g., Confucianism and capitalism) and struggles for new forms of liberation. I accentuate "liberation" because I am arguing here from the perspective of the external borders of the modern/colonial world system. And we all know that "emancipation" is the word used for the same purpose within the internal borders of the modern/colonial world system.

In any case, the point I would like to make could be stressed by Tu Wei-ming's elegant and deadly sentence at the end of the introduction to *Confucian Thought*:

> The nine essays, written over a fairly long period of time for a variety of purposes, are in the kind words of Robert C. Neville, "attempts at transmission and interpretation, Confucius' own self-understanding." *However, these attempts, far from transmitting and interpreting the Confucian conception of selfhood, suggest ways of exploring the rich resources within the Confucian tradition so that they can be brought to bear upon the difficult task of understanding Confucian selfhood as creative transformation.* [1985] (1996, 16)

If Confucianism offers the possibility of desubalternizing knowledges and expanding the horizon of human knowledge beyond the academy and beyond the Western concept of knowledge and rationality, this possibility is also open to forms of knowledge that were hit harder by the colonial tempest, including the knowledge of Amerindians and Native Americans. Vine

Deloria Jr., as intellectual and activist has been insisting (since the 1970s) on the cracks (or the colonial difference) between Native American knowledge and the structure of power in the hands of Anglo-Americans. Deloria has been criticized for essentializing the difference by presenting it in dichotomous terms. I do not have the time here to dispel a form of criticism when it comes from a postmodern leftist position that is just blind to the colonial difference. Of course, America is not a two-sided struggle between Anglo and Native Americans. The force of the national ideology in scholarship and, as a consequence, the lack of comparative works (that will place Native Americans in the context of Amerindians in Latin America, Aborigines in New Zealand and Australia, but also in comparison with Islam and Hinduism) hide the fact that what really matters is the colonial difference. As Deloria (1978) argues, "world views in collision" have been a fact of the past five hundred years and they have been in collision in the sixteenth century and today. However, neither of the world views in collision remained the same and they were not just between Anglos and Native Americans. World views in collision have been many, at different times around the planet. That is precisely the geohistorical density of the modern/colonial world system and the diachronic contradictions of its internal (conflicts between empires within the same world view) and external borders (world views in collision).

In chapter 7 I return to this topic by a different route: the future of a diverse planetary civilization beyond the universalisation of either Western neoliberalism or Western neo-Marxism. However, I need to state now that my references to Wei-ming and Deloria were not done with the intention of proposing that Confucianism or Native American religions are alternatives to Protestantism. They were made to suggest, quite to the contrary, that Protestant ethics was not necessarily an alternative to neither Confucianism or Native American religions (Deloria, 1999; Churchill 1997), and, above all, to stress one of this book's main arguments. If nation-states are no longer conceived in their homogeneity, if production of commodity is no longer attached to one country (e.g., think of the many places involved in the car industry), then we should no longer conceive Confucian or Protestant ethics or Native American religions as homogeneous systems either. Therefore, the relationships between faith and knowledge, a distinction we owe to the modern and secular conception of epistemology, needs to be rethought. That is mainly the reason I compared Tu Wei-ming and Deloria with Weber. Although I would enroll myself among the second possibility if I had no other choice. The good news is that we have other choices, even the possibility of choosing to think in and from the borders, to engage in border thinking as a future epistemological breakthrough. Tu Wei-ming and Deloria are not interpreting, translating from the Western hegemonic perspective, or transmitting knowledge from the perspective of area studies. Their analytic and critical reflections (rather than "religious studies") are engaged in a powerful exercise of border thinking from the perspective of epistemological subalternity. Alternatives to modern epistemology can hardly come only from *modern* (Western) epistemology itself.

II

Let me explain my notion of border thinking by introducing "gnosis" as a term that would take us away from the confrontation—in Western epistemology, between epistemology and hermeneutics, between nomothetic and ideographic "sciences"—and open up the notion of "knowledge" beyond cultures of scholarships. *Gnosis* and *gnoseology* are not familiar words nowadays within cultures of scholarship. The familiar words are those like epistemology and hermeneutics, which are the foundations of the "two cultures," sciences and the humanities. Indeed, hermeneutics and epistemology are more familiar because they have been articulated in the culture of scholarship since the Enlightenment. Since then, hermeneutics has been recast in secular, rather than in biblical terms, and epistemology has also been recast and displaced from its original philosophical meaning (referring to true knowledge, *episteme*, as distinct from opinion, *doxa*, and located as a reflection on scientific knowledge). Hermeneutics was assigned the domain of meaning and human understanding. Thus, the two cultures discussed by Snow (Snow 1959) came into being as a reconversion of the field of knowledge in the second phase of modernity, located in northern Europe and developed in the three main languages of knowledge since then (English, French, German). This frame is central to my discussion throughout this book. Gnosis was part of this semantic field, although it vanished from the Western configuration of knowledge once a certain idea of rationality began to be formed and distinguished from forms of knowledge that were considered dubious. Gnosis indeed was appropriated by the Gnostics (Jonas 1958), a religious and redemptive movement opposed to Christianity, from which comes the bad press received by "gnosticism" in the modern colonial world (from the Renaissance to the post–cold war). However, this is not the genealogy I am interested in.

Although the story is more complex, the following summary intends to map my use of gnosis and gnoseology. The verb *gignosko* (to know, to recognize) and *epistemai* (to know, to be acquainted with) suggest a different conceptualization of knowledge and knowing. The difference, in Plato's work, between doxa and episteme is well known, the first indicating a type of knowledge guided by common sense and the latter a more second-order knowledge, a systematic knowledge guided by explicit logical rules. Gnosis seems to have emerged as a response to the need to indicate a secret or hidden kind of knowledge. Greek philologists, however, recommend not to establish a rigid distinction between gnosis and episteme but to look at specific uses of them by specific authors.

Now, the *Oxford Companion of Philosophy* links gnoseology with the Greek word for "knowledge" and, therefore, does not make a clear distinction with episteme. But here an important and modern distinction is introduced as far as gnoseology refers to a kind of knowledge that is not available to sense experience—knowledge either attained by mystic contemplation or by pure logical and mathematical reasoning. Interestingly enough, the *Oxford Companion of Philosophy* reveals its own location when it clarifies that gnoseology is an archaic term and has been superseded by epistemology, (in the modern, post-Cartesian sense of reason and knowledge), and by metaphysics, a form and conceptualization of knowledge that has become (in Heidegger and Gadamer, for instance) linked with meaning and hermeneutics. Thus, gnoseology in the early modern colonial world became a term to refer to knowledge in general, while epistemology became restricted to analytical philosophy and the philosophy of sciences (Rorty 1982). In German the word *Erkenntnistheori*, in French *théorie de la connaissance*, and in Spanish *teoría del conocimiento* became expressions equivalent to gnoseology. Ferrater Mora ([1944] 1969), for example, distinguished in Spanish "teoría del conocimiento" from "epistemología" by the fact that the latter refers to scientific knowledge while the former to knowledge in general.

It is interesting to note that Valentin Y. Mudimbe employed gnosis in the subtitle of his book *The Invention of Africa: Gnosis, Philosophy and the Order of Knowledge* (1988). This book emerged from a request to write a survey on African philosophy. How do you, indeed, write such a history without twisting the very concept of philosophy? Mudimbe states the discomfort he found himself in when he had to survey the history of philosophy as a disciplined kind of practice imposed by colonialism and, at the same time, to deal with other undisciplined forms of knowledge that were reduced to subaltern knowledge by colonial disciplined knowing practices called philosophy and related to epistemology. The "African traditional system of thought" was opposed to "philosophy" as the traditional was opposed to the modern: philosophy became, in other words, a tool for subalternizing forms of knowledge beyond its disciplined boundaries. Mudimbe introduced the word gnosis to capture a wide range of forms of knowledge that "philosophy" and "epistemology" contributed to cast away. To seize the complexity of knowledge about Africa, by those who lived there for centuries and by those who went to Westernize it, the knowledge produced by travelers in the past and by the media in the present, underlining at the same time the crucial relevance of the "African traditional system of thought," needed to conceptualize knowledge production beyond the two cultures. He noted that gnosis etymologically is related to *gnosko*, which in ancient Greek means "to know." But, more specifically, Mudimbe notes, it means "seeking to know, inquiry, methods of knowing, investigation, and even acquaintance with someone. Often the word is used in a more specialized sense, that of higher and esoteric knowledge" (Mudimbe 1988, ix). Mudimbe is careful enough to specify that gnosis is not equivalent to either doxa or episteme. Episteme, Mudimbe clarifies, is understood as both science and intellectual configuration about systematic knowledge, while doxa is the kind of knowledge that the very conceptualization of episteme needs as its exterior: episteme is not only the conceptualization of systematic knowledge but is also the condition of possibility of doxa; it is not its opposite.

Following the previous configuration of the field of knowledge in Western memory, I will use gnoseology as the discourse about gnosis and I will understand by *gnosis* knowledge in general, including doxa and episteme. Border gnosis as knowledge from a subaltern perspective is knowledge conceived from the exterior borders of the modern/colonial world system, and border gnoseology as a discourse about colonial knowledge is conceived at the conflictive intersection of the knowledge produced from the perspective of modern colonialisms (rhetoric, philosophy, science) and knowledge produced from the perspective of colonial modernities in Asia, Africa, and the Americas/Caribbean. Border gnoseology is a critical reflection on knowledge production from both the interior borders of the modern/colonial world system (imperial conflicts, hegemonic languages, directionality of translations, etc.) and its exterior borders (imperial conflicts with cultures being colonized, as well as the subsequent stages of independence or decolonization). By interior borders I mean, for instance, the displacement of Spain from hegemonic position by England, in the seventeenth century, or the entry of the United States. in the concert of imperial nations in 1898. By exterior borders I mean the borders between Spain and the Islamic world, along with the Inca or Aztec people in the sixteenth century, or those between the British and the Indians in the nineteenth century, or the memories of slavery in the concert of imperial histories. Finally, border gnoseology could be contrasted with territorial gnoseology or epistemology, the philosophy of knowledge, as we know it today (from Descartes, to Kant, to Husserl and all its ramifications in analytic philosophy of languages and philosophy of science): a conception and a reflection on knowledge articulated in concert with the cohesion of national languages and the formation of the nation-state (see chapter 6).

"Gnosticism," said Hans Jonas (1958, 32), was the name for numerous doctrines "within and around Christianity during its critical first century." The emphasis was on *knowledge (gnosis)* with salvation as the final goal. As for the kind of knowledge gnostic knowledge is, Jonas observes that the

term by itself is a formal term that doesn't specify what is to be known or the subjective aspect of possessing knowledge. The difference with the gnostic context can be located in the concept of reason.

> As for *what* the knowledge is about, the associations of the term most familiar to the classically trained reader point to *rational* objects, and accordingly to natural reason as the organ for acquiring and possessing knowledge. In the gnostic context, however, "knowledge" has an emphatically religious or supranatural meaning and refers to objects which we nowadays should call those of faith rather than of reason. . . . *Gnosis* meant pre-eminently knowledge of *God*, and from what we have said about the radical transcendence of the deity it follows that "knowledge of God" is the knowledge of something naturally unknowable and therefore itself not a natural condition. . . . On the one hand it is closely bound up with revelationary experience, so that reception of the truth either through sacred and secret lore or through inner illumination replaces rational argument and theory. . . . on the other hand, being concerned with the secrets of salvation, "knowledge" is not just theoretical information about certain things but is itself, as a modification of the human condition, charged with performing a function in the bringing about of salvation. *Thus gnostic "knowledge" has an eminently practical object.* (Jonas 1958, 34)

We are obviously no longer at the beginning of the Christian era and *salvation* is not a proper term to define the practicality of knowledge, and neither is its claim to truth. But we need to open up the space that epistemology took over from gnoseology, and aim it not at God but at the uncertainties of the borders. Our goals are not salvation but decolonization, and transformations of the rigidity of epistemic and territorial *frontiers* established and controlled by the coloniality of power in the process of building the modern/colonial world system.

But since my focus is on forms of knowledge produced by modern colonialism at the intersection with colonial modernities, border gnosis/gnoseology and border thinking will be used interchangeably to characterize a powerful and emergent *gnoseology*, absorbing and displacing hegemonic forms of knowledge into the perspective of the subaltern. This is not a new form of synchretism or hybridity, but an intense battlefield in the long history of colonial subalternization of knowledge and legitimation of the colonial difference. By "subalternization of knowledge" I intend, through this book, to do justice and expand on an early insight by the Brazilian "anthropologian" (as he called himself, instead of "anthropologist") Darcy Ribeiro. "Anthropologian" was indeed a marker of subalternization of knowledge: an anthropologist in the "Third World" (Ribeiro was writing at the end of the 1960s and in the middle of the cold war and the consolidation of area studies) is not the same as an anthropologist in the First World, since the former is in the location of the object of study, not in the location of the studying subject. It is in this precise tension that Darcy Ribeiro's observation acquires its density, a density between the situation being described and the location of the subject within the situation he or she is describing:

> In the same way that Europe carried a variety of techniques and inventions to the people included in its network of domination . . . it also introduced to them its equipment of concepts, preconcepts, and idiosyncrasy which referred at the same time to Europe itself and to the colonial people.
>
> The colonial people, deprived of their riches and of the fruit of their labor under colonial regimes, suffered, furthermore, the degradation of assuming as their proper image the image that was no more than the reflection of the European vision of the world, which considered colonial people racially inferior because they were black, Amerindians, or "mestizos." Even the brighter social strata of non-European people got used to seeing themselves and their communities as an infrahumanity whose destiny was to occupy a subaltern position because of the sheer fact that theirs was inferior to the European population. (Ribeiro 1968, 63)

That colonial modernities, or "subaltern modernities" as Coronil (1997) prefers to label it, a period expanding from the late fifteenth century to the current stage of globalization, has built a frame and a conception of knowledge based on the distinction between epistemology and hermeneutics and, by so doing, has subalternized other kinds of knowledge is the main thesis of this book. That long process of subalternization of knowledge is being radically transformed by new forms of knowledge in which what has been subalternized and considered interesting only as object of study becomes articulated as new loci of enunciation. This is the second thesis of this book. The first is explored through a cultural critique of historical configurations; the second, by looking at the emergence of new loci of enunciation, by describing them as "border gnosis" and by arguing that "border gnosis" is the subaltern reason striving to bring to the foreground the force and creativity of knowledges subalternized during a long process of colonization of the planet, which was at the same time the process in which modernity and the modern Reason were constructed.

By "colonial differences" I mean, through my argument (and I should perhaps say "the colonial difference"), the classification of the planet in the modern/colonial imaginary, by enacting coloniality of power, an energy and a machinery to transform differences into values. If racism is the matrix that permeates every domain of the imaginary of the modern/colonial world system, "Occidentalism" is the overarching metaphor around which colonial differences have been articulated and rearticulated through the changing hands in the history of capitalism (Arrighi 1994) and the changing ideologies motivated by imperial conflicts. The emergence of new areas of colonization that had to be articulated within the conflictive memory of the system (e.g., France's colonization of North Africa four hundred years after the Spanish expulsion of the Moors from the Iberian Peninsula).

In my own intellectual history, a first formulation of border gnosis/gnoseology could be found in the notion of "colonial semiosis" and "pluritopic hermeneutics," which I introduced several years ago (Mignolo 1991) and which became two key notions in the argument and analysis of my previous book on coloniality in the early modern period (Mignolo 1995a). Colonial semiosis (which some readers found to be just more jargon, although the same readers would not find "colonial history" or "colonial economy" extravagant) was needed to account for a set of complex social and historical phenomena and to avoid the notion of "transculturation." Although I do not find anything wrong with the notion of transculturation, and while I endorse Ortiz's corrective of Malinowski's "acculturation," I was trying to avoid one of the meanings (indeed, the most common) attributed to the word: transculturation when it is attached to a biological/cultural mixture of people. When Ortiz suggested the term, he described Malinowski's acculturation as follows:

> Acculturation is used to describe the process of transition from one culture to another, and its manifold social repercussions. But transculturation is a more fitting term. I have chosen the word transculturation to express the highly varied phenomena that come about in Cuba as a result of the extremely complex transmutation of culture that has taken place here, and without a knowledge of which it is impossible to understand the evolution of the Cuban folk, either in the economic or in the institutional, legal, ethical, religious, artistic, linguistic, psychological, sexual or other aspects of its life. (Ortiz [1940] 1995, 98)

Ortiz conceived the entire history of Cuba as a long process of transculturation. And he summarized this idea in the following dictum: "The whole gamut of culture run by Europe in a span of more than four millenniums took place in Cuba in less than four centuries" (Ortiz [1940] 1995, 99). Ortiz was interested in defining a national feature of Cuban history. I am more interested in critically reflecting on coloniality and thinking from such an experience, than in identifying national (or subcontinental, e.g., "Latin American") distinctive features. This is the main reason why I prefer the term colonial semiosis to transculturation, which, in the first definition provided by Ortiz, maintains the shadows of "mestizaje." Colonial semiosis emphasized, instead, the conflicts engendered by coloniality at the level of social-semiotic interactions, and by that I mean, in the sphere of signs. In the sixteenth century, the conflict of writing systems related to religion, education, and conversion was a fundamental aspect of coloniality (Gruzinsky 1988; 1990; Mignolo 1995a). Colonial semiosis attempted, although perhaps not entirely successfully, to dispel the notion of "culture." Why? Because culture is precisely a key word of colonial discourses classifying the planet, particularly since the second wave of colonial expansion, according to sign system (language, food, dress, religion, etc.) and ethnicity (skin color, geographical locations). Culture became, from the eighteenth century until 1950 approximately, a word between "nature" and "civilization." Lately, culture has become the other end of capital and financial interests.

While Ortiz defined transculturation mainly in terms of contact between people, he suggested also that tobacco and sugar, beyond their interest for the study of Cuban economy and historical peculiarities, offer, in addition, certain curious and original instances of transculturation of the sort that are of great and current interest in contemporary sociological sciences (Ortiz [1940] 1995, 5). This kind of transculturation is closer to my own notion of colonial semiosis. Let's explore why. In the second part of the book, and after exploring in detail tobacco's features in comparison with sugar, Ortiz explores the historical aspects of both and observes:

> Tobacco reached the Christian world along with the revolutions of the Renaissance and the Reformation, when the Middle Ages were crumbling and the modern epoch, with its rationalism, was beginning. One might say that reason, starved and benumbed by theology, to revive and free itself, needed the help of some harmless stimulant that should not intoxicate it with enthusiasm and then stupefy it with illusions and bestiality, as happens with the old alcoholic drinks that lead to drunkenness. For this, to help sick reason, tobacco came from America. And with it chocolate. And from Abyssinia and Arabia, about the same time, came coffee. And tea made its appearance from the Far East.
>
> The coincidental appearance of these four exotic products in the Old World, all of them stimulants of the senses as well as of the spirit, is not without interests. It is as though they had been sent to Europe from the four corners of the earth by the devil to revive Europe when "the time came," when that continent was ready to save the spirituality of reason from burning itself out and give the senses their due once more. (Ortiz [1940] 1995, 206)

I am not interested in discussing here the historical validity of Ortiz's assertion but in looking at transculturation from the realm of signs, rather than from that of people's miscegenation, and in displacing it toward the understanding of border thinking and the colonial difference. When people's blood enters in the definition of transculturation, it is difficult to avoid the temptation to understand miscegenation and biological mixtures. It is not the blood or the color of your skin but the *descriptions* of blood mixture and skin color that are devised and enacted in and by the coloniality of power that counts. Blood mixture and skin color, as far as I can ascertain, do not have inscribed in them a genetic code that becomes translated into a cultural one. Rather, the descriptions made by those living organisms who can make descriptions of themselves and of their surroundings (Mignolo 1995a, 1–28) are the ones that establish an organization and a hierarchy of blood mixture and skin color. In this regard, the notion of transculturation is not relevant so much because it describes a given reality as it is because it changes previous descriptions made by living organisms making descriptions of themselves (and sometimes following "disciplinary" norms in order to get such descriptions "right"). Transculturation offers a different view of people interaction. It is, in other words, a principle to produce descriptions that changes the principle in which similar descriptions have been made up to the point of its introduction in cultures of scholarship's vocabulary. Instead, the encounter of exotic products coming into Europe from the four corners of the world to enter in a new social and gnoseological setting is a good image of transculturation without mestizaje. What is missing in Ortiz's analysis is coloniality, and it is missing because for Ortiz the main question is nationality. Thus, colonial semiosis frames the issue within but also beyond the nation in the sense that nation-states are firmly established in the horizon of coloniality: either you find a nation-state that becomes an empire (like Spain or England) or one undergoing uprisings and rebellions to become autonomous, working toward the foundation of a nation (e.g., the Americas at the end of eighteenth and the beginning of the nineteenth centuries).

Perhaps some of the resistance to colonial semiosis from people who will readily accept colonial history or economy is due to the fact that colonial semiosis goes together with pluritopic hermeneutics. And this, for sure, not only complicates the matter but also introduces more obscure jargon. Sometimes, however, jargon is necessary, for how would you change the terms, and not only the content, of the conversation without it? I needed the combination of these two notions to move away and not get trapped by the opposite danger: the platitude of colonial economy or colonial history starting from the surface of what is "seen" and avoiding the risks of looking for what Rolph-Trouillot called the "unthinkable" in the Haitian Revolution. Thus, it is not always the case that jargon is unnecessary, and often uncommon words show us the invisible. In any event, pluritopic hermeneutics was necessary to indicate that colonial semiosis "takes place" in between conflict of knowledges and structures of power. Anibal Quijano (1997) has developed the notion of "coloniality of power," a phenomenon I just described as a "conflict of knowledges and structures of power." My understanding of coloniality of power presupposes the colonial difference as its condition of possibility and as the legitimacy for the subalternization of knowledges and the subjugation of people.

III

Coloniality of power is a story that does not begin in Greece; or, if you wish, has two beginnings, one in Greece and the other in the less known memories of millions of people in the Caribbean and the Atlantic coast, and better-known memories (although not as well known as the Greek legacies) in the Andes and in Mesoamerica. The extended moment of conflict between people whose brain and skin have been formed by different memories, sensibilities, and belief between 1492 and today is the crucial historical intersection where the coloniality of power in the Americas can be located and unraveled. Quijano identifies coloniality of power with capitalism and its consolidation in Europe from the fifteenth to the eighteenth centuries. Coloniality of power implies and constitutes itself, according to Quijano, through the following:

1. The classification and reclassification of the planet population—the concept of "culture" becomes crucial in this task of classifying and reclassifying.

2. An institutional structure functional to articulate and manage such classifications (state apparatus, universities, church, etc.).

3. The definition of spaces appropriate to such goals.

4. An epistemological perspective from which to articulate the meaning and profile of the new matrix of power and from which the new production of knowledge could be channeled.

This is, in a nutshell, what for Quijano constitutes the coloniality of power by way of which the entire planet, including its continental division (Africa, America, Europe), becomes articulated in such production of knowledge and classificatory apparatus. Eurocentrism becomes, therefore, a metaphor to describe the coloniality of power from the perspective of subalternity. From the epistemological perspective, European local knowledge and histories have been projected to global designs, from the dream of an *Orbis Universalis Christianus* to Hegel's belief in a universal history that could be narrated from a European (and therefore hegemonic) perspective. Colonial semiosis attempted to identify particular moments of tension in the conflict between two local histories and knowledges, one responding to the movement forward of a global design that intended to impose itself and those local histories and knowledges that are forced to accommodate themselves to such new realities. Thus, colonial semiosis requires a pluritopic hermeneutics since in the conflict, in the cracks and fissures where the conflict originates, a description of one side of the epistemological divide won't do. But that is not all, because while the first problem was to look into the spaces in between, the second was how to produce knowledge from such in-between spaces. Otherwise, it would not have been a pluritopic hermeneutics, but a monotopic one (i.e., a persepective of a homogenous knowing subject located in a universal no-man's-land), describing the conflict between people made of different knowledge and memories. "Border thinking" is the notion that I am introducing now with the intention of transcending hermeneutics and epistemology and the corresponding distinction between the knower and the known, in the epistemology of the second modernity. To describe in "reality" both sides of the border is not the problem. The problem is to do it from its exteriority (in Levinas's sense). The goal is to erase the distinction between the knower and the known, between a "hybrid" object (the borderland as the known) and a "pure" disciplinary or interdisciplinary subject (the knower), uncontaminated by the border matters he or she describes. To change the terms of the conversation it is necessary to overcome the distinction between subject and object, on the one hand, and between epistemology and hermeneutics on the other. Border thinking should be the space in which this new logic could be thought out. In chapter 1, I explore Abdelkebir Khatibi's concept of "an other thinking" as a response to this problem. In chapter 6 I explore the possibility of "an other tongue" following Alfred Arteaga's expression.

IV

This book came into existence when I realized that today's emergence of "border thinking" was a consequence of the modern world system, as originally described by Imannuel Wallerstein (1974), and expanded and complicated later on by Eric Wolf (1982), Janet L. Abu-Lughod (1989), Giovanni Arrighi (1996), not to mention the debates on the very idea of "world system" that took place in the past twenty years, of which the journal *Review* (published by the Ferdinand Braudel Center at Binghamton) has been a visible medium (see *Review* 15, No. 4, [1992], for instance). I began to piggyback on modern world system analysis and, in doing so, I followed the example of Edward Said on the one hand and the South Asian Subaltern Studies Group on the other. In both cases, there was piggybacking on Michel Foucault, first, and Karl Marx and Antonio Gramsci, second, whose debates on colonialism were located in a "universal" domain of discussion, promoting it from the more local and descriptive site it occupied until the 1980s. But then, why am I not piggybacking on South Asian subaltern studies, or on Said's *Orientalism*, or even on German critical theory or French post structuralism, which have more clout in cultural studies and postcolonial debates than modern world system theory? And why the modern world system model or metaphor that has been much criticized and looked at with suspicion by many within the social sciences, and went almost unnoticed within the humanities?

One of the possible answers to this question is at the same time my justification to start with this paradigm: the modern world system model or metaphor has the sixteenth century as a crucial date of its constitution, while all the other possibilities I just mentioned (Said, Guha, critical theory, poststructuralism) have the eighteenth century and the Enlightenment as the chronological frontier of modernity. Since my feelings, education, and thinking are anchored on the colonial legacies of the Spanish and Portuguese empires in the Americas, to "begin" in the eighteenth century would be to put myself out of the game. This is also an answer to Valentin Mudimbe, who asked me once, "What do you have against the Enlightenment?" The Enlightenment comes second in my own experience of colonial histories. The second phase of modernity, the Enlightenment and the Industrial Revolution, was derivative in the history of Latin America and entered in the nineteenth century as the exteriority that needed to be incorporated in order to build the "republic" after independence from Spain and Portugal had been gained (see chapter 3).

Border gnosis or border thinking is in this book in dialogue with the debate on the universal/particular, on the one hand, and with Michel Foucault's notion of "insurrection of subjugated knowledges," on the other. Furthermore, border thinking/gnosis could serve as a mediator between the two interrelated issues I am introducing here: subjugated knowledges and the universal/particular dilemma. A link between Foucault's notion of subjugated knowledges and Darcy Ribeiro's subaltern knowledges allows me to reframe the dilemma of the universal/particular through the colonial difference.

In his inaugural lecture in the College of France (1976), Foucault introduced the expression "insurrection of subjugated knowledges" to describe an epistemological transformation he perceived at work in the fifteen years or so previous to his lecture. He devoted a couple of paragraphs to specify his understanding of subjugated knowledges: "By subjugated knowledges I mean two things. On the one hand, I am referring to the historical contents that have been buried and disguised in a functionalist of formal systematization" (81). By "historical content." Foucault was referring to something that has been buried "behind" the disciplines and the production of knowledge, that was neither the semiology of life nor the sociology of delinquency but the repression of the "immediate emergence of historical contents."

His second approach to subjugated knowledges was expressed in the following terms:

> I believe that by subjugated knowledges one should understand something else,
> something which in a sense is altogether different, namely, a whole set of knowl-

edge that has been disqualified as inadequate to its tasks or insufficiently elaborated: naïve knowledges, located low down on the hierarchy, beneath the required level of cognition of scientificity. I also believe that it is through the
re-emergence of these low-ranking knowledges, these unqualified knowledges
(such as that of the psychiatric patient, of the ill person, of the doctor—parallel
and marginal as they are to the knowledge of medicine—that of the delinquent,
etc.) which involve what I would call a popular knowledge [*le savoir des gens*]
though it is far from being a general common sense knowledge, *but on the contrary a particular, local, regional knowledge, a differential knowledge incapable of
unanimity and which owes its forces only to the harshness* with which it is opposed
by everything surrounding it—that is through the re-appearance of this knowledge, of these local popular knowledges, these disqualified knowledges, that
criticism performs its work. (Foucault [1976] 1980, 82; emphasis added)

Foucault was certainly aware of the disparity between the kinds of knowledges he was confronting, academic and disciplinary knowledge, on the one
hand, and nonacademic and popular knowledge on the other. He was also
aware that he was not attempting to oppose the "abstract unity of theory" to
the "concrete multiplicity of facts" (83). Foucault was using the distinction
between disciplinary and subjugated knowledges to question the very foundation of academic/disciplinary and expert knowledge without which the
very notion of subjugated knowledge would not have sense. He called *genealogy* the union of "erudite knowledge and local memories" and specified
that what *genealogy* really does is to "entertain the claims to attention of
local, discontinuous, disqualified, illegitimate knowledges against the claims
of a unitary body of theory which would filter hierarchies and order them
in the name of some true knowledge and some arbitrary idea of what constitutes a science and its objects" ([1972–77] 1980, 83).

My intention in this introduction and throughout the book is to move
subjugated knowledge to the limits of the colonial difference where subjugated become subaltern knowledges in the structure of coloniality of power.
And I conceive subaltern knowledges in tandem with Occidentalism as the
overarching imaginary of the modern/colonial world system: Occidentalism
is the visible face in the building of the modern world, whereas subaltern
knowledges are its darker side, the colonial side of modernity. This very
notion of subaltern knowledges, articulated in the late 1960s by Darcy Ribeiro, makes visible the colonial difference between anthropologists in the
First World "studying" the Third World and "anthropologians" in the Third
World reflecting on their own geohistorical and colonial conditions. Allow
me to repeat, with a distinct emphasis, Ribeiro's paragraph quoted already
on page 13:

In the same way that Europe carried a variety of techniques and inventions to
the people included in its network of domination . . . *it also introduced to them*

its equipment of concepts, preconcepts, and idiosyncrasy that referred at the same time to Europe itself and to the colonial people. The colonial people, deprived of their riches and of the fruit of their labor under colonial regimes, suffered, furthermore, the degradation of assuming as their proper image the image that was no more than the reflection of the European vision of the world, which considered colonial people racially inferior because they were black, (Amer) Indians, or mestizos. . . . Even the brighter social strata of non-European people got used to seeing themselves and their communities as an *infrahumanity whose destiny was to occupy a subaltern position* because of the sheer fact that theirs was inferior to the European population. (Ribeiro 1968, 63; emphasis added)

Although the introduction of "subalternity" by Antonio Gramsci pointed toward a structure of power established around class relations in the modern (industrial) Western societies, ethnoracial relations (as I suggested) were crucial for the establishment of class relations structured around labor, the exploitation of the Amerindians, and the increasing slave trade from sub-Saharan Africa. On the other hand, a hierarchical relation and consequently a subalternization of knowledge occurred at a different level, the level of religion. Christianity established itself as intolerant to Judaism and Islam as well as to the "idolatry" of the Amerindians, whose extirpation became a major goal of the church in the sixteenth and seventeenth centuries (Duviols 1971; MacCormack 1991). Christianity became, with the expulsion of Jews and Moors and the "discovery" of America, the first global design of the modern/colonial world system and, consequently, the anchor of Occidentalism and the coloniality of power drawing the external borders as the colonial difference, which became reconverted and resemantized in the late eighteenth and early nineteenth centuries with the expansion of Britain and France to Asia and Africa. Global designs are the complement of universalism in the making of the modern/colonial world.

Today, *a* world history or *a* universal history is an impossible task. Or perhaps both are possible but hardly credible. Universal histories in the past five hundred years have been embedded in global designs. Today, local histories are coming to the forefront and, by the same token, revealing the local histories from which global designs emerge in their universal drive. From the project of the *Orbis Universalis Christianum,* through the standards of civilization at the turn of the twentieth century, to the current one of globalization (global market), global designs have been the hegemonic project for managing the planet. This project changed hands and names several times, but the times and names are not buried in the past. On the contrary, they are all still alive in the present, even if the most visible is the propensity toward making the planet into a global market. However, it is not difficult to see that behind the market as the ultimate goal of an economic project that has become an end in itself, there is the Christian mission of the early modern (Renaissance) colonialism , the civilizing mission of the secularized modernity, and the development and modernization projects after World War II. Neoliberalism, with its emphasis on the market and consumption, is not just a question of economy but a new form of civilization. The impossibility or lack of credibility of universal or world histories today is not advanced by some influential postmodern theory, but by the economic and social forces generally referred to as globalization and by the emergence of forms of knowledge that have been subalternized during the past five hundred years under global designs I just mentioned—that is, during the period of planetary expansion I call here modern colonialisms and colonial modernities. To simplify things, I refer to this double edge as modernity/coloniality. The coexistence and the intersection of both modern colonialisms and colonial modernities (and, obviously, the multiplication of local histories taking the place occupied by world or universal history), from the perspective of people and local histories that have to confront modern colonialism, is what I understand here as "coloniality," quite simply, the reverse and unavoidable side of "modernity"—its darker side, like the part of the moon we do not see when we observe it from earth.

The overarching, and necessary, concept of coloniality/modernity implies the need, indeed, the strong need, for building macronarratives from the perspective of coloniality. And this is one of the main goals of this book. Macronarratives from the perspective of coloniality are not the counterpart of world or universal history, but a radical departure from such global projects. They are neither (or at least not only) revisionist narratives nor narratives that intend to tell a different truth but, rather, narratives geared toward the search for a different logic. This book is intended as a contribution to changing the terms of the conversation as well as its content (persuaded by Trouillot's insistence on the issue) to displace the "abstract universalism" of modern epistemology and world history, while leaning toward an alternative to totality conceived as a network of local histories and multiple local hegemonies. Without such macronarratives told from the historical experiences of multiple local histories (the histories of modernity/coloniality), it would be impossible to break the dead end against which modern epistemology and the reconfiguration of the social sciences and the humanities since the eighteenth century have framed hegemonic forms of knowledge. Western expansion since the sixteenth century has not only been a religious and economic one, but also the expansion of hegemonic forms of knowledge that shaped the very conception of economy and religion. That is to say, it was the expansion of a "representational" concept of knowledge and cognition (Rorty 1982) that I will be attempting to displace from the perspective of emerging epistemologies/gnoseologies, which I explore and conceive as border gnosis/gnoseology and link to modernity/coloniality.

V

The book is then a series of interconnected essays on the *imaginary* of the modern/colonial world system. I use imaginary in the sense of Edouard Glissant. Following the translator of *Poétique de la rélation* ([1990] 1997), I read Glissant *not* to mean by imaginary "the now widely accepted Lacanian sense in which the Imaginary is contrasted with the Symbolic and the Real." For Glissant the imaginary is all the ways a culture has of perceiving and conceiving of the world. Hence, every human culture will have its own particular imaginary" (Wing 1997). In a terminology already introduced in the *Darker Side of the Renaissance* (Mignolo 1995a), the imaginary of the modern/colonial world is its self-description, the ways in which it described itself through the discourse of the state, intellectuals, and scholars. I also submit, and discuss throughout the book, "Occidentalism" as the overarching metaphor of the modern/colonial world system imaginary. It is fitting that an updated article published by Wallerstein in 1992 is titled "The West, Capitalism and the Modern World-System." By "border thinking" I mean the moments in which the imaginary of the modern world system cracks. "Border thinking" is still within the imaginary of the modern world system, but repressed by the dominance of hermeneutics and epistemology as keywords controlling the conceptualization of knowledge.

But let me tell you first how I do conceive of the modern/colonial world system in this book. I do not discuss whether the "world system" is five hundred or five thousand years old (Gunder Frank and Gills 1993; Dussel 1998a; 1998b). It is important for my argument to make a distinction between the "world system" Gunder Frank and Gills theorize and the "modern/colonial world system," whose imaginary is the topic of this book. This imaginary is a powerful one, not only in the sociohistorical economic structure studied by Wallerstein (1974; 1980; 1989) and what he calls "geoculture" (Wallerstein 1991a), but also in the Amerindian imaginary.

"Imaginary" shall be distinguished from "geoculture." For Wallerstein, the geoculture of the modern world system shall be located between the French Revolution and May 1968 in France (as well as around the world) is defined in terms of France's intellectual hegemony—a most interesting location of the geoculture of the modern world system, since its economic history as the history of capitalism (from Venice and Genoa, to Holland and England) (Arrighi 1994) does not include France, as a special chapter of this narrative. France, then, provided the geoculture of modernity since the French Revolution, although France's participation in the history of capitalism was marginal (Arrighi 1994). On the other hand, Wallerstein stated that there is no geoculture of the system until the French Revolution. How can we describe then the Christian global and geo-ideological perspective from the sixteenth to the eighteenth centuries? I prefer, therefore, to think in terms of the imaginary of the Atlantic commercial circuit, which is extended, and thus includes what Wallerstein calls "geoculture," to the end of the twentieth century and is resemantized in the discourse of neoliberalism as a new civilizing project driven by the market and the transnational corporations. In my argument, the imaginary of the modern/colonial world system is the overarching discourse of Occidentalism, in its geohistorical transformation in tension and conflict with the forces of subalternity that were engendered from the early responses of the Amerindian and African slaves to it, to current intellectual undoing of Occidentalism and social movements looking for new paths toward a democratic imaginary.

Laguna writer Leslie Marmon Silko includes a "five hundred year map" at the beginning of her novel, *The Almanac of the Dead* (1991); (fig. 1), and the first sentence of the Zapatista declaration from the Lacandon Forest in January 1994 reads "we are the product of 500 years of struggle" (EZLN, CG 1995). October 12 is commemorated by Spaniards and officially in the Americas as the day of the "discovery." Amerindians have recently begun to commemorate October 11, instead, as the last day of "freedom." I suppose that a similar image can be created, if it is not yet at work, among the Afro-Caribbean and Afro-American population.

Glissant's use of the concept of "imaginary" is sociohistorical rather than individual. Spanish philosopher José Ortega y Gasset, concerned with the same question of the density of collective memory, conceived every act of saying as inscribed in a triple dimension: the ground ("suelo"), the underground ("subsuelo"), and the enemy ("el enemigo") (Ortega y Gasset 1954). The underground is what is there but is not visible. The Christian T/O was invisibly inscribed since the sixteenth century in every world map where we "see" fourth continents. We may not "know" that the fourth continents are not "there" in the world map but the symbolical inscription "fourth" in the tripartite Christian division of the world in Asia/Shem, Africa/Ham, and Europe/Japeth began to be accepted in and since the sixteenth century. And we may not know that the Americas were considered the daughter and the inheritor of Europe because it was, indeed, a fourth continent but not like the others. Noah did not have four sons. Consequently, the Americas became the natural extension of Japeth, toward the West. The imaginary of the modern/colonial world system is not only what is visible and in the "ground" but what has been hidden from view in the "underground" by successive layers of mapping people and territories.

However, I'm not arguing for the "representation" of the invisible or for "studying" the subalterns. To argue in that direction would be to argue from the perspective of a "denotative" epistemic assumption that I rejected in my previous book. (1995a; 16–28) and that I continue to reject here. Denotative epistemic assumptions are presupposed in what I call here "territorial episte-

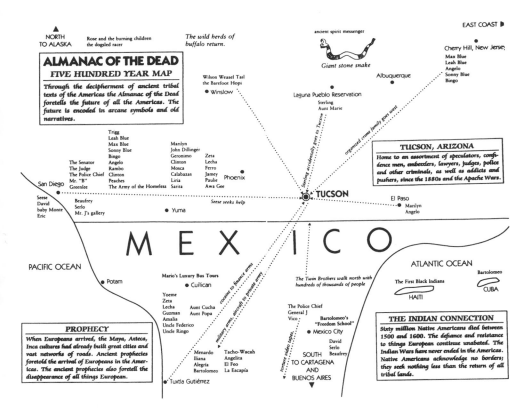

Figure 1. Leslie Marmon Silko's map reinstalled the colonial difference by introducing the temporal dimension within a spatial configuration, showing in a transnational perpective the history of the modern/colonial world system from a particular local history. As we know, Amerindians did not make a strict distinction between space and time. The "five hundred year map" joins Amerindians' and Native Americans' claim for memory, for land, for human dignity, for the desubalternization of knowledge, and for erasure of the colonial difference. (From Leslie Marmon Silko. 1982. *Almanac of the Dead*. New York: Simon and Schuster, Inc.)

mology" and which is, in terms of Ortega y Gasset, "the enemy." Ortega y Gasset assumed that every act of saying was a "saying against." In my argument this is not a necessary restriction. It would be more accurate to say that every act of saying is at the same time a "saying against" and a "saying for." This double movement will acquire a complex dimension when viewed at the intersection of local histories and global designs, and at the intersection of hegemonic and subaltern grounds and undergrounds. From this perspective, recent discussions on the "facts" and "fictions" component of Rigoberta Menchú's (1984) narrative fall within a denotative and territorial epistemology. Rigoberta Menchú's story is no less "fact and fiction" than any other known narrative from the Bible to *The Clash of Civilizations*. The better question would be: What are the ground, the underground, and the enemy of these or other narratives? To argue in this direction requires a change of terrain: to move, first, from a denotative to an enactive epistemology, and, second, to move from a territorial to a border epistemology which presupposes an awareness of and a sensibility for the colonial difference. Rigoberta Menchú argues from an enactive and border epistemology. Her critics are located instead in a denotative and territorial epistemology. This tension between hegemonic epistemology with emphasis on denotation and truth, and subaltern epistemologies with emphasis on performance and transformation shows the contentions and the struggle for power. It also shows how the exercise of the coloniality of power (anchored on denotative epistemology and the will to truth) attributes itself the right to question alternatives whose will to truth is preceded by the will to transform—a will to transform, like in Rigoberta Menchú, emerging from the experience of the colonial difference engrained in the imaginary of the modern/colonial world since 1500.

Janet L. Abu-Lughod (1989) described the world order between A.D. 1250 and 1350 in eight dominant commercial circuits, extending from Peking to Genoa (fig. 2). At this point I am interested in two aspects from this map. One is the fact that during that period, Genoa, Bruges, and Troyes were in the margins of the commercial circuits, dominated by circuit viii. This is one of the reasons why Spaniards and Portuguese were interested in reaching China, but there is no record of the Chinese being irresistibly attracted by Christendom as it was emerging in the West after the failure of the Crusades. My second point of interest is that figure 2 completely ignores what figure 3 shows. The map shown in figure 3 includes two more commercial circuits "hidden" from Eurocentric narratives. The first commercial circuit had its center in Anahuac, in what is today Mexico, and extended toward today's Guatemala and Panama in the south and to today's New Mexico and Arizona in the north. The other had its center in Tawantinsuyu, in what is today Peru, and extended north toward present-day Ecuador and Colombia, east to present-day Bolivia and south to the northern part of today's Argentina and Chile.

Enrique Dussel (1998a) has suggested that, given the world order described in figure 2, the fact that it was the Spaniards and not the Chinese or the Portuguese who "discovered" America responds to an obvious historical logic. China was in a dominant position. Therefore, even if Chinese navigators reached the Pacific coasts of America before the Spaniards, it was not an event to be qualified as the most important since the creation of the world, as historian López de Gómara did toward 1555. The Portuguese did not need to try the Atlantic route because they had been controlling the coast of Africa, from north to south, and around to the Indian Ocean, with

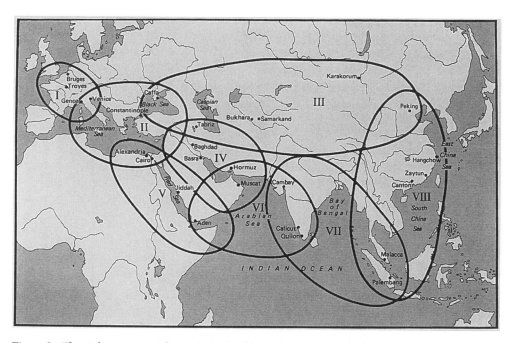

Figure 2. The eight commercial circuits in the thirteeth century in a multicentered world, according to Janet L. Abu-Lughod. Notice that although Abu-Lughod writes at the end of the twentieth century, the Atlantic and the "Americas" are not in the picture of the scholar because they were not in the picture of those living in the thirteenth century from Genova to Adend and to Peking; from Palembang to Karakorum. (From Janet L. Abu-Lughod. 1989. *Before European Hegemony*. Copyright © 1989 by Oxford University Press. Used by permission of Oxford University Press, Inc.)

easy access to Malaca, Canton, and Peking. It is not by chance that Columbus went first to the court of Portugal, and only after his plans were rejected did he approach Isabelle and Ferdinand of Spain. What Columbus did, in this context, was to open the gates for the creation of a new commercial circuit connecting circuit I, in Abu-Lughod's map, with the one in Anahuac and the other in Tawantinsuyu. I am retelling this well-known story because it is the story that connects the Mediterranean with the Atlantic, begins to displace the commercial forces (mines and plantations) to the latter, and lays the foundation of what is today conceived as the modern world system. Now the inception of a new commercial circuit, which would be the foundation of Western economy and dominance, goes together with a rearticulation of the racial imaginary, whose consequences are still alive today. Two ideas became central in such rearticulation: "purity of blood" and "rights of the people."

The "purity of blood" principle was formalized at the beginning of the sixteenth century, in Spain, and established the final "cut" between Chris-

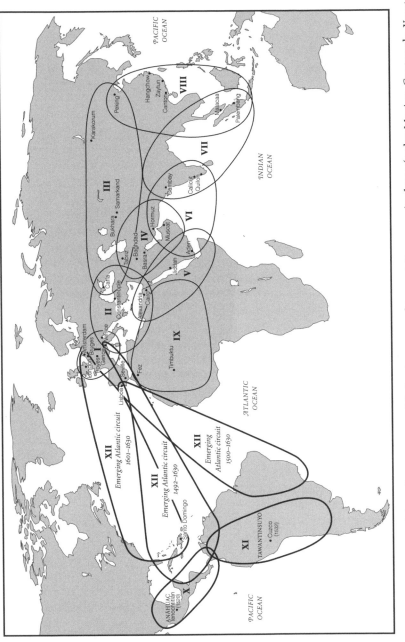

Figure 3. The emergence of the Atlantic commercial circuit connected two existing ones: Anahuac (today Mexico, Guatemala, Yucatan, Nicaragua) and Tawantisuyu (today Bolivia, Peru, north of Chile and Argentina, Ecuador and Columbia). Until the middle of the fifteenth century, the Atlantic commercial circuit was not yet hegemonic, although Christians' global designs and map making provided a global conception of the world not available until then. The Atlantic commercial circuit became hegemonic with the expansion of England and France to Asia and Africa, after the Dutch transitional period in the second half of the seventeenth century. This moment corresponded also with the tracing of the imperial (internal) borders and the making of the European South.

tians, Jews and Moors (Sicroff 1960; Netanyahu
Harvey 1990, 307–40; Constable 1997). At the s   , .. created the
concept of "converso." While the expulsion of the Moors demarcated the
exterior of what would be a new commercial circuit and the Mediterranean
became that frontier, the expulsion of the Jews determined one of the inner
borders of the emerging system. The converso instead opened up the borderland, the place in which neither the exterior nor the interior frontiers apply,
although they were the necessary conditions for borderlands. The converso
will never be at peace with himself or herself, nor will he or she be trustwor-
thy from the point of view of the state. The converso was not so much a
hybrid as it was a place of fear and passing, of lying and terror. The reasons
for conversion could as easily be deep conviction or sheer social convenience. Whatever the case, he or she would know that the officers of the
state would be suspicious of the authenticity of such a conversion. To be
considered or to consider oneself a Jew, a Moor, or a Christian was clear. To
be a converso was to navigate the ambiguous waters of the undecided. At
the time, the borderland was not a comfortable position to be in. Today, the
borderland is the place of a desired epistemological potential (see chapters
1, 5, 6, and 7) and the "discomfort" generated by Rigoberta Menchú.

While "purity of blood" rearticulated the three religions of the book and
the field of force in the Mediterranean, later it was adapted to the Spanish
colonies in the Americas too, and it was carried over the republican period.
My interest here in underlining "purity of blood" is due to the fact that in
the Iberian Peninsula in the sixteenth century the Atlantic was organized
according to a different and opposed principle: the "rights of the people,"
which emerged from the Valladolid early debates between Gines de Sepúlveda and Bartolomé de las Casas on the humanity of the Amerindians
and was followed up by the long debates in the School of Salamanca on
cosmopolitanism and international relations (Höffner 1957; Ramos et al.,
1984). Contrary to "purity of blood," which was a punitive principle, "rights
of the people" was the first legal attempt (theological in nature) to write
down a canon of international law, that was reformulated in a secular discourse in the eighteenth-century as the "rights of men and of the citizen"
(Ishay 1997, 73–173). One of the important differences between the two
("rights of the people" and "rights of men and of the citizen") is that the
first is at the heart of the colonial, hidden side of modernity and looks for
the articulation of a new frontier, which was similar neither to the Moors
nor to the Jews. The second, instead, is the imaginary working within the
system itself, looking at the "universality" of man as seen in an already
consolidated Europe, made possible because of the riches from the colonial
world flowing west to east, through the Atlantic.

The "Rights of the People" had another important consequence in building the imaginary of the modern world system, which would be revealed
after the declaration of the "rights of men and of the citizen." "Rights of
the People" was a discussion about Amerindians, and not African slaves.
Amerindians were considered vassals of the king and servants of God; as
such they, theoretically, could not be enslaved. They were supposed to be
educated and converted to Christianity. African slaves were not in the same
category: they were part of the Atlantic "commerce" (Manning 1990, 23–
37) rather than natives of a New World where complex social organizations
have been achieved, as in Anahuac and Tawantinsuyu. However, and perhaps because of the difference in status, Amerindians failed in their revolutionary attempt. The most well known revolt, that of Tupac Amaru, in the
eighteenth century was unsuccessful. The Haitian Revolution, which anticipated the movements of independence in Spanish America, was successful
but "silent" in the self-description of the modern world system (Trouillot
1995) for which only the independence of New Englanders from England
and the French Revolution counted.

The extension of the Spanish domain in the Americas, as can be seen in
figure 4 (Wolf 1982, 132) significantly changed during the nineteenth century. Its shape was transformed first with the independence of Spanish
American countries and, second, with the displacement of the frontier between the United States and Mexico when Mexico lost its northern territories in 1848 and then Cuba and Puerto Rico in 1898. The modern/colonial
world system was profoundly altered at the end of the nineteenth century.
The United States (a former British colony) became a leading power, and
Japan detached itself from China and was admitted to the family of nations
abiding by the standards of civilizations. By the beginning of the twentieth
century (as shown in fig. 5; Huntington 1996), the imaginary of the "modern" world system reduced the "West" to practically just English-speaking
countries. On the other hand, a complementary perspective from the hidden
side of "coloniality" (fig. 6, Osterhammel 1997) underlines the colonized
areas of the world, instead of underlining the "West." These two maps (figs.
5 and 6), suggest once more that modernity and coloniality are looked at
separately, as two different phenomena. There could be no other reason why
Wallerstein conceived a "modern" and not a "modern/colonial" world system, and why all his more recent analyses are done from within the history
of the "modern" (Wallerstein 1991a), which he locates in the French Revolution.

At this point, a new and crucial turn in the imaginary of the modern/
colonial world system shall be mentioned. If the sixteenth and the seventeenth centuries were dominated by the Christian imaginary (whose mission
extended from the Catholics and Protestants in the Americas, to the Jesuits
in China), the end of the nineteenth century witnessed a radical change.

Figure 4. The Spanish Empire, until 1848, extended through almost all the Americas. (From Eric R. Woolf. 1982. *Europe and the People without History.* Berkeley: The University of California Press. Used by permission of The University of California Press.)

"Purity of blood" was no longer measured in terms of religion but of the color of people's skin, and began to be used to distinguish the Aryan "race" from other "races" and, more and more, to justify the superiority of the Anglo-Saxon "race" above all the rest (de Gobineau 1853–55; Arendt [1948] 1968, 173–80). I submit that the turning point took place in 1898 when the U.S.-Spanish War was justified, from the U.S. perspective, with reference to

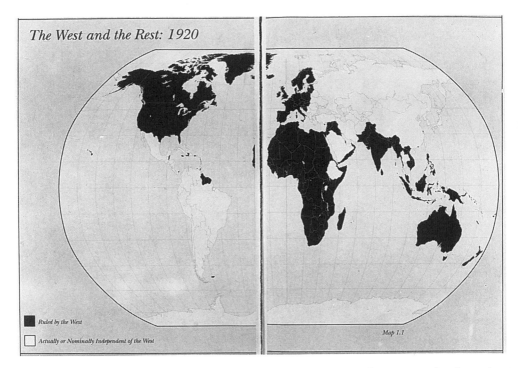

Figure 5. By 1920 hegemony has moved North and West as the United States was already on the way to becoming the new imperial country. Central and South America and the Caribbean (roughly "Latin America") became "marginal" in the imaginary of the modern/colonial world. (From Samuel P. Huntington. 1996. *The Clash of Civilians and the Remaking of the World Order.* Used by permission of Simon and Schuster.)

the superiority of the "white Anglo-Saxon race" whose destiny was to civilize the world (Mahan 1890; Burgess 1890, vol. 1; Fiske 1902b) over the "white Catholic Christians and Latins," a term introduced by the French political intelligentsia and used at that time to trace the frontiers in Europe as well as in the Americas between Anglo-Saxons and Latins. A significant turn of events took place whose consequences for today's racial and multicultural discourse in the United States cannot be overlooked. Not only did W.E.B. Du Bois write *The Souls of the Black Folk* ([1905] 1990) in the initial years of the twentieth century when racial discourse on white supremacy was justifying U.S. imperial expansion, but also the year 1898 became the anchor for the U.S. perspective on "Latinos" continuing until today. I have argued elsewhere (Mignolo, forthcoming) that 1898 provided the ideological and historical justification to recast 1848 and the Treaty of Guadalupe-Hidalgo between the United States and Mexico in an ideological discourse that was still not available at the time (Oboler 1997).

British Territory
French Territory
German Territory
Belgian Territory
Netherlands Territory
Portuguese Territory
Spanish Territory
Italian Territory

Figure 6. By the same years (beginning of the twentieth century), a look from the colonial perspective helps also in understanding the colonial difference. In contrast with figure 4, Spanish territory has been reduced to Spain itself. British and French territories reversed the sixteeth to mid-nineteeth century modern/colonial map: territorial possessions are now located in Africa and Asia, not in America. "British" territory in the Americas, as drawn on the map, is no longer British at the time but independent United States. (From Jürgen Osterhammel. 1997. *Colonialism: A Theoretical Overview*, used by permission of Markus Wiener Publishers.)

The changes in the modern/colonial world imaginary I have in mind throughout this book are illustrated in figures 7, 8, and 9. The reader should make an effort to "see" beyond the maps the colonial differences, framed in the sixteeth century and reframed ever since until the current scenario of global coloniality.

VI

There are, finally, several differences I would like to underline between the terminology and assumptions of the modern world-system model or metaphor and my own conception of the modern/colonial world-system. In the first place, I conceive of the system in terms of internal and external borders rather than centers, semiperipheries, and peripheries. Internal and external borders are not discrete entities but rather moments of a continuun in colonial expansion and in changes of national imperial hegemonies. The emer-

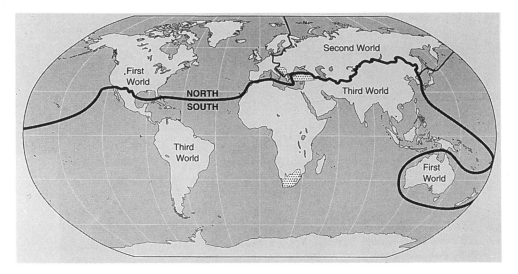

Figure 7. The cold war redrew the map of the early modern/colonial world and displaced the colonial difference from the dichotomy between Occident and Orient to North and South. The North-South geopolitical distinction is curious since Australia and Argentina are so far South as you can get, but the colonial difference has been located, this time, in First and Third Worlds. These developments explain again why "Latin America" began to fade away in the 1920s (see fig. 5). (From Martin W. Lewis and Karen E. Wigen. 1997. *The Myth of Continents: A Critique of Metageography.* Berkeley: The University of California Press. Used by permission of The University of California Press.)

gence of a new commercial circuit centered in the Atlantic and inclusive of both Spain and its domain in the Americas and the Philippines is one of the basic changes triggering a new imaginary. If Islam was situated in the exteriority of the commercial circuit, the Americas were located halfway between the otherness of the Amerindian and the African slaves, on the one hand, and the Spanish and Creole (born in America from Spanish descent) population, on the other. In the sixteenth century, Russia and Spain were two powerful Christian centers. Soon, they became its margin. Leopoldo Zea (1957) described how Russia and Spain became borders (his expression) of the West: "border countries where Western habits and customs are blurred and mingle with non-Western ones" ([1957] 1992, 103). For Zea, the increasing secularization of the hegemonic Western imaginary relegated Russia and Spain to the fringes of the West:

> Russia because of her Byzantine orthodoxy and Spain because of her Catholicism did not take the path pursued by the West, when she began to follow a new trend, renouncing her Christian past as an experience she had undergone but had no desire to repeat. During this phase Russia had to readjust to the new

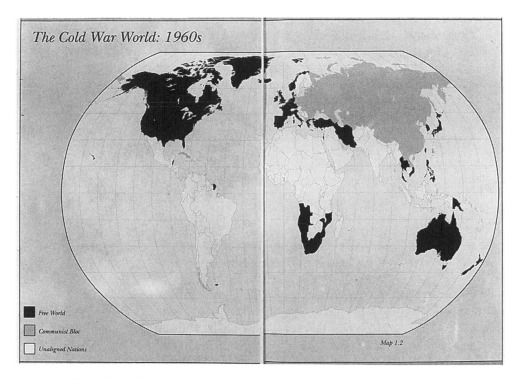

Figure 8. The cold war also witnessed massive decolonization that radically transformed the face of the world as depicted in figures 5 and 6. A new form of colonialism, nonterritorial, arose in the West (or "free world"), in wich power was no longer visible and measured in territorial possessions. A new form of colonialism arose in the East (or "Communist bloc"), leaving a zone of nations in between (or "unaligned nations"). (From Samuel P. Huntington. 1996. *The Clash of Civilizations and the Remaking of the World Order.* Used by permission of Simon and Schuster.)

> trend, become Westernized, and abandon that part of the past which no longer
> had any meaning for Western man. (Zea 1992, 104)

The Marxist-Leninist revolution in 1918 redrew the borders and the place of the Soviet Union in the modern world system and began a colonialism of its own. Although I do not pursue this line of thought in this book, it is important to mention it not only as an explanation of my understanding of "borders of the modern/colonial world system" but also because in 1959 Cuba entered into the reconfiguration initiated by the Russian Revolution and forced a redrawing of the geopolitical map of the Americas. It is also important to keep in mind that the Russian Revolution brought the emerging Soviet Union into a new relation with western Europe through the incorporation of Marxism, all the while maintaining its memory and its "difference" with the secular imaginary of the core countries of western Europe

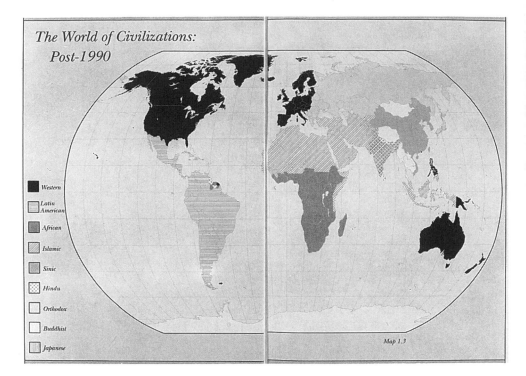

Figure 9. The end of the cold war made more visible what is still graphically invisible: the global colonialism enacted by the transnational corporations. The colonial difference is no longer located in the geographic arena. The colonial difference is displaced here to "civilizations," not to cardinal points in map. "Latin America" suddenly became a "civilization" whose configuration can hardly be understood without understanding the colonial difference as was played out in the complex spatial history of the modern/colonial world. (From Samuel P. Huntington. 1996. *The Clash of Civilizations and the Remaking of the World Order*. Used by permission of Simon and Schuster.)

(Wallerstein 1991a, 84–97). The "speed with which Russia was assimilated into European international society increased at the end of the seventeenth century" (Gong 1984, 101), but by the end of the nineteenth century, two positions (Westerners and Slavophiles) disputed Russia's relation to Europe. Westerners considered Russia European, whereas to Slavophiles it was both European and Eastern, "with native principles of life which had to be worked out without influence from Western Europe" (Gong 1984, 106). Similar considerations could and should be pursued in other borders, like the Ottoman Empire, Japan, China, and Islamic countries. Borders install in the imaginary of the modern/colonial world system an other logic, a logic that is not territorial, based on center, semiperipheries, and peripheries.

The decision to frame my argument in the modern/colonial world model rather than in the linear chronology ascending from the early modern, to the modern, to the late modern (as I did in *The Darker Side of the Renaissance*) was prompted by the need to think beyond the linearity of history and beyond Western geohistorical mapping. The geohistorical density of the modern/colonial world system, its interior (conflicts between empires) and exterior (conflicts between cosmologies) borders, cannot be perceived and theorized from a perspective inside modernity itself (as is the case for world system analysis, deconstruction, and different postmodern perspectives). On the other hand, the current and available production under the name of "postcolonial" studies or theories or criticism starts from the eighteenth century, leaving aside the crucial and constitutive moment of modernity/coloniality that was the sixteenth century.

Starting from the premises of world system analysis, I move toward a perspective that, for pedagogical purposes, I specify as modern/colonial world system analysis. If we bring to the foreground subaltern studies also as a perspective, as Veena Das suggests (Das 1989), then modern/colonial world system analysis introduces the subaltern perspective articulated on the basis of memories and legacies of the colonial experience, that is, the colonial experiences in their historical diversity. At this point the concept "coloniality of power," introduced by Anibal Quijano (1992, 1997, 1998) is displaced, shifting from a "modern world" to a "modern/colonial world." Once coloniality of power is introduced into the analysis, the "colonial difference" becomes visible, and the epistemological fractures between the Eurocentric critique of Eurocentrism is distinguished from the critique of Eurocentrism, anchored in the colonial difference—being articulated as postcolonialism—and which I prefer (because of the singularity of each colonial history and experience) to conceive and argue as post-Occidentalism (see chapter 2). Thus, the geopolitic of knowledge becomes a powerful concept to avoid the Eurocentric critique of Eurocentrism and to legitimize border epistemologies emerging from the wounds of colonial histories, memories, and experiences. Modernity, let me repeat, carries on its shoulders the heavy weight and responsibility of coloniality. The modern criticism of modernity (postmodernity) is a necessary practice, but one that stops where the colonial differences begin. The colonial differences, around the planet, are the house where border epistemology dwells.

There is, finally, another clarification to be made. Within the discussion among theoreticians and historians adhering to modern world system, the "origins" of capitalism and the "origins" of the modern world system constitute a point in question. Giovanni Arrighi's discussion of the nondebate between Ferdinand Braudel and Immanuel Wallerstein (Arrighi 1998, 113–29) is about the origin of capitalism that Braudel locates in thirteenth-century Italy. When Wallerstein takes 1500 as a reference point, it is not clear whether he is referring to the origin of capitalism or to the origin of the modern world system, which implies, but goes beyond, capitalism.

My own emphasis is on the emergence of a new commercial circuit that had, in the foundation of it's imaginary, the formalization of "purity of blood" and the "rights of the people." These two principles were contradictory in their goals: the first was repressive, the second was expansive (in the sense that a new logic and new legal principles were necessary to incorporate unknown people to the imaginary). The principles of "purity of blood" and the "rights of the people" connected the Mediterranean with the Atlantic. A new imaginary configuration was coalescing, one that complemented the transformation of the geopolitical world order brought about by the "discovery" of America: the imaginary of the emerging modern/colonial world system.

VII

Finally, a note on local histories and global designs, which are so crucial to understanding border thinking, at the intersection of both, but from the perspective of local histories, and above all, to understanding the limits of world system analysis, the variety of postmodern perspectives, and deconstruction confronted with the colonial difference and the emergence of border thinking. I suggested before that world system analysis, postmodern theories, and deconstructive strategies (even if there are differences between them) are all valuable critical enterprises of and within the imaginary of the modern world, but that they are blind to the colonial difference. They are blind not to colonialism, of course, as an object of study, but to the epistemic colonial difference and the emergence of border thinking as a new epistemological (or gnoseological) dimension. Let me offer some preliminary highlights of an emerging conceptualization from the experience of the colonial difference.

Hélé Béji, a writer and philosopher who divides her life between Paris and Tunisia, and who wrote a disenchanted book about the failures of nation-building after decolonization (Béji 1982), in her latest book makes a strong distinction between civilization and culture. Civilization, like for Norbert Elias (Elias 1937), is for Béji linked to modernity, progress, technology. Culture, on the other hand, is conceived as the domain of tradition, the domain and spheres of life against which civilizing designs attempt to tame. Culture is also linked with passion, whereas civilization is portrayed in terms of reason:

> Le triomphe des passions culturelles en dit long sur la désaffection des individus pour les promesses de la civilization . . . L'Occident est aujourd'hui confronté a cette nostalgie d'une identité qui se présente comme l'enjeu essentiel de notre humanité. De plus en plus, le mot *culture* recouvre une acception de l'humain où chaque identité, pour échapper à sa dissolution mondiale, se resserre dans

une tradition, une religion, une croyance, une origine, jusqu'à se réduire à une figure rudimentaire de la memorie que la civilization continue d'éffacer inélucta-blement. (Béji 1997, 46)

The triumph of cultural passions is very revealing of the disappointments that people experience when confronted with the promises made in the name of civilization. The West is today confronted with the nostalgic revival of identity that presents itself as the true face of humanity. The word *culture* discloses, more and more, a sense of being human where each identity, to avoid being dissolved by globalization, closes itself on a given tradition, a given religion, a belief, an origin, to the point of reducing itself, as identity, to a rudimentary figure of memory that civilization continues to erase relentlessly. (1997, 46)

The notion of "culture mondiale" introduced by Béji (1997, 47) has to be translated as "worldly culture" and not as "global culture," which will be a translation complicit with Béji's notion of civilization, technology, progress, and homogeneity. "Worldly culture," which for Béji is a new form of civiliza-tion (and I would say a post-Occidental notion of civilization), distinguishes itself from the concept of civilization associated with modernity in that "worldly culture" does not imply a "universal reason." "Worldly culture" would be, in my own argument, the outcome of border thinking rearticulat-ing, from the subaltern perspective of "cultural reason," the "universal rea-son of civilization." In a previous article I have attempted to express a similar idea under the concept of the "postcolonial reason" (1994, 1996a, 1997a) and, in chapter 2 of this book, as "post-Occidental reason," that I also ex-plore under the heading of border thinking/gnoseology.

The tensions between culture and civilization staged by Béji, parallel my own concept of subaltern knowledge in the constitution of the modern/colonial world system. Her concept of "worldly culture" parallels my own of border thinking as, precisely, the multiplication of epistemic energies in diverse local histories (different spaces and moments in the history of capi-talism; Arrighi 1994) and its unavoidable obscure companion, the history of colonialism (still to be written from the perspective I am displaying here). In the obscurity of the company, in the cracks between modernity and colo-niality, dwells the colonial difference(s). Béji's "culture" parallels my own "local histories" and, therefore, "worldly culture" could be translated to my vocabulary as the rearticulation and appropiation of global designs by and from the perspective of local histories. Let me offer you another quotation from Béji where my own notion of border thinking from the subaltern per-spective becomes the epistemic potential that remaps colonial difference(s) toward a future "culture mondiale" (worldly culture). Here the hegemony (face) of civilization and the subalternity of cultures would become the mul-tiple diversity of local histories (without faces) but no longer subaltern to global designs.

La *culture mondiale*, qui est une nouvelle forme de civilisation, se distingue de celle-ci en ce qu'elle n'a plus de raison universelle. La civilisation avait un visage, tandis qu'elle n'en a pas. Elle est une entité anonyme où l'Orient et l'Occident, tout en s'affrontant, développent de mystérieux traits communs. Les retombées de la civilization son entrées dans le métamorphorses sans nom, sans lieu, sans époque, de la culture mondiale. (Béji, 1997, 47; see my chapter 7 for an exploration of this last idea)

"Worldly culture" is a new form of civilization that distinguishes itself from the former in that "worldly culture" does not claim a universal reason. Civilization was provided with a face, while "worldly culture" doesn't have one. "Worldly culture" is an anonymous entity where the East and the West in confrontation cultivate [*developpent*] intriguing common traits. The periodic rise and fall of civilization are entering now in a metamorphosis of a worldly culture without name, without place, without epoch.

In a similar line of thinking, Martinican writer and philosopher, Edouard Glissant ([1990] 1997, 1998), distinguished between "globalization" (Béji's civilization, my global designs) and "mondialization" (Béji's culture, my local histories). A similar distinction in terms of vocabulary has been advanced, independent from Béji and Glissant, by Brazilian sociologist Renato Ortiz. Let me offer an example of each that will help in understanding the double articulation and the subsequent the epistemic potential of border thinking (from a subaltern perspective) emerging from the cracks between civilization and culture, between globalization and "mondialization" (worldness), between global designs and local histories. Here is Glissant on "globalization" and "worldness":

Worldness is exactly what we all have in common today: the dimension I find myself inhabiting and the relation we may well lose ouselves in. The wretched other side of worldness is what is called globalization or the global market: reduction to the bare basics, the rush to the bottom, standardization, the imposition of multinational corporations with their ethos of bestial (or all too human) profit, circles whose circumference is everywhere and whose center is nowhere. (Glissant 1998, 2)

From the clash between the worldness and the global, Glissant extracts the positive fact of "plural, multiplying, fragment identities" that is no longer perceived as a lack or a problem but as a "huge opening and as a new opportunity of breaking open closed gates" (1998, 2). The opening up of new and diverse worldness identities emerging from the clash between current global designs (the market civilization) is for Glissant the becoming of a "world in Creolization," to which I return in chapter 5. Glissant has been criticized for using "Créolization," a local Caribbean concept, and giving it a planetary (not universal) scope. However, the concept has also been used by anthropologist Ulf Hannerz (1987a) thinking precisely of globalization from the perspective of "peripheral cultures" (Hannerz 1991) and, furthermore, it has been the "normal" procedure in modern epistemology to delocalize concepts and to detach them from their local histories (e.g., "logocentrism," "archaeology," "capitalism," "cogito," etc.). By a different route, Glissant arrives at an image and description of the future similar to that of Hélé Béji, a perspective of a worldly culture as a new civilization without hegemony:

> What will historical consciousness be then, if not the chaotic pulsing towards these meetings of all histories, none of which can claim (thanks to the inherent qualities of chaos) to have an absolute legitimacy?. . . I call creolization the meeting, interference, shock, harmonies and disharmonies between the cultures of the world, in the realized totality of the earth-world. . . . Creolization has the following characteristics: the lightning speed of interaction among its elements; the "awareness of awareness" thus provoked in us; the reevaluation of the various elements brought into contact (for creolization has no presupposed scale of values); unforeseeable results. Creolization is not a simple cross breeding that would produce easily anticipated results. (Glissant 1998, 4)

If Creolization is not a "cross breeding," it is because it is conceived not as hybrid but, once again, as a rearticulation of global designs from the perspective of local histories. The local history Glissant is talking about and from is the colonization of the Caribbean. He is thinking from the colonial difference. And from the colonial difference hybridity is the visible outcome that does not reveal the coloniality of power inscribed in the modern/colonial world imaginary.

I conclude this discussion with Renato Ortiz because while Ortiz's distinction between "globalization" and "worldness" is similar to Glissant's (and also close to Béji's distinction between culture and civilization), he does not foresee a future in Creolization—a future of a "wordly culture" without one face, but with many of them. I explore this difference in more detail in chapter 3. I would like to note here, however, the differences between decolonization in Tunisia in the late 1950s, the fact that Martinique is, still a French "protectorate" after the wave of decolonization after World War II, and that Brazil's complex decolonization and subsequent nation-building took place during the nineteenth century. Ortiz, contrary to Béji, is thinking almost a century after decolonization in Brazil. His own approach to globalization has been shaped by both a local history and a colonial language (Portuguese) distinct from Béiji's.

But Ortiz has another aspect in common with my argument. His is a critic of the limits of the notion of world system, particularly when it comes to the notion of "culture." Ortiz ([1994] 1997, 23–98) is correct in pointing out that the notion on "geoculture" introduced later by Wallerstein (1991a) is restricted to the geoculture of the system. That is, it leaves in the dark other cultural manifestations or dimension. Wallerstein himself will agree with Ortiz's appraisal that this is precisely the meaning Wallerstein attributes to geoculture: the geoculture of the modern world system and not as the culture of the world. But in any case, Ortiz's debate with Wallerstein from Brazil and in Portugese (and translated into Spanish) is more a process of building his own argument than engaging in a dialogue with Wallerstein. What his argument amounts to is the need to distinguish between "globalizaçao" and "mondialiçaçao" (globalization and worldness).

From here Ortiz moves to differentiating, on the one hand, economic and technologic globalization from cultural worldness and, on the other, to distinguish between the restricted meaning of geoculture, in Wallerstein, and a world cultural diversity beyond and betwixt the geoculture of the modern world system. The establishing of these different levels allows Ortiz to disentangle, when thinking about capitalism in China and Japan, the level of globalization (economic, technologic) from the level of worldness. The Confucian intellectual legacy offered, for instance, a model for the adaptation of local culture to the global economy different from the training of workers in England after the industrial revolution. In this respect, the "traditional" European societies were less prepared for the advent of capitalism than the "traditional" societies in China or Japan. This comparison allows Ortiz to remap the concept of modernity and apply it to the multiplication of modernity as illustrated by the displacement of capitalism to East Asia. This move, in Ortiz's argument, is crucial since it represents the view of an intellectual in the "Third World" sensitized and attentive to the fractures of the geoculture of the modern/colonial world system when it enters in conflict with the diverse geocultures of the world. This is Ortiz's strength. His weakness is his blindness to the colonial difference. Ortiz's criticisms of Wallerstein's notion of geoculture have been argued from the very perspective of modernity itself, not of coloniality. Coloniality doesn't enter in his argument. Like in Wallerstein, modernity is the center and coloniality is relegated to the periphery of the history of capitalism. But coloniality is not a protagonist. Ortiz is more concerned with the transformation of life-style by what he calls "world modernity." "World modernity" (Ortiz [1994] 1997, 99–144), much like Béji "worldly culture," is not a European or North Atlantic modernity but is precisely worldly.

But contrary to the views of Béji and Glissant, Ortiz's worldly modernity is deprived of the memory of colonial differences and the forces, still at work today in the mass media, of the coloniality of power. Ortiz focuses his attention on examples such as airports or malls around the world and, from this vantage point, attempts to dismantle the easy opposition between global homogeneity and local heterogeneity (as well as other common oppositions). The argument—and sometimes the celebration of "world modernity"—is indeed against the defense of national values and cultures. The fact that Ortiz overlooks the colonial difference leads him to draw his "world" examples mainly from the United States, Japan, and Europe. Argentina and Brazil may enter the picture, but as a point of comparison, not as the location of the coloniality of power. For that reason, Africa, Asia, and the Caribbean are largely absent from his examples and statistics. For the same reason, when capitalism is considered, Ortiz's main examples are China and Japan, but not Algeria, Indochina, India, or even the Caribbean. Finally, and with the purpose of locating the different arguments, I would like to add that Ortiz's concern with epistemology is located in his departure from world system analysis. His is a signal contribution on the limitations of the social sciences when transposed from their place of "origin" to the colonial world. But Ortiz does not reflect critically on this issue (see my chapters 4 and 6), as other sociologists do (Quijano 1998; Lander 1998a; 1998b). In Latin American intellectual and academic production, this is a significant difference between intellectuals caught in the net of European legacies (like Ortiz himself) and intellectuals like Quijano, Dussel, and Rivera Cusicanqui for whom coloniality is a starting point of their intellectual production.

From this perspective, let's go back to the question of modernity. If, as Quijano and Dussel claim, modernity is not a European phenomenon, then modern colonialism has different rhythms and engery according to its spatial and historical location within the modern/colonial world system. Global designs thought out and implemented from the local history of Europe, first, and then the North Atlantic in the twentieth century were influential in the making of colonial modernities in different localities and temporalities of the modern/colonial world system. This book is not a new history of the modern/colonial world system but a series of reflections on the question of knowledge in the colonial horizon of modernity. My main aim is to make an epistemological point rather than to tell the story anew.

VIII

The book's architectonic is the following: by starting with and departing from the modern world system metaphor and introducing parallel expressions such as modernity/coloniality, modern/colonial world system, coloniality at large I intend to stress that there is no modernity without coloniality, that the coloniality of power underlines nation building in both local histories of nations that devised and enacted global designs as well as in those local histories of nations that had to accommodate themselves to global designs devised with them in mind but without their direct participation. Thus, two pervasive and simultaneous topics that run through the book are subaltern knowledges and border thinking, in their complex and diverse intersections at different stages of the modern/colonial world system. The Americas, for example, were part of the system from its very inception; the Islamic world, on the contrary, was cast out at the very inception of the system, while India came into the picture in the late eighteenth century; China and Japan, for their part, were never colonized in the way the Americas and India were, and their very existence and tardy entrance into the picture not only make the picture more complex, but also create new possibilities for thinking from and about the exterior borders of the system. President Clinton's 1998 visit to China was a preview of such possibilities.

Chapter 1 is devoted to developing in more detail the basic concepts and scenarios I have introduced thus far. The three chapters in Part Two revolve around the ratio between geopolitical configurations and knowledge production. Chapter 3 starts a dialogue with postcolonial theorizing, bringing "Occidentalism" and "post-Occidentalism" into the picture, post-Occidentalism serving as a local and overarching concept in the imaginary of the modern/colonial world system on which postcolonialism and post-Orientalism depend. Chapter 4 brings the overall discussion of chapter 2 to the Americas and their place in the modern/colonial world system, articulated by overlapping imperial conflicts and their relations with Amerindians and with African slavery and its legacy. It attempts to remap the Americas in the modern/colonial world system, rather than to reproduce it in the national imaginary, be it in Bolivar or the early version of the Monroe Doctrine. Chapter 4 brings the previous discussion to an epistemological terrain and explores, on the basis of subaltern studies, the tensions between local histories and global designs at the epistemological level. While in Part One the argument is underlined by the ratio between geopolitical configurations, knowledge, and the coloniality of power, Part Two focuses on language, knowledge, and literature (as a transdisciplinary site of knowledge production). In chapter 5 I focus on the crisis of national languages and literatures in a transnational world. Chapter 6 expands the same argument in the domain of epistemology and discusses the complicity between the hegemonic languages of the modern/colonial world system and the social sciences. Both chapters constantly bring to the foreground the dialectics between subaltern knowledges and border thinking. In chapter 7 I reconstruct the larger picture in which the issues discussed in chapters 5 and 6 take place. In it I discuss the role of "civilization" and "civilizing mission" in the modern/colonial world system. I consider border thinking at the intersection of the "barbarian" and the "civilized," as the subaltern perspective appropriates and rethinks the double articulation of "barbarian" and "civilized" knowledge.

All in all, this is an extended meditation that started from the recognition of any critique of modernity from inside modernity itself (e.g., postmodernity, deconstruction, world system analysis) and, above all, of its limits. That is why I start and depart from world system analysis (as well as from postmodernity and deconstruction). The internal variability of "differe/a/nce" cannot transcend the colonial difference, where deconstruction has to be subsumed and transformed by decolonization. In other words, the transcending of the colonial difference can *only* be done from a perspective of subalternity, from decolonization, and, therefore, from a new epistemological terrain where border thinking works (see the end of chapter 1, where I explore this idea through the work of Khatibi and Derrida). Border thinking can only be such from a subaltern perspective, never from a territorial (e.g., from inside modernity) one. Border thinking from a territorial perspective becomes a machine of appropriation of the colonial differe/a/nces; the colonial difference as an object of study rather than as an epistemic potential. Border thinking from the perspective of subalternity is a machine for intellectual deconolonization.

Part One

IN SEARCH OF AN OTHER LOGIC

CHAPTER 1

Border Thinking and the Colonial Difference

IN MARCH 1998, I participated in a workshop jointly organized by the University of Tunisia and the Mediterranean Studies Group, from Duke University. The subject of my talk, which is a recurrent theme of this book, was the mapping of the racial foundation of modernity/coloniality. Basically, I explored the reconversion and formalization of the "purity of blood" principle in sixteenth-century Spain (and, therefore, in the Mediterranean), which locked a long-lasting history of conflicts between the three religions of the Book and, parallel to it, the legal-theological debates, in the School of Salamanca, of the "rights of the people"—debates that turned around the vexing question of the location of Amerindians in the natural order of things and, therefore, in the Atlantic. The joint exploration of "purity of blood" with the "rights of the people" allowed me to put my finger on a crucial moment in the construction of the imaginary of the modern world system (e.g., the moment of emergence of a new commercial and financial circuit linking the Mediterranean with the Atlantic) and, at the same time, to look at it not only from the interiority of its formation and expansion but also from its exteriority and its margins. I was assuming, with Quijano and Wallerstein (1992) and Dussel ([1992] 1995; 1998a), that the particular moment I was looking at marked at the same time the emergence of a new world system and also of modernity/coloniality. In other words, the historical coexistence between the expulsion of the Jews and the Moors from Spain and the "discovery" of America was at the same time a landmark for both modern colonialism and colonial modernities—that is, of modernity/coloniality.

This historical logic was so obvious to me (as it would be to those working within world system theory or on the history of Spain and of Latin America) that I did not pay attention to the fact that most of my audience was from North Africa, and the history of Maghreb is significantly different from the history of Spain and (Latin) America. At the end of my talk I was asked a question, by Rashida Triki, art historian from the University of Tunisia, about precisely this coupling of modernity/coloniality. I did not understand the question very well and, obviously, I did not answer it, even if I did spend a few minutes talking around the question I did not fully understand. After the session was over, I approached Rashida and asked her to formulate the question and, finally, I understood! The misunderstanding was in our respective presuppositions: Rashida was thinking the history of colonialism, from the perspective of French (and modern, post-Enlightenment European) history, while I was looking at the "same" scenario from the perspective of Spain and (Latin) American history—that is, from the perspective of a national history marginalized from post-Enlightenment Europe (Spain) and a colonial moment (Indias Occidentales, later on Latin America), which was also erased from the construction of the idea of colonialism and the modern world (post-Enlightenment). From my perspective it was "natural" that modernity and coloniality are two sides of the same coin. For Rashida, coloniality not only came "after" modernity, but it was not easy for her to understand that for me they are two sides of the same coin—that is, to understand that from the perspective of the Americas, coloniality is constitutive of modernity. The colonial difference is here at work, revealing at the same time the difference between French colonialism in Canada and the Caribbean before the French Revolution and Napoleon era, and French colonialism thereafter. The colonial difference, in other words, works in two directions: rearticulating the interior borders linked to imperial conflicts and rearticulating the exterior borders by giving new meanings to the colonial difference.

Several years before, I had a somewhat similar conversation with the Mexican-based Argentinean anthropologist, Nestor García-Canclini, about colonialism and modernity in Latin America. For García-Canclini, colonialism is linked to the colonial period, roughly from early sixteenth century until the beginning of the nineteenth century. Since this time, what we have is the beginning of modernity, the nation-building process after several countries attained independence from Spain or autonomy from Portugal. In this linear fashion, colonialism structured the *past* of Latin America. Once again, from that perspective, the "colonial period" is perceived before "modernity," not as its hidden face. I found a different view articulated by Andean intellectuals (sociologist Silvia Rivera Cusicanqui in Bolivia; sociologist Aníbal Quijano in Peru) as well as in the Argentinean philosopher Enrique Dussel. Basically, for Rivera Cusicanqui, the history of Bolivia could be divided in three periods: the colonial period, roughly until mid-nineteenth century; the period of the republic, until 1952; and the period of modernization (which coincides with U.S. politics of progress and modernization in Latin America), until today. However, Rivera Cusicanqui (1992) does not conceive of these periods as successive, but as simultaneous: they all coexist today in diachronic contradictions, and what coexists is the colonial remora of Bolivian history, the different articulations of colonizing forces and colonized victims. Quijano (1992; 1997) talks, instead, of the coloniality of power. And Dussel ([1992] 1995) writes of a planetary and a European modernity whose inception coincides with, and is a consequence of, the "discovery" of America and the making of the Atlantic commercial and financial circuit.

COLONIALITY OF POWER: THE MODERN WORLD SYSTEM
FROM THE COLONIAL PERSPECTIVE

As I explain in the introduction, I start and depart from the modern world system model or metaphor. As a starting point it simplifies my argument: the connection of the Mediterranean with the Atlantic through a new commercial circuit, in the sixteenth century, lays the foundation for both modernity and coloniality. The new commercial circuit also creates the condition for a new global imaginary built around the fact that the new "discovered" lands were baptized "Indias Occidentales." The Occident, the West, was no longer European Christendom (as distinguished from Eastern Christians in and around Jerusalem) but Spain (and by extension the rest of Europe) and the new colonial possessions. "Occidentalism" was the geopolitical figure that ties together the imaginary of the modern/colonial world system. As such, it was also the condition of emergence of Orientalism: there cannot be an Orient, as the other, without the Occident as the same. For this very reason, the Americas, contrary to Asia and Africa, are not Europe's difference but its extension. This motif did not change when French and German naturalists, historians, and philosophers in the eighteenth century replaced the early descriptions of America provided by missionaries, soldiers, and men of letters with their own impressions: from Buffon to Hegel, America was conceived as the daughter of Europe and its promised future. Asia and Africa were the past, America the future. This motif lasted until the second half of the nineteenth century when "America" (Anglo-America) had really "grown up" and began to take over the leadership of the world order. One can say that Spain was the beginning of modernity in Europe and the beginning of coloniality outside of Europe. This view remains the canonical view today: there are books about colonialism and about modernity, but they do not interact—their genealogies are different. The reason for such a division is either the belief (contested by Quijano and Dussel) that modernity is only a European business and coloniality something that happens outside of Europe (provided that Ireland is not considered Europe), or the conception that coloniality is from the national perspective of the colonizing country. Algeria, for example, will seldom be included as part of French national history, although a history of Algeria, as a nation, cannot avoid France.

In this chapter I explore theoretical responses to and departures from the modern world system. I make an effort to connect and draw a genealogy of thinking from local histories subsuming global designs. First, I look into Anibal Quijano's concept of "coloniality of power" and Enrique Dussel's "transmodernity" as responses to global designs from colonial histories and legacies in Latin America. The second part is devoted to Abdelkhebir Khatibi's "double critique" and "une pensée autre" (an other thinking) as a re-

sponse from colonial histories and legacies in Maghreb. I also examine
Edouard Glissant's notion of "Créolization," proposed to account for the
colonial experience of the Caribbean in the horizon of modernity and as a
new epistemological principle. These perspectives, from Spanish America,
Maghreb, and the Caribbean, contribute today to rethinking, critically, the
limits of the modern world system—the need to conceive it as a modern/
colonial world system and to tell stories not only from inside the "modern"
world but from its borders. These are not only counter or different stories;
they are forgotten stories that bring forward, at the same time, a new epistemological dimension: an epistemology of and from the border of the mod-
ern/colonial world system.

I close the chapter by discussing two indirect criticisms of the type of
argument I am proposing. One, indirectly related, is by a sociologist of Marxist persuasion and Arabic/Muslim descent, Aziz Al-Azmeh, whose attach-
ment to disciplinary principles would make it difficult for him to understand
or accept positions and proposals as those advanced by Quijano, Dussel,
Khatibi, and Glissant. Al-Azmeh doesn't engage personally any of the thinkers I have discussed. I am interested, however, in Al-Azmeh's rejection of the
possibility of cross-cultural understanding that reestablishes the monotopic
principle of modern epistemology and, therefore, casts a doubt about transdisciplinary perspectives of those introduced by Glissant or Dussel. The second is Jacques Derrida's critique of Khatibi's concept of bilingualism and,
consequently, of double critique. In closing the chapter, I open it up to a
new dimension of thinking from the border of the modern/colonial world
system by bringing into the discussion Du Bois's "double consciousness"
and Gloria Anzaldúa's "new mestiza consciousness" grounded in the experience of the borderlands.

The "hidden" aspect of the "modern" world system was recently brought
to light by the Peruvian sociologist Anibal Quijano and by the Argentinian
philosopher of liberation, Enrique Dussel. Quijano came up with the
concept of coloniality, while Enrique Dussel originated the different
but complementary idea of transmodernity. What both concepts share,
however, is a sense that the modern world system or modernity, for that
matter, is being thought out and through from the "other end," that is,
from "colonial modernities." Quijano insists on the fact that, in Latin
America, the "colonial period" should not be confused with "coloniality,"
and that the nation building that followed it during the nineteenth
century in most Latin American countries (with the exception of Cuba
and Puerto Rico) cannot be understood without thinking through coloniality of power. And this is so, precisely, because modernity and coloniality are the two sides of the modern world system, although in Wallerstein's
version this double side was not clearly articulated. It was only
recently, when Quijano and Wallerstein cosigned an article ("Americanity

as a Concept, or the Americas in the Modern World-System," 1992), that coloniality made its appearance and brought to light the articulation of modernity/coloniality and the relevance of the Americas, and the sixteenth century in it.

> The modern world-system was born in the long sixteenth century. The Americas as a geosocial construct were born in the long sixteenth century. The creation of this geosocial entity, the Americas, was the constitutive act of the modern world system. The Americas were not incorporated into an already existing capitalist world-economy. There could not have been a capitalist world-economy without the Americas. (Quijano and Wallerstein, 1992, 549)

This emendation applies to two of the three basic items that Wallerstein originally singled out as constitutive of a capitalist world economy: an expansion of the geographical size of the world, the development of variegated methods of labor control for different products and different zones, and the creation of the relatively strong state machinery in the core states of the world economy (Wallerstein 1974, 38). The variegated methods of labor control were tied to the first racial mapping of the modern world system. The well-known debate of Valladolid—between Bartolomé de las Casas and Juan de Sepúlveda and, later on, the legal-theological scholarship in the School of Salamanca devoted to finding the place of the Amerindians in the chain of being and in the social order of an emerging colonial state—culminated in the enunciation of the "rights of the people" (a forerunner of the "rights of man and of the citizen") as vassals of the king and servants of God. Labor was needed for two reasons: first, to facilitate the massive death of Amerindians and, second, for the partial implementation of the crown legislation, helped by the church vigilance over the liberties taken by the *conquistadores* with Amerindians under their tutelage.

In what sense is coloniality of power helpful in understanding the current reconfiguration of the world economy and world imaginary in the history of Spanish control over the Indias Occidentales and the emergence of Latin America as a group of countries whose common denominators are the Spanish and Portuguese colonial legacies? In his 1997 article, Quijano presents the following argument. "Coloniality of power" and "historico-structural dependency" are two interrelated key words tracing the particular, local history of Latin America, not so much as an existing entity where events "happened" and "happen," but as a series of particular events whose location in the coloniality of power and in the historicostructural dependency has made Latin America, what Latin America has been and is today, from the colonial period in Peru to Fujimori as the paradigmatic articulation of neoliberalism. Coloniality of power underlines the geo-economic organization of the planet which articulates the modern/colonial world system and manages the colonial difference. That distinction allows Quijano to link

capitalism, through coloniality, to labor and race (and not only class) as well
as to knowledge:

> La colonialidad del poder y la dependencia histórico-estructural, implican
> ambas la hegemonía del eurocentrismo como perspectiva de conocimiento. . . .
> En el contexto de la colonialidad del poder, las poblaciones dominadas de todas
> las nuevas identidades fueron tambien sometidas a la hegemonía del eurocen-
> trismo como manera de conocer, sobre todo en la medida que algunos de sus
> sectores pudieron aprender la letra de los dominadores. (Quijano 1997, 117)

> Coloniality of power and historico-structural dependency: both imply the he-
> gemony of eurocentrism as epistemological perspective. . . . In the context of
> coloniality of power, the dominated population, in their new, assigned identi-
> ties, were also subjected to the Eurocentric hegemony as a way of knowing
> ([Quijano explains how "Indian" and "Black" were homogenizing identities es-
> tablished by the coloniality of power, erasing the diversity of "Indian" and
> "black" identities]).

A note on "dependency theory" and its mark in the imaginary of the
modern/colonial world system is here necessary for two reasons. One, is the
fact that dependency theory was one of the responses, from Latin America,
to a changing world order that in Asia and in Africa took the form of "decolonization." In the Americas, independence from colonial powers (Spain and
England) was obtained long before in what can be labeled the first wave of
decolonization (U.S. and Haitian revolutions; Spanish American independence). Dependency theory "preceded"—on the one hand—by a few years
Wallerstein's "modern world system" metaphor as an account from the perspective of modernity. It was "followed"—on the other hand and in Latin
America—by a series of reflexions (in philosophy and the social sciences)
as an account from the perspective of coloniality. Both Quijano and Dussel
are indebted to the impact of dependency theory in its critique to "development" as the new format taken by global designs once the "civilizing mission" was winding down with the increasing process of decolonization. Although dependency theory has been under attack from several fronts
(Cardoso 1977), it is important not to lose sight of the fact that from the
perspective of Latin America, it clearly and forcefully put in the agenda the
problems involved in "developing" Third World countries. The impact of
dependency theory in Latin American philosophy was remarkable too. Peruvian philosopher A. Salazar Bondy saw in dependency theory an epistemological provocation and a model to put an end to a long "imitative" tradition
and dependency of Latin America over European philosophy (Salazar Bondy
1969). It was a crucial moment of self-discovery, of understanding philosophy in Latin America and the Third World as part of a global system of
domination. In this regard, dependency theory was for philosophy, in Latin

America, what Father Placide Tempels's *Bantu Philosophy* (1945) was for the self-discovery of African philosophy (Mudimbe 1988; Eze 1997, 10–14; Serequeberhan 1994).

In the preceding pages, I hope to have suggested that the modern world system looks different from its exteriority as Quijano, following Juan Carlos Mariátegui, tries to show.[1] At the same time, underlining particular local histories that have been constructed around the density of "Indias Occidentales" and "Latin America" (constructions that could be explained through coloniality of power and as historicostructural dependency), I hope to have suggested and it will be clear as my argument proceeds, that Occidentalism was a planetary rearticulation during the sixteenth century, which continued as the overarching imaginary of the modern/colonial world system and of modernity/coloniality. "Indias Occidentales" and "Latin America" became crucial pieces in that redistribution and, indeed, made Orientalism possible. However, and paradoxically enough, the emergence of Orientalism (in Said's analysis; see Said 1978) coincided with the second stage of modernity as an interimperial transformation of capitalism and the modern/colonial world system with England and France expanding toward Asia and Africa. This is also the moment in which "modernity" and "modernization" began to make a difference in an emerging Latin America composed by several nations gaining independence from Spain and Portugal. A few years after the United States of North America gained independence from England, the French Revolution took place and the Haitian Revolution followed suit. However, at this moment of transition in the modern world system, U.S. independence and the French Revolution became the standards of modernity and modernization, and set the economic, political, and epistemological standards. Thus, it was clear that "Latin America" was not the Orient but the "extreme Occident," and its own intellectuals, like Domingo Faustino Sarmiento of Argentina, appointed themselves as the leaders of a civilizing mission in their own country, thus opening up the gates for a long history of intellectual internal colonialism, which began to break apart in 1898 when the system reaches a turning point. The United States entered the planetary scene as the new imperial power, and, in Latin America, a tradition of "peripheric intellectuals" contesting imperialism and the civilizing mission made its appearance (José Martí in Cuba, at the end of the nineteenth century; Juan Carlos Mariátegui in Peru, in the 1920s—see chapter 3). The emergence of "civilizing mission" displacing the "Christian mission" of early colonalism summarizes this switch in the modern world sys-

---

[1] The reader not familiar with Juan Carlos Mariátegui and the work of Aníbal Quijano since the late 1960s, should think in terms of something equivalent to the South Asian Subaltern Studies Group, although its focus was not the subaltern but colonialism and ethnicity in Mariátegui, from a Marxist perspective, Nietzsche and Sorel (for more details, see chapter 3).

tem and establishes the first articulation of internal borders, the borders
between two empires in decay (Spain and Portugal), the raising of the British
Empire and French colonialism, and the consolidation of Germany as a third
powerful nation in western Europe. The standards of knowledge and its
exportation were established mainly in these three countries and in these
three languages (see chapter 7).

Whereas Quijano began his intellectual production in the late 1960s in
sociology, Enrique Dussel began writing during the same years but in philosophy. Coming from their respective disciplines and trajectories and working
independently of each other, they arrived after 1990 at similar conclusions
and perspectives, as is often the case in Latin America where genealogies
are regularly broken by a new wave of ideas and intellectual production from
the center of the world system (in German, French, and English). In 1992,
Quijano published "Colonialidad y modernidad-racionalidad" (Quijano
1992) and Dussel came out with "Eurocentrism and Modernity" (Dussel
[1993] 1995). In his article, Dussel insists that what is today Latin America
was the first periphery of modern Europe and that the concept of modernity
that was framed after the Enlightenment occluded the role of Europe's own
Iberian periphery, and particularly Spain, in its formation (Dussel [1993]
1995, 67). This occlusion was such that even Wallerstein, who clearly states
that the modern world system began to be articulated in 1500 developing
new economic areas (mines and plantations), is blind to the Spanish contribution to the epistemological imaginary of the modern world system:

> Geo-cultures come into existence at one moment and, at a later moment, may
> cease to hold sway. In the case of the modern world-system, it seems to me that
> its geo-culture emerged with the French Revolution and then began to lose its
> widespread acceptance with the world revolution of 1968. The capitalist world-
> economy has been operating since the long sixteenth century. *It functioned for*
> *three centuries, however, without any firmly established geo-culture. That is to say,*
> *from the sixteenth to the eighteenth century, no one set of values and basic rules*
> *prevailed within the capitalism world-economy, actively endorsed by the majority*
> *of the cadres and passively accepted by the majority of the ordinary people. The*
> *French Revolution, lato senso, changed that.* It established two new principles:
> (1) the normality of political change, and (2) the sovereignty of the people. . . .
> The key point to note about these two principles is that they were, in and of
> themselves, quite revolutionary in their implications for the world-system. . . .
> It is in this sense that I have argued elsewhere that the French Revolution repre-
> sented the first of the antisystemic revolutions of the capitalist world-economy,
> in a small part a success, in larger part a failure. (Wallerstein 1995, 1163; empha-
> sis added)

Wallerstein is here also blind to the colonial difference and prisoner of the
very self-imaginary constructed by the intellectuals of the second stage of

modernization, once France, Germany, and England displaced Spain and Portugal from the economic and intellectual arena. He is missing the point of the constitutive character of the Americas for the imaginary of the modern/colonial world, as Quijano will make clear in an article coauthored with Wallerstein (Quijano and Wallerstein 1992). Said, with all his contributions to the politics of cultures of scholarship, fell into the same trap at the very inception of his definition and contextualization of Orientalism:

> Americans will not feel quite the same about the Orient [!], which for *them* is much more likely to be associated very differently with the Far East (China and Japan, mainly). Unlike the Americans, the French and the British—less so the Germans, Russians, Spanish, Portuguese, Italians, and Swiss—have had a long tradition of what I shall be calling *Orientalism*, a way of coming to terms with the Orient that is based on the Orient's special place in European Western experience. *The Orient is not only adjacent to Europe; it is also the place of Europe's greatest and richest and oldest colonies, the source of its civilizations and languages, its cultural contestant, and one of its deepest and most recurring images of the Other.* (Said 1978, 1; emphasis added)

I have no intention of ignoring the tremendous impact and the scholarly transformation Said's book has made possible. Nor do I intend to join Aijaz Ahmad (1992) and engage in a devastating critique of Said because the book doesn't do exactly what I want it to. However, I have no intention of reproducing the enormous silence that Said's book enforces: without Occidentalism there is no Orientalism, and Europe's "greatest and richest and oldest colonies" are not the "Oriental" but the "Occidental": the Indias Occidentales and then the Americas. "Orientalism" is the hegemonic cultural imaginary of the modern world system in the second modernity when the image of the "heart of Europe" (England, France, Germany) replaces the "Christian Europe" of the fifteenth to mid-seventeenth century (Italy, Spain, Portugal). It was from the "Indias Occidentales" that the great flow of riches, in gold and silver, reached Spain and the rest of Europe. One example suffices to sustain the argument: between 1531 and 1660 a minimum of 155,000 kilograms of gold and 16,985,000 of silver entered Spain legally; the illegal amount, of course, cannot be calculated (Céspedes del Castillo 1985, 133). These amounts transformed the economic relations between Spain and the rest of Europe and also the commerce with the "extreme" Orient. Céspedes del Castillo observes:

> De este modo América hizo posible el rápido crecimiento del comercio mundial y determinó su volúmen. Los grandes beneficiarios de ese tráfico fueron los intermediarios europeos: mercaderes, banqueros, la construcción naval y otras industrias. Además, una parte de los metales preciosos permaneció en Europa, bien atesorada para usos no económicos (haciendo posible el esplendor del arte barroco en escultura, orfebreria y vestido), bien acuñada, aumentando asi la

circulación monetaria, lo que influyó considerablemente en el desarrollo económico Europeo. (Céspedes del Castillo 1985, 133)

For this reason, America made the rapid growth of world trade possible, and
determined its volume. The great beneficiaries of such intense trading were the
European intermediaries: merchants, bankers, naval constructions, and other
industries. Furthermore, a great deal of gold and silver remained in Europe and
was directed toward noncommercial uses (which made the splendor of sculp-
ture and baroque art possible), although it was contributed to increase the circulation of money, which, as it turns out, was influential in the subsequent European economic development.

The situation began to change around 1630. Europe went through a period of depression between 1620 and 1680, and at the beginning of this
period devastating religious wars ravaged the area. Castilian colonial mo-
nopoly began to crumble and with it the power and prestige of Seville as a
commercial center of the new Atlantic commercial circuit. During the seventeenth century, Holland emerged as a new hegemonic power (Arrighi 1994).
Amsterdam, in the seventeenth century at the periphery of the new commercial circuit and under the control of Spain, replaced Seville as the world trade
center (Wallerstein 1980, 36–73). Whereas until this period the Atlantic was
the main focus of attention, as was piracy, on the part of the British, the
French, and the Dutch, in the seventeenth century Europeans under Dutch
leadership began to establish themselves in the East Indies. The interest of
the period for my argument, which I expand in chapter 7, is that colonial
mercantile economy was somewhat detached from the hegemonic Christian
ideology still dominant in its Puritan and Catholic conflicts. It was, in other
words, a colonial mercantile economy that would be linked to secularization
and the civilizing mission 150 years later.

It is true, as Said states, that the Orient became one of the recurring images
of Europe's Other after the eighteenth century. The Occident, however, was
never Europe's Other but the difference within sameness: Indias Occidentales (as you can see in the very name) and later America (in Buffon, Hegel,
etc.), was the extreme West, not its alterity. America, contrary to Asia and
Africa, was included as part of Europe's extension and not as its difference.
That is why, once more, without Occidentalism there is no Orientalism.
Occidentalism was a transatlantic construction precisely in the sense that
the Americas became conceptualized as the expansion of Europe, the land
occupied by the descendants of Japheth whose name has inscribed his own
destiny: "breath," "enlargement," and, as such, they will rule over Shem
(located in Asia) and Ham ("hot not in wisdom but in willfulness," located
in Africa) (Hay 1957, 12). During the sixteenth century, when "America"
became conceptualized as such not by the Spanish crown but by intellectuals
of the North (Italy and France, Mignolo 1982; 1995a, chap. 6), it was im-

plicit that America was neither the land of Shem (the Orient) nor the land of Ham (Africa), but the enlargement of the land of Japheth. There was no other reason than the geopolitical distribution of the planet implemented by the Christian T/O map to perceive the planet as divided into four continents; and there was no other place in the Christian T/O map for "America" than its inclusion in the domain of Japheth, that is, in the West (Occident). Occidentalism, in other words, is the overarching geopolitical imaginary of the modern/colonial world system, to which Orientalism was appended in its first radical transformation, when the center of the system moved from the Iberian Peninsula to the North Sea, between Holland and Britain.

Quijano and Dussel, as well as Brazilian "anthropologian" Darcy Ribeiro (1968; [1969] 1978), have been at pains to find a location "beyond eurocentrism" (Dussel 1998a) or "beyond occidentalism" as Coronil (1996) has recently restated the issue. One of the main concerns of these scholars is knowledge: Occidentalism—as I said—as the overarching imaginary of the modern world system was, at the same time, a powerful machine for subalternizing knowledge (from the early missionaries of the Renaissance to the philosophers of the Enlightenment), and the setting up of a planetary epistemological standard. Quijano addresses this issue explicitly in his article "Colonialidad y modernidad-racionalidad" (Quijano 1992) and Dussel does so in his "Eurocentrism and Modernity" ([1993] 1995) as well as in his book *The Underside of Modernity* (1996a). The basic argument in Dussel reads as follows:

> Kant's answer to the question posed by the title of his essay "What Is Enlightenment?" is now more than two centuries old: "Enlightenment is the exodus of humanity by its own effort from the state of guilty immaturity. . . . Laziness and cowardice are the reasons why the greater part of the humanity remains pleasurably in state of immaturity. . . . Today we would ask him: an African in Africa or as a slave in the United State in the eighteenth century; and an Indian in Mexico or a Latin American *mestizo*, should all of these subjects be considered to reside in a state of guilty immaturity? (Dussel [1993] 1995, 68)

Of course the answer will be no in most cases, although the fact remains that today Kant's dictum has all its force in its spirit, and not necessarily in Kant's precise words. There is no question that Quijano, Dussel, and I are reacting not only to the force of a historical imaginary but also to the actuality of this imaginary today. Quijano has a similar perspective on the subalternization of knowledge when he writes: "At the same time that the colonial domination was asserting itself, a cultural complex under the name of rationality was being put in place and established as the universal paradigm of knowledge and of hierarchical relations between the 'rational humanity' (Europe) and the rest of the world" (1992, 440). As a sociologist, Quijano assigns himself the task of analyzing the epistemological crises that he locates in the epistemological principle splitting the knowing subject from the known object. He concerns himself with this paradigm where the accent is placed on the individual character of the knowing subject, thus suppressing the intersubjective dimension in the production of knowledge. Quijano establishes a link between the epistemological relation between a subject and an object, and the economical relation between a subject and its private property. But what is really relevant in Quijano's analysis of the subalternization of knowledge is not so much the complicity with modern economic ideology (either private property in Renaissance mercantilism or in Enlightenment capitalism), but the fact that once a correlation between subject and object was postulated, *it became unthinkable to accept the idea that a knowing subject was possible beyond the subject of knowledge postulated by the very concept of rationality put in place by modern epistemology* (Quijano 1992, 442). That is the reason Orientalism was possible, as well as area studies after World War II (see chapters 2 and 7).

THE LOCAL HISTORIES OF GLOBAL DESIGNS

This epistemological configuration, regularly located in Descartes, was a turning point in relation to the epistemology of the Renaissance, significantly alien to the subject-object distinction. As a matter of fact, the dominant tendency in the Renaissance was expressed in the *Studia Humanitatis* and its concerns with education, the nature of Man and ethics. Thus, grammar, rhetoric, poetry, and history (as rhetorical and ethical enterprise) were the dominant disciplines (Cassirer, Kristeller, and Randall 1948; Kristeller 1965). In general, Aristotle was not a major figure because of his emphasis on logic and science (as with the Italian Aristotelian Pietro Pomponazzi [1462–1525], the Renaissance concept of science was far from the idea that was to be introduced at a later date by Galileo and, philosophically, by Descartes). It was, so to speak, a humanistic conceptualization of science and philosophy, based in logic rather than in observation and experimentation. Furthermore, the perception of the Arab world at this time was not a perception that we can call "Orientalism" and not even the perception of the "Other," but rather the perception of an enemy whose knowledge had the same foundation: Greek thought. In a letter of November 17, 1370, Petrarch pronounces to his physician and friend, Giovanni de Dondi, a strong judgment against the Arabs:

> Before I close this letter, I implore you to keep these Arabs from giving me advice about my personal condition. Let them stay in exile. . . . I know that the Greeks were once most ingenious and eloquent men. Many very excellent philosophers and poets; outstanding orators and mathematicians have come

from Greece. That part of the world has brought forth princes of medicine. You know what kind of physicians the Arabs are. I know what kinds of poets they are. . . . The minds of men are inclined to act differently; but, as you used to say, every man radiates his own peculiar mental disposition. To sum up: I will not be persuaded that any good can come from Arabia. (Cassirer et al. 1948, 142)

In the fourteenth century the Arabs were not the subaltern "Other" they would become, relocated from the sixteenth century on with the victory of Christianity over Islam and the conflation of Arabs with Islam. Padua was a peripheral place in a world order whose commercial circuits (Abu-Lughod 1989, 34; see fig. 2 on page 27) extended from Genoa to Peking with Baghdad, Alexandria, and Cairo as more "central" locations. It was only the triumph of Christian Spain at the inception of a new circuit, the Atlantic circuit, that will place the "Arabs" in a subaltern position, making them the Other and contributing to the configuration of the object of study in the eighteenth century that prompts what Said named Orientalism.

Orientalism, in other words, was a particular rearticulation of the modern/colonial world system imaginary in its second phase, when Occidentalism, structured and implemented in the imaginary of Spanish and Portuguese empires, began to fade away. But to say it was fading away does not mean that it vanished. Occidentalism lost the imaginary hegemonic power. However, in Petrarch's dictum, the value ascribed to Arab knowledge, from a Christian perspective, became a yardstick to judge and subalternize forms of knowledge that cannot be justified within the Greco-Roman and Christian epistemological configuration. The so-called discovery of the New World was a foundational moment in this respect: while the *Studia Humanitatis* was producing and establishing the rule of knowledge, chiefly in theology, ethics, and education in an emerging Christian western Europe, the emergence of a "new world" forced a rearticulation of the principle of knowledge in the realm of ethics and in the "scientific" (e.g., Aristotelian) aspect of the Renaissance.

In the domains of ethics, I underline one of Dussel's basic observations:

The first Hispanic, Renaissance, and humanist modernity produced a theoretical and philosophical reflection of the highest importance, which has gone unnoticed by so-called modern philosophy (which is only the philosophy of the second modernity). The theoretical-philosophical thought of the sixteenth century has contemporary relevance because it is the first, and only, that lived and expressed the originary experience during the period of the constitution of the first world-system. Thus, out of the theoretical "recourses" that were available . . . , the central philosophical ethical question that obtained was the following:

what right has the European to occupy, dominate and manage the recently discovered
cultures, conquered by the military, and in the process of being colonized? (Dussel
1998a, 15)

Dussel is referring here to the discussions in the School of Salamanca on the
"rights of the people," a legal-theological debate forgotten, in the eighteenth
century, when the declaration on the "rights of men and of the citizen" came
into existence. The enormous difference between the two ethical moments
in the imaginary of the modern world system is that in the declaration of
the "rights of men and of the citizen" the colonial question has vanished;
consequently, the concept of man and of the citizen universalized a regional
issue and erased the colonial question. It was precisely at that intersection,
and due to the erasure of the colonial conflict, that the Haitian Revolution,
which was enacted as an implementation of the rights of man and of the
citizen, was unthinkable, as Trouillot eloquently argued (Trouillot 1995).
And it was unthinkable, I would submit—and suggest that Quijano and
Dussel have been making a similar point from a different perspective—because the eighteenth century redefined the imaginary of the modern/colonial
world system in a way that was consistent with the new imperial power
(Holland, Britain, France). It was self-conceived as a new beginning that
erased—for the future generation—the crucial importance of the Renaissance and the Reformation. D'Alembert made this point very clear at the
beginning of his "Élements de philosophie" (1759):

> If one examines carefully the mid-point of the century in which we live, the
> events which excite us or at any rate occupy our minds, our customs, our
> achievements, and even our diversions, it is difficult not to see that in some
> respects a very remarkable change in our ideas is taking place, a change whose
> rapidity seems to promise an even greater transformation to come. . . . Our cen-
> tury is called . . . the century of philosophy par excellence. . . . *The fruit or sequel*
> *of this general effervescence of minds has been to cast new light on some matters*
> *and new shadows on others, just as the effect of the ebb and flow of the tides is to*
> *leave something on the shore and to wash others away.* (Quoted in Cassirer 1951,
> 4; emphasis added)

The turning point was, for D'Alembert, the *"mid-point of the century in*
which we live" and he was right. The entire theologicolegal debate on colonization and the "rights of the people" has vanished from sight and, today,
postcolonial thinking has promoted an imaginary that "begins" also in the
eighteenth century. This is one of the reasons why it is not obvious for Said
that "Occidentalism" is the condition of possibility of "Orientalism" and
"Orientalism" accepted as an emerging field without preconditions. In the
same vein, we could explain that the South Asian Subaltern Studies Group
attempted to bring Marx into the rewriting of colonial history at the same

time—and for very understandable historical reasons—to locate the limits of colonialism in the British colonization of India, toward the end of the eighteenth century. This is why, once again, Kant's reflections on the Enlightenment is so important to the group leader, Ranajit Guha (Guha 1996). My first intention here in piggybacking my own analysis on world system theory is precisely to bring back to the shore memories that have been washed away and that are so "fundamental" in today's global imaginary. My second intention is to take advantage of the modern/colonial world system to locate the emergence of "border thinking" from the colonial difference as a revolution equivalent to the one described by D'Alambert but happening in several locations at the same time, responding to an amazing diversity of local histories and inverting the post-Enlightenment tendency to refer all kinds of knowledge to "the century of philosophy par excellence" convincingly described by D'Alembert.

My observations on Quijano and Dussel could be complemented by a significant amount of work being done in African philosophy during the past three decades, mainly by a new generation of philosophers who assigned to themselves the task of reading major figures of Western thought (Kant, Hegel, Marx, Heidegger, Foucault) from the point of view of coloniality. Eze (1997b) and Serequeberhan (1997), for example, provide a revealing reading of what is "behind" Kant's "What Is Enlightenment" as well as his theory of pure and practical reason and the sublime. Eze shows a double movement in Kant's theoretical reflections: on the one hand, the spatial organization of people by the color of their skin and their planetary location in the four continents that Kant developed in his lectures on *Anthropology from a Pragmatic Point of View* (delivered between 1756 and 1797); and, on the other, Newton's theories of the natural world applied to the history and morality. The end result is a search for the transcendental as the ultimate grounding of reason, knowledge, and philosophy. Kant was able to classify and describe four races: white (Europeans), yellow (Asians), black (Africans), and red (American Indians). In the American Indians, the Negroes, and the Hindus (in which he included Persians, Chinese, and Turks), he also found the potential for reason, passion, and sensibility that he found in the white Europeans. (It is notorious, incidentally, that when Kant talks about the Americans he talks about North America, as South America undeniably slides out of the picture.) Serequeberhan, for his part, discovers the same prejudice in Kant's "What Is Enlightenment" and in "Idea of a Universal History from a Cosmopolitan Point of View," both pieces published in 1784. The task African philosophers assign to African philosophy is complemented by the new task Continental philosophers assign to Continental philosophy in dialogue with Africans (i.e., Bernasconi 1997), showing the limits of Derrida's deconstruction from the perspective of African philosophy.

While this geopolitical distribution of intellectual tasks and disciplinary projects may look suspect, it is unavoidable precisely because of the constitution of the imaginary of the modern/colonial world system. "Philosophy" has to be appropriated as a word and as an activity from Africa or Latin America (Salazar Bondy 1966; 1969) in order to interrogate Europe and European philosophy as the local history in which such global designs were conceived and imposed by force or by seduction. But there is still another level in which African philosophy must reorganize its task beyond rereading the key figures of Western philosophers in their blindness to the colonial difference and to the coloniality of power. This task is to mediate between philosophical practices within colonial modern histories (e.g., the practice of philosophy *in* Africa, Latin America, North America, as we will see in chapter 2) and "traditional" forms of thoughts—that is, forms of thought coexisting with the institutional definition of philosophy but not considered as such from the institutional perspective that defines philosophy. "Tradition" here doesn't mean something "before" modernity but rather the persistence of memory. In that regard, there is no difference between African and European "traditions." Both Africa and Europe have them, and both have "modernities" and "colonialities," although in different configurations. While the first concern could be conceived as intellectual decolonization, the second concern leads to "border thinking," as has been clearly argued by Wiredu (1997, 303–12), Eze (1997c), and Makang (1997).

In the next section I explore both decolonization as a form of deconstruction and border thinking in the works of Moroccan philosopher, essayist, and novelist Abdelkebir Khatibi, and Martinican writer and thinker Edouard Glissant.

THE LOCAL HISTORIES OF BORDER THINKING

I turn now to the emergence and epistemological potential of "border thinking," whose planetary and local historical conditions have been outlined in the first section and linked to the colonial difference as articulated in its variance along the spacial history of the modern/colonial world. By planetary and local historical conditions I mean a double movement: on the one hand, the expansion of the modern world system since the end of the fifteenth century; on the other, the parallel construction of its imaginary both from inside and from outside of the system. By local historical conditions I refer also to both the local histories "within" the modern world system (e.g., the local histories of the "metropolitan centers," the local histories of Europe and the United States, the local histories of Spain and England) and the local histories of its margins (e.g., the Andes under colonial rule, the independence of Latin American countries from Spain and nation building under a new global order, the local history of India under British rule or of Algeria and Tunisia under French colonialism). I am not, therefore, setting a stage in which local histories are those of the colonized countries, or the Third World, and global designs are located in the colonizer countries of the First World. Global designs, in other words, are brewed, so to speak, in the local histories of the metropolitan countries; they are implemented, exported, and enacted differently in particular places (e.g., in France and Martinique, for instance, in the nineteenth century).

This description corresponds to the canonical moment of the modern world system. After the 1970s and more so after the 1990s, however, it becomes more difficult to locate global designs in particular "countries" since transnational corporations are, precisely, undermining the power of the state (even of the state of developed countries) to produce and "export" global designs. To the extent that global designs are no longer situated in one territory (e.g., those of British colonialism), local histories are correspondingly affected. In this regard, countries that had colonial possessions until the 1960s (like Britain and France) are becoming subject to the transformation of their own local histories in relation to their previous location in the coloniality of power. This scenario also applies to the United States. today. The U.S. position in the world order is radically different from the position that, for instance, Spain occupied in the sixteenth or England in the nineteenth century, due mainly to the power of transnational corporations and its consequences: the expansion of capitalist economy to those regions of the planet that have been identified, from the local histories where capitalism emerged, as "Oriental" and, therefore, not likely to become capitalist. That was, precisely, the entire point made through the "Orientalist" imaginary. Capitalism was linked to the "Occidental" imagination, not to the "Oriental" one. But, of course, it was linked to a certain dimension of Occidentalism: an Occidentalism located in northern and western Europe (France, England, Germany) and the United States, but not to southwestern Europe (Italy, Spain, Portugal) and their legacy in Latin America.

I needed the preceding geopolitical map to point out the external and internal borders of the modern world system in order to locate, in both, the emergence of border thinking. Now I can consider some of the central ideas advanced by Abdelhebir Khatibi (Khatibi 1983, [1983] 1990), a Moroccan philosopher, along with those of Carribean writer and essayist, Edouard Glissant (Glissant [1981] 1989; [1990] 1997). The main reasons to select Khatibi in relation to my previous argument are several. First, Khatibi's arguments bring to the foreground the early history of the modern world system and the conflict between the Christians and the Moors in the sixteenth century in the ideology of the Renaissance, which Khatibi refers to as "Occidentalism." Second, he rearticulates this conflict with the second, post-Enlightenment moment of the modern world system: the French colonization of

Maghreb. Third, Khatibi has a critical perspective on "Orientalism" independent of Said's : his article "L'orientalisme désorienté" was originally published in 1974. Fourth, Khatibi's essay on "La decolonization de la sociologie," written in 1981, advances important perspectives on the decolonization of knowledge that have been brought out to a larger audience, more recently (although not necessarily with the same critical force) by the report of the Gulbenkian Foundation, *Open the Social Sciences* (Wallerstein et al., 1996). I will expand on these issues one at a time. Finally, although Khatibi is piggybacking on Derrida's deconstruction and on Foucault's archaeology, because he does not have the same concern with opposing one to the other, he is also clearly detaching himself from both of them. Khatibi procedes in the same manner with Nietzsche and Heidegger, embracing their proposal to a certain point: the point where an internal critique of modernity is blind to the critical perspectives from the Arabic language, knowledge, and memory and the Islamic world. It is precisely here that border thinking emerges in full and plain force. Edouard Glissant, for his part, will provide a multilayered, comparative perspective: the Afro-Caribbean experience of French colonialism, with the repressed memory of Spanish early colonization; and the memory of African slavery contrasted with the Arabic-Islamic density of Maghreb.

An Other Thinking

The general ideal of decolonization of knowledge, in Khatibi, is grounded in two of his crucial concepts: "double critique" and "une pensée autre" ("an other thinking"). In the course of exploring these concepts I will be defining my own conceptualization of border thinking (border gnosis, or border epistemology). By so doing, I am not attempting to find the only and correct concept that captures the "thing," the (master) empty signifier that will house the entire diversity of particulars. To do so would go against my own conception of border thinking, changing the content, but not the terms, of the conversation (as I learned from Rolph-Trouillot's "Global Flows, Open Cultures," a paper presented at Stanford University in May 1998). I would be falling into a modern, universal view of knowledge and epistemology, where concepts are not related to local histories but to global designs, and global designs are always controlled by *certain* kinds of local histories. My conception of border thinking emerges not from a universal conceptual genealogy that can be traced to Plato (or Aristotle, for that matter), or linked to some enlightened philosopher in the eighteenth century and back to some influential thinker of the present (who more certainly will be linked to a national genealogy and write in French, German, or English), but from the local histories of Spanish legacies in America. More specifically, my conceptualization emerges from the imperial conflict between Spain and the United States, in the nineteenth century, which has generated the physical borderland between Mexico and the United States, but also the metaphorical borders as enacted in the histories of Cuba/United States, Puerto Rico/United States that basically define the configuration of Latino/as or Hispanics in this country. However, Spain is also the missing link between Khatibi's double critique, an other thinking and my own border gnosis. The early expulsion of the Moors out of the Iberian Peninsula, where they lived for several centuries, and across the Mediterranean (Harvey 1990) was in keeping with the need to find a place for the Amerindians in the planetary, and Christian order of being, and with the exportation of African slaves to take up the jobs that Amerindians—as vassals of the king—were not legally allowed to do.

In Khatibi's local history, the West (*l'Occident*) is defined in opposition to "notre patrimoine" (*l'Islam*). However, he is quick to get out of the dichotomy necessary to set the stage for an other thinking ("une pensée autre") since, and curiously enough, an other thinking is a way of thinking without the Other. Since the conflict between Europe and the Arab world goes back many centuries, Khatibi argues, this conflict becomes a machine of mutual misunderstanding (1983, 15)—thus, the necessity of a double critique to both Occidental and Islamic fundamentalism. A double critique becomes at this intersection a border thinking, since to be critical of both, of Western and Islamic fundamentalism, implies to think from both traditions and, at the same time, from neither of them. This border thinking and double critique are the necessary conditions for "an other thinking," a thinking that is no longer conceivable in Hegel's dialectics, but located at the border of coloniality of power in the modern world system. Why? Because Hegel's dialectics presuppose a linear conception of historical development, whereas "an other thinking" is based on the spatial confrontations between different concepts of history. Or, shall I say, "an other thinking" is possible when different local histories and their particular power relations are taken into consideration. In this case, Arabic philosopher Ibn Khaldun becomes canonical in his difference from German philosophers. Linear progress and progression are not within the scope of a double critique, and a dialectical synthesis is no longer recommended once "an other thinking" becomes available. The epistemological potential of border thinking, of "an other thinking," has the possibility of overcoming the limitation of territorial thinking (e.g., the monotopic epistemology of modernity), whose victory was possible because of its power in the subalternization of knowledge located outside the parameters of modern conceptions of reason and rationality. A double critique releases knowledges that have been subalternized, and the release of those knowledges makes possible "an other thinking." In the case of Khatibi, we are at the intersection of French and Arabic, at the intersection of Western and Arabic knowledge, but not in a happy synthesis that will lead us to a natural reproduction of Western epistemology.

The second opposition Khatibi attempts to undo (after the opposition between the Christian West and the Islamic East), and I would say the very foundation of his need for a double critique, is the postcolonial situation in the Maghreb. "What did we do," asks Khatibi, reflecting on Maghrebian intellectuals' attitude in the process of decolonization, "other than reproduce a rather simplistic version of Marx's thought, on the one hand, and the ideological theology of Arabic nationalism, on the other?" (1983, 16). A way out of these dichotomies presupposes a double critique and the search for "an other thinking" that will go beyond certain limitations of Marxist thinking, which maintains a geopolitics of knowledge according to the knowing subject in the First World (the Occident) and the known subject in the dogmatism and Arabic nationalism: "An other thinking is formulated as a response to the large questions and issues that are shaking the world today, to the questions emerging from the places where the planetarization of science, of technique and of strategies are being disclosed" (13). What emerges from this formulation is that "an other thinking" is no longer located in either of the two alternatives into which Orientalism, and later area studies, organized the distribution of scholarly labor from the eighteenth century to the cold war. "An other thinking" implies a redistribution of the geopolitics of knowledge as organized by both Occidentalism (as the overarching imaginary and self-definition of the modern world system) and Orientalism (one particular instance in which the difference from the same was located), along with area studies and the triumph of the social sciences in the geopolitics of knowledge. It also entails an effort to escape the domain of Western metaphysics and its equivalent, the theological realm of Islamic thought. "An other thinking" locates itself in all of these, and in none, in their borderland (as Gloria Anzaldúa frames it).

The potential of "an other thinking" is epistemological and also ethical: *epistemological* because it is constructed on a critique of the limitations of two metaphysical traditions—the Christian/secular Western and the Islamic. Two historical moments are relevant here: one, the sixteenth century and the rearticulation of the conflict between Christianity and Islam, through the "purity of blood" principle (see the introduction); two, the eighteenth century and the secularization of philosophy and knowledge, the formation of capitalism, and the rise of French colonialism. Thus, a consequent description of "an other thinking" is the following: a way of thinking that is not inspired in its own limitations and is not intended to dominate and to humiliate; a way of thinking that is universally marginal, fragmentary, and unachieved; and, as such, a way of thinking that, because universally marginal and fragmentary, is not ethnocidal (Khatibi 1983, 19). Thus, the *ethical* potential of an other thinking. Dussel, independently of Khatibi, has characterized modern, instrumental reason by its genocidal bent. He tries to reveal this in his concept of the "myth of modernity": "Modernity includes a rational "concept" of emancipation that we affirm and subsume. But, at the same time, it develops an irrational myth, a justification for genocidal violence. The postmodernists criticize modern reason as a reason of terror; we criticize modern reason because of the irrational myth it conceals" (Dussel [1993] 1995, 67). Interestingly, Khatibi and Dussel not only coincide in their critique of modernity without knowing each other, but both define their enterprise in relation to modernity and to European philosophers (Nietzsche, Heidegger, Foucault, Derrida for Khatibi; Apple, Marx, Habermas, Levinas for Dussel). The consequences of coloniality of power and subalternization of knowledge can be perceived at work from the colonial difference nourishing Khatibi's and Dussel's ethical and epistemic reflections. And this is the situation that "an other thinking" addresses at the same time that it opens a new perspective for a geopolitical order of knowledge production.

Khatibi's double critique of two kinds of "metaphysics" (Western and Islamic) has a geohistorical locus of enunciation called "Maghreb." But what does he mean by this claim to a location and a true being ("tel qu'il est") of the Maghreb? The Maghreb, far from being constructed as an ontological site, similar to the idea of the nation, is, on the contrary, thought out as the location of what I will elaborate as an epistemic irreducible difference. I want to indicate a geohistorical location that is constructed as a crossing instead of as a grounding (e.g., the nation). Located between Orient, Occident, and Africa, the Maghreb is a crossing of the global in itself. On the other hand, in order to think of the Maghreb as the difference that cannot be told, and not as an "area" to be studied, we need a kind of thinking beyond the social sciences and positivistic philosophy, a kind of thinking that moves along the diversity of the historical process itself. Such a way of thinking should first be attentive, "listening to Maghreb in its plurality (linguistic, cultural, political)"; and, second, it should be attentive to "Maghreb exteriority." This is an exteriority that shall be decentered from its dominant determinations in such a way that would make it possible to think beyond the ontologization of an area to be studied and move to a reflection of the historicity of differences. In this sense, a double critique is the criticism of the imperial discourses (the exteriority from which the Maghreb was constituted as an area) as well as of national discourses asserting identity and differences articulated in and by imperial discourses (Khatibi 1983, 39).

At this point, double critique is a crucial strategy to build macronarratives from the perspective of coloniality. As such, these macronarratives are not predestined to tell the truth that colonial discourses did not tell. That step is already implied in double critique. Macronarratives from the perspective of coloniality are precisely the places in which "an other thinking" could be implemented, not in order to tell the truth over lies, but to think otherwise, to move toward "an other logic"—in sum, to change the terms, not just the content of the conversation. Such narratives make it possible to think coloniality, and not only modernity, at large. The epistemological implications of these possibilities are enormous. I explore some of them here, specifically those that allow Khatibi to position himself in relation to the social sciences (e.g., his claim for the decolonization of sociology) and those that allow him to distance himself from his own allies (e.g., internal criticism of Western metaphysics, as represented by Nietzsche, Heidegger, Derrida, or Foucault).

With respect to sociology, Khatibi underlines the fact that sociohistorical decolonization (with all its difficulties) did not produce a critical way of thinking. It did not result in, as Khatibi puts it, a decolonization that would have been, at the same time, a deconstruction. By playing decolonization together with deconstruction, and underlining that his is a perspective from the Third World (1983, 47), Khatibi is indeed making a move of boundless significance. On the one hand, he distinguishes a critique of modernity from the perspective of modernity itself; on the other, he enacts a critique of modernity from the perspective of coloniality. Thus, he marks his alliance with Foucault or Derrida at the same time as his detachment. With sociology, however, Khatibi's position is one-sided: "We have still a lot to think about the structural solidarity linking imperialism, in all its dimensions (political, cultural, military), to the expansion of what is called 'social sciences' " (1983, 48). The implications for double critique are these: (1) a decolonizing deconstruction (e.g., from a Third World perspective) of Western logo- and ethnocentrism that has been exported all over the planet, and that will complement a postmodern deconstruction à la Derrida or in the form of Foucault's archaeology or Nietzsche's genealogy; and (2) a criticism, from the same perspective (e.g., a decolonizing deconstruction from the Third World) of the knowledges and discourses produced by the different societies of the Arab world. A decolonizing deconstruction could be better understood, perhaps, from Khatibi's positioning in relation to Nietzsche's criticism of Christianity. At the same time that Khatibi finds in Nietzsche an ally for his criticism of Christianity (from inside Nietzsche's own history, I would add), Khatibi realizes he has to depart from him. While he places Nietzsche in the enormous fight that the German thinker developed against Christianity, he also locates himself as a Arab/Islamic thinker against Christianity, a position that cannot be subsumed under the presumable universal location of Nietzsche's criticism: "Mais nous sommes *aussi* musulmans par tradition; ce qui fait changer la position stratégique de notre critique" (1983, 21: We are *also* Muslims by tradition; a fact that changes the strategic position of our critique).

Knowledge becomes, in Khatibi's argument, entrenched in language, and, therefore, translation acquires a signal importance both for double critique and for "an other thinking." Khatibi's departure from Derrida and Foucault takes place, precisely, when language and translation are brought into the realm of knowledge and epistemology, into the realm of coloniality and the double critique and away from the linguistic translation within the same overarching metaphysics that ignores what is at stake in translating knowledge (in this case, from Greek to Arabic, from Arabic to Spanish, or from French to Arabic). Translation allows Khatibi to explore his idea of an other thinking as "thinking in languages." Khatibi explores the discontinuity of knowledge in Arabic language since Ibn Khaldum (fifteenth century) (Khatibi 1983, 63–111) and from there moves to the intersection, in the realm of knowledge, in the French language in which the canon and the tradition (from Greece to Rome to France) silenced knowledge production in Arabic. Here, Khatibi introduces a powerful metaphor to describe this situation: parallel to "underdeveloped societies" there are "silenced societies." Silenced societies are, of course, societies in which talking and writing take place but which are not heard in the planetary production of knowledge managed from the local histories and local languages of the "silencing" (e.g., developed) societies. In the case of the Maghreb, a language like Arabic, with a longer history than French, with a greater number of speakers (French speakers represent 2.1 percent of the population of the world while Arabic speakers constitute 3.5 percent), and with a legacy of knowledge linking Arabic to Greek philosophy, became epistemologically marginal in the coloniality of power. Until the eighteenth century, Latin and Spanish eclipsed it; since the eighteenth century, French took a leading position and, recently, English is overcoming French. "Silenced societies" even when they speak, says Khatibi, are not listened to in their difference ("Même quand elles parlent, elles ne sont pas entendues dans leur différence" [1983, 59]). The sentence may resonate in a later formulation ("Can the subaltern speak?") of great currency. If Khatibi was not listened to, it may be due to the very fact that he was denouncing in French at the same moment in which English was taking the place that French occupied in relation to Arabic. Or perhaps it was also due to the fact that knowledge in the French language that has been heard has in recent history been knowledge recognized as global (or universal). So knowledge from local histories where intellectual projects are produced at the intersection of silenced and silencing languages, as in Khatibi and Glissant, did not receive the same attention. This situation is not trivial. It opens up a space for the multiplication of interconnected projects at the intersection of local histories and global designs, both at the "center" and the "periphery." This means that the dichotomy is no longer sustainable since "an other thinking," as Khatibi proposes it, could be enacted both in the Maghreb as well as in France, as Khatibi himself and other Maghrebien intellectuals bear witness.

Epistemic Decolonization and the Colonial Difference

Since on two occasions I have been asked why I don't mention nomadism (à la Deleuze and Guattari) when speaking about this subject, and, as I understood it, the question presupposed that I was not paying attention to the universal or, at least, more "cogent" conceptual solution to the problem, I pause to address this issue. In addition, this issue is important in understanding the differences between deconstruction and intellectual decolonization as articulated by Khatibi. Winifred Woodhull (1993) describes different kinds of exile in Britain and France, particularly since the 1970s, that is to say, since the years of decolonization of French and British colonies and also since the emergence of the transnational corporation. He links migrants with nomads, whereas Deleuze and Guattari make a clear distinction between the two. Let's initially accept the more simple conception of nomad and say that expatriates, immigrants, and refugees are nomads with different "local histories," some from situations of violence internal to the world systems, others, generated in the places once exterior to it and now becoming a conflictive part of it (e.g., the problem of citizenship for a Maghrebian in France, for Mexicans in the United States, or for South Asians in Britain). And let's take advantage of Woodhull's distinction and exemplification of different kinds of exiles in France in the past thirty or so years:

> It is essential to draw distinctions within and between groups of expatriate intellectuals who have come to France at different times and in various circumstances: Those from other Western European countries, or from the United States and Canada, who have come mainly for reasons of intellectual or cultural affinity (such as Nancy Huston), and those for whom oppression in their native land is a central factor (as for James Baldwin); those who have come from Eastern European countries as political and intellectual dissidents (Julia Kristeva, Tzvetan Todorov), and those who have come from third world countries, particularly former colonies (Abdelkebir Khatibi, Nabile Fares), to take up residence in France permanently or intermittently for political, cultural, or intellectual reasons. *Exile means something different in each case, and figures in the work of these individuals and groups in very different ways.* (Woodhull 1993, 89; emphasis added)

In this book I am mainly concerned with border thinking produced by the last kind of intellectuals, either living in the former colonizing or the former colonized countries and moving between the two, as is the case for Khatibi. But I am also concerned with those who did not move, but around whom the world moved. Amerindian intellectuals in Latin America or Native Americans in the United States are in a border position not because they moved but because the world moved to them. On the other hand, the Chicano/a intellectuals are in between both possibilities: in the nine-teenth century, the United States frontier moved south and circled a large Mexican population within U.S. territory. In the twentieth century, particu-larly in the past thirty years, massive migration from Mexico is generating, within the United States, a type of intellectual who thinks in the border, although his or her situation is different from that of a migrant intellectual such as Khatibi. This is another type of situation (somewhere in between that of the Amerindians and Native Americans and that of Khatibi), since the Chicano/a are such in part because of migration but also in part because the world moved around them (the southern frontier in the nineteenth cen-tury) or because they descend from immigrants but they are not immigrants themselves (e.g., Gloria Anzaldúa, Cherrie Moraga).

Let's move now to the more complex definition of nomadism and no-madology in Deleuze and Guattari ([1987] 1996, 351–423), which is related to science and to thinking beyond science. I understood that the question I was asked a couple of times could be summarized as follows: "What is the difference, after all, between border thinking or border gnosis and nomadology? And if there is no difference, as I suspect, why not just go ahead and talk about (or 'apply') nomadology to the issue you are dealing with?" I felt myself in the same situation as Khatibi when he articulated his relation to Nietzsche, who criticized Christianity while inhabiting it. For Khatibi, instead, criticism of Christianity was performed from a subaltern (and exterior) Muslim perspective in the conflictive imaginary of the modern/colonial world system. There is no universal location from which to talk about Christianity: it is one thing to deconstruct Western metaphysics while inhabiting it, and it is quite another to work on decolonization as a form of deconstruction (see also Outlaw 1997), from the historical exteriority of Western metaphysics; that is, from those places that Western metaphysics transformed into "si-lenced societies" or "silenced knowledges" (e.g., subaltern knowledges; Ber-nasconi 1997, 186–87). It is one thing to criticize the complicity between knowledge and the state while inhabiting a particular nation-state (in this case France), and another to criticize the complicity between knowledge and the state from the historical exteriority of a universal idea of the state forged on the experience of a local history: the modern, European, experi-ence of the state. The same argument could be made—as we can see—if we replace Christianity with language. Thus, nomadology is a universal state-ment from a local history, while an other thinking is a universal statement from two local histories, intertwined by the coloniality of power: that is why one of the first articulations of double critique and "an other thinking" in Khatibi is an analysis of French Marxism and Arabic postcolonial national-ism. There is no reduction of "an other thinking" to nomadology and vice versa. Both are entrenched in local histories: nomadology is a universal history told from a local one; "an other thinking" is a universal history of the modern/colonial world system that implies the complementarity of modernity and coloniality, of modern colonialism (since 1500 and its internal conflicts) and colonial modernities, in their diverse rhythms, temporalities, with nations and religions coming to conflict at different periods and in different world orders.

But I think that the most striking differences between nomadology and "an other thinking" is similar to the difference between "an other thinking" and deconstruction along with the importance that Khatibi attributes to "thinking in languages," "cette parole tierce" (this third word). This move is at the same time an effort to delink from the tyranny of Occidental reason its sciences and technologies articulated in Occidental languages (from Latin to French, German, and English) and a critique of Islamic fundamentalism articulated in Arabic language. Different from Derridean deconstruction, Khatibi's decolonizing version works in between French and Arabic; that is, "an other thinking" is thinking in language, in between two languages and their historical relations in the modern world system and the coloniality of power. Translation is again inevitably invoked. But translation is also given a particular function in the structure of thinking and in the production of knowledge. As such, there is a risk of which Khatibi is aware, and he explicitly tries to respond to it. This is the risk, in the structure of knowledge and the coloniality of power, of translating French into Arabic as importation of knowledge and Arabic into French as exportation of an "Oriental" exotic commodity. To that real danger Khatibi responds as follows:

> Disons, d'une façon descriptive, que le savoir arabe actuel est une interférence conflictuelle entre deux epistèmes dont l'une (l'occidentale) couvre l'autre; elle la restructure de l'intérieur, en la détachant de sa continuité historique. A tel point que le chercheur arabe, rompu au savoir occidental, risque toujours de ne pas préssentir de quel lieu il parle, et d'où viennent effectivement les problèmes qui le tourmentent. (Khatibi 1983, 59)

> Let's say, in a descriptive manner, that Arabic knowledge is a conflictive interference between two epistemologies where one (Western epistemology) covers the other. It [Western epistemology] restructures Arabic knowledge from its own interior and detaches it from its historical continuity. To the extent that the Arab scholar, attached and detached at the same time from Western knowledge, risks not knowing from which location he speaks, and where the problems that torment him come from.

Translation (Mignolo and Schiwy, forthcoming), from the perspective of the Arabic language and knowledge, has two singular moments: the first taking place when Arab intellectuals translated from Greek to Arabic and created the conditions for the future translation from Arabic into Spanish, with Alfonso el Sabio and the School of Toledo, in the thirteenth century. Alfonso el Sabio, king of Castile between 1252 and 1284, arrived in a moment of hope and enthusiasm for Christianity. In the long battle between Christianity and Islam in the Iberian Peninsula, which lasted from the eighth to the fifteenth century, Alfonso el Sabio came to power right after three major Christian victories against Islam: Cordoba was reconquered in 1236; Valencia, in 1238; and Seville, in 1248. Alfonso was instrumental in surrounding himself with men of wisdom, Jews and Muslims, who translated from Arabic and Hebrew into Spanish, and through Arabic and Hebrew, Greek knowledge was recast. But the thirteenth century was crucial also in other aspects related to translations. Metaphorically speaking, but of real serious consequences, the thirteenth century was the moment in which Ibn Sina's (Avicenna's) philosophy began to be displaced by that of Ibn Rushd (Averroes). If both draw from Aristotle, it was the Aristotelian physics pressed onward by Averroes, rather than the metaphysics explored by Avicenna, that would be rearticulated later, in the sixteenth century, as a method and form of objective knowledge designed by Galileo and Descartes (Sardar 1987, 102; Durand 1969, 45–93). In this trajectory of translation, of thinking in languages, a form of knowledge became hegemonic in complicity and complementarity with the economic history of the modern/colonial world system: from mercantilism based on slavery, coupled with a Christian mission, until its consolidation with the industrial revolution and capitalism, coupled with the civilizing mission and development (Étienne 1987).

The second aspect of translation for Arabic intellectuals would take place within the modern/colonial world system, when the original situation was inverted. First, during the nineteenth century, the "mission civilizatrice" toward Maghreb demanded translation of French texts into Arabic, and the goal was not to reinforce Arabic language and Islamic domain in a period of expansion but, on the contrary, to reinforce the expansion of the new local and epistemic imperialisms of the modern world system. In other words, while the first moment of translation took place before European hegemony, the second took place during European and North Atlantic hegemony. But what is important for our argument is that the second moment of translation coincided with the restructuration of knowledge in the eighteenth and nineteenth centuries, along with the emergence of the social sciences in the nineteenth century and their rise to prominence after 1945. Translation at large was, after 1945, related to the rise of the social sciences coupled with area studies in the United States. Khatibi's call for the decolonization of sociology, in 1980, implies this moment of epistemic translation and the monolingualism of the social sciences to which Khatibi offers the alternative of "an other thinking," a thinking in languages that intervenes in the social sciences as a mirror of the social world in which language is the neutral instrument of an objective and triumphant epistemology.

Mondialité, Creolization, and the Colonial Difference

The difference between the two positions is obvious: whereas the monolinguism of the social sciences implies the purity of the language and the transparency of the knowing subject describing and explaining a knowable object, an other thinking is instead the opacity, as Glissant ([1990] 1997, 114) proposes in a different but parallel argument, across language: "Language has no mission," Glissant states ([1990] 1997, 114), other than the mission assigned to it by the state and the metaphysical belief in the transparency of language in the sciences to mirror the reality of the "social" and "natural" worlds. The spiritual world, in this view, becomes marginal in its irreconcilable difference with the objectivity claimed by the scientific enterprise. The end of nationhood's dream about the unity of the language and the purity of the corresponding culture questions, on the one hand, the confident activities of Western disciplinary knowledge cast in the hegemonic languages of the second modernity and opens up, on the other hand, the anachronism of such belief, as Khatibi's thinking in languages hints.

I have brought Glissant into this argument for two reasons. One is his habitation in the French language, although he differs from Khatibi in that, coming from the Caribbean, the alterity of French is Creole and not Arabic (see chapter 5); second, Glissant, who also thinks from the experience of coloniality of power, reaches conclusions similar to Khatibi:

> It is, therefore, an anachronism, in applying teaching or translation techniques, to teach *the* French language or to translate into *the* French language. It is an epistemological anachronism, by means of which people continue to consider as classic, hence eternal, something that apparently does not "comprehend" opacity or tries to stand in the way of it. Whatever the craven purist may say . . . there are several French languages today, and languages allow us to conceive of their unity according to a new mode, in which French can no longer be monolingual. If language is given in advance, if it claims to have a mission, it misses out on the adventure and does not *catch on* in the world." (Glissant [1990] 1997, 119)

I close this third part of the chapter by quoting Khatibi in a paragraph that echoes Glissant's exploration of Creolization of the languages of the world and, consequently, the Creolization of epistemology (or gnoseology)—that is, an other thinking that is a thinking in language:

> Une pensée-autre, telle que nous l'envisageons, est une pensée en langues, une mondialisation traduisantes de codes, des systèmes et des constellations de signes qui circulent dans le monde et au-dessus de lui. . . . Chaque societé ou group de societés est un relais de cette mondialisation. Une stratégie qui ne

travaille pas activement à transformer ces relais est, peut être, condomnée à se
devorer, à tourner sur elle même, entropiquement. (Khatibi 1983, 61)

An other thinking, as I conceive it, is a thinking in languages, a globalization
by means of translating different codes, as well as systems and constellations of
signs that go around and under the world. . . . Each society or ensemble of
societies is a halt and a crossroads of global structuring. Any strategic project
that doesn't address and actively engage these locations is, perhaps, condemned
to be devoured, to turn upon itself, entropically.

Glissant introduced a distinction between "mondialité" (globality) and
"mondialisation" (globalization). In my view, globalization is the dimension
of global designs while globality is articulated in local histories. Globality,
on the other hand, reveals local histories in their complexity: the perspective
of the architects of global designs interacting with the perspective of the
"nomad" or "minor designs" (Deleuze and Guattari [1987] 1996, 361), as
well as the emerging perspective of "an other thinking" or the epistemological Creolization, as articulated from the exterior of the universal history of
the modern world system (Khatibi, Glissant).

Let's go back now to the distinction between "nomadism" and "an other
thinking," which I call the "irreducible difference." The clinamen, "as the
minimum angle, has meaning only between a straight line and a curve, the
curve and its tangent, and constitutes the original curvature of the movement of the atom," said Deleuze and Guattari (1996, 361), following Michel
Serres. The clinamen allows for a model of becoming and heterogeneity, as
opposed to "the stable, the eternal, the identical, the constant" (1996, 361).
The same perspective allows them to define "minor languages" and "minor
literatures." "Major" and "minor" qualify two different uses of languages, in
literature and science: the German of Prague, for instance, "functioned as a
potentially minor language in relation to the German of Vienna or Berlin"
(Deleuze and Guattari [1987] 1996, 104). Such a formulation may look, at
first glance, as one "applicable" to French Creole or Chicano/a English and
Spanish. But such a move will hide the irreducible difference. Glissant and
Khatibi arrive, in fact, at a similar view, but not from a local history of knowledge built from the perspective of modernity, as is the case in Deleuze and
Guattari, but from local histories of knowledge built also from the perspective of coloniality. It is the coloniality of power and knowledge as articulated
in languages that lead Khatibi and Glissant to a critique of Western epistemology and to the articulation of the irreducible difference with their "alias,"
European thinkers practicing a monotopic critique of modern epistemology.
Glissant's version of "Creolization of the world" in this context moves along
the lines of Khatibi's "an other thinking": both are complementary and irreducible to a "nomadic" or "minor science":

Creolization is not a synthesis. . . . Creolization is not the simple mechanics of a crude mixture of distinct things, it goes much farther, what it creates is new, unheard-of and unexpected.

And this is what is difficult for us to imagine and to accept. We live behind the formerly fertile certainties of Being and enter into the variability of what it is. The permanence of Being, now so mortal, yields to the movement and change of what it is. . . .

. . . creolization opens for everyone the unfenced archipelago of the world-totality (e.g., globality). I see a sign of this in the fact that certain oppressed communities, such as the Amerindians of Chiapas in Mexico or the Gypsies of the former Yugoslavia are motivated to fight this oppression in the name of an openness, or a relation, of an intertwining that could be more just and more balanced. (Glissant 1998; 6, 7)

Both perspectives (Deleuze and Guattari in France, on the one hand, Khatibi and Glissant between Maghreb and France, between the Caribbean and France, on the other) are complementary but irreducible—let me insist—to one another because of the colonial difference. Their local histories, as you can imagine, are intertwined through coloniality, by the internal tensions of the coloniality of power (France and Spain both in the Mediterranean and the Atlantic), but irreducible to a nomadic universal history as the one proposed by Deleuze and Guattari or to the deconstructive universalism claiming the law of language and erasing the coloniality of power entrenched in language and epistemology (Derrida 1996). It is this complementary and irreducible (colonial) difference that I would like to explore quickly in the next section and take it as the frame for the entire book.

BETWEEN DISCIPLINARY NORMS AND COLONIAL MODERNITIES

Perhaps the point I am trying to make could be better argued if we bring to the foreground a social scientist, this time, of Marxist persuasion, Arabic/Muslim descent, and working in the European academy. I am mentioning all these constituents as relevant for Aziz Al-Azmeh, whose studies on Islam and modernities were published in the book series *Phronesis*, edited by Ernesto Laclau (Al-Azmeh 1993). In a strong argument against the possibility of cross-cultural conversations and as a response to the tensions created by the spectrum of Islam in current European affairs and everyday life, Al-Azmeh positions himself—although indirectly—against what Khatibi and Glissant propose. However, Al-Azmeh's argument against culturalism—which he characterizes as based on an organismic and metaphysical notion of culture, as entities defined by analogy to biological systems (1993, 25)—

could instead be complemented by Khatibi's concepts of "double critique" and "an other thinking" and by Glissant's "epistemological Creolization." Al-Azmeh, emphatically arguing against the rhetoric of "culturalism," states:

> The fact remains that the rhetoric of culturalism, a rhetoric of identity which views difference as antithesis, can only subsist naturally in the context of revivalism. . . . There is at work a sort of conceptual irredentism, which claims to be recovering matters occluded by the falsity of actual history, the history of modernity, the Enlightenment and the world. Matters such as identity, indeterminacy, subjectivity and authenticity, asserted in the spirit of *revanchisme*, often by former Marxists settling accounts with an erst-while philosophical consciousness. It is, finally, the same *revanchisme* that some Third-World intellectuals are reclaiming as a sort of saviour, a continuation of nationalism by other means. . . . What is normally absent from this celebration of primal innocence is the fact that its mode of expression and articulation is so much part of modernity. (Al-Azmeh 1993, 28).

From this general frame, Al-Azmeh goes on to three components underlining culturalist rhetoric: Western xenophobia, postmodernist xenophilia, and, finally, retrograde and xenophobic nationalism, including political Islamism and Hindu communalism (Al-Azmeh 1993, 28). I am insisting on Al-Azmeh's position against culturalist rhetoric because I see a risk of a quick transposition of this kind of argument to Khatibi and Glissant and the consequent risk of losing sight of the fact that both, Khatibi and Glissant, could be criticized from a seemingly culturalist rhetoric (the rhetoric of identity and authenticity), and from an affirmation of the rationality of the social sciences as a remedy to culturalist rhetoric. As a matter of fact, Al-Azmeh's final argument against the possibility of cross-cultural conversations is predicated on the fact that the defender of cross-cultural conversation assumes a monolithic, consistent, unified, and ontological concept of culture that is alien, as we have seen, to Khatibi's "an other thinking" and Glissant's "epistemological Creolization."

Now there is a second point I would like to tackle in Al-Azmeh's argument: the way he establishes a dichotomy between Western epistemology and culturalist rhetoric. He assumes, on the one hand, that the tropes and notions of political and social thoughts available today "form a universal repertoire that is inescapable, a repertoire which, *though of Western origin*, has in the past century and a half become a *universal patrimony* beyond which political and social thought is inconceivable, except very marginally" (1993, 33; emphasis added). According to Al-Azmeh such a situation was due, through education and legal systems, to "universal acculturation," to global forms of communication. This repertoire became "native not only to their points of origin, but worldwide" (1993, 34), as there is no longer geopolitical location for the universal principles governing knowledge in the social sciences (I come back to this issue when discussing Wallerstein et al. 1996 in subsequent chapters). To this globality of epistemology, which is no longer Western, Al-Azmeh opposes the "discourse of authenticity" that is characterized for its regionalism, for reaching back into a reworked past, toward a deliberate primitivism and nativism (see also Gerholm 1994). This primitivism has two components, according to the author. One is symbolic and specific to each group (e.g., songs of Serbian nationalists), while the other is universal as modules of social and political thought, such as "organismic culturalism." But according to the author,

> *No authentic social science or social philosophy is therefore possible*, not only be-
> cause its formal and institutional elements are no longer historically available,
> but also because what it implies is the collapse of knowledge into being in the
> monotony of solipsism and of self-reference. . . .

> It goes without saying that the language of primitivism subtends a project of
> cultural hegemony and of primitivist social engineering. . . . Desirous of creat-
> ing novel and anti-modernist (but only ambiguously so) conditions of social,
> cultural and intellectual life, fascistic political groups in the South propound a
> culturalism which is consonant with their political formation and renewed elite
> formation, and which is simultaneously consonant with the international infor-
> mation system as it has come to be in the last two decades. (Al-Azmeh 1993,
> 34; emphasis)

Al-Azmeh underlines, on the one hand, the role of daily exoticism deliv-
ered to the countries of origin and nourishing the culturalist advocacy of right-wing groups. On the other hand, he points out the analogue of foreign exotica in Western countries, which leads toward forms of ghettoization, reinforced by "policies of ethnic confinement and by ethnic stratification of labor" (Al-Alzmeh 1993, 35). The author is interested in calling attention to what, for him, is an objective complicity "between libertarian postmodernism and *tiers-mondisme* in the West, that is conducive to retrogression in the South and to archaic leadership of Southern people in the North." As a way out from this unhappy complicity, Al-Azmeh proposes to "understand other cultures" in the same way we understand madness, the unconscious, the ancient past, or ethnographic objects—that is, without confining them to exoticism and taking them for partners in "conversation"(1993, 36). In order to do so, he suggests that

> We need to look at them with the realities of history in view, if we are to go
> beyond politely listening and talking at cross-purposes, with due respect for the
> right of others to be impermeable to the understanding and abhorrent to the
> sensibility. Conversation should cease to be a form of cross-cultural etiquette if
> it is to preserve any liberating potential. Otherwise, by turning culturalist, it

will leave the setting of terms to the most retrograde and violent forces of livid hatred both in Europe and beyond, and concede to them the claim that they represent all of us. (Al-Azmeh 1993, 36)

My insistence on "an other thinking" and "epistemological Creolization" as different possibilities of border thinking is precisely due to the need of getting away from the opposition set up by Al-Azmeh, which leads him to a blind celebration of the social sciences, preserving a hegemonic epistemology without which "no *authentic social science is possible*," an epistemology that takes authenticity away from culturalist rhetoric in order to appropriate it for the rhetoric of the social sciences.

The argument I am building in this book is that both positions, as described by Al-Azmeh, are right and wrong at the same time, since one presupposes the other. But to get out of the dilemma that Al-Azmeh has no choice but to argue (a dilemma that was forced by the very violence of a universal form of knowledge that provoked the reactive violence of the culturalist rhetoric), a double critique is needed. A double critique, "an other thinking," would lead to the openness of the "unforeseeable diversity of the world" and of "unheard and unexpected" forms of knowledge, as argued by Glissant (1998).

I am not arguing here "against" Al-Azmeh, since his criticism of the culturalist rhetoric I truly endorse. I am indeed bringing to the discussion the example of Third World intellectuals who embrace the social sciences and react against dangerous (in their view) forms of culturalist rhetoric, cultural authenticity, and *tiers-mondisme*. At the same time, such a position could be blind to the alternative such as the one Khatibi and Glissant offer. As a matter of fact, I have heard social scientists sympathetic to Glissant's position, although making clear that Glissant was a "poet and a writer." I do not see Al-Azmeh in the same group as, say, Fukiyama or Samuel Huntington. But I see his position defending a universality of the social sciences, "an authenticity of social thought" that is as risky as the "authenticity of the culturalist rhetoric." What seems to be at stake here are the irreducible differences as well as the complementarity I underlined earlier, between the positions of Deleuze and Guattari on the one hand and Khatibi and Glissant on the other. A formulation by Glissant shows, indirectly of course, the limits of Al-Azmeh's claim for the "authentic" cross-cultural understanding as a previous condition for cross-cultural conversation:

If we examine the process of "understanding" people and ideas from the perspective of Western thought, we discover that its basis is this requirement for *transparency*. In order to understand and thus accept you, I have to measure your solidity with the ideal scale providing me with grounds to make comparisons and, perhaps, judgments. . . . But perhaps we need to bring an end to the very notion of a scale. (Glissant [1990] 1997, 190)

The way out for Glissant is the dialectic between *transparency* (which is how I understand "authentic social sciences" in Al-Azmeh's formulation) and *opacity*. If we accept opacity in tandem with a double critique, and with "an other thinking," Glissant's argument situates the irreducible difference that cannot be appropriated either by the social sciences or by what Al-Azmeh identifies as culturalist rhetoric:

> Agree not merely to the right to difference but, carrying this further, agree also to the right to opacity that is not enclosure within an impenetrable autarchy but subsistence within an irreducible singularity. Opacities can coexist and converge, weaving fabrics. *To understand these truly one must focus on the texture of the weave and not on the nature of its component.* (Glissant [1990] 1997, 190)

The last part of my argument in this chapter brings Jacques Derrida into the picture in his dialogue with Abdelkebir Khatibi. Derrida's *Le monolinguisme de l'autre* (1996) illuminates another aspect of the irreducible difference between a defense of the universal diversity of the social sciences, their delinking from the place of origin and their expansion to become a global patrimony (Al-Azmeh): a universal framing of human history attempts to escape from the lineal, universal macronarratives of modernity (Deleuze and Guattari), albeit remaining blind to the possibility of the need of macronarratives from the perspective of coloniality (Khatibi, Glissant). What Derrida illuminates is the limit of deconstruction of Western metaphysics (in its variety), when facing a double critique and "an other thinking" as the irreducible difference of the coloniality of power and of thinking in languages. The variety of Western metaphysics (there is not one but several) is, as Derrida himself states, monolingual. Khatibi, instead, underlines that his, unlike Derrida's, is a *bilingual situation* related to two (forms of) methapysics, Western and Islamic (Khatibi 1983, 57). Such a bilingual situation, which allows for a double critique and border thinking, places the Arabic language (and Islamic knowledge in Arabic language) in a new dimension, a planetary dimension of which Arabic was deprived at least since the sixteenth century.

The bilingual situation in Maghreb is described by Khatibi as follows (1983, 59–60). The Arab intellectual or scholar is, by necessity, a *translator* of a set of disciplines and knowledge that have been formed elsewhere. Al-Azmeh would prefer to think about the planetary patrimony of disciplines and knowledges, instead of an "original" and its "translations." For Khatibi, instead, the imposing intellectual and scientific production in the West makes the bilingual and epistemological situation an asymmetric one, and knowledge produced in Arabic language a subaltern kind of knowledge. On the other hand, the fact that Arab intellectuals of the past translated from the Greek in order to found an autonomous philosophical and scientific language makes it difficult to accept Arabic as a flexible language, capable of *speaking in languages* ("parler en langues") and producing knowledge at the intersection of languages and thoughts that become inscribed in their own Arabic memory. "An other thinking" becomes, in this perspective, a *translation* machine that is at the same time a way of thinking in languages, a form of globality (in Glissant's expression) that operates by translating codes and sign systems circulating in, above, and below the world. Now, this bilingual situation, thought out by Khatibi in the relation between Arabic and French, will be valid for any other planetary bilingual situation, where speaking in languages is at the same time a way of empowerment and of decolonization of knowledge (1983, 59–60).

Derrida, instead, takes a different route. I would say, first, that the irreducible difference between both positions is between a Judeo-Franco-Maghrebian genealogy (Derrida 1996, 133) and an Occidental genealogy, which is at the same time Islamic-Arabo-Maghrebian (Khatibi 1983, 11–39). Derrida has problems speaking about and using the word "colonialism."

> Je ne peux pas, là encore, analyser de front cette politique de la langue et je ne voudrais pas me servir trop facilement du mot "colonialism." Toute culture est originairement coloniale. (Derrida 1996, 68)

> I cannot analyze straightforwardly this politic of language here, and would not like to abuse the word "colonialism." All culture is originally colonial.

I surmise that Derrida's problems with colonialism are related to his resistance, and perhaps blindness, to the colonial difference. The question is not, therefore, the coloniality of universal culture ("Toute culture est originairement coloniale"), but the coloniality of the modern/colonial world system and, in this case, the colonial difference and the role of France after the nineteenth century in North Africa. While Khatibi is clearly thinking and writing from the colonial difference in the modern/colonial world, Derrida insists on a universal perspective supported by his monotopic radical criticism of Western logocentrism understood as a universal category uncoupled from the modern/colonial world. His argument on the "monolinguisme de l'autre" misses the point of the colonial world. His argument on the "monolinguisme de l'autre" misses the point of the colonial difference that supports Khatibi's entire work. One can say that Khatibi and Derrida are not on the same side of the colonial difference.

Of course, Derrida is not blind to "la guerre coloniale moderne" but insists that what is at work in it and what it reveals is the "colonial structure of every culture" (1996, 69). Consequently,

> Le monolinguisme de l'autre, ce serait *d'abord* cette souveraineté, cette loi venue d'ailleurs, sans doute, mais aussi et d'abord la langue même de la Loi. Et la Loi comme Langue. (Derrrida 1996, 69)

> The monolingualism of the other will be, without a doubt, a kind of sovereignty, a kind of law coming from elsewhere; but it will also be foremost the very language of the Law. And the Law as Language.

From Khatibi's perspective it is irrelevant whether every culture is colonial. What is at stake is the complicitous coloniality of the modern world system: not the universality of the law (as may be the case with the universality of nomadology) stated from a regional experience (clearly manifested in the examples and the authors quoted and commented on by Derrida), but the historicity of a particular colonial experience, and the location of Maghreb first in relation to the Spanish Empire, then to French colonialism—two moments of the modern/colonial world system. To insist on the colonial structure of every culture, as Derrida does, means to lose track of the historical perspective in which Khatibi's double critique (an other thinking as a thinking in language) is situated. Furthermore, the epistemological potential is this time on the side of Khatibi who can talk, at the same time, of deconstruction and decolonization, of decolonization as a particular kind of deconstruction. The epistemological potential is underlined by the historical coincidence between the years in which Derrida articulated the deconstruction project and the years in which political decolonization was taking place in Maghreb (Khatibi 1983, 47–48). And yet, the question is not to choose between one or the other but to understand the irreducible difference between both and the epistemological potential of border gnosis (epistemology) of Khatibi's "an other thinking." Derrida (or Deleuze and Guattari, for that matter) remains "in custody" of the universal bent of the modern concept of reason—a perspective that border thinking is changing as it moves toward a "fragmentation as universal project (Hinkelammert 1996, 238), instead of the reproduction of "abstract universals" (e.g., Language is the Law; or the war machine is exterior to the state apparatus).

CONCLUDING REMARKS

I close this chapter by bringing to the foreground the notion of "double conciousness" (Du Bois [1905] 1990), "double vision" (Wright 1993), "new mestiza consciousness" (Anzaldúa 1987), "borderlands of theory." (Calderón and Saldívar 1991), "double translation" (Subcomandante Marcos 1997a). All of these key words belong to the same family as "double critique" and "Creolization." All of them are changing the perspective, the term rather than the content, of the conversation. All of them critically reflect on the imaginary of the modern world system from the perspective of the coloniality of power and from particular, local histories of modernity/coloniality: Maghreb from the sixteenth century with the expulsion of the Moors from

the Iberian Peninsula, to the French colonization at the beginning of the
nineteenth century, to political decolonization in the second half of the
twentieth century (Khatibi). Afro-Americans in the French Caribbean (Glissant) and in the United States (Du Bois, Wright) reflect on the local histories
of slavery since the sixteenth century, when slavery became identified with
Africans and with blacks; on being black and (North) American or black
and belonging to Western civilization (Wright); or on the "double rape" (the
colonization of New Spain by the Spanish in the sixteenth century and the
colonization of Mexico by the United States, in 1948; Anzaldúa 1987),
which creates the conditions for the emergence of a "new mestiza consciou-
ness." Or they reflect on the "double translation" allowing for an intersection between incommensurable (from the perspective of modernity) forms
of knowledge: Marxism modified by Amerindian languages and cosmology
and Amerindian epistemology modified by the language of Marxist cosmology in a cross-epistemological conversation that is rewriting and enacting a
history of five hundred years of oppression (as in the Zapatistas movement).
What all these key words have in common is their disruption of dichotomies
through being themselves a dichotomy. This, in other words, is the key configuration of border thinking: *thinking from dichotomous concepts rather than
ordering the world in dichotomies.* Border thinking, in other words, is, logically, a dichotomous locus of enunciation and, historically, is located at the
borders (interiors or exteriors) of the modern/colonial world system, as all
the previous cases indicate.

Although I do not go into a detailed exploration of each of these key
words and the particularity of each intellectual project, I return to them
throughout the book. Here I would like to stress, however, that in all these
cases (as well as in others I may not be aware of), the subalternization of
knowledge in the modern world system seems to be creating the conditions
for an "otherwise than epistemology" out of several articulations of border
thinking, in its exterior and interior borders. All of these key words participate in a similar epistemological project, linked by their critique of the epistemic coloniality of power. All of them can also be linked by their irreducible difference to critical forms of knowledge from the interior perspective
of modernity itself.

When Fanon states, in *Black Skin, White Masks* ([1952] 1967), that for a
Negro who works on a sugar plantation the only solution is to fight but that
he "will embark on this struggle, and he will pursue it, not as the result of
a Marxist or idealistic analysis but quite simply because he cannot conceive
of life otherwise" (1952, 224), he is not denying Marx's powerful analysis
of the logic of capitalism. He is pointing out the difficulties of jumping from
an analysis of the logic of capitalism to the truth of social solution. Fanon
is calling attention to the force of black consciousness, not just of class
consciousness. And I would guess that Fanon is referring to "Marxist idealis-

tic analysis," not to Marx himself. In like manner, when Khatibi (1983, 47–48) criticizes Marx for his blindness to colonialism and for suggesting that the colonization (and industrialization) of India was the necessary step toward the international proletarian revolution, he is not denying the powerful analysis of the logic of capitalistic economy. At the same time, the recognition of Marx's contribution and its validity today should not obscure the fact that even if Marx could be dissociated from Hegel and in a certain way from the core of Western metaphysics (Khatibi 1983, 53), he would still be grounded on the belief of a total knowledge "mapping the world in an inexorable dialectic," "in custody" of the tyranny of the universal abstracts of modern rationality. Thus, the need of "an other thinking" that "is neither Marxist in the strict sense of the term, nor anti-Marxist in the meaning that the right-wing could be, at the limits of these possibilities" (Khatibi 1983, 54). It is coherent with the planetary emergence of border thinking that Subcomandante Marcos would make almost the same statement fifteen years later, in Spanish, and in a situation that is neither that of the slave plantations nor that of the Maghrebien intellectual reflecting on the history of colonialism and its aftermath: "The Zapatismo," stated Subcomandante Marcos, "is and is not Marxist-Leninist. The Zapatismo is not fundamentalist or milenarist indigenous thinking; and it is not indigenous resistance either. It is a mixture of all of that, that crystallizes in the EZLN" (1997a, 338–39).

When Fanon mentions that his patient "is suffering from an inferiority complex" or when he quotes a participant during the Twenty-Fifth Congress of Catholic Students protesting against the dispatch of Senegalese troops while, on the other hand, it was known from other sources that one of the torturers in the police headquarters was Senegalese, and it was known also what the archetype of the Senegalese could represent for the Malagasy, Fanon concludes that "the discoveries of Freud are of no use to us here" ([1952] 1967, 104). Certainly Fanon is not denying Freud's contribution, he is just marking its limit beyond the type of psychological disorders, of a particular social class of a particular sector of western Europe at the end of the nineteenth century in a Christian and Victorian type of society. That that type of social structure and psychological disorder could be revealed in another part of the planet, particularly where European society was transplanted without much interference of "native" population, is undeniable. The fact that the impotence of an Algerian man following the rape of his wife by a French soldier cannot be easily resolved with the tools provided by psychoanalysis is also rather obvious: the human unconscious as described by Freud is based on a particular kind of man and woman, in a particular kind of society, in a particular language structure (German, Indo-European languages) that proved difficult to *translate* into Arabic, in the tension between Arabic and French (Fanon [1961] 1963, 249–310). Once again, it is not Freud's contributions that are in question, but rather the limits of their usefulness that are revealed by revealing the colonial difference. Similar situations abound. Paul Gilroy (1993, 159–60) tells the story told by C.L.R. James about Richard Wright, in Wright's house in France, showing to James the numerous volumes of Kierkegaard's work on his bookshelves and saying: "Look Nello, you see those books there?. . . Everything that he writes in those books I knew before I had them." James concludes that "What (Dick) was telling me was that he was a black man in the United States and that gave him an insight into what today is the universal opinions and attitude of the *modern* personality" (Gilroy 1993, 159). In the same spirit Gloria Anzaldúa will say, "I have known things longer than Freud" (Anzaldúa 1987, 33), not because Freud's contribution is invalid, but because it cannot be taken as a hegemonic form of knowledge reproducing the epistemic subjugation that the coloniality of power enacted in the formation of the modern/colonial world system.

Briefly, I found in all these examples the sense that border thinking structures itself on a double consciousness, a double critique operating on the imaginary of the modern/colonial world system, of modernity/coloniality. As such, it establishes alliances with the internal critique, the monotopic critique of modernity from the perspective of modernity itself (e.g., Kierkegaard, Nietzsche, Heidegger, Marx, Freud, Derrida) at the same time that it marks the irreducible difference of border thinking as a critique from the the colonial difference. If, as Peruvian sociologist Aníbal Quijano argues, geopolitical coloniality of power and its consequences, historicostructural dependencies, implies "eurocentric hegemony as epistemological perspective" (1997, 117), "double critique," "an other thinking," "epistemological Creolization," "double consciousness," and "new mestiza consciousness," are all theoretical articulations of border thinking breaking away from "eurocentrism as epistemological perspective." The form that this breaking away is taking is the irreducible difference established between the monotopic critique of modernity from the perspective of modernity itself, still "in custody" of the monotopic of abstract universals (e.g., a critique of the imaginary of the modern world system from its interior) and the pluritopic and double critique of modernity from the perspective of coloniality (e.g., a critique of the epistemic imaginary of the modern world system from its exterior). It is precisely this perspective that, in the last analysis, could be articulated in the context of the coloniality of power ingrained (but invisible) in the epistemological imaginary of the modern world system.

Coloniality of power shall be distinguished from the colonial period, in Latin America extending itself from the early sixteenth century to the beginning of the nineteenth, when most of the Spanish-speaking countries and Brazil gained independence from Spain and Portugal and began to be constituted as new nation-states. Colonialism, as Quijano observes, did not end with independence because coloniality of power and knowledge changed hands, so to speak, and became subordinated to the new and emerging epistemological hegemony: no longer the Renaissance but the Enlightenment (as will be seen in chapter 2). The emergence of border thinking is, again, breaking away from post-Enlightenment instrumental reason, whose current manifestation is palpable in what Pierre Bourdieu (1998a) calls "the essence of neoliberalism" and describes as a program for the destruction of possible collective enterprises that can be considered an obstruction to the logic of the pure market, in what Franz Hinkelammert defines as the "rationality of the market only" (1996), and in what Subcomandante Marcos labels "the fourth world-war" (1997b) and is breaking away as well from its consequences—the auspicious, advantageous, and helpful deconstruction, nomadology, Marxist legacy, and postmodern critique of modernity. Border thinking brings to the foreground the irreducible epistemological difference, between the perspective from the colonial difference, and the forms of knowledge that, being critical of modernity, coloniality, and capitalism, still remain "within" the territory, "in custody" of the "abstract universals."

Part Two

I AM WHERE I THINK:
THE GEOPOLITICS OF KNOWLEDGE
AND COLONIAL EPISTEMIC
DIFFERENCES

Post-Occidental Reason: The Crisis of Occidentalism and the Emergenc(y)e of Border Thinking

"POSTCOLONIAL REASON" was the expression I used in the first version of this chapter (Mignolo 1994; 1996a; 1997c), but I soon realized that "postcolonial" criticism and theory was mainly employed by critics and intellectuals writing in English and in the domain of the British Empire and its ex-colonies (Australia, New Zeland, India). The entire Americas, including the Caribbean, North Africa, and most of the time sub-Saharan Africa were left out of the picture. "Post-Occidental reason" appears to be more satisfying for the geohistorical scenario I was seeking, from the Spanish empire since the sixteenth century to the emergence of the United States as a new colonial power toward the end of the nineteenth century. In this period the imaginary of the modern/colonial world system moved from "Indias Occidentales," the name allocated by the Spanish crown to the "Western Hemisphere," the name introduced in the early United States, to relocate the Americas in the spectrum of a modern/colonial system dominated until the nineteenth century by European colonial countries and powers.

In this chapter my aim is to bring border thinking into conversation with postcoloniality through the colonial difference. Anthony Appiah asked several years ago whether the "post" in postcolonial was the same as that in "postmodern" (Appiah 1991). My answer is tied to the modern/colonial world system I use as a general frame of this book. Consequently, the first answer is obvious: "post" means the same in both postmodern and postcolonial, as far as they are both two sides of the same coin, of the same geohistorical configuration. However, the very idea of "post" is entrenched within the logic of the "modern" side of the imaginary, since "modernity" has been conceived in terms of progress, chronology, and superseding a previous stage. In this sense, "post" attached to coloniality follows the same logic. On the other hand, "beyond" instead of "post" has a spatial connotation that underlines the side of coloniality rather than that of modernity. This is perhaps the reason why Enrique Dussel and Fernando Coronil, whose thoughts are ingrained in local histories of colonial modernities, prefer "beyond" to "post." "Beyond Eurocentrism" and "Beyond Occidentalism" are the titles of their articles, titles that carry the weight of an ideological and political position (Dussel 1998a; Coronil 1996). Dussel ([1993] 1995) also prefers "transmodernity" to "postmodernity." Ramon Grosfoguel, a sociologist from Puerto Rico working in the United States, has advanced a similar interpretation, comparing the uses of the "TimeSpace" category in sociologist and economist thinking from "inside" the world system imaginary and sociologists and economists thinking from its "periphery." Theories of development originating in the center "usually assume an eternal TimeSpace framework. By contrast, most theories emerging from the periphery assume an episodic-geopolitical TimeSpace framework" (Grosfoguel 1997a, 535). But this is not all. The colonial difference reveals other dimensions of the space/time complex beyond Western epistemology, as Vine Deloria noticed. His observation could find an easy echo in all Amerindian communities in South America—that one of the main differences between Christianity and Amerindian religions is that between "time and space, between time and places, between a remembered history and a sacred location" ([1990] 1999, 118).

I also want to distinguish between "postcoloniality" on the one hand and "post-Occidentalism," "postcolonialism," "post-Orientalism," or their corresponding "beyond." What they all have in common is the colonial difference in all its spatial historicities in the modern/colonial world. By postcoloniality I refer in general to different modalities of critical discourse of the imaginary of the modern/colonial world system and the coloniality of power. Postmodernity did not detache itself from postcoloniality. Their relation has been slightly displaced. On the other hand, in each of the different "-isms" I refer to the particularity of critical discourses within specific local histories. For instance, post-Occidentalism is ingrained in the local history of the Americas (Retamar [1974]; 1995 Gruzinsky 1988; Dussel 1993; Coronil 1996); postcolonialism has been used by cultural critics entrenched in the local histories of the Commonwealth and British colonialism (Barker, Hulme, and Iversen 1994; Adam and Tiffin 1990; Chambers and Curti 1996), and by post-Orientalism I refer to criticism of the coloniality of power on and from local histories of what is today the "Middle East" (Said 1978; Behdad 1994; Lowe 1991). However, I am not positing postcoloniality as an empty signifier that can contain and accommodate the rest. Postcoloniality is embedded in each local history and more than an empty signifier is a link between them all. It is the connector, in other words, that can bring the diversity of local histories into a universal project, displacing the abstract universalism of ONE local history, where the modern/colonial world system was created and imagined (I explore this idea further at the end of chapter 4). In sum, diversality as universal project (see chapter 7).

It is my contention that one of the main contributions of the academic conversation around postcoloniality and its equivalent, beyond Eurocentrism and Occidentalism, was to relocate the ratio between geohistorical locations and knowledge production. The imaginary of the modern/colonial world system located the production of knowledge in Europe. The early versions of Occidentalism, with the discovery of the New World, and the later version of Orientalism, with the ascension of France and Britain to world hegemony, made non-Western epistemologies something to be studied and described. In the very act of describing Amerindian or Oriental knowledge and customs, they were detached from the grand Greco-Roman tradition that provided the foundation of modern epistemologyand hermeneutics. "Modernity" was imagined as the house of epistemology. The central role that the social sciences began to occupy after World War II was parallel to the configuration of area studies and extended the geopolitics of knowledge production to the North Atlantic. Paradoxically, a colonial object of description in the sixteenth century (the Americas) became a central geohistorical location for the production of knowledge in the twentieth century. This cycle is the historical foundation of most of the conversations under the label of postmodernity, as I further elaborate in this chapter. Thus, postmodernity is both a critical discourse on the assumption of the imaginary of "modernity" and a characterization of the historical present in which such a discourse is possible. Postcoloniality (and its equivalents) is both a critical discourse that brings to the foreground the colonial side of the "modern world system" and the coloniality of power imbedded in modernity itself, as well as a discourse that relocates the ratio between geohistorical locations (or local histories) and knowledge production. The reordering of the geopolitics of knowledge manifests itself in two different but complementary directions:

1. the critique of the subalternization from the perspective of subaltern knowledges (e.g., Dussel 1996); and

2. the emergence of border thinking (as described in the previous chapter) as a new epistemological modality at the intersection of Western and the diversity of categories that were suppressed under Occidentalism (as an affirmation of Greco-Roman tradition as the locus of enunciation in the sixteenth and seventeenth centuries), Orientalism (as an objectification of the locus of the enunciated as "Otherness"), and area studies (as an objectification of the "Third World," as producer of cultures but not of knowledge).

These two directions establish the main historical framework of my argument throughout the book, as I already discussed it in chapter 1.

OCCIDENTALISM IN THE COLONIAL HORIZON OF MODERNITY

It has been observed that postcolonial is an ambiguous expression, sometimes dangerous, other times confusing, and generally limited and unconsciously employed (McClintock 1992; Shohat 1992; Radhakrishnan 1993; Dirlik 1994). It is ambiguous when used to refer to sociohistorical situations linked to colonial expansion and decolonization across time and space. For example, Algeria, nineteenth-century United States, and nineteenth-century Brazil are all referred to as postcolonial countries. The danger arises when this term is used as one more "post-" theoretical direction in the academy and becomes a mainstream played against oppositional practices by "people of color," "Third World intellectuals" or "ethnic groups" in the academy. It is confusing when "hybridity," "mestizaje," "space-in-between," and other equivalent expressions become the object of reflection and critique of post-colonial theories, for they suggest a discontinuity between the *colonial con-figuration* of the object or subject of study and the *postcolonial position* of the locus of theorizing. Postcoloniality is unconsciously employed when uprooted from the conditions of its emergence (e.g., as a substitute of "commonwealth literature" in certain cases, as a proxy of "Third World literature" in others). Thus, postcoloniality or the postcolonial becomes problematic when applied to either nineteenth- or twentieth-century cultural practices in Latin America.

Occidentalism rather than colonialism was the main concern of, first, the Spanish crown and men of letters during the sixteenth and seventeenth centuries and, second, the state and intellectuals during the nation-building period, which defined the Latin American selfsame in its difference with Europe and Occident. America, contrary to Asia and Africa, became the "daughter" and "inheritor" of Europe during the eighteenth century. Post-Occidentalism better describes Latin American critical discourse on colonialism. José Martí's compelling expression "Nuestra América" summarized the debate among nineteenth-century Latin American intellectuals, at the moment when the force of the European Enlightenment, which inspired both the revolutionaries of independence and subsequent nation builders, was being replaced by the fear of a new colonialism from the north during the second half of the nineteenth century. The three colonial legacies, Spanish/Portuguese, French/British, and United States, were clearly described, some thirty years after José Martí in Cuba, by José Carlos Mariátegui in Peru, who saw in the Peruvian school system the "herencia colonial" (Spanish colonial legacy) and the "influencia francesa y norteamericana" (French and U.S. influence). Mariátegui's distinction between "herencia" and "influencia" (the past and the present) is based on the linear historicism of modernity that hides, even today at the end of the twentieth century, the synchronic coexistence of different colonial legacies. The Cuban Revolution brought a new perspective to Latin American history and inspired Fernández Retamar in Cuba (following the path of Martí and Mariátegui) to write his canonical piece, "Nuestra América y Occidente" (Our America and Occident), in which he introduced the key word post-Occidentalism (Fernández Retamar [1974]; 1995, Mignolo 1996a; 1996b).

I would submit that, in spite of the difficulties implied in the term postcolonial and the less familiar post-Occidentalism, we should not forget that both discourses contribute to a change in theoretical and intellectual production, that I have described as "border gnosis," linked to "subalternity" and "subaltern reason." It is not so much the historical postcolonial condition that should retain our attention, but rather the postcolonial loci of enunciation as an emerging discursive formation, and as a form of articulation of subaltern rationality. In this chapter, I propose that the most fundamental transformation of the intellectual space at the end of the twentieth century is taking place because of the configuration of critical subaltern thinking as both an oppositional practice in the public sphere and a theoretical and epistemological transformation of the academy (Prakash 1994). In this context, I find Ella Shohat's description of postcolonial theories compelling, and I will add to it post-Occidentalism as a site of enunciation and "subaltern reasons" as variations:

> The term "post-colonial" would be more precise, therefore, if articulated as "post-First/Third Worlds theory," or "post-anticolonial critique," as a movement beyond a relatively binaristic, fixed and stable mapping of power relations between "colonizer/colonized" and "center/periphery." Such rearticulations suggest a more nuanced discourse, which allows for movement, mobility and fluidity. Here, the prefix "post" would make sense less as "after" than as following, going beyond and commenting upon a certain intellectual movement—third worldist anti-colonial critique—rather than beyond a certain point in history— colonialism; for here "neo-colonialism" would be a less passive form of addressing the situation of neo-colonized countries, and a politically more active mode of engagement. (Shohat 1992, 108)

Despite all the ambiguities of the term analyzed by Shohat, she underlines an important aspect of contemporary theoretical practices identified as postcoloniality, which could be extended to encompass all critical reflection on diversity as universal project. Consequently, I suggest that subaltern reason be understood as a diverse set of theoretical practices emerging *from* and responding *to* colonial legacies at the intersection of Euro/American modern history. I do not go so far as talking about or looking at the postcolonial as a new paradigm but of viewing it as part of a larger one, precisely what I characterize as border gnosis, an other thinking from and beyond disciplines and the geopolitics of knowledge imbedded in area studies; from and beyond colonial legacies; from and beyond gender divide and sexual prescriptions; and from and beyond racial conflicts. Thus, border gnosis is a longing to overcome subalternity and a building block of subaltern ways of thinking. Thus seen, the "post" in postcolonial is significantly different from other "posts" in contemporary cultural critiques. I will further suggest that there are two fundamental ways of critiquing modernity: one, from colonial histories and legacies (postcolonialism, post-Occidentalism, post-Orientalism); the other, the postmodern, from the limits of the hegemonic narratives of Western history.

I began by making references to Shohat's and McClintock's concerns with "postcoloniality" because of their publications in the English-speaking world. But these issues go beyond U.S. academic and political concerns. In the Andes, the present forces of colonial legacies have been a constant assumption and a starting point in understanding hidden and overt violence in the area (Rivera Cusicanqui 1993), in not being afraid of speaking of "internal colonialism" (instead of the more common "post-beyond-Occidentialism" or the more fashionable "postcoloniality"), and in openly and theoretically articulating scholarship with activism (see chapter 4 for more details). I shall pause to explain in what sense I understand postcolonialiality. First, I am limiting my understanding of "colonialism" to the geopolitical and geohistorical constitution of western European (in Hegel's conception) modernity in its double face: the economic and political configuration of the modern world as well as the intellectual space (from philosophy to religion, from ancient history to the modern social sciences) justifying such configuration. Subaltern reason opens up the countermodern as a place of contention from the very inception of Western expansion (e.g., Waman Puma de Ayala's *Nueva corónica y buen gobierno*, finished around 1615), making it possible to contest the intellectual space of modernity and the inscription of a world order in which the West and the East, the Same and the Other, the Civilized and the Barbarian (see chapter 8), were inscribed as natural entities. Since about 1500, the process of consolidation of western Europe as a geocultural entity (Morin 1987; Fontana 1994) coincided with transatlantic travels and the expansion of the Spanish and Portuguese empires. Italy, Spain (or Castile), and Portugal were, during the sixteenth and the first half of the seventeenth centuries, the "heart of Europe," to borrow an expression that Hegel eventually applied to England, France, and Germany toward the beginning of the nineteenth century. I limit my understanding of postcolonial situations/conditions to any sociohistorical configuration emerging from people gaining independence or emancipation from Western colonial and imperial powers (such as Europe until 1945 or the United States from the beginning of the twentieth century). Here, the postcolonial condition is synonymous with neocolonial, the process of building the nation after colonial independence. Neocolonialism is the political and economical context in which "internal colonialism" was enacted (Stavenhagen 1990). Subaltern reason instead precedes and coexists with postcolonial/neocolonial situations/conditions.

One of the first difficulties we encounter in this map of colonial legacies and subaltern theorizing is that the United States is not easily accepted as a postcolonial/neocolonial country and, consequently, as a reality that could be accounted for in terms of postcolonial theories (Shohat 1992, 102; McClintock 1992, 86–87). Because of its surface postmodern appearance of being the place where postcoloniality found a shelter and because of its deep colonial past, one can say that it all came together in the United States. The difficulty arises not only because of the differences between colonial legacies in the United States and, let's say, Jamaica, but also because postcoloniality (both in terms of situation or condition and of discursive and theoretical production) tends to be linked mainly with Third World countries and experiences. The fact seems to be that even if the United States doesn't have the same kind of colonial legacies as Peru or Indonesia, it is nonetheless a consequence of European colonialism and not just one more European country in itself. Due to American leadership in the continuity of Western expansion, postmodern rather than postcolonial critics would be more easily linked to the history of the United States. One could say that U.S. colonial history explains postmodern theories such as those formulated by Fredric Jameson (Jameson 1991), where the space of contestation comes from the legacies of capitalism rather than from the legacies of colonialism. The already classic discussion between Jameson and Ahmad could easily be reread in this context (Jameson 1986; Ahmad 1987).

Postcolonial theorizing in the United States, as Dirlik noted, found its house in the academy among intellectual immigrants from the Third World (John 1996). But, of course, postcolonial theorizing *is not* an invention of Third World intellectuals migrating to the United States and *should not* be limited to this enclave. On the other hand, there is nothing wrong with the fact that migrating Third World intellectuals found themselves comfortable in the space of postcolonality. What Third World intellectuals and scholars in the United States (and I am one of them) contributed to was the marketing of postcoloniality among an array of available theories and a spectrum of "post" possibilities. On the other hand, Afro-American studies in the United States, whose emergence is parallel to postmodern and postcolonial theories, is deeply rooted in the African diaspora and, consequently, in the history of colonialism and slavery (Eze 1997a; 1997b). Dirlik has a point if we interpret his dictum as the marketization of postcolonial theory within the U.S academy. His point loses its poise when we consider, for instance, Stuart Hall and Paul Gilroy in England, or we go beyond the U.S. academy and take seriously Ruth Frankenberg's dictum that in the United States the question is not the postcolonial (as it is, e.g., for England and India) but civil rights (Frankenberg and Mani 1993). In this sense, the concept of civil rights has not been used to claim an identity and, similarly, civil rights in the United States will have more similarities with post-dictatorships in the Southern Cone: neither of them is the locus of subjectivity and identity formation, although both are extremely helpful to understand the political landscape in the United States and the Southern Cone, contemporary with the movement of decolonization in Asia, Africa, and the Caribbean. Once more, the bottom line is the subaltern reason in the geopolitical distribution of knowledge that could be explained by colonial legacies and local critical histories.

Subaltern reason, or whatever you want to call it, nourishes and is nourished by a theoretical practice prompted by movements of decolonization after World War II, which at its inception had little to do with academic enterprises (Césaire, Amilcar Cabral, Fanon) and had at its core the question of race. If Marxist thinking could be described as having class at its core, postcolonial theorizing could be described as having race at its core. Two of the three major genocides of modernity (the Amerindian and the African diaspora in the early modern period; the Holocaust as closing European modernity and the crisis of the civilizing mission) are, in my understanding, at the root of colonial and imperial histories—which is to say, at the root of the very constitution of modernity. The subaltern reason is what arises as a response to the need of rethinking and reconceptualizing the stories that have been told and the conceptualization that has been put into place to divide the world between Christians and pagans, civilized and barbarians, modern and premodern, and developed and underdeveloped regions and people, all global designs mapping the colonial difference.

But if one more example from U.S. intellectual history is needed to conceive of postmodernity as complementary with subaltern reason, one may take seriously Cornel West's (1989) argument about the American evasion of philosophy as a genealogy of pragmatism. By reading Emerson, Pierce, Royce, Dewey, Du Bois, James, and Rorty (among others), West convincingly suggests that the American evasion of philosophy is precisely the outcome of a philosophizing out of place—that is to say, of practicing a philosophical reflection whose foundations were not grounded in the needs of a breakaway settler colony but rather in the needs of colonial countries. Thus, when West states that "[p]rophetic pragmatism emerges at a particular moment in the history of North Atlantic civilization—the moment of postmodernity"—he further specifies that "postmodernity can be understood in light of three fundamental historical processes":

   1. The end of the European age (1492–1945) that decimated European self-confidence and prompted self-criticism. According to West, "this monumental decentering of Europe produced exemplary intellectual reflections such as the demystifying of European cultural hegemony, the destruction of the Western metaphysical traditions, and the

deconstruction of North Atlantic philosophical systems." Notice here the parallel between Cornel West's chronology and the modern world system frame.

2. The emergence of the United States as the world military and economic power, offering directions in the political arena and cultural production.

3. The "first stage of decolonization of the Third World" enacted by the political independence in Asia and in Africa. (West 1993, 9–11)

Notice also that the three fundamental historical processes that West offers for understanding postmodernity could also be invoked to understand post-coloniality. Playing with words, one could say that postmodernity is the discourse of countermodernity emerging from the metropolitan centers and *settler colonies*, while postcoloniality is the discourse of countermodernity emerging from *deep-settler* colonies (e.g., Algeria, India, Kenya, Jamaica, Indonesia, Bolivia, Guatemala) where coloniality of power endured with particular brutality.[1] Notice, too, that if decolonization after 1945 is taken into account (which mainly places decolonization in relation to the British Empire and German and French colonies), then nineteenth-century Latin America (e.g., Hispanic and Luso America) would not be considered as an early process of decolonization and its status as a set of Third World countries would not be easily accepted. This is another reason why the postcolonial question in Latin America only recently began to be discussed in academic circles in the United States and is still mostly ignored in Latin American countries, while modernity and postmodernity already have an ample bibliography in Latin America, particularly in those countries with a large population of European descent (e.g., Brazil and the Southern Cone). However, as we shall see, *in* Latin America dependency theory and philosophy of liberation were the critical responses to the colonial difference since the late 1960s (see chapter 3).

The map presented by West suggests a threefold division of colonial legacies: settler colonies; deep-settler colonies; and colonialism/imperialism without settlements after 1945. Thus, Cornel West states that "It is no accident that American pragmatism once again rises to the surface of North Atlantic intellectual life at the present moment. . . . The distinctive appeal of American pragmatism in our postmodern moment is its unashamedly moral emphasis and its unequivocally ameliorative impulse" (1989, 4). The emphasis on postmodernity (instead of postcoloniality) in a settler colony that became a world power helps us to understand the attention that post-

---

[1] I am borrowing the distinction between "settler colonies" (the United States, Australia, New Zealand, etc.) and "deep-settler colonies" (Algeria, Peru, India, etc.) from McClintock (1992, 88–89).

modernity has received in Latin America, particularly in Atlantic continental coast countries close to Europe and far away from the Pacific coast and dense Amerindian population. That we are beginning to see articles mixing postcoloniality and Latin America seems to stem from the fact that postcoloniality has become an important topic of discussion in academic circles in the same settler colony that arose to a world power, although the distinction between the emergence and uses of both postmodernity and postcoloniality is not always made nor are its consequences evaluated. When Dirlik, for instance, blatantly and provocatively states "the postcolonial begins when Third World intellectuals have arrived in the First World academy" (Dirlik 1994, 329), two parallel issues should be addressed: when and where does the postmodern begin? The answer, following Dirlik's statement, would be: when metropolitan and settler colony intellectuals frame as "postmodern" the drastic changes in the logic of late capitalism (Jameson), in the condition of knowledge in the most highly technological societies (Lyotard), or in the continuation of the critique of modernity in Western metaphysics (Vattimo). On the other hand, we should be able to distinguish *postcolonial theories* as an academic commodity (in the same way that postmodern theories were and are commodified), from *postcolonial theorizing*, as critiques subsumed under subaltern reason and border gnosis: a thinking process in which people living under colonial domination had to enact in order to negotiate their life and subaltern condition. Postcolonial theorizing may have "entered" in the academic market with the arrival of Third World intellectuals to the United States but certainly did not "begin" then. Postcolonial theorizing as a particular enactment of the subaltern reason coexists with colonialism itself as a constant move and force toward autonomy and liberation in every order of life, from economy to religion, from language to education, from memories to spatial order, and it is not limited to the academy, even less to the U.S. academy!

RESPONSES FROM THE EXTERNAL MARGINS OF THE WEST

Let's turn then to the "post-Occidental question" in Latin America. If one looks back to the deep-settler colonies in Latin American countries with a large indigenous population, concerns with issues that today would be identified as postcolonial discourses coexisting with neocolonial conditions can be found after the Russian Revolution, and different manifestations can be singled out: intellectuals like José Carlos Mariátegui in Peru (around 1920) and Enrique Dussel in Argentina (from the 1970s on) as well as philosophers such as Leopoldo Zea and Edmundo O'Gorman (from 1960 to today) in Mexico.

In 1958 Zea published *América en la historia*, in which "Occidentalism" was at the core of his concerns. Zea's problematic was rooted in a long-lasting tradition among Hispanic American intellectuals since the nineteenth century: the conflictive relationship with Europe and, toward the end of the nineteenth century, with the United States—in other words, with Occidentalism. Zea portrayed both Spain and Russia as marginal to the West. Two chapters are called, significantly, "España al margen de occidente" (Spain at the margin of the West) and "Rusia al margen de occidente" (Russia at the margin of the West). One can surmise that deep-settler colonies (type b) in neocolonial situations in Latin America have some similarities with the transformation of Russia into the Soviet Union, although almost a century elapsed between Latin American decolonization and the Russian Revolution. One obvious similarity that Zea points out comes from the marginal modernity of Spain and Russia during the eighteenth and nineteenth centuries. There are, however, enormous differences because of the separate era in which each historical process occurred and because of the fact that, while in Latin America decolonization took place in former deep-settler Spanish and Portuguese colonies, some interacting with deep indigenous cultures (e.g., the Andes [Bolivia, Peru, Ecuador, Colombia] and Mesoamerica [Mexico, Guatemala] and others) dealing with slavery as forced migrations, the Russian Revolution took place at the very heart of the empire. Both Spain and Russia had a similar relationship with "Eurocentrism," to which Zea devotes a chapter of his most recent book (Zea 1988), locating them in the foundation and aftermath of Cartesian and Hegelian conceptualizations of "reason," as well as in Marx and Engels' inverted Hegelianism as a socialist utopia materializing not in Europe but in its margins. Historical inheritances and their revolutionary implementations in the Soviet Union are not, however, linked to colonial legacies and postcolonial thinking, for reasons I will soon describe.

During the same years that Zea was writing his *América en la historia*, Edmundo O'Gorman (1961; Mignolo 1993b) was dismantling five hundred years of colonial discourse building and manipulating the belief that America was discovered when, as O'Gorman clearly demonstrates, there was no America to be discovered in the first place, and, for those who were already living in the lands where Columbus arrived without knowing where he was, there was nothing to be discovered at all. Certainly, neither Zea nor O'Gorman paid much attention to the contribution of people from Amerindian descent to the constant process of decolonization. However, there is a common dictum today among indigenous social movements, in both the Americas and the Caribbean, that "Columbus did not discover us." While two key concepts for Zea and O'Gorman in their postcolonial theorizing were "Occidentalism" and "Eurocentrism," Mexican-American scholar Jorge

Klor de Alva critically examined the meaning of the term "colonialism" and its misapplication to Latin America:

> The first part of my thesis is simple: Given that the indigenous populations of the Americas began to suffer a devastating demographic collapse on contact with the Europeans; given that the indigenous population loss had the effect, by the late sixteenth century, of restricting those who identified themselves as natives to the periphery of the nascent national polities; given that the greater part of the mestizos who quickly began to replace them fashioned their selves primarily after European models; given that together with Euro-Americans (*criollos*) and some Europeans (*peninsulares*) these Westernized mestizos made up the forces that defeated Spain during the nineteenth-century wars of independence; and, finally, given that the new countries under criollo/mestizo leadership constructed their national identities overwhelmingly out of Euro-American practices, the Spanish language, and Christianity, it is misguided to present the pre-independence *non-native* sectors as colonized, it is inconsistent to explain the wards of independence as anti-colonial struggles, and it is misleading to characterize the Americas, following the civil wars of separation, as postcolonial. In short, the Americas were neither Asia nor Africa; Mexico is not India, Peru is not Indonesia, and Latinos in the U.S.—although tragically opposed by an exclusionary will—are not Algerians. (Klor de Alva 1992, 3)

Klor de Alva formulated this thesis, as he himself makes clear, based on his inquiries into the construction of identities of contemporary U.S. Latinos and Mexican Americans. Furthermore, although he doesn't make this point as clear, his conception of "the Americas" excludes the Caribbean (English, French, Spanish), whose consideration would radically change the picture of the colonial and the postcolonial, since the French and English Caribbean are not the same type of colonies as the Spanish Caribbean. Basically, Klor de Alva's idea of "the Americas" is purely Hispanic and Anglo-American. Nevertheless, his effort to detach the Spanish/Portuguese from the British/ French/Dutch invasion of the Americas and the Caribbean looks to me like a sheer semantic game, similar to the argument that Spanish nationalists used to enact in order to save Spain from the brutalities of the conquest or to emphasize the civilizing (i.e., Christian) mission of the crown and the missionary orders. But even if "colonization" is misapplied to Latin America, we should not lose sight that we are talking about European and Western expansion ("Eurocentrism" and "Occidentalism" in terms of Zea and O'Gorman), and we should not lose sight of the internal colonial conflicts, mainly between Spain, England, and Holland toward the end of the seventeenth century, when Seville was no longer the center of global commerce and Amsterdam took its place. The change of hands in colonial power should be kept in mind if we are to understand the transformations and, at the same time, the continuities from the early modern/colonial period (Spain, Portugal, Renaissance) to the modern/colonial period (Holland, England, France, Enlightenment).

Moreover, colonialism is a notion denoting and describing colonial experiences after the eighteenth century (the stages of mercantile capitalism and the industrial revolution, according to Darcy Ribeiro [1968]) and, consequently, the Spanish and Portuguese expansion toward the Atlantic and the Pacific, mainly during the sixteenth and the first half of the seventeenth centuries, cannot properly be called as such. Klor de Alva underlines the anachronism of colonialism applied to historical events and processes in an imprecise "Latin America" under Spanish and Portuguese banners. While I sympathize with Klor de Alva's effort to avoid academic colonialism by reframing Spanish and Portuguese in a conceptualization that mainly emerged from the experiences of decolonization of British and French colonialism, I also feel uncomfortable with his argument because it falls next to an unwritten and officialist discourse of postimperial Spain, in which the term "viceroyalty" is used to avoid the political (and negative, from the Spanish perspective) implications of the term "colonialism."

To echo Klor de Alva's concerns of avoiding academic colonialism (a concern I have also found in several Latin American countries, where I lectured on issues of coloniality and postcoloniality, and of which I will make references throughout this book), by framing Latin American colonial and cultural histories in the vocabulary of English and Commonwealth criticism, it would be necessary to regionalize colonial legacies and postcolonial theorizing, to avoid the trap of the epistemology of modernity, in which colonial languages (such as English, French, or German) in complicity with theoretical and academic discourses produce the effect of universal knowledge for the sheer fact that the knowledge produced in the languages of late colonial powers has indeed the right to be exportable to every corner of the planet. The commodification and exportability of knowledge are perhaps the reason for Klor de Alva's discomfort with using colonialism and postcolonialism in and about Latin America.

What really remains as paradigmatic examples of subaltern/colonial criticism in Latin America is located in the Caribbean (part of it belonging to the Commonwealth), in Mesoamerica, and in the Andes. Zea and O'Gorman, although living in Mexico, were detached from these epistemological locations. The Caribbean contribution to postcolonial theorizing is already well known, basically because a good deal of writing is in English and French (e.g., George Lamming, Aimée Cesaire, Frantz Fanon, Edouard Glissant, Raphael Confiant), the dominant languages of the modern/colonial period. The Spanish Caribbean contribution is less familiar (Fernández Retamar, José Luis González), since Spanish as the dominant language of the early modern/colonial period lost its prestigious place as a "thinking language" with the fall of Spain and the rise of England and France (Mignolo 1995a;

1995b). It should be remembered, however, that while colonial legacies in the Caribbean are entrenched with the African diaspora, in Mesoamerica (mainly Mexico and Guatemala) and the Andes their profile is obtained from the long-lasting interaction between dense Amerindian populations and Spanish institutions and settlements.

In the late 1960s two Mexican sociologists, Pablo González Casanova and Rodolfo Stavenhagen, proposed the concept of "internal colonialism" to account for the relationship between the state and the Amerindian population since Mexico's independence from Spain in 1821. As one could expect, the concept was criticized from a scientific-oriented sociology, as if the needs to which González Casanova (1965) and Stavenhagen (1965) were responding would have been solely disciplinary! The vigor of the concept shall be situated in mapping the social configuration of nation building in the Spanish ex-colonies, rather than in whether or not it fulfills the demands of a disciplinary system of control and punishment. However, since the concept has been criticized from the hegemonic disciplinary perspective, it vanished from the scene, and few will remember it as an early manifestation of postcolonial theorizing in Latin America. More precisely, "internal colonialism," a concept introduced by Third World sociologists to account for the social realities of their country and region, carries the trace of the colonial difference, the subaltern reason.

Certainly, the need of further elucidation of "internal colonialism" should not be denied. For instance, when the concept is used in the context of U.S. history, the differences between North and South colonial legacies (as it was pointed out earlier) cannot be ignored. In fact, who in U.S. national communities are in subaltern positions: Native Americans, Asian Americans, Mexican Americans? And in Argentina, are Italian communities in the same subaltern positions as Amerindian communities? Be that as it may, "internal colonialism," as used by González Casanova and Stavenhagen in Mexico and, more recently, by Silvia Rivera Cusicanqui (1984; 1993) in the Andes, is clearly applied to the double bind of the national state after independence: on the one hand, to enforce the colonial politics toward indigenous communities and, on the other, to establish alliances with metropolitan colonial powers. Chiefly, in nineteenth-century Mesoamerica and the Andes, the question was to break the ties with Spanish colonialism and to build a nation with the support of England and France, and this is perhaps the main profile of neocolonialism in the ex-Spanish and Portuguese colonies. Above all, "internal colonialism" is relevant in Rivera Cusicanqui's work (as well as in other Bolivian intellectuals, such as Xavier Albó [1994]) to understanding a society in which more than 50 percent of the population is of Amerindian descent, speaks Aymara or Quechua, and maintains a socioeconomic organization inherited from Inca and Aymara legacies, which coexisted for five hundred years with Western people and institutions. The concept of "internal colonialism" also helps to establish a balance between class and ethnicity. In Rivera Cusicanqui's conception, one explanation of the crisis in Andean social sciences and their failure to understand social movements such as "Shining Path" was due mainly to their blindness to ethnicity, colonial legacies, and "internal colonialism" (Rivera Cusicanqui 1992).

A CUBAN PERSPECTIVE ON POST-OCCIDENTALISM

Occidentalism as the overarching imaginary of the modern/colonial world system can be understood in Coronil's proposal:

> To the extent that "the West" remains assumed in Said's work, I believe that Said's challenge, and the ambiguity in his discussion of Orientalism, may be creatively approached by problematizing and linking the two entities that lie at the center of his analysis: the West's Orientalist representations and the West itself.
>
> I would like to take a step in this direction by relating Western representations of "Otherness" to the implicit constructions of "Selfhood" that underwrite them. This move entails reorienting our attention from the problematic of "Orientalism," which focuses on the deficiencies of the West's representations of the Orient, to that of "Occidentalism," which refers to the conceptions of the West animating these representations. It entails relating the observed to the observers, products to production, knowledge to its sites of formation. (Coronil 1996, 56)

On the other hand, as the overarching imaginary, "Occidentalism" works in reverse: from the "Orient" to the "West," so to speak. When "Occidentalism" is related to modernization, it can be perceived as a model to follow or as an evil to kill. These two perceptions are at work in China and have been analyzed recently by Xiaomei Chen (1995; Keping 1994). A similar perspective could be located in Latin America where Occidentalism can either provide the model for modernization or be the colonial evil that reproduces colonization. Thus, following on the steps of Coronil, I also propose to look at Occidentalism from inside the modern world system as well as from its exteriority (in Levinas's sense). The modern/colonial world system is and has been made in these constant double interactions. Such a perspective is twice as important from the (Latin) American perspective since the Americas have never been considered part of the Orient or the Other, but an extension of the same, as I have already mentioned in the introduction and will pursue in the following chapter (Mignolo 1995c; 1996b).

Post-Occidentalism was introduced, as I have already mentioned, by Cuban intellectual Roberto Fernández Retamar in 1976. In introducing the term, he was assuming that Occidentalism was the key word in Latin American cultural history. Occidentalism, contrary to Orientalism, was created from the very beginning as the extension of Europe, not as its otherness: "Indias Occidentales" (the legal expression used by the Spanish crown all through its possessions from the continent to the Philippines) set the stage for the relationships between Europe and what would later become the Americas, the "extreme Occident." Thus, the constant tension between the extreme Occident as the "empty" continent where Europe extended itself, and the Amerindians, already inhabiting the "empty" continent. Thus, Fernández Retamar recognizes that "Amerindians and Blacks far from being foreign bodies in 'our America' (e.g., Latin America) because they are not Western, they belong to it with full right, with more right than the foreign and outcast agents of the civilizing mission" (Fernández Retamar [1974] 1995). Thus the exteriority of the colonial difference.

Fernández Retamar makes a link between this observation and Marxism, since Marxism emerged as the critical voice of capitalism, which, for him, is equivalent to Occidentalism. For Fernández Retamar, Marxism is no longer an Occidental ideology but a post-Occidental one. What is interesting to note here is his assumption—from the Cuban and Caribbean experience—that Marxism allows going beyond Western imaginary. In fact "Amerindians and Blacks," crucial in the Caribbean experience, were not much so in the European context in which Marxism originated. The crossing-over of colonialism and capitalism in Latin America allows Fernández Retamar to propose post-Occidentalism as a Marxist category although incorporated to the colonial history of Amerindian exploitation and African slave trade. Post-Occidentalism could have been linked to "internal colonialism" and to "dependency theory." However, the isolation impinged by colonial geohistorical distribution, complemented with the scientific distribution of knowledge located in the metropolitan centers, made of the local histories and knowledge a curious and sometimes folkloric incident in the larger map of global designs.

There are two issues here that need to be untangled. One is the distinction between neocolonial situations and the other between neocolonial discourses and post/Occidental/colonial criticism. My first inclination would be to define "neocolonial situations and discourses" as a configuration arising from the liberation of colonial rules and the different stages of the modern period, such as the independence of Anglo- and Hispanic America at the end of the eighteenth and the beginning of the nineteenth centuries, respectively, as well as the decolonization of Indonesia and the Algerian or the Cuban Revolution—that is to say, neocolonial situations and discourse types (a), (b), and (c). This may be too schematic for certain tastes, but it helps in sorting out some of the confusion and ambiguities of the expression.

Post/Occidental/colonial criticism as subaltern theorizing, by contrast, mainly emerges in the aftermath of decolonization after World War II and parallels new forms of neocolonialism and dictatorship. Furthermore, it is the critical consciousness on colonialism and neocolonialism that created the conditions for subaltern theorizing. Now, if subalternity (understood as theory building and cultural critic) emerges from different types of colonial and neocolonial legacies, then post/Occidentalism/colonialism and postmodernism are countermodern moves responding to different kinds of colonial legacies and neocolonial states that have in common the process of Western expansion identified as modernity/coloniality/Occidentalism.

The reader could object, at this point, by saying that postmodernity is not a particularly Anglo-American or even a European phenomenon but of peripheral modernities as well. Using similar logic, one can argue that the same observation could be made about post/Occidentalism/colonialism, saying that it is not just an issue of modernity and colonized countries between 1492 and 1945 but rather a global or transnational issue. Modernity is both the consolidation of empire and nation/empires in Europe, a discourse constructing the idea of Occidentalism, the subjugation of people and cultures, as well as the counterdiscourses and social movements resisting Euro-American expansionism. Thus, if modernity consists of both the consolidation of European history (global design) and the silenced critical voices of peripheral colonies (local histories), postmodernism and post/Occidentalism/colonialism are alternate processes of countering modernity from different colonial legacies and in different national or neocolonial situations: (1) legacies from/at the center of colonial empires (e.g., Lyotard); (2) colonial legacies in settler colonies (e.g., Jameson in the United States); and (3) colonial legacies in deep-settler colonies (e.g., Said, Cusicanqui, Spivak, Glissant, Albó, Bhabha, Quijano). In other words, postmodernity and post/Occidentalism/colonialism are both parts of subaltern reason and an extended critique of subalternity.

It is my contention that post/Occidental/colonial theorizing allows for a decentering of theoretical practices in terms of the politics of geohistorical locations (Mignolo 1995; see also chapters 2 and 4), and the distinction between post/Occidental/colonial discourses and theories becomes difficult to trace. Cultures of scholarship become part of a political domain of discourses, and social concerns, coupled with knowledge oriented toward emancipation/liberation. Thus, it would have been difficult to conceive Fanon as a post/Occidental/colonial theoretician in the late 1950s. His discourse, attractive and seductive as it was (and still is), was not part of the conceptual framework that, at the time, was seen in terms of theoretical discourse in the academy. Theory in the humanities was conceived then mainly in terms of linguistic models and in the social sciences, in terms of the covering law model. Fanon became a post/Occidental/colonial theoretician once the academy conceptualized a new kind of theoretical practice, invented a name to distinguish it from others, and placed it within a specific academic battlefield.

"Theory" (in quotation marks) becomes necessary to distinguish between an inherited concept of theory (from the social sciences, linguistics, and semiotics and sometimes from the transposition from the natural to social sciences and the humanities) and a type of self-reflective and critical practice in the academy. There are two takes in the use of the term theory that I would like to point out, comparing "critical theory" with post/Occidental/colonial theorizing and the emergence of subaltern reason.

In the first take, Craig Calhoun described the use of critical theory by Frankfurt School philosophers as a displacement of the canonical concept of theory in philosophy, by adapting it to the social sciences:

> They challenged the presumed absolute identity of the individual as knower embodied famously in the Cartesian cogito ("I think, therefore I am"). Influenced by Freud, Romanticism, and thinkers of the "dark side" of Enlightenment like Nietzsche and Sade, they knew the individual person had to be more complex than that, especially if he or she was to be the subject of creative culture. They also say the individual is social in a way most ordinary theory did not, constituted by intersubjective relations with others, all the more important where they furthered a sense of non-identity, of the complexity of multiple involvements with others, that enabled a person to reach beyond narrow self-identity. (Calhoun 1995a, 16)

But perhaps more important to my purpose is Calhoun's observation that most of the early key Frankfurt theorists were Jews (Calhoun 1995, 17). Here we touch on a crucial issue in the formation of subaltern reason and post/Occidental/colonial theorizing: the inscription of the colonial/subaltern experience of the theoretician in his or her theoretical practices, similar to the inscription of the Jewish experience in Frankfurt early critical theory (e.g., Horkheimer and Adorno's reading of the Jews' experience against the Enlightenment ideals, [1947] 1995, 168–208). Calhoun's reading of the connection between the ethnicity of the theoretician and the building of critical theory is the following:

> Most of the early key Frankfurt theorists were Jews. If this did not produce an acute enough interest in politics of identity to start with—most of them coming from highly assimilated families and assimilating further themselves in the course of their studies—the rise of Nazism and broader anti-Semitic currents brought the issue home. Faced with the question why Jews were not just one minority group among many—for the Nazis certainly but also for most of modernity—Horkheimer and Adorno sought the answer in a characteristic way: Anti-Semitism represented the hatred of those who see themselves as civilized, but could not fulfill the promises of civilization for all those who reminded them of the failures of civilization. (Calhoun 1995a, 17)

In a sense, then, critical theory as practiced by the Frankfurt School theoretician is, like post/Occidental/colonial theorizing, a kind of "barbarian theorizing": a theoretical practice by those who oppose the clean and rational concept of knowledge and theory and theorize, precisely, from the situation they have been put in, be they Jewish, Muslim, Amerindian, African, or other "Third World" people like Hispanics in today's United States. But not only that: the link between theory and ethnicity in the early Frankfurt School detected by Calhoun is also similar to the awareness of being a "Third World" philosopher, like Leopoldo Zea or O'Gorman, who have to write (using Zea's title of his latest book) from "marginalization and barbarism" (Zea 1988). Zea and O'Gorman placed themselves at the margin of the discipline, as historians and philosophers, although the ethnic question did not reach their own thinking. Frankfurt philosophers were at the center stage of disciplinary, epistemological, and theoretical transformations, although the ethnic question was inscribed in their thinking and transformed theoretical practices into "critical theory." Zea and O'Gorman contributed, nonetheless, to value thinking "from marginalization and barbarism"—or, as Kusch would say, from the "philosophical location" where location is not only geographic but historical, political, and epistemological (1978, 107–14). In other words, they contributed to show the limits of civilization and the rise of "barbarian" (Jewish, marginalized postcolonial, female, Afro-European or American, Amerindian, homosexual, etc.) theorizing.

In the second take, Mary John (1996), unlike Craig Calhoun, looks at the inscription of the subject position in "doing theory" in France in the 1960s, and also at the radical transformation of doing theory since the late 1970s. That radical transformation comes mainly from the awareness that theory is where you can find it. There is no geographical or epistemological location that holds the property rights for theoretical practices but "the philosophical location," in Kusch's terms (see chapter 3)—that is, the starting point and the road orienting our thinking with alterity constantly intervening, suggesting, or showing at the same time the unthinkable (Kusch 1978, 109). John, like Calhoun, looks for the inscription of subjectivity at the intersection of feminism and postcoloniality, in whatever form this intersection can manifest itself. The awareness and the inscription of feminism and postcoloniality in John's concept of "doing theory" is equivalent to the awareness of Jewishness in the Frankfurt School's "critical theory." But it is more: it is also an awareness that the very concept of theory, linked to the modern reason, cannot be accepted, rehearsed, and applied to feminist concerns and postcolonial issues. If John's disbelief is in the dichotomy between linking theories to their context of origin or taking them in their universal scope and making them travel to illuminate alien contexts, then the question remains that the very concept of theory is interpellated (John 1996). What I am arguing in this chapter and the rest of the book is that we should delink the concept of theory from its modern epistemological version (to explain or to make sense of unconnected facts or data) or its postmodern version (to deconstruct reified conceptual networks). One of the aims of post/Occidental/colonial theorizing, in my understanding, is to reinscribe in the history of humankind what was repressed by modern reason, either in its version of civilizing mission or in its version of theoretical thinking that was denied to the noncivilized that Gilroy theorizes in the concept of double consciousness in Frederick Douglass (Gilroy 1993). As such, one of the versions of theorizing I envision and argue for is that of thinking from the borders and the perspective of subalternity. In this case, from the border of the modern concept of theory and those unnamed ways of thinking that have been silenced by the modern concept of theory but not repressed: to think theoretically is a gift and a competence of human beings, not just of human beings living in a certain period, in certain geographical locations of the planet, and speaking a small set of particular languages. If postcoloniality is not able to break away from modern epistemology, it would become just another version of it with a different subject matter. It would be, in other words, a theory *about* a new subject matter but not the constitution of a new epistemological subject that thinks *from and about* the borders.

Subaltern reason and border thinking go beyond the Occidental/colonial and rejoin Frederick Douglass's inversion of the dialectic master/slave, analyzed by Paul Gilroy (1993, 58–64). The allegorical relations of master and slave to portray independent and dependent self-consciousness in relation to consciousness and knowledge, can be thought out—in Hegel—within a disembodied epistemology that assumes the locus of enunciation of the master as the universal one. Hegel's allegory is located within a Cartesian and disembodied concept of reason. As such, reason could be described and conceptualized with independence of gender and sexual relations, social hierarchies, national or religious beliefs, or ethnic prejudices. However, the silence implied in the disembodied (both individual and social) is at the same time the assumption of position of a universal position of power in relation to which sexual relations, social hierarchies, national or religious beliefs, and ethnic prejudices are subaltern categories. Hegel's allegorical speculations of the master/slave relations shall be confronted constantly with the embodied reflection on consciousness and self-consciousness narrated and theorized by Douglass: "A few months of his discipline tamed me. Mr. Covey succeeded in breaking me. I was broken in body, soul and spirit. My natural elasticity was crushed; my intellect languished; the disposition to read departed; the cheerful spark that lingered about my eye died; the dark night of slavery closed in upon me; and behold a man transformed into a brute" (quoted by Gilroy 1993, 61).

At the moment that Douglass reflects on his experience and tells the story, he is no longer a slave, and one could say that he possesses a "consciousness that exists for itself," while Covey becomes the representative of "a consciousness that is repressed within itself" (Gilroy 1993, 60). At this point, Douglass is in a position to understand both the slave and the master from the perspective (and experience) of the slave, while Covey lacks the experience of the slave in his understanding of the relationship between both. Hegel's allegory is located on the side of Covey, not Douglass. Douglass thinks from the experience of the subaltern who has liberated himself from that position and can analyze slavery as a form of subalternity from that perspective. By so doing, Douglass introduces the perspective of the slave into the analysis of the relation master/slave. But now the questions asked and issues raised are no longer those of understanding a disincorporated consciousness and self-conscioumess, but that of understanding from the historical experiences made possible by the very concept of Reason that Hegel was trying to elucidate in his *Phenomenology of the Spirit.*

We all know that the concept of Reason introduced by René Descartes did not only have philosophical and metaphysical import, but was a crucial principle to develop and manage the larger spectrum of society (Taylor 1989, 285–304). Consequently, one should expect that new forms of rationality, emerging from subaltern experiences, will not only have an impact in philosophy and social thought but in the reorganization of society. Thinking from subaltern experiences should contribute to both self-understanding and public policy, creating the condition for precluding subalternity. Thus, it seems that the possibilities of theorizing colonial legacies could be carried out in different directions: from a strictly disciplinary location, from the location of someone for whom colonial legacies are a historical but not a personal matter, and, finally, from the site of someone for whom colonial legacies are entrenched in his or her own history and sensibility, like slavery for Douglass. Some of the confusion and ambiguity of the term today is due, I believe, to the various possibilities of engaging oneself in postcolonial criticism. I am also convinced that the opposite prejudice is the common belief that persons who *are from* some place in the heart of the empire have the necessary competence to theorize, no matter where they *are at* because theorizing is taken to be the universal practice of the modern reason. This prejudice is anchored in the ideological distribution of knowledge in the social sciences and the humanities, parallel to the geopolitical distribution of the world into First, Second, and Third. Or, to put it another way, while *subaltern reason* discloses a change of terrain regarding its very foundation as a cognitive, political, and theoretical practice, modern reason speaks for the foundation of the humanities and the social sciences during the nineteenth century, grounded in Renaissance and Enlightenment (rather than colonial) legacies. In this sense, subaltern reason is both postmodern *and* postcolonial.

AREA STUDIES AND THE WESTERN DISTRIBUTION OF
KNOWLEDGE AND CULTURES

I owe the preceding insight to Carl Pletsch (1981). Pletsch traced the division of social scientific labor related to First, Second, and Third Worlds between 1950 and 1975, a time in which social scientific labor was reorganized according to a new world order and, coincidentally, a time in which the emergence of colonial discourses and the foundations of postcolonial theories are now being located. Colonial discourses and theories were not yet an issue at the time Pletsch wrote his article, which was mainly devoted to the social sciences. The period chosen by Pletsch is also relevant for the implied connections between decolonization and the emergence of the cold war, which brought Russia/the Soviet Union back into the picture on the fringes of Western modernity as the Second World. Pletsch's thesis is simple: Western anxiety due to the emergence of socialist nations and, above all, the Soviet Union prompted the division of the world into three large categories: technologically and economically developed countries that are democratically organized; technologically and economically developed countries ruled by ideology; and technologically and economically underdeveloped countries. The foundation of such a distribution cannot necessarily be bonded to the properties of the objects classified but rather to the site of enunciation constructing the classification: the enunciation is located in the First World and not in the Second or the Third. Since the classification originated in democratically developed and capitalistic countries, it naturally became a First World decision and the measuring stick for subsequent classifications. My first assumption, in this context, is that postcolonial criticism strives for a displacement of the locus of theoretical enunciation from the First to the Third World, claiming for the legitimacy of the "philosophical location."[2]

My assumption can be better understood if we pursue Pletsch a little further. The thrust of his argument lies in the fact that the academic redistribution of scientific labor is not parallel with the political and economical relocation of cultural worlds. Or, as Pletsch explains:

> Terms evoking ethnocentrism, condescension, imperialism, and aggression were systematically replaced by apparently neutral and scientific terms—euphemisms. Not only did former colonies become "developing nations" and primi-

---

[2] I was told on a couple of occasions that I should not talk about First, Second and Third Worlds because such entities never existed. I would like to emphasize that I am not talking about the entity, but the conceptual division of the world, which, as such, existed and still exists, even when the configuration of the world is no longer the one that prompted the distinction. I feel the need to apologize for introducing this note, but at the same time I cannot avoid it.

tive tribes become "traditional people," the War and Navy Departments of the United States Government were transformed into the "Defense" Department. . . . It would have been simply impossible to explain the need for foreign aid and vast military expenditures in a time of peace with categories any more differentiated than those marshaled under the three worlds umbrella. (Pletsch 1981, 575)

From an epistemological perspective, the classic distinction between traditional and modern societies was relocated and redistributed. The modern world was divided in two: the First World was technologically advanced, free of ideological constraints, utilitarian thinking, and thus *natural*. The Second World was also technologically advanced but encumbered with an ideological elite that prevented utilitarian thinking and free access to science. The traditional Third World was economically and technologically underdeveloped, with a traditional mentality obscuring the possibility of utilitarian and scientific thinking. Thus, the epistemological distribution of labor was part and parcel of the ideological distribution of the world and the reconceptualization of science, ideology, and culture:

Western social scientists have reserved the concept of culture for the mentalities of traditional societies in their pristine states. They have designated the socialist societies of the second world the province of ideology. And they have long assumed—not unanimously, to be sure—that the modern West is the natural haven of science and utilitarian thinking. Consistent with this scheme, one clan of social scientists is set apart to study the pristine societies of the third world (anthropologists). Other clans—economists, sociologists, and political scientists—study the third world only insofar as the process of modernization has already begun. The true province of these latter social sciences is the modern world, especially the natural societies of the West. But again, subclans of each of these sciences of the modern world are specially outfitted to make forays into the ideological regions of the second world. Much as their fellow economists, sociologists, and political scientists who study the process of modernization in the third world, these students of the second world are engaged in area studies. What distinguishes their area is the danger associated with ideology, as opposed to the now innocent otherness of traditional cultures. But the larger contrast is between all of these area specialists, whether of the second or third world, and the disciplinary generalists who study the natural societies of the first world. (Pletsch 1981, 579)

I quoted Pletsch at length because of the substantial redistribution of the order of things and of the human sciences since the nineteenth century, described by Michel Foucault (1966; 1969), and because it helps to clarify the location of postcolonial and postmodern theoretical practices at the close of the twentieth century, following the collapse of the three-world order and the end of the cold war. One can surmise that one substantial characteristic of the postcolonial as legitimate *loci* of theoretical enunciation articulated on particular colonial legacies is the emergent voices and actions from Third World countries, reversing the backward image produced and sustained by a long colonial legacy until the redistribution of scientific labor. If, according to the distribution of scientific and cultural production in First, Second, and Third Worlds, someone is *from* an economically and technologically underdeveloped country, and he or she has a mentally obscure mind, then he or she cannot produce any kind of significant theoretical thinking because theory is defined according to First World standards. Theory and sciences are produced, according to this logic, in First World countries where there are no ideological obstructions to scientific and theoretical thinking. Thus, the ideology of the civilizing mission was still at work in the distribution of scientific labor between the three worlds.

My second assumption is that the locus of postmodern theories (as articulated by Jameson [1991] is in the First World, although in opposition to the epistemological configuration of the social sciences vis-à-vis the Third World analyzed by Pletsch. One could argue that postmodern reason blends theoretical practices and training from the First World with the ideological underpinnings of the Second (not in terms of state policy, but in terms of its Marxist-Leninist foundations). But, as such, it maintains its difference with postcolonial reason in which the alliance is between the cultural production of the Third World and the theoretical imagination of the First: a powerful alliance in which the restitution of "secondary qualities" in theoretical production displaces and challenges the purity of the modern reason, conceived as a logic operation without interference of sensibility and location. The restitution of sensibility and location is postcolonial theorizing empowering those who have been suppressed or marginalized from the production of knowledge and understanding.

There is no reference to literature in Pletsch's article. One must remember, however, the enormous impact of literary production of Third World countries (e.g., García Márquez, Assia Djebar, Salman Rushdie, Naguib Mahfouz, Michelle Cliff). The fact that such an impact took place in the literary domain (i.e., in the domain of "cultural" production rather than in the social sciences) supports Pletsch's scheme of the distribution of knowledge. It also explains why magical realism became the imprint of the Third World's high-cultural production. However, when "literary narratives" are also taken as theories in their own right, the distinction between the location of theoretical and cultural production begins to crumble.

Let's rethink now the distinction between *coming from, being at,* and *being from* (Gilroy 1990–91). If postcolonial discourses (including literature and theories) are associated with people (*coming) from* countries with colonial legacies, it is precisely because of the displacement of the locus of intellectual production from the First to the Third World. However, while literary output can easily be attributed to the cultural production of the Third World, theory is more difficult to justify because—according to the scientific distribution of labor analyzed by Pletsch—the locus of theoretical production is the First rather than Third World. My third assumption is that postcolonial theoretical practices are not just changing our vistas of colonial processes; they are also challenging the very foundations of the Western concept of knowledge and understanding by establishing epistemological links between geohistorical locations and theoretical production.

By insisting on the links between the place of theorizing (*being from, coming from,* and *being at*) and the locus of enunciation, I am emphasizing that loci of enunciation are not given but enacted. I am not assuming that *only* people coming from such and such a place could do X. Let me insist that I am not casting the argument in deterministic terms but in the open realm of logical possibilities, of historical circumstances and personal sensibilities. I am suggesting that for those whom colonial legacies are real (i.e., they hurt), that they are more (logically, historically, and emotionally) inclined than others to theorize the past in terms of coloniality. I am also suggesting that postcolonial theorizing relocates the boundaries between knowledge, the known and the knowing subject (which was my reason for stressing the complicities of postcolonial theories with "minorities"). While I perceive the location of the knowing subject in the social economy of knowledge and understanding as the main contribution of postcolonial theorizing, I also believe that the description or explanation of the known is the main contribution of postmodern theories.

THE RATIO BETWEEN KNOWLEDGE AND
ITS GEOHISTORICAL LOCATION

I move now to particular cases of countermodernity and differential loci of enunciation, where the differences are related to coming *from* different colonial legacies and being at different geocultural locations.

Enrique Dussel, an Argentinian philosopher associated with the philosophy of liberation, has been articulating a strong countermodern argument. I quote from the beginning of his Frankfurt lectures:

> Modernity is, for many (for Jürgen Habermas or Charles Taylor, for example), an essentially or exclusively European phenomenon. In these lectures, I will argue that modernity is, in fact, a European phenomenon, but one constituted in a dialectical relation with a non-European alterity that is its ultimate content. Modernity appears when Europe affirms itself as the "center" of a World history that it inaugurates; the "periphery" that surrounds this center is consequently

part of its self-definition. The occlusion of this periphery (and of the role of Spain and Portugal in the formation of the modern world system from the late fifteenth to the mid-seventeenth centuries) leads the major contemporary thinkers of the "center" into a Eurocentric fallacy in their understanding of modernity. If their understanding of the genealogy of modernity is thus partial and provincial, their attempts at a critique or defense of it are likewise unilateral and, in part, false. (Dussel [1993] 1995, 65)

The construction of the idea of modernity linked to European expansion, as forged by European intellectuals, was powerful enough to last almost five hundred years. Postcolonial discourses and theories began effectively to question that hegemony, a challenge that was unthinkable (and perhaps unexpected) by those who constructed and presupposed the idea of modernity as a historical period and implicitly as *the* locus of enunciation—a locus of enunciation that in the name of rationality, science, and philosophy asserted its own privilege over other forms of rationality or over what, from the perspective of modern reason, was nonrational. I would submit, consequently, that postcolonial literature and postcolonial theories are constructing a new concept of reason as differential loci of enunciation. What does "differential" mean? Differential here first means a displacement of the concept and practice of the notions of knowledge, science, theory, and understanding articulated during the modern period.[3] Thus, Dussel's regionalization of modernity could be compared with Homi Bhabha's, both speaking *from* different colonial legacies (Spanish and English respectively): "Driven by the subaltern history of the margins of modernity—rather than by the failures of logocentrism—I have tried, in some small measure, *to revise the known, to rename the postmodern from the position of the postcolonial*" (Bhabha 1994, 175; emphasis added).
I find a noteworthy coincidence between Dussel and Bhabha, albeit with some significant differences in accent. The coincidence lies in the very important fact that the task of postcolonial reasoning (i.e., theorizing) is not only linked to the immediate political needs of decolonization (in Asia, Africa, and the Caribbean) but also to the rereading of the paradigm of modern reason. This task is performed by Dussel and Bhabha in different, although complementary ways.

---

[3] A revealing example of what I am trying to articulate is Norma Alarcón's counterreading of Jean-Luc Nancy's theoretical allocating of meaning. While Nancy allocates meaning to Chicano culture by reading it from the space where ethnicity and language do not interfere with his own discourse (e.g., the total absence of reference to the Maghreb in French language and culture), Alarcón's discourse is a necessary relocation from the space in which ethnicity and language dislocate the production of knowledge and understanding (Alarcón 1994; Nancy 1994).

After a detailed analysis of Kant's and Hegel's construction of the idea of Enlightenment in European history, Dussel summarizes the elements that constitute the myth of modernity:

(1) Modern (European) civilization understands itself as the most developed, the superior, civilization; (2) This sense of superiority obliges it, in the form of a categorical imperative, as it were, to "develop" (civilize, uplift, educate) the more primitive, barbarous, underdeveloped civilizations; (3) The path of such development should be that followed by Europe in its own development out of antiquity and the Middle Ages; (4) Where the barbarians or the primitive opposes the civilizing process, the praxis of modernity must, in the last instance, have recourse to the violence necessary to remove the obstacles to modernization; (5) This violence, which produces in many different ways, victims, takes on an almost ritualistic character: the civilizing hero invests his victims (the colonized, the slave, the woman, the ecological destruction of the earth, etc.) with the character of being participants in a process of redemptive sacrifice; (6) From the point of view of modernity, the barbarian or primitive is in a state of guilt (for, among other things, opposing the civilizing process). This allows modernity to present itself not only as innocent but also as a force that will emancipate or redeem its victims from their guilt; (7) Given this "civilizing" and redemptive character of modernity, the suffering and sacrifices (the costs) of modernization imposed on "immature" peoples, slaves, races, the "weaker" sex, et cetera, are inevitable and necessary. (Dussel [1993] 1995, 75)

The myth of modernity is laid out by Dussel to confront alternative interpretations. While Horkheimer and Adorno, as well as postmodernist thinkers such as Lyotard, Rorty, or Vattimo, all propose a critique of reason (a violent, coercive, and genocidal reason), Dussel proposes a critique of the Enlightenment's irrational moments as sacrificial myth not by negating reason but by asserting the reason of the other—that is, by identifying postcolonial reason as differential locus of enunciation. The intersection between the idea of a self-centered modernity grounded in its own appropriation of Greco-Roman (classical) legacies and an emerging idea of modernity from the margins (or countermodernity) makes clear that history does not begin in Greece, and that different historical beginnings are, at the same time, anchored to diverse loci of enunciation. This simple axiom is, I submit, a fundamental one for and of postsubaltern reason. Finally, Bhabha's project to rename the postmodern from the position of the postcolonial also finds its niche in postsubaltern reason as a differential locus of enunciation.

While Dussel redraws the map of modernity by including in its geography the expansion of the Spanish and Portuguese empires after 1500 and revises the Enlightenment narrative by bringing in the phantom of colonial stories, Bhabha works toward the articulation of enunciative agencies. Dussel's programmatic suggestion that the accession of modernity lies today not necessarily in a process that will transcend modernity from inside (e.g., postmodernity) but rather as a *process of transmodernity*, seems to concur with Bhabha's concerns. Let's read Dussel first:

> Transmodernity (as a project of political, economic, ecological, erotic, pedagogical and religious liberation) is the co-realization of that which it is impossible for modernity to accomplish by itself: that is, of an incorporative solidarity, which I have called analeptic, between center/periphery, man/woman, different races, different ethnic groups, different classes, civilization/nature, Western culture/Third World cultures, et cetera. (Dussel [1993] 1995, 76)

If, as he claims, the overcoming of these dichotomies presupposes that the darker side of modernity (e.g., the colonial periphery) discovers itself as innocent, that very discovery will presuppose asserting loci of enunciation at the borders of colonial expansion and constructing postcolonial reason out of the debris of European modernity and the transformed legacies of world cultures and civilizations.

In my understanding, Bhabha's contribution to the articulation of postcolonial reason lies in the loci of enunciation taking ethical and political precedence over the rearticulation of the enunciated. Therefore, Bhabha has to play enactment against epistemology and to explore the politics of (enunciative) locations, which he does by introducing Charles Taylor's concept of "minimal rationality,"[4] an effort to bring to the foreground human agency instead of representation:

> Minimal rationality, as the activity of articulation, embodied in the language metaphor, alters the subject of culture from an epistemological function to an enunciative practice. If culture as epistemology focuses on function and intention, then culture as enunciation focuses on signification and institutionalization; if the epistemological tends towards a reflection of its empirical referent or object, the enunciative attempts repeatedly to reinscribe and relocate the political claim to cultural priority and hierarchy . . . in the social institution of the signifying activity. (Taylor 1989, 177)

The postcolonial as the signpost of a differential locus of enunciation organizes Bhabha's discourse of countermodernity. These sites of enunciation are not, however, dialectical opposites to the locus of enunciation created by modernity (e.g., modern subject and subjectivity) in the constant invention and reconstruction of the self and of the monotopic concept of reason. They are, instead, places of interventions, interruptions of the self-invention

---

[4] Although Taylor doesn't elaborate the concept of "minimal rationality" in the book quoted by Dussel (*Sources of the Self*, 1989), epistemological considerations emerging from colonial trajectories are not the paradigmatic examples of Taylor's arguments.

of modernity. Bhabha is responding, from the legacies of colonial British India, to the same concerns expressed by Dussel from the legacies of colonial Hispanic America.

> I am posing these questions from within the problematic of modernity because of a shift within contemporary critical traditions of postcolonial writings. There is no longer an influential separatist emphasis on simply elaborating an anti-imperialist or black nationalist tradition "in itself." There is an attempt to interrupt the Western discourses of modernity through these displacing, interrogative subaltern or postslavery narratives and the critical theoretical perspectives they engender. (Bhabha 1994, 241)

Furthermore, in the following paragraph, he states: "The power of the postcolonial translation of modernity rests in its *performative, deformative* structure that does not simply revalue the contest of a cultural tradition, or transpose values 'cross-culturally' " (241).

Bhabha's emphasis on agency over representation is reinforced by his concept of "time lag": in a revealing footnote in the conclusion to his *The Location of Culture* (note 16), Bhabha reminds the reader that the term time lag was introduced and used in previous chapters (8 and 9) and that he sees this concept as an expression that captures the "splitting" of colonial discourse. Time lag becomes, then, a new form of colonial discourse and a new location of postcolonial theorizing. Postcolonial theorizing assumes both the splitting of the colonial subject (of study) as well as the splitting of postcolonial theorizing (the locus of enunciation). A similar epistemological quarrel was underlined by Norma Alarcón in the context of women studies, of gender and ethnicity in particular, when she states that "The subject (and object) of knowledge is now a woman, but the inherited view of consciousness has not been questioned at all. As a result, some Anglo-American feminist subjects of consciousness have tended to become a parody of the masculine subject of consciousness, thus revealing their ethnocentric liberal underpinning" (357). The epistemological controversy in postcoloniality is that the split subject of colonial discourse mirrors the split subject of postcolonial theorizing; likewise, women as understanding subjects mirror women as subjects to be understood. Because of this, an epistemological twist is in the making where enunciation as enactment takes precedence over enactment as representation. However, the location of postcolonial theorizing requires a temporal articulation. Time lag is Bhabha's relevant concept to explore the decentered epistemology of postcolonial reason. The concept emerges from the intersection of two nonexplicit and disparate theoretical frameworks. One comes from the aftermath of the formal apparatus of enunciation (theorized by Benveniste in the early 1960s) and, independently, by Bakhtin's concept of hybridization and dialogisme, and—directly—from the colonial bent introduced by Gayatri-Spivak, who

asked the influential question, "Can the subaltern speak?" The other resonates in Fabian's (1983) analysis of the denial of coevalness in colonial discourse. When the denial of coevalness is cast not in terms of comparing
cultures or civilization stages based on a presupposed idea of progress, but
is applied to the locus of enunciation, time lag allows for a denial of enunciative coevalness and, therefore, to a violent denial of freedom, reason, and
qualification for political and cultural intervention. It is through concepts
such as "the denial of the denial of coevalness" (Mignolo 1995, 249–58,
329–30) and enunciative time lag that the restitution of the intellectual force
emanating from colonial legacies could be enacted and the distribution of
intellectual labor relocated.

The discussion of Foucault's colonial forgetting, at the end of Bhabha's
chapter on the postmodern and the postcolonial, highlights a complex argument he develops throughout the book: "There is a certain position in the
Western ratio that was constituted in its history and provides a foundation
for the relation it can have with all other societies, *even with the society
in which it historically appeared*" (quoted by Bhabha, 1994, 195). Bhabha's
interpretation of Foucault's statement points toward the fact that by "dis-
avowing the colonial moment as enunciative present in the historical and
epistemological condition of Western modernity," Foucault closes the possibility of interpreting Western ratio in the conflictive dialogue between the
West and the colonies. Even more, according to Bhabha, Foucault "disavows
precisely the colonial text as the foundation for the relation the Western
ratio can have, 'even with the society in which it historically appeared' "
(Bhabha 1994, 196). The enunciative present, in other words, is the present
of Western time and its locus of enunciation. Colonial loci of enunciation
have been dissolved or absorbed by colonial discourse, including the production and distribution of knowledge for their lack of contemporaneity:
colonies like the Third World produced culture while metropolitan centers
produced intellectual discourses interpreting colonial cultural production
and reinscribing themselves as the *only* locus of enunciation. Bhabha contributes to relocate—finally—the dialogue between modernity and postmodernity, on the one hand, and of colonialism and postcolonial critical discourse
and theorizing, on the other:

> Reading from the transferential perspective, where the Western ratio returns to
> itself from the time lag of the colonial relation, we see how modernity and
> postmodernity are themselves constituted from the marginal perspective of cul-
> tural difference. They encounter themselves contingently at the point at which
> the internal difference of their own society is reiterated in terms of the difference
> of the other, the alterity of the postcolonial site. (Bhabha 1994, 196)

By extending the concept of time lag from the subject in psychoanalysis
and its fracture between the sign and the symbol (Bhabha 1994, 191–98) to

cultural differences under colonialism, Bhabha is clearly underscoring Fanon's locus of enunciation: "He [Fanon] too speaks from the signifying time lag of cultural difference that I have been attempting to develop as a structure for the representation of subaltern and postcolonial agency" (Bhabha 1994, 236). This is not the occasion to comment on time lag and its relation to "the representation of the subaltern." I am more comfortable with time lag and postcolonial agency. In other words, the denial of coevalness that Fabian (1983) identified as a strategy of colonial discourse to undermine other cultures by locating them in a lower scale in the ascending march of (European) civilization and progress is being contested (i.e., by denying the denial of coevalness), precisely by postcolonial agencies and postcolonial theorizing.

The aftermath of the Enlightenment project that Bhabha critiques in Foucault is also underlined by Paul Gilroy (1993) in his critique of Jürgen Habermas and Marshall Berman. Gilroy claims, in opposition to the belief in the unfulfilled promises of modernity, that the history of African diaspora and, consequently, a reassessment of the role of slavery in the construction of modernity, "require a more complete revision of the terms in which the modernity debates have been constructed than any of its academic participants may be willing to concede" (Gilroy 1993, 46). The decentered and plural configuration of modern subjectivities and identities embraced by Gilroy runs against Berman's belief in the "intimate unity of the modern self and the modern environment" (Gilroy 1993, 46). Bhabha and Gilroy join Dussel in their critique of the construction of modernity in postmodern thinking. What differentiates their postcolonial theorizing are their colonial legacies: Spanish and Latin American for Dussel; African diaspora, French, German, and British empires for Gilroy; British Empire and the colonization of India for Bhabha.

Santiago Castro-Gómez (1996) expressed serious reservations about my comparison of Dussel and Bhabha as critics of the coloniality of power from different local histories. In my view, Castro-Gómez's reservations are based on a misunderstanding of what I take as "postcoloniality," in part due to the manner I built the argument in articles published in Spanish (Mignolo 1996a; 1996b; 1997a; 1997c), and in part to his own "progressive" conception of postcolonial theorizing. For Castro-Gómez the names of Edward Said, Gayatri Spivak, and Homi Bhabha are the paradigmatic stages of postcolonial theories and all theorizing under that heading has to be measured from the perspective of its "last stage." That is, Castro-Gómez maintains a linear, progressive, and modernist conception of knowledge production. My comparison between Bhabha and Dussel was done precisely to counter such a perspective and to accentuate the ratio between geohistorical locations and knowledge production. I am not blind to the fact that Bhabha and Spivak are "better known" and "more popular." But it is precisely that difference which should be interrogated in relation to the coloniality of power and knowledge. It is not my intention to take anything away from the contributions made by Spivak and Bhabha. It is my intention to get away from the modern/colonial world system imaginary regarding the production and conceptualization of knowledge, which in the case of Castro-Gómez undermines its own solidarity with postcoloniality.

There is, however, one point in Castro-Gómez's argument that deserves careful attention. For him, Said, Spivak, and Bhabha advance a postcolonial argument whereas Dussel should be understood as a countermodern one. Castro-Gómez starts from Michel Foucault's critique of the order of knowledge and underlines the fact that the modern *épistéme* starts from the assumption that knowledge cannot be conceived as representation of the properties imbedded in the object. Knowledge also depends on the formal conditions located in the cognitive structure of a transcendental subject, the knowing subject. Castro-Gómez takes advantage of Foucault's uncovering the paradox of modern epistemology according to which the knowing subject is part of the knowledge production but, as transcendental subject, cannot be represented in the same way that the object of knowledge is. As it is known, Foucault explains the emergence of the human sciences upon this paradox. Castro-Gómez concludes by stressing that knowledge, in the conceptualization of modern epistemology (and I mean by "modern" interiority the exercise of the coloniality of power in drawing the colonial difference), was founded on the projection of an empirical western European subject, white, male, heterosexual, and from the middle class, to a transcendental knowing subject (1996, 154–55). He further stresses that the illusion of observing and capturing a totality is only possible under the condition of the blindness regarding the observation of one locus of observation. Thus, modern epistemology, which was able to subalternize other forms of knowledge, built itself assuming a universal perspective of observation and a privileged locus of enunciation (155).

As the reader who has followed my argument to this point can imagine, I cannot but endorse Castro-Gómez's rendering of a crucial aspect of modern epistemology, through Foucault's analysis. As far as he links Foucault with Umberto Maturana and Francisco Varela visibly in the last sentence of the previous paragraph, I agree with Castro-Gómez since Maturana and Varela have been a guide for my theoretical reflection since the 1970s (Mignolo 1978; 1991, 1995a). Castro-Gómez's critique of Latin American philosophy is anchored in the paradox of modern epistemology. He observes that one limitation of the human sciences and of modern philosophy was their incapacity to disclose that the universality of their discourse was, indeed, deeply anchored in the sociocultural particularity of the observers as knowing subject (1996, 155). I have the impression, once again, that something of the sort is the point I am stressing in this book, and that I have stressed in previous publications, some of them commented on by Castro-Gómez in his article. So, what is the point and where is the difference? Let's follow Castro-Gómez's argument a little bit further since he introduces the case of postindependence intellectuals, in Latin America, which will constitute a leading thread of the argument in chapter 3.

If modern epistemology narcotized its own locus of enunciation and projected an idea of knowledge as universal designs from particular and hidden local histories, what happens when global epistemological designs enter in other, colonial, local histories? Castro-Gómez takes the example of Domingo F. Sarmiento and Juan B. Alberdi—thinkers, essayists, and politicians of great influence in nineteenth-century Argentina and in Spanish America as well. Castro-Gómez correctly points out that Sarmiento and Alberdi established a differential locus of enunciation (Mignolo 1995a, 316–37) from the periphery but *within* the epistemology of modernity. I said "correctly" because it is precisely the reason why independence in Latin America went together with internal colonialism. Castro-Gómez proposes to describe positions such as those established by Sarmiento and Alberdi as "second degree observations" in the sense that they open up the possibility of several loci of observation and enunciation, even though they remain faithful to the philosophy of the Enlightenment they try to emulate. However, the limitations of Sarmiento and Alberdi are the same limitations of modern epistemology: the blindness or the incapacity to observe themselves observing themselves (Castro-Gómez 1996, 156; Mignolo 1991, 357–95; 1995a, 1–28). To make this possible, Castro-Gómez posits, we need a "third degree of observation," that is, "an observation of the order of knowledge from which European observations observe themselves—a possibility that will require an *epistemological break* with that very order" (1997, 156), that is, with the order of modern epistemology. This, indeed, is Castro-Gómez's crucial point. Here is where he locates postcolonial reason and postcolonial thinking. The difference rests in the fact that I attribute a postcolonial position to Argentinian philosophers Kusch and Dussel and to a Mexican philosopher of history, Zea, a position that Castro-Gómez sees as countercolonial, second-degree observations rather than postcolonial, third-degree observations.

This point remains valid for some of the discussion in this chapter and in the following one. There is a difference, however, between Sarmiento and Alberdi, on the one hand, and Kusch, Dussel, and Zea on the other. Whereas the former took Europe as a model for the future of Latin American, the latter took it as a hindrance. If both are different loci of enunciation, Sarmiento and Alberdi proposed it as a local continuation of a universal design. Kusch, Dussel, and Zea, instead, proposed a differential locus of enunciation as an affirmation of the difference, even if they remained within the epistemological foundation to whose content they objected. Thus, postcoloniality as a critical discourse on the imaginary of the modern/colonial world system could be understood at two levels, as I specified at the beginning of the chapter: a critique of subaltern knowledges (second-order observation); and postcolonial reason as border thinking (third-order observation). Clearly, Kusch, Dussel, and Zea contributed to the first but not Sarmiento and Alberdi.

One question remains, however: although one can find epistemological articulation in Latin America closer to what Castro-Gómez labels third-degree observation (like in Fanon or Glissant), in Spanish America that step has not been clearly devised from the 1960s to the 1990s. Why is this so? Why is it that Castro-Gómez's suggestion to identify postcolonial thinking and postcolonial reason as a third-degree observation can be found in English and French but not in Latin American philosophy? Is it that Latin American philosophy, which is written in Spanish and within Spanish intellectual legacies, keeps sliding to the margin of modernity since the second half of the nineteenth century? Is Castro-Gómez's correct theoretical observation not to overlook one aspect of the history of the modern/colonial world system in which language and knowledge maintain, until today, an articulation of the coloniality of power and knowledge that is still entrenched in the epistemology of modernity? I return to these questions in chapters 5, 6, and 7.

Up to this point, my observations have focused mainly on language, ethnicity, and the geopolitics of knowledge. I have not addressed the question of gender in the coloniality of power and knowledge. I close this chapter by bringing gender to the foreground, and return to it in chapters 5 and 6.

GENDER AND THE COLONIALITY OF POWER

I conclude by opening up the discussion to emerging domains of subaltern metatheoretical inquiry and the critique of the patriarchal dimension of the coloniality of power. I have been limiting the discussion to loci of enunciation and geohistorical categories. This is the terrain in which colonial legacies and postcolonial theories have been mainly discussed in the recent past. Concepts such as First and Third Worlds, West and East, margin and periphery, and Spanish or British colonialism, are all geohistorical categories. When I elaborated on what I think is an epistemological breakthrough, I did so assuming that one of the motivations of postcolonial theorizing is the geohistorical location of the production and distribution of knowledge. The politics and sensibilities thus formed are comparable, in my argument, with the politics and sensibilities of gender, race, or class configuration. In all these cases, the production of knowledge and the need for theories are no longer driven by an abstract and rational will to tell the truth, but also (perhaps mainly) by ethical and political concerns with structure of domination and of human emancipation. It should be added that if production of knowledge was always driven toward human emancipation (as the Renaissance and Enlightenment projects claimed), one should make the qualification that postcolonial theories promote "liberation" both social and epistemic. And, we should add, knowledge production is not only for the liberation of subjugated people, but also for the self-liberation of those who live and act within the structure of belief of modernity and colonialism, two sides of the same coin. Emancipation *as* liberation means not only the recognition of the subalterns but the erasure of the power structure that maintains hegemony and subalternity.

Thus, we have the important chronological distinction introduced by Sara Suleri that cuts across geocultural categories. By highlighting "English India," she is able to bring the colonial and the postcolonial (situations, discourses) under a new light:

> If English India represents a discursive field that includes both colonial and postcolonial narratives, it further represents an alternative to the troubled chronology of nationalism in the Indian subcontinent. As long as the concept of nation is interpreted as the colonizer's gift to its erstwhile colony, the unimaginable community produced by colonial encounter can never be sufficiently read. (Suleri 1992a, 3)

What should retain our attention in this quotation is the fact that the chronological rearticulation of colonial/postcolonial is anchored in the connivance between language and empire. To say "English India" is similar to saying "Hispanic America" or "Anglo-America," and the conceptualization of geocultural categories is very much connected to imperial languages.

Furthermore, Suleri brings to the foreground the connections between geocultural categories and gender, sexuality, and the politics and sensibilities of geocultural locations (Suleri 1992a; 1992b). Suleri's arguments join those of other critics of gender and colonialism such as Trinh Minh-ha (1989) and Chandra Mohanty (1988). Their writings contribute very much to redirecting postcolonial theoretical practices toward the encounter with issues raised by women of color as well as with those theorizing borders (e.g., Anzaldúa [1987]; Saldívar [1992]; and African diaspora [e.g., Gilroy 1993]). From this perspective, Suleri sees two major issues haunting the future of cultural criticism and postcolonial theorizing: one is the realignment of the polarities ("East-West," "colonizer-colonized," "us-them," etc.) in which early postcolonial theorizing was founded; the other is the question of the articulation of gender and the postcolonial condition:

> If the materiality of cultural criticism must now locate its idiom in the productive absence of alterity, it must realign its relation to the figure of gender. The

figurative status of gender poses a somewhat uncritical discourse reliant on metaphors of sexuality, or does it merely reify the sorry biologism that dictates
traditional decodings of the colonial encounter? Since the "feminity" of the
colonized subcontinent has provided Orientalist narratives with their most pre-
vailing trope for the exoticism of the East, contemporary reading of such texts
is obliged to exercise considerable cultural tact in the feminization of its own
discourse. In other words, a simple correlation of gender with colonizer and
colonized can lead only to interpretive intransigence of a different order,
through which an attempt to recognize marginality leads to an opposite replica-
tion of the uncrossable distance between margin and center. The taut ambiva-
lence of colonial complicity, however, demands a more nuanced reading of how
equally ambivalently gender functions in the tropologies of both colonial and
postcolonial narratives. (Suleri 1992a, 15)

Introducing gender and feminism into colonial cultural studies confirms the
epistemological breakthrough being enacted by postcolonial theorizing in
at least two different and complementary directions: one, by discovering the
complicities between modernity and the violence of reason and by recov-
ering the suppressed secondary qualities from the domain of knowledge; the
other, by opening up scholarly work and academic pursuit to the public
sphere (Moya 1997; Mohanty, Russo, and Torres 1991). The strength of postcolonial theorizing (as well as other theoretical practices transforming
knowledge-as-representation into knowledge-as-enactment, and of erasing
the subject/object destruction) resides in its capacity for epistemological as
well as for social and cultural transformation. It is helping, furthermore, to
redefine and relocate the task of the humanities and the cultures of scholarship in a transnational world—that is, to take the humanities and cultures
of scholarship beyond the realm of modernity and their complicity with
national and imperial states (see chapter 6).

CHAPTER 3

Human Understanding and Local Interests:
Occidentalism and the (Latin) American Argument

IN THE FALL OF 1997 Irene Silverblatt and I cotaught an undergraduate seminar on "Modernity and Coloniality in Latin America." In the spring of 1998
we repeated the seminar at the graduate level, as one of the core courses for
the Latin American Cultural Studies certificate. Between the two seminars
we changed the title slightly. In the spring of 1998 the title was "Modernity,
Coloniality and Latin America." We realized that the first title presupposed
a fixed and existing entity where "things" like modernity and coloniality
happened "inside" it or "to it," while our argument was oriented toward
showing that "Latin America" is indeed part of the geopolitical process today
described as modernity/coloniality. "Indias Occidentales," later on America
and then Latin America, was twice constitutive of modernity from its particular colonial difference. First, in the sixteenth century, the "discovery" of
America was constitutive of the formation of the modern/colonial world.
Second, during the early nineteenth century, the Americas were constitutive
of the second stage of modernity/coloniality. Although "history" emphasized
the French Revolution, the Enlightenment, and the formation of the modern
nation-states, decolonization in the Americas goes hand in hand with the
shorter history of modernity (from the eighteenth century to today). That
is, during the period that India began to be colonized by England and North
Africa was falling under French colonialism, the Americas witnessed a long
period of decolonization from England (the United States), France (Haiti),
and Spain (Argentina, Mexico, Colombia, Chile, Peru, Ecuador). Here you
have, in a nutshell, a variegated spectrum of the variances of the colonial
difference in the modern/colonial world.

The chapter's goal is to map this process—not to describe it in detail, but
to identify moments, historical events, social movements, and ideas that
shaped the image of the Americas, of the two Americas, of the Americas and
the Caribbean, in the colonial horizon of modernity. This process, of making
and unmaking the Americas, is part of the larger one, the formation and
transformation of the modern/colonial world system, of imperial allocation
of cultures (e.g., territorializing people in relation to their language and their
location in the planet) and subaltern relentless relocation. The most telling
case—in the geopolitical arena—is that of the United States moving from a
subaltern position in the world order, at the beginning of the nineteenth

century, to an imperial force during the twentieth century. In this regard, the argument develops keeping in mind the density of geohistorical locations in the making of the modern/colonial world. For instance, decolonization in India took place in 1947 and in North Africa between the end of the 1950s and the beginning of the 1960s. In Latin America decolonization at the beginning of the nineteenth century occurred in a different world order, with the ascending imperial power of England and France after the Napoleonic defeat. Therefore, theories of decolonizaton by Indian or North African intellectuals who were born shortly before or shortly after decolonization were prompted by a historical and emotional experience significantly different from Latin American intellectuals who theorize decolonization between a century and a century and a half after decolonization. Furthermore, it should be remembered, the Americans were considered, from the colonial European perspective, as its extension rather than as its difference (as was the case with Africa and Asia). The Haitian Revolution in the early nineteenth century and the significant reconfiguration of the modern/colonial world system in 1898 set the state for both the location of Hispanic/Latinos today in the United States and for the rethinking of people of African descent, in the Americas, beyond the United States. Last but not least, the Zapatistas uprising in 1994 in a long chain of Amerindian protests since the sixteenth century added to the complexity of the map of coloniality of power, decolonization, and struggle with the colonial difference in the Americas, which I try to remap in this chapter.

Consequently I navigate through dates, events, and thinkers in the nineteenth and twentieth centuries, assuming that their conflicting and diverse local histories are all entrenched in colonial legacies, in building the imaginary of the modern world system, and dealing with the colonial difference. In the first part of the chapter, I explore the imaginary that made of the Americas the "Western Hemisphere" and divided it into two languages and two "races." Bolivar, Jefferson, and Chilean intellectual Francisco Bilbao are the main protagonists of this first part. I move then to Marxist Peruvian intellectual José Carlos Mariátegui, who rearticulated, in the early twentieth century, the previous debate from a Marxist perspective and brought Amerindian cultures, which had been absent in the nineteenth-century debates, into the picture. Focusing on the Argentinean polemical thinker Rudolfo Kusch, I discuss his contribution of a particular kind of border thinking in the 1970s, articulating Amerindian with western European categories of thought (including Heidegger, Nietzsche, and Hegel). I do not pursue, but I would like to state, that the reflections initiated by Kusch could now be followed by an emerging Amerindian intellectuality, which was absent until the 1970s. Finally, I pause on Cuban anthropologist Fernando Ortiz and his concept of transculturation for several reasons: first, because he began to think "about" the border of the nation in terms of "mestizaje" and the border of cultures in terms of the transculturation of objects and commodities in the modern/colonial world system; second, because he introduced into the homogenous Creole imaginary of Latin America the contribution of Afro-Americans in Cuba and the Caribbean; and, third, because his notion of transculturation of the social (and more particularly of the national) did not challenge—indeed, maintained the purity of—disciplinary discourse. This tension in Ortiz allows me to introduce Afro-Caribbean thinkers, like Edouard Glissant and Frantz Fanon, both of them reflecting from the experience of slavery rather than from a particular discipline, and joining Du Bois, who introduced the concept of "double consciousness" in the early twentieth century. "Double consciousness," taken to the level of disciplinary foundation, introduces an epistemological fissure that I am attempting to describe as border thinking.

RETELLING A STORY ALREADY WELL KNOWN

I am telling this story with Aymara intellectual and political activist Fausto Reinaga's observation in mind: "The Andean Republics, Ecuador, Peru, Bolivia, Chile and Argentina were born as a consequence of 500 years of kheswaymara [Quechua and Aymara] war against the Spanish invaders. The so-called 'independence war' was an episode sixteen years long" (Reinaga 1969, 159). This silenced story has continued from independence until today. The Zapatistas, as I have already mentioned, began the first declaration from the Lacandon Forest by referring to five hundred years of oppression. This silenced but present background, which includes the Haitian Revolution, should be kept in mind as the hidden side of the Creole intellectual's nineteenth-century aspirations of modernizing Latin America. I return to this background in chapter 7 in order to analyze indigenous movements in the context of current globalization.

This chapter expands on chapter 2, using as its starting point Quijano's and Wallerstein's thesis on the Americas in the imaginary of the modern colonial world system. "Americanity" is a concept that developed at least two centuries after the "discovery" and was consolidated after the independence of the state of New England, New Spain, the Viceroyalty of Peru, and New Granada from England and Spain respectively. At that point, the places known by their inhabitants as Tawantinsuyu in the south, Anahuac in the north, and Abya-Yala in the center, were rebaptized "Indias Occidentales." One of the reasons for this name was Columbus's belief that he reached the Indies and the later Vespucci's hypothesis that the lands reached by Columbus were a New World. As it is well known, it was a German man of letters and cosmographer, Martin Waldseemuller, who belonged to the Gimnasio Vosgense (the name assigned to a humanist circle in the city of Saint Die, Lorene), who suggested the name "America" in honor of Amerigo Vespucci. However, what is of interest is the gender transformation suggested by Waldseemüller in order to fit a "fourth" continent in the world picture of the time, which was, basically, a Christian world picture. In the fifteenth century, among all known cosmologies (Islamic, Chinese, Aztec, Inca), the Christian cosmology was the only one to conceive the world divided in three continents (Asia, Africa, and Europe) and to assign to each continent one of Noah's sons (Japhet, Shem, Ham) (Hay 1957). The Spanish crown could not call Indias Occidentales "America" because it was not interested in continental identity but in the administration of the colonial possessions, and the colonial possessions were both Indias Occidentales (today the Americas and the Caribbean) and Indias Orientales (the Pacific islands with the Philippines as its center).

"America," interestingly enough, is a name that became the territorial identification not for the Spanish crown, or for the Spanish in the Indias Occidentales, but for the Creole population and intellectuals, born in "America" from Spanish descent and leaders of the independence during the nineteenth century. It was also the Creole population and its intellectuals who initiated a process of self-definition as "Americans" with all its possible variations ("Spanish," "Indo," "Latin"), as we will see. The importance of the discourse of geocultural identity lies in the fact that it filled a space that was broken in the process of conquest and colonization. As I have argued elsewhere (Mignolo 1996d), the conquest and colonization generated forms of "saying out of place": the relation the indigenous population felt with the place from which their saying had been articulated through the centuries (cosmology, memories, social relations, labor, etc.) was broken. Their saying became a "saying out of place" in their relationship with the colonizers; and it became also "out of place" in their own communities because of their knowing that foreign elements had been introduced in their space. For the Spanish, their saying was equally "out of place" in the sense that they were alien and foreign to the knowledge, cosmology, people, and memories they were describing when they described the Amerindian populations. On the other hand, their own memories in the new land were also "new," and quite different from the memories Castile and Castilian historians were invoking to build their territoriality (i.e., the process of constructing a place formed by geographical boundaries and common memories). The emergence of the "Creole" population and its intellectuals filled that empty space, building on a new territoriality that became, through the years, named "Latin America": a territoriality whose geographical contours are, more or less, continental South America, and the common memories based on Spanish colonization of Indias Occidentales, which lead to the inclusion of Puerto

Rico, Santo Domingo, and Cuba, with the same language as continental Spanish America. On the other hand, and in an inverted relation, Brazil is included in Latin America not because of the language (as in the case of the islands), but because it is continental!

The end result is that the current image of (Latin) America has been mapped on the colonial legacies of the first modernity (e.g., the early modern period of the "Annales" historians), mainly the sixteenth century when the Atlantic commercial circuit was established—the economical foundation of the modern world system, but a forgotten and silenced component, once the history of the second modernity (mid-seventeenth to World War I approximately) became entrenched with national historiography and dominated by England, France, and Germany. Thus, for instance, while any single history of "Latin America" will begin with 1492, the "Indian Question," and the beginning of African slavery (which forced an important reconversion of the very concept of slavery, since prior to this it was not common to identify slavery with Africa), "Anglo-American" history will begin in 1600 (Slotkin 1973; 1985; Stephanson 1995). This date (1600) is not, however, the "starting" date for Native American intellectuals for whom 1492 is still relevant (e.g, the "Five Hundred Year Map" of Marmon Silko, *Almanac of the Dead*, 1991; see my introduction). The reason is simple: Native Americans are not bound to the Anglo (British America) national history for which the "beginning" is the time of the Pilgrims' arrival. In any event, what is crucial to keep in mind for the geopolitical formation and transformation of the "Americas" are the differences between 1600 and 1776 in the colonial history of Anglo-America, on the one hand, and the British colonization of the Caribbean islands on the other. The year 1655 is a significant date in the history of the Caribbean, when England conquered Jamaica and broke up the Spanish design to control the entire Caribbean. From then on, until the Utrecht Treaty in 1713, when a Spanish colonialism in decline was able to retain Puerto Rico, Cuba, and Santo Domingo (the eastern part of Hispaniola—the western part, Saint Domingue, was under French control), the colonial history of the Caribbean is the history of new emerging powers (Holland, England, and France) taking over and establishing themselves in the plantation economy. But also the year 1655 marks an important difference with north, continental "America": England never took possession of the continent in the same way that it took possession of Jamaica or the Spaniards took possessions of the Caribbean, Mesoamerica, and the Andes. This difference would establish a closer parallel between England and France, in the Caribbean, from the point of view of colonization. And this difference would also be at the heart of situating Afro-Americans in the Caribbean and their relation to London, and to Afro-Americans in the continental United States.

You may wonder why I have insisted so much on dates. I have already mentioned, in the introduction, that the model or metaphor "modern world system" is a great deal based on dates. Wallerstein, for example, states:

> The imbrication of the three concepts (three realities?) [the West, capitalism, and the modern world system] reached its apogee in the nineteenth century. But how even do we delimit this nineteenth century? 1815–1914?; or 1789–1917?; or 1763–1945? Or even 1648–1698? Within any of these time-frames, but particularly as we narrow them, there seemed little doubt for most people in most parts of the globe that the "West" (or "Europe") had "risen," and that it was exercising, particularly after 1815, effective political and economic domain over the rest of the world, at least until this dominance began to recede in the twentieth century. (Wallerstein 1992, 561–62)

These are indeed dates that mark the contours of the "modern" but not the "modern/colonial" world system. None of those dates implies the Americas, not to mention China, Japan, or any country of the Islamic world or of North and sub-Saharan Africa. I have provided some of the significant dates at the intersection of modernity/coloniality for the local histories of the Americas. I could have provided other dates as well: 1804 and the Haitian Revolution; 1868 and the Meiji Restoration, for Japan, which dismantled an old political order and prepared Japan for its request to be accepted into the family of nations ruled by the standard of civilization, at the end of the nineteenth century (Gong 1984; Najita 1974); or 1930, when in China the debate on modernization and Occidentalism rearticulated the relation between China and the West (Howlland 1996; Kang and Xiaobing 1997). Although neither China nor Japan was properly "colonized" in the sense that the Americas or India or Africa was, the coloniality of power was at work. The modern world system was constituted as such in its articulation of its exteriority and its different form of hegemonic leadership or direct and open domination. The articulation of the modern/colonial world system, in its diverse local histories, is not only a question of economic transactions and networks, but also of its imaginary. Discussion around "modernization as Westernization" in China in 1930 (Yu Keping 1994) or the debate around "civilization and barbarism" in nineteenth- and early twentieth-century Latin America (mainly in Argentina, Brazil, and Venezuela) are examples of the successful imaginary of the modern world system in its colonial horizons (its exteriority).

MODERNITY, COLONIALITY, AND (LATIN) AMERICA

The idea that there is such a thing as "Latin America" came about as a complex process in the nineteenth century. This process was not "original" to the Creole population but a necessity at the crossroads of imperial conflicts. There are several studies about who first came up with the idea and the name of Latin America (Ardao 1980; 1993; Rojas Mix 1992). Although these studies mainly focus on intellectual discourses of the time (and I follow the same pattern in this chapter), it is also clear in their analyses (and I hope to maintain it in my own), and as it is also historically known, that the geopolitical configurations of the subcontinent imaginary and the name were not the inventions of enlightened Latin American intellectuals in search of their identity, but also of a new configuration of an imperial field of forces: Spain and Portugal in decay; France and England in their hegemonic imperial stage; and the United States, with a clear perspective of their "manifest destiny" and project of their future imperial power. "Latin American" identity, as any other geopolitical and ethnic identity, was the result of a double discourse: the discourse of imperial state allocation of identity filtering down to civil society, and the discourse of relocation produced from the sectors of the civil society (e.g., intellectuals, social movements) dissenting with the former. "Latin America" was a postcolonial identity, within the liberal dominant forces in the modern world system during the nineteenth century. In the historical context I described in the preceding section, the United States was also within a "postindependence" mentality. Postcolonial nations after 1950, contrary to postindependence nations in the early nineteenth century, defined themselves on the conflicting horizons of decolonization and Marxism (Béji 1982; Chatterjee 1986; 1993), while postindependence nations articulated themselves within the liberal ideology of the modern world system. "Decolonization" as final horizon was still not available in the nineteenth century.

If the differences between U.S. independence from England and that of Latin American countries from Spain and Portugal are clear in several respects, it should also be emphasized that the United States constituted itself as an independent nation from a rising empire (Britain), whereas Latin American countries obtained their independence from two empires in decay (Spain and Portugal). Between 1820 and 1830, two symptomatic events took place north and south of the American continent. While several Spanish American countries obtained independence between 1810 and 1821, the United States negotiated the possession of Louisiana with the French government, and between 1812 and 1819 Florida was annexed to the states of the union. All this took place while Bolivar in South (and later on Latin) America was planning a congress in Panama (in 1826) to work on the legal unity of the American Confederation (and Bolivar was indeed thinking America from the extreme south to the extreme north). And, no doubt, Bolivar had the right vision of the new world order when he decided to hold the Congress in Panama. He foresaw the opening of a canal, or a series of canals, that would connect the Atlantic with the Pacific and become, with

time, the center of the planet. He went on to imagine that if the world needed
a capital city, Panama should be it because of its strategic position connecting Europe with America and Asia and bringing to "such a happy region the
tributes from the four parts of the globe" (Blanco y Azpurúa, *Documentos
para la historia del Libertador*, vol. 6). The Panama Congress was, indeed, a
new idea: a congress of new nations was something without precedent since
the rise of nation-states, as Benedict Anderson ([1983], 1990) has shown
us. Postindependence should be understood then as (economic, political,
epistemological) rearrangements of the coloniality of power, and the emergence of new projects in conflictive tension with global design.

In fact, if Bolivar was original in imagining an American confederation
and in having an American congress in Panama, he was not so original in
seeing the Panama canal as a strategic point in the future of the global world
order. The year of 1823 has a particular significance from the perspective of
the United States, when the convergence of the Monroe Doctrine with the
ideology of the Manifest Destiny brought about the idea of a Pan-Americanism (see my subsequent comments on Du Bois and Pan-Africanism). A
united America was also envisioned, but under the hegemony of the United
States. The difference between Bolivar's idea in the south and the proclamation of the Monroe Doctrine in the north was that while the latter was the
proclamation of a number of states that had recently gained independence
from a leading empire (Britain), Bolivar's vision relied on an idea of
"America" based on a set (and not just one) of Spanish American independent republics that had recently gained independence from an empire in
decay. From Bolivar's perspective, given his admiration for the United Kingdom, an imperial project was not in his horizon. There was no design equivalent to the Monroe Doctrine or the Pan-American idea linked to it. Why the
United States emerged with the idea of a "manifest destiny" and the Spanish
American republics with an idea of unity that is more "defensive" than "of-
fensive" could be explained in relation to the imperial powers from which
independence was obtained. From the historical standpoint of today, it is
clear that between 1820 and 1830 the future historical paths of the two
Americas, Anglo and Latin, were being decided. Before then, roughly from
1500 to 1800, the differences between the two Americas were the differences
dictated between the Spanish and British empires in the modern/colonial
world system. Language and race, as we will see, were two crucial components in the articulation of the modern/colonial world system imaginary.

The commonality of the difference, however, lies in the way that, at the
beginning of the nineteenth century, "America" was appropriated by intellectuals of the emerging states as different from Europe but still within the
West. As Quijano and Wallerstein (1992) have pointed out, the "Americas,"
contrary to Asia and Africa, were constituted as part of the modern/colonial
world system. The old Spanish colonial territories conceptualized as Indias

Occidentales, and the fourth continent imagined as "America" within the Christian division of the planet in three continents before 1500, which dominated the geopolitical imaginary of the modern/colonial world until the end of the eighteenth century, began to change due to the emergence of a new community of intellectuals (the New World intellectuals) for whom "America" and its future should become autonomous from Europe. That is to say, political independence was accompanied by a symbolic independence in the geopolitical imagination. President Thomas Jefferson wrote in 1808 that the common interests between the independent United States and the emerging social movements in the Spanish colonies were the goals of excluding European influence from "this hemisphere" (Whitaker 1954, 28). "This Hemisphere" will soon become the "Western Hemisphere." That is, "Western" but at the same time independent from "Europe." Local histories (in this case, the rise of national histories) came together with the projective articulation of global designs. Jefferson was extremely clear in 1811 about the need for a double articulation of local histories, with global designs replacing an outdated world order:

> What, in short, is the whole system of Europe towards America but an atrocious and insulting tyranny? One hemisphere of the earth, separated from the other by wide seas on both sides, having a different system of interests flowing from different climates, different soils, different productions, different modes of existence. . . .
>
> History . . . furnishes no example of a priest-ridden people maintaining a free civil government. . . . But in whatever governments they end, they will be *American* governments, no longer to be involved in the never-ceasing broils of Europe. *The European nations constitute a separate division of the globe; their localities make them part of a distinct system; they have a set of interests of their own in which it is our business never to engage ourselves. America has a hemisphere to itself. It must have a separate system of interest which must not be subordinated to those of Europe.* (Whitaker 1954, 28–29; emphasis added)

However, Jefferson was reacting to a degraded concept of America by European intellectuals and scientists from Buffon to De Paw (Gerbi [1955] 1982, 315–37). One can recognize here a general principle that will be incorporated, a decade later, into the Monroe Doctrine in the problematic sense of "America for the Americans" as the spirit of Pan-Americanism. Within Pan-Americanism the Isthmus of Panama acquired, toward 1850–60, a meaning that could not have been dreamed by Bolivar. By then the United States had not only annexed Louisiana and Florida, but also Texas in 1845, and with the Guadalupe-Hidalgo Treaty of 1848, moved the frontier to the south. What is today New Mexico, Arizona, California, Nevada, Utah, and a part of Colorado became part of the United States. This last annexation had a particular relevance in relation to previous ones: the Guadelupe-Hidalgo Treaty was a conflict between new emerging nations and not between a new emerging empire the (United States) and a decaying one (Spain), as it was, for instance, in the case of Puerto Rico and Cuba in 1898. From today's standpoint, 1848 was decisive for the imaginary configurations of the two Americas and of "Latinidad" in the United States (the emergence of a Chicano/a consciousness within the larger context of Latino/as in the United States) and, therefore, the reconfiguration of the Anglo and Latin Americas (Oboler 1997, 31–54). In 1857, Senator Buchanan restated the Monroe Doctrine in the new spirit of the Manifest Destiny nourished by all the previous annexations. Regarding the Isthmus of Panama as a subcontinental divide, an idea perceived already by López de Velasco (cosmographer of Philip the Second) toward 1570, Buchanan stated that it was the destiny of the Saxon race to extend itself through all the North American continent, as the Isthmus marked the southern frontier. He was projecting a massive migration toward the south and therefore projecting that Central America would have in a short period of time a significant Anglo-American population and that such a population will carve the future of the indigenous people, by which term he was not referring to Amerindians but rather to the Creole population (e.g., Spanish descendants) in Nicaragua (Torres Caicedo 1869, in Ardao 1980, 197).

In 1898 the apparently good intentions of the Monroe Doctrine toward Latin America vanished when the United States went beyond continental expansion, and began to conceive of itself as a future imperial power. The Isthmus of Panama, seen by Bolivar as a crucial geopolitical location, became also crucial for the United States in a new world order in which European imperial powers were expanding all over the globe. Cuba and Puerto Rico were strategic islands, from the military point of view, to control the Caribbean, and the United States took advantage of the belated independence movements from Spain in both islands (Rodriguez-Beruff 1988; Herwig 1976). From the point of view of my argument, 1898 and 1848 redraw the early division between Anglo and Latin America. Although the part of the population labeled "Hispanics" or "Latino/as" today in the United States could originate from any place in Latin America or Spain, the fact of the matter is that basically the imperial relations between the United States, Mexico, Puerto Rico, and Cuba are at the historical core of an ethnic conflict, regardless of the place of origin of those called "Hispanics" or "Latino/as." In other words, 1848 and 1898 are turning points in the colonial horizon of modernity, which muddled the clear division between Latin and Anglo America, maintaining people in specific territories and attributing to them a set of fixed cultural properties (Romero, Hondagneu-Sotelo, and Ortiz 1997; Bonilla, Meléndez, Morales, and Angeles Tórres 1998).

COLONIALITY AND THE MODERN WORLD SYSTEM

As we have seen in chapter 2, Jorge Klor de Alva made an interesting point in his efforts to differentiate Latin America from Africa and Asia, in their respective relationships with Spain, France, and England: the independence in Latin America (or the equivalent of what is called decolonization after World War II) was not achieved by "indigenous" Amerindians but by "indigenous" Creoles, the population of Spanish descent born and raised in continental South America. The same argument can indeed be extended to the independence of Anglo-America. Native Americans, in the North, like Amerindians in the South, did not participate in the decision-making process leading to independence from Spain and England. However, Anglo-Americans did not "Creolize" themselves as Latin Americans did. There are, then, several aspects to be considered when comparing decolonization in the first part of the nineteenth century and the second part of the twentieth century as different moments in the articulation and rearticulation of the modern world system. In this context, Klor de Alva's argument is inconsequential since it is not a semantic but a historicostructural problem: both moments of decolonization are part of the colonial horizon of modernity or, if you wish, of the colonial structure and imaginary of the modern world system. Consequently, while nineteenth-century intellectuals, in Latin America, had the U.S. independence and the French Revolution as their horizon, twentieth-century intellectuals in Asia and Africa were in the middle of the cold war (Fanon [1964] 1988, 108–10), which was their general frame of reference. Therefore, what were Latin American intellectuals thinking during the cold war more than a century after early nineteenth-century decolonization and fifty years or so from the end of the Spanish dominion in America, and the transfer of Cuba and Puerto Rico, in 1898, about a new form of colonialism, generally identified as "imperialism"?

To answer this question I'll go back first to the Chilean dissident philosopher and essayist Francisco Bilbao (1823–65), born in the troubled years of the war for independence in Spanish America. Decolonization at the beginning of the nineteenth century could not have been undertaken with a national-state project in mind, since nation-states as known today were not available. When Benedict Anderson (1992, 67) talks about "national liberation movements in the Americas" between 1820 and 1920, we should keep in mind the changes between these two dates: "Before 1884 the word nación simply meant <the aggregate of the inhabitants of a province, a county or kingdom> and also <a foreigner>" (Hobsbawn 1990, 15). Reading Bolivar's "Carta de Jamaica" 1815, (a significant crossing of imperial locations), the "nation" was conceived as the ensemble of "Americanos meridionales" (South American) under the Spanish ruler and not as singular nation-states.

No revolutionary intellectual in the United States at the end of the eighteenth century or in Latin America at the beginning of the nineteenth could have written what Frantz Fanon wrote about the pitfalls of national consciousness or about national culture (Fanon 1961): both were in the future, to be constructed, to be made available. As Hobsbawn has described, it is only at the end of the nineteenth century that a self-conceptualization of the nation-state took place (Hobsbawn 1990). For that reason, Bolivar's idea of an American Union is what takes, until the first half of the nineteenth century, the place of the national consciousness. A "Creole" republic, as opposed to the alternative of a "Creole" monarchy, occupied the discourse of American intellectuals of the time. There is a second reason why independence in the Americas was not like decolonization in Asia and Africa in the geopolitical world order of the cold war pointed out by Klor de Alva: the fact that America, as implied in the previous section, was constructed as the extension of Europe, and of Occidentalism, and not as its opposite. Jefferson did not hesitate in defining the location of the America in the Western Hemisphere.

But let's go back to Bilbao (1823–65). One year before his death he published *Evangelio Americano*, a fascinating essay in which he explored the differences between America and Europe, between the revolution of the states of New England and the Spanish colonies, the rise of the United States, the Spanish colonization, and the difficulties in maintaining the revolutionary spirit of independence in building the new republics. In the language of the time, Bilbao spoke heavily of race to characterize different groups of people. He spoke, chiefly, of the black race, the Indian race, the Creole race (referring to those born in America of Spanish descent). Thus, he talked also about the Franks in Gaul or the Normans in England, the Aztecs in Mexico, and the Incas in Peru. On the basis of these characterizations he observed something peculiar to the Americas:

> Todos los ejemplos que la historia nos presenta de invasiones de razas y conquistas, son, puede decirse, uniformes en cuanto al resultado. La raza invasora que triunfa, se instala, se apodera y divide la tierra, y ella y sus descendientes se constituyen soberanos. . . . En ese fenómeno hay, puede decirse, una identificación entre el conquistador y la tierra conquistada. En la colonización española en particular, sucede que la raza dominante gobierna, administra, explota, no como si fuese cosa propia o la misma patria, sino como cosa ajena que puede perder y de la que es necesario sacar el quilo. . . . Más la América no fue considerada como una agregación de territorio sino como una explotación. . . . Existía profunda diferencia entre el español de nacimiento y el americano, aunque descendiente de español. *No se verifica este fenómeno en la India con los hijos de los ingleses. Son ingleses, no asiáticos.* (Bilbao [1864] 1988, 138–39; emphasis added)

All the historical examples of conquests and racial invasions are, one could say, uniform in their final results. The invading and triumphant race appropriated and divided the land and the descendants of this race constituted themselves as sovereign of this land. . . . There is in that phenomenon, one could say, an identification between the conqueror and the conquered land. In the Spanish conquest, particularly, it happened that the dominant race governed, administered, exploited, but not as if all these things were their own or belonged to their own country, but—on the contrary—as something that it was not theirs and that they could lose in any moment. . . . Therefore, America was not considered as a territorial addition but as exploitation. . . . There was a deep difference between those born Spanish and those born Americans, even when the latter descended from the former. *The situation is completely different in India with the children of the British population. They are British, not Asiatic.*

Bilbao's observation in 1864 was repeated, several decades later (in 1924) by the Peruvian intellectual and essayist of Marxist persuasion, José Carlos Mariátegui. Mariátegui also remarked that independence from Spain was not a social movement coming from the "indigenous" but from the "indigenous" Creole population. For them, the French Revolution (and also the independence of the colonies in New England) was a source of inspiration (Mariátegui [1924] 1991, 360). Neither Bilbao nor Mariátegui mentioned the Haitian Revolution (1804), a Revolution that could have been taken as a model by Amerindians, if Amerindians could have been in a position to revolt after the failed uprising of Tupac-Amaru (Valcárcel 1947; Valcárcel and Flórez 1981). When this particular element is coupled with the fact that, first, independence was gained without having a model of nation-state to follow (like India in 1947 or Algeria in 1962), and, second, that decolonization in Africa and in Asia coincided with a series of dictatorial regimes in Latin America, the postcolonial argument takes a different route. Furthermore, the path the postcolonial argument takes will depend on the moment of local history and colonial legacy in which it is grounded: in the Andes (José Carlos Mariátegui) it will be different from the Spanish Caribbean (Fernando Ortiz), and this differs from the French (Edouard Glissant) and the English Caribbean (George Lamming), as well as from the North African (Khatibi).

Now we are in a position to address the question of the concern of Latin American intellectuals in the twentieth century vis-à-vis decolonization. Anibal Quijano, whose very concept of coloniality of power owes much to Mariátegui, characterized one of the major lines of his thought as a tension between Marxism and the indigenous question in Peru. A second line was Mariátegui's intellectual enthusiasms for thinkers such as Nietzsche or Sorel, not always accepted by intellectuals claiming themselves as Marxists. Quijano explains the actuality of Mariátegui in part through tensions set up in a local history in which he was living, experiencing, and observing the capitalist society on which, while different from Marx's specific society, Marx based his work and analysis. Colonialism and racism were not crucial components of Marx's analysis of capitalism from "inside" and also, as Marxist intellectual José Aricó (1988) showed, Marx failed to understand Bolívar's project, a project that remains today exemplary in Latin American official as well as oppositional histories. I would suggest, following Quijano's explanation, that the actuality of Mariátegui today is due to the fact that his thinking moved from local histories to global designs (like Marxism), and not the other way around. In so doing, he encountered (like Fanon in *Peau noir, masque blancs*, 1952) the limits of Marxism in the domain of colonialism and racism. All these tensions put Mariátegui at odds with both nationalist Peruvians and international Marxists: Haya de la Torre, a Peruvian intellectual and politician, accused Mariátegui of Eurocentrism due to his introduction of Marxism and the notion of social class to reflect on the national history of Peru, while European Marxists suspected him of mysticism for the attention he paid to the indigenous question and for the fact that he attempted to present Marxism as a myth to the indigenous population. Mariátegui took the first step toward a dialogue that Subcomandante Marcos (and other urban intellectuals) found in the form of translation: the Zapatismo as such emerged at the moment in which Marxist cosmology is transformed by the translation of indigenous cosmology into it, and indigenous cosmology is transformed by the translation of Marxist categories into it (Mignolo forthcoming).

In other words, as an intellectual from the margin of the modern colonial world system, Mariátegui worked within Marxist global designs at the same time that he encountered its limits in the local history. The fruitful and persuasive tension that Quijano later perceived could be recast in terms of the epistemological potential of border thinking lived by Mariátegui as a tension, and theorized by Subcomandante Marcos and the Zapatista movement (Mignolo 1998; see also my concluding remarks on translation in this chapter). It was from that very border between Western and Amerindian cosmologies that Mariátegui's work emerged. Mariátegui, like Fanon, was a thinker of the border; Bilbao was a thinker of the margins. This is one of the crucial differences between postcolonial thinking in the nineteenth and twentieth centuries. The former intellectual production sustained itself in the conflict between local histories of colonialism and racism and the new path opened up by U.S. independence and the French Revolution. Bilbao in Chile and, later, Cuban revolutionary intellectual José Martí (1853–95) saw a double danger: the expansion of the United States toward the south, the intervention of France in Mexico, and the constant presence of England in the South American economy. Martí's interests in the indigenous question, which was more a concern with the history of ancient civilization, was related to the definition of "Our America" rather than being a move toward a dialogue with the indigenous population of his time. Certainly, for Martì in Cuba the indigenous question was not as pressing as for Mariátegui in Peru. But, above all, the times were different: Bilbao was concerned with building the republic; Martì with obtaining Cuba's independence from Spain. Mariátegui, in the 1920s, a century after the independence of most Spanish-American countries and a few years after the Russian Revolution, was in a position to reflect critically both on the history of Spanish colonialism and on the history of nation building in Peru (as well as other Spanish American countries during the nineteenth century). His sensibility toward the indigenous question was the first move I know of, however, toward the emergence of border thinking in the local history of the Andes and in the making of Latin America, this time between colonial legacies and local national designs.

In this sense, Mariátegui was specifically speaking of an "Indo-Spanish" America. That is, he was not concerned either with Brazil or with the non-Spanish Caribbean, even if Spanish colonialism left its traces in the islands, which became, in the seventeenth century, British, Dutch, or French possessions. Mariátegui, as is common in any intellectual works with geopolitical content or implications, thought about the world from the burning experience of Spanish colonial legacies in Peru and the Andes:

> The nations of Spanish America they all move in the same direction. The solidarity of their historical destiny is not an illusion created by pro-American literature. These nations have a brotherhood relation not only in their rhetoric but also in their histories. They proceed from a common matrix: Spanish conquest, by destroying indigenous cultures and autochthonous social formations, imposed a homogeneous pattern in the ethnic, political and moral aspect of Spanish America. (Mariátegui [1924] 1991, 360)

We should not conclude from this quotation that Mariátegui was in support of Spanish colonization. On the contrary, he was once again perhaps the most violent critic, up to his time, of the crimes and exploitation of Spanish colonialism. He was here just recognizing the basic facts in the making of the local histories of areas with dense indigenous populations like Peru, Bolivia, Mexico, Ecuador, and Guatemala.

Mariátegui was, because of the vantage point of a century elapsed since independence, in a position to ask an epistemological question: "Is there a thinking which is particularly Hispanic American?" And he responded in the negative. For him, it was obvious that there existed a German and a French "way" of thinking in Western culture, but not an Hispanic American way. He expanded on his negative answer by saying:

> La producción intelectual del continente [by which, of course, he meant the part of the continent which was under Spanish colonialism] carece de rasgos propios. No tiene contornos originales. El pensamiento hispano-americano no

es generalmente sino una rapsodia compuesta con motivos y elementos del pensamiento europeo . . . El espíritu hispano-americano está en elaboración. El continente, la raza, están en formación también. Los aluviones occidentales en los
cuales se desarrollan los embriones de la cultura hispano o latino-americana
(. . .) *no han conseguido consustanciarse ni solidarizarse con el suelo sobre el cual
la colonización de America los ha depositado.* (Mariátegui [1924] 1991, 366)

The intellectual production of the continent is far from having a well-defined
profile. It lacks original contours. Hispanic American thought is no more than
a song composed with motifs and elements from European thought. . . . The
Hispanic American spirit is in progress. The continent and its racial formation
are also in their formative process. The Western inundation from where the
embryos of the Hispanic or Latin American cultures develop . . . has not yet
reached its point of accommodation and solidarity with the soil on which the
colonization of America deposited them.

But, of course, as with any form of identification, Spanish American identity
is not something we should understand as the intrinsic spirit of a local history (e.g., Spain's colonial legacies), but as something in conflictive dialogue
with other forces at work at the time a form of identification is being discussed and the colonial difference negotiated. Thus, for Mariátegui, as for
other intellectuals of the time, "Indo-Americanism," sometimes "Ibero-
Americanism," was a form of identification in confrontation with "Pan-
Americanism." Thinking from the borders allowed Mariátegui to transcend
the dichotomy set up by the title itself. First, Ibero-Americanism is an intellectual movement grounded in traditions and sensibilities, while Pan-Americanism is grounded in business and economic interests. However, he quickly
introduces a nuance to his position by recognizing that, on the one hand,
the interests that motivate Pan-Americanism have their counterparts in busi-
nessmen and government officers in Spanish American countries, subservi-
ent to imperial designs and practitioners of internal colonialism. On the
other hand, Mariátegui forcefully argued that the new Ibero-American intellectuals should establish a dialogue with the new American intellectuals
(dead or alive) such as Ralph Waldo Emerson, Waldo Frank, William James,
and Walt Whitman. Thinking from the border emerges here as a contradiction and a challenge to the very unity of the Ibero-America Mariátegui posited at the beginning of his argument. First, he stated the opposition between
Ibero- and Pan-Americanism; second, he distinguished political and economic "Pan-Americanism" from the work of (North) American intellectuals;
and, third, he distinguished, within Ibero-Americanism, political/economic
interests from intellectual ones:

El trabajo de la nueva generación ibero-americana puede y debe articularse y
solidarizarse con el trabajo de la nueva generación yanqui. Ambas generaciones

coinciden. Las diferencian el idioma y la raza; pero las comunica y las manco-muna la misma emoción histórica. La América de Waldo Frank es tambien, como nuestra América, adversaria del Imperio de Pierpont Morgan y del Petróleo.

En cambio, la misma emoción histórica que nos acerca a esta América revolucio-naria nos separa de la España reaccionaria de los Borbones y de Primo de Rivera. Que puede enseñarnos la España de Vásquez de Mella y de Maura . . .? Nada; ni siquiera el método de un gran Estado industrialista y capitalista. La civiliza-ción de la potencia no tiene sede en Madrid ni en Barcelona; la tiene en Nueva York, Londres, en Berlin. (Mariátegio [1924] 1991, 369–370)

The intellectual work of the new Ibero-American generation should and ought to establish solidarity with the intellectual work of the new Yankee generation. Both generations coincide in their interest. Language and race differentiate them, but there is a common historical sensibility that establishes a common ground among them. Waldo Frank's America is, like our America, against Pier-pont Morgan and the oil empires.

Instead, the same historical sensibility that gets us close to Waldo Frank's revolutionary America cuts us off from the Borbones and Primo de Rivera's reactionary Spain. What can the Spain of Vásquez de Mella y de Maura teach us. . .? Nothing. It can't even teach us the method of a capitalist and great indus-trial state. The civilization of potency doesn't have its office in Madrid or Barce-lona. It has it instead in New York, London, and Berlin.

Alliances, in the last analysis, are not established by languages or traditions only, but by common goals and interests in the field of forces established by and in the coloniality of power. What Mariátegui identifies, in the last analy-sis, is the coloniality of power that intellectuals of both Americas oppose and reject. If their language (Spanish, English) is different, they have a common history (the critique of the coloniality of power). But, in order to reach such a conclusion, as Mariátegui did, it was necessary to transcend territorial thinking (establishing frontiers and creating dichotomies) and locate oneself in the borders, erase frontiers (mainly those created by the consolidation of national ideologies, national languages, national cultures, and their imperial consequences), and transcend dichotomies.

In the next chapter I pursue the answer to the question about intellectual production in Latin America at the time of decolonization during the cold war. The essay as a genre of intellectual production was displaced, after the 1950s, by the increasing relevance of the social sciences. Area studies during the cold war managed to transform the Third World into an object of study at the same time that it exported the social sciences as a tool for a neutral and objective understanding of social reality. Critical thinking became en-trenched and in dissidence with the social sciences; next, problems were cast in terms of "dependency," "internal colonialism," and "liberation." In the next section, however, I explore Rodolfo Kusch's contribution as an effort to think from the borders of Western and Amerindian categories.

BORDER THINKING AND THE TRANSFORMATION OF KNOWLEDGE
(OR, HOW TO BENEFIT FROM AMERINDIAN CATEGORIES OF THOUGHT
AND AFRO-CARIBBEAN EXPERIENCES WITHOUT CONVERTING THEM
INTO EXOTIC OBJECTS OF STUDY)

In the final chapter of his book *Knowledge and Human Interests* ([1968] 1971), Jürgen Habermas describes Schelling's *Lectures on the Method of Academic Study,* delivered in the summer semester of 1802 at Jena (only a few years after the independence of the New England colonies, and a few years before independence in Spanish America). Habermas points out that Schelling, although using the language of German idealism, drastically renewed the concept of theory "that has defined the tradition of great philosophy since its beginning." And he quotes Schelling: "The fear of speculation, the ostensible rush from the theoretical to the practical, brings about the same shallowness in action that it does in knowledge. It is by studying a strictly theoretical philosophy that we become most immediately acquainted with Ideas, and only Ideas provide action with energy and ethical significance" ([1968] 1971, 301).

Habermas interprets this paragraph by saying that "The *only* [Habermas's emphasis] knowledge that can truly orient action is *knowledge that frees itself from mere human interests and is based on Ideas* [my emphasis]—in other words, knowledge that has taken a theoretical attitude" ([1968] 1971, 301). However, Habermas wrote this chapter (an appendix of his book) to disprove the trajectory of Schelling's dictum in the positivistic self-justification of the natural and the social sciences as well as in the humanities. Taking, on the one hand, the division of scientific labor and knowledge in which academic disciplines have been organized after the nineteenth century, and celebrating the need of disengaging knowledge from "immediate" interests (like a fascist national physics or a Soviet genetics), Habermas develops a brilliant argument to demonstrate that, in the last analysis, there is no, and there can be no, knowledge without interests. He mentions, and subsequently forgets, Max Horkheimmer's critique of the concept of theory that promoted the very concept of "critical theory" in the Frankfurt School (Horkheimer [1950] 1972)—Edmund Husserl's reflection on the crisis of the European sciences, coincidentally published the same year as Horkheimer's essay (Husserl [1950] 1970). Husserl's doubt was not with the crisis of the sciences but with "their crisis as sciences" (Habermas [1968] 1971, 302). More specifically, Husserl was concerned, according to Habermas, with the "scientific culture" (or with "cultures of scholarship," as I develop in chapter 6 and 7). Habermas, interpreting Husserl, states:

> What ultimately produces a scientific culture is not the information content of theories but the formation among theorists themselves of a thoughtful and enlightened mode of life. *The evolution of the European mind seemed to be aiming at the creation of a scientific culture of this sort.* After 1933, however, Husserl saw this historical tendency endangered. He was convinced that the danger was threatening not from without but from within. He attributed the crisis to the circumstance that the most advanced disciplines, especially physics, had degenerated from the status of true theory. (Habermas [1968] 1971, 302; emphasis added)

By locating the problem in the "evolution of the European mind," Husserl distances himself—according to Habermas—from possible trivial accusations of building a "European mind," equivalent to, say, fascist genetics or Soviet physics. However, Husserl's "European mind" was a geohistorical location of the problem similar to those raised in colonial geopolitics of knowledge, such as "Latin American or African philosophy." Husserl was referring to a community of interests defined by history, language, tradition, and self-construction of the very idea of science and knowledge, which, as Schelling and Habermas (among others) delineated, "began" in Greece. But of course, the same "beginning" cannot be claimed for a "(Latin) American," "African," or "Asian" mentality. Or at least a similar claim (often made in Latin American philosophy) is not as transparent as Husserl's claims could be: Greece is indirectly related to memories and the past in Latin America, whose "beginning" has to be located in the violence of coloniality. Human interest shall be defined in that conflictive horizon of understanding: the coloniality of power and the colonial difference of colonial modernities.

This is one part of the story that gets lost in Habermas's argument. The other is the manner in which Habermas demonstrates that knowledge without interests is an impossibility, and that the natural sciences' self-description as objective knowledge detached from human interest was a positivistic self-description that favored the instrumental reason and the use of knowledge for social management rather than for creativity, intellectual pursuit, and human "emancipation" (Habermas's use of a post-Enlightenment word), or for human "liberation" as Enrique Dussel and other Third World thinkers will prefer. Nevertheless, there are two theses in Habermas's argument that are helpful in linking knowledge, interest, and emancipation/liberation. One thesis sustains that "*in the power of self-reflection* (and Habermas is thinking here of academic disciplines, of natural and social sciences as well as of the humanities), *knowledge and interests are one*" ([1968] 1971, 314). The other thesis states that "*the unity of knowledge and interest proves itself in a dialectic that takes the historical traces of suppressed*

dialogue and reconstructs what has been suppressed" ([1968] 1971, 315). Both
theses link knowledge with emancipation. But emancipation from what?
From authoritarianism, of course, in a relentless march of "mankind's evolution toward autonomy and responsibility," or "we all" learned from the Enlightenment: "only in an emancipated society, whose members' autonomy
and responsibility had been realized, would communication have developed
into the non-authoritarian and universally practiced dialogue from which
both our model of reciprocally constituted ego identity and our idea of true
consensus are always implicitly derived" ([1968] 1971, 315, 314).

At this point of his analysis, Habermas has lost track of his beginning:
Horkheimer's critical take on the notion of theory and its connection between critical theory and oppression, as was the case with the Jews in Germany, 450 years after their expulsion from Spain at the "beginning" of the
modern/colonial world system and of the colonial differences. Habermas
forgot also to pursue further Husserl's idea of the "European mind" forming
a community, a scientific culture that will be linked to "a thoughtful and
enlightened mode of life." The formation of cultures of scholarship and of
intellectual pursuit linked with "enlightened mode of life" beyond the "European mind" had, all along the configuration of the modern/colonial world
system, a complicated history. In fact, what could a scientific culture be
beyond the "European mind" (from its formation in the Renaissance
through the Enlightenment) since the hegemonic epistemological imaginary
of the modern world system, particularly its scientific authority and credibility, was so powerful as to make Fernando Ortiz emphasize, several times,
that his study of slavery was objective and nonpassionate. Ortiz was making
this observation just after his return to Cuba from his advanced studies
abroad. However, the force of local histories that the thinker inhabits (in
the case of Mariátegui, Ortiz, Du Bois) and the distance of the "scientific"
model of knowledge he or she adopts end up, in creative thinkers, defining
a community of interest that in the case I'm analyzing could be described as
"knowledge and interest in local colonial histories."

In this book my argument goes in the last direction: the distinction between local histories and global design makes it possible to understand
Schelling's (and Habermas's) project in a local history in which the universality of their interest was taken for granted and was the foundation of global
designs. The very structure of the modern world system goes together with
a changing imaginary in which the universal (logically and historically) is
its aim: there is a long-lasting discussion in Christian philosophy on the
problems of the "universals" (Beuchot 1981) which became the epistemological foundations of the practical project of Christianizing the world. This
complicity made it possible first to conceive Christianity, and knowledge
under Christian philosophy, as a global project, and, second, with the secularization of the world, knowledge became attached to Reason and Theory

(instead of to God) and supported a new global design, the civilizing mission. The exportation of epistemological global designs filled the space of knowledge as the civilizing mission became central in the domain of education (Gonzalbo Aizpurú 1990; Viswanathan 1989; Osorio Romero 1990). Within local histories of colonial mercantilism (sixteenth and seventeenth centuries) and colonial capitalism (late eighteenth to twentieth century), in Latin America, Asia, and Africa, the explicit connections between knowledge and interest is more difficult to hide: the links between knowledge and interests are motivated by the need for liberation, for decolonization, instead of emancipation. *That is, knowledge is linked to liberation and decolonization from the subaltern perspective, as emancipation was during the nineteenth century in Europe.* There cannot be knowledge detached from interest from a subaltern perspective since all subaltern perspective is "critical" in the sense that Horkheimmer and Khatibi gave to the word. By questioning the emancipation view linking knowledge and interest, as argued by Habermas, I am not questioning the validity of his argument in the local history he is quarreling with. My point is that his argument implicitly and nonintentionally disqualifies other possibilities of linking knowledge with interests from a subaltern position for which Habermas's discussion is tangentially relevant.

In an early article, Angel Rama (1926–83), the Uruguayan literary and cultural critic who extended Ortiz's notion of "transculturation" to the literary field, traced an anatomy of Latin American literary and cultural contribution, as a region of the Third World. The article in question was written for a meeting, in Geneva, whose goal was to examine Latin American cultural history in relation to the Third World and to universal history. Rama's analysis is most useful to summarize my argument up to this point, as well as to chart what follows (Rodolfo Kusch, Ortiz, and the concept of "transculturation," Du Bois's notion of "double consciousness," Glissant et al.'s "Creolité," and Anzaldúa's "new mestiza consciousness").

The first point of interest is that the Third World is in this instance a geopolitical reference, rather than the imperial dangers of the United States, as was evident in the war with Mexico in 1847 and the Guadalupe Hidalgo Treaty of 1848, as well as the French invasion of Mexico in 1861, which had a great deal to do with the adaptation of the name of "Latin America" (Ardao 1980; 1993; Rojas Mix 1992). Both events were Francisco Bilbao's concern in the second half of the nineteenth century. Underlining two dates, 1810, Bolivar's ideal, and 1910, the Mexican Revolution, Rama stressed the Spanish American Creole intellectual identification of Latin American particularities. He recognized, after the work of Mariátegui, the plurality of Latin American culture, an aspect that would have been more difficult to recognize for Bilbao. Bilbao described the Americas as a unique configuration in the history of humankind. With celebratory and emphatic prose, Bilbao stated that neither in the ancient Orient nor in Europe could be seen such a vast span of land "dominated only by two races, with two languages, with two religions, and one political structure" (Bilbao [1862] 1988, 273). This apocalyptic vision set the stage for a long-lasting tradition, reaching to Angel Rama, in which "Latin America" is defined by the expansion of the ideology of the independence, mainly by a Creole mentality. It is precisely this imaginary that Angel Rama reproduced in 1965 when he stated:

> Ni las culturas africanas tienen posibilidad visible de desarrollo autónomo dentro del continente americano, ni las culturas indígenas pueden cubrir el salto en el tiempo necesario para alcanzar y superar a las culturas europeas acriolladas. *Estas han ocupado América y allí se mantienen sólidamente. Tanto las primeras como las segundas están destinadas a morir, y solo pueden insertar elementos propios dentro de esta cultura europea americana, u occidental y atlántica, como se quiera:* es para lo africano el ejemplo de la poesía Cubana, desde Martí a Guillén; es para lo indígena peruano, la novela indigenista en sus muy diversos ejemplos y niveles. (Rama [1965] 1993, 3:62)

> Neither did the African cultures have the possibility of autonomous development in the American continent, nor would the indigenous culture be able to fill the necessary jump in time to reach and to go beyond European "Creolized" cultures. These latest ones had occupied America and maintained themselves solidly grounded in it. Instead, African and indigenous cultures are destined to disappear, and can only survive by inserting elements proper to each culture within this Euro-American culture, Occidental and Atlantic, or whatever you would like to call it: such is the case, for the African culture, poetry in Cuba, from Mart\ to Guillen, and for the indigenous culture in Peru, the indigenous novel in its variety of forms and levels.

Readers familiar with Rama's contribution in the 1970s and early 1980s (Rama 1996; Moraña 1997) may be surprised by such statements, uncharacteristic of a thinker of Marxist persuasion and one of the most distinguished literary and cultural critics of the second half of the twentieth century, together with Antonio Cándido (1995) and Roberto Schwarz (1992) in Brazil, Fernández Retamar (1981) in Cuba, or Cornejo Polar (1994) in Peru. I am not quoting it to develop a critique ad hominem but because I believe the paragraph describes a common belief, even among Creole intellectuals, in Spanish America, of Marxist persuasion. And when I say Creole I do not only mean blood related to Spaniards, but, mainly, the legacy of Spanish colonialism as worked out to define a (Latin) American imaginary out of that tradition and in confrontation with Europe, the United States, the history and consequences of African slavery, and the long-lasting repression of Amerindian communities. It is in this context that the latest work of Rodolfo Kusch, Argentinian philosopher of German descent, acquires enormous relevance. I devote the following section to Kusch and the Amerindian question stated by Rama and, in the following one to the Afro-American question by exploring the writing of Cuban anthropologist Fernando Ortiz and Afro-American thinker W.E.B Dubois, French Caribbean writer and essayist Edouard Glissant, and Chicana writer and essayist Gloria Anzaldúa.

Thinking from the Ruins of Amerindian Categories

To grasp better the implications of Rama's dictum, it would be helpful to start with a parallel between indigenism and Indianism. "Indigenism" is defined as a set of cultural and political practices, by Creole intellectuals as well as non-Amerindian organizations (such as nongovernmental organizations, or NGOs), in defense and alliance with Amerindians (or "indigenous" Amerindians). Indigenism covers a wide spectrum of political persuasions, from the state politics of integration to oppositional intellectuals who perceived in Amerindian communities the future of the social revolution. "Indianism," instead, is defined by the belief that "lo indio" (difficult to translate into English with the neutral pronoun "lo") is characterized by its pre-Columbian configuration. Such a belief could be shared by Amerindians as well as by non-Amerindians. Indianism when assumed by Amerindian people in their long history of upheaval against external and internal colonialism, has been perceived as a symbolic restitution of the past in view of a better future. I would like to advance an argument that I will make later and to suggest that "the Zapatismo," in Mexico, has defined a space beyond both indigenism and Indianism and such a new space, which I called elsewhere "the Zapatistas's theoretical revolution," (Mignolo 1997d; forthcoming) is an attainment and at the same time a coming into being of border thinking: a new space coming out of a double translation, a translation of Marxism into Amerindian cosmology and Amerindian into Marxist cosmology, involving in the process both Amerindian and urban-Creole intellectuals. Of course, Rama did not have the chance to witness this third crucial moment in his genealogy marked by the early independence in 1810 and the Mexican revolution in 1910. In the 1990s, the failure of the Mexican Revolution has its continuation in the Zapatistas who have also introduced a new discourse and have given a new meaning to "Indianity." But it is certainly what is being articulated, although from a different perspective, by Creole intellectuals who can look at the limits of Indigenism and Indianism at the crossroads of globalization (Mires 1991; Varesse 1997) and the emergence of Amerindian intellectuals (Rappaport [1990] 1998; Varesse 1996b).

I would argue that Rodolfo Kusch's work, since and after *América profunda* (1963), is not only a contribution to a reconfiguration of Indianity, in the common work of Amerindian and Creole intellectuals, but also a contribu-

tion toward a new epistemological landscape from which Amerindian categories have been ignored or taken as objects of study, not as "energy" for
thinking. Kusch makes it possible to start from the assumption that the
name "philosophy" may be of Greek origin (and in that sense, it marks a
"beginning") but "thinking" has no origin in any particular culture: there is
no beginning for "thinking," although there are beginnings of the names
that "thinking" has taken in the history of human beings (see Dussel [1992]
1995 and Mignolo 1995a; 1995b, for similar attempts). Furthermore, we
should keep in mind that for historical reasons related to education there is
not yet in regions of Latin America with a dense Amerindian population a
significant and public cultural production of transnational impact (with the
exception of Rigogerta Menchu in Guatemala) by intellectuals from Amerindian descent (with the exception of people like Fausto Reynage, Roberto
Choque, and Fernando Untoja in Bolivia; or Demetrio Cujti Cuxil in Guatemala), as it is the case in the United States, where literary, artistic, and intellectual activists have had a long trajectory and a visible presence (Deloria
1999; Coltelli 1990). In this regard, Kusch's latest work has a more telling
dimension.

But before we take up Kusch's work, let me outline the context in which
his thoughts were shaped, as well as how my own descriptions of Kusch's
ideas are being articulated. This caution is necessary because of the controversial political figure that Kusch was in Argentinian circles and still is in
the history of Latin American philosophy. No doubt, this was due in some
part to his proximity to Martin Heidegger (of whom Kusch was a critic
rather than a blind follower). Kusch's thinking was at the edge of a pro-Nazi
attitude, which, one can surmise, was already at its inception in the early
nineteenth century a romantic ideologue for whom J. G. Herder's ideas of
the "national" and the "popular" were not only translated in political but
also in metaphysical and ideological terms. The romantic legacy incarnated
in the early Kusch and his celebration of "barbarism" (a book written shortly
before the fall of Juan Domingo Perón (Kusch 1953) has its immediate continuation in *América profunda*, in which Kusch articulates his ideas in the
context of Aymara civilization and colonial legacies. Arturo A. Roig, an Argentinian philosopher of leftist persuasion, who—like Kusch, though for
different reasons—has been a victim of the military government that took
over in 1976 (Kusch was fired from the university that very year and died
in 1979; Roig returned to the university after 1984 following the return of
democracy in Argentina), harshly criticized Kusch's philosophy as a reduction of (Latin) American identity to a metaphysics of the "land," the inertia
of the flora, which, according to Roig, Kusch matched with the passivity of
the feminine as a complement to the celebration of the illiterate peasant,
perceived as the root and the authenticity of (Latin) America. It is from this
standpoint, according to Roig, that Kusch found his way to read Heidegger

"à l'Américaine" without avoiding the pattern toward a fascist ideology (Roig 1993, 82–84). I am persuaded that Roig's reading of Kusch, if not completely wrong, is completely misleading. In the following pages I look into the positive aspects of Kusch's philosophy and to a new reading of his work, beyond *América profunda*, which is where his critics seem to have stopped reading.

When Kusch began writing, anthropologists had not yet recognized the implications of the scene of writing or the complex, complicitous relationship between the anthropologist and his informant or between the anthropologist and his audience; nor did they recognize the fractures created by the informant's narrative being addressed to the anthropologist instead of to the people of his or her community. However, when anthropologists did become aware of the ethical and political issues involved in practicing anthropology (i.e., "writing culture"), the context in which their reflections took shape was basically that of the North American anthropologist doing fieldwork in Asia, Africa, or Latin America—that is, contexts in which the informant's culture was alien to the anthropologist. Kusch, however, found himself in quite a different situation. The people and communities he contacted, both historically and at that time, were simultaneously "they" and "we" vis-à-vis himself. The Andean people and cultures he was trying to understand were foreign to his Argentinian urban, middle-class background, yet "they" were also "we": (Latin) Americans. And Kusch's "selfsame" was also his "other," in that he had grown up amid the fragments of the European tradition at the colonial periphery. (Whether the Andean people would have considered themselves American and counted Kusch as one of them is a different question.) The point here is that Kusch found himself on shifting ground, even groundless ground, and his entire intellectual life thereafter was directed toward understanding "America" as a locus of enunciation, which he conceived as a conflictive politics of difference. He viewed himself as a member of the middle class and as a philosopher on the margins of the West, whereas he viewed the Andean people as central to American culture, although displaced by marginalizing economic and political forces of Western culture. To Kusch, "the West" meant (Hegel's) Europe and the United States. Thus, his work (up to *América profunda*) is marked by the constant tension of identifying an "American" locus of enunciation.

In his first volume of essays, *La seducción de la barbarie* (1953), Kusch traced what was uniquely, specifically American to the landscape, a landscape that had been considered, from a "civilized" perspective, a wilderness or site of anticivilization (see chapter 8). In positing this landscape as "seductive," Kusch suggests something similar to what Roberto Fernández Retamar, speaking from a Caribbean rather than an Andean locus, would later term the "seduction" of Caliban:

Our symbol then is not Ariel . . . but rather Caliban. This is something that we, the mestizo inhabitants of these same isles where Caliban lived, see with particular clarity: Prospero invaded the islands, killed our ancestors, enslaved Caliban, and taught him his language to make himself understood. What else could Caliban do but use that same language—today he has no other—to curse him, to wish that the "red plague" would fall on him? I know no other metaphor more expressive of our cultural situation, our reality. . . . What is our history, what is our culture, if not the history and culture of Caliban? (Fernández Retamar [1973] 1989, 14)

In *América profunda* (Deep America), Kusch continues along the same lines of thought, connecting the Quechua and Aymara languages and knowledges, via the lands and mountains of Bolivia and Peru, with the much older traditions of a powerful and extensive Inca Empire. This is when Kusch realized that his conception of nature in *La seducción de la barbarie* was inadequate for the apprehension of the "America" for which he was striving. He needed to understand the indigenous people (i.e., their descendants), not just the landscape. More to the point, he needed to understand how these people understood and related themselves to nature. Kusch approached this new task he set for himself from the perspective of both a (Western) philosopher and a middle-class Argentinian of German descent, realizing that if one's *thought* is grounded in one's *place*, then migration must bring about a different configuration, since it creates a groundless ground from which to think and speak—an insight that Kusch would later elaborate as the "place of philosophy" (1978).

América profunda opens with Kusch's description of walking around the streets of Cuzco, once the center of the Inca Empire and later an important place in the Spanish administration of colonial Peru. Since independence (i.e., the early nineteenth century), Cuzco has become a major Peruvian city with a complex and conflictive past. Kusch's sensibility as a person born and raised in a country basically populated by descendants of the Spanish colonizers or nineteenth-century European immigrants is reflected in his observations on the filth and the unbearable smell that he identifies as the stench of America. He sees in himself and his class the cleanliness associated with the ideas of progress and civilization—thus the two sides of America:

On the one hand, America with its deep layers, its Messianic roots and its divine wrath at the surface layer, and, on the other, the progressive, Westernized citizens. Both are like the two extremes of an ancient human experience. One is bound to the stench and brings with it the fear of extermination, and the other, conversely triumphant and clean, points toward a limitless, although impossible, triumph.

But this same opposition, instead of appearing tragic, has an outlet that makes a dramatic interaction possible, like a kind of dialectic, which later we call phagocytosis. It deals with the absorption of the clean things of the West by the things of America, like a kind of equilibrium or reintegration of what is human in these lands. (Kusch 1963, 17; my translation)

For Kusch, America no longer seemed to be a place constructed in opposition to Europe, but rather a place where an extended (and colonial) Occident coexisted with the Amerindian—that is, with those ancestral memories, lifestyles, and thought patterns of Amerindian cultures that had survived the colonial and postcolonial (or neocolonial) periods. The conflictive encounters between Old World Europeans and pre-Columbian peoples of the Andes, Mesoamerica, and the Caribbean created a (new) world in which the dialectic of the filthy and the clean, the fetid and the fresh, continued. But fetid or fresh to whom? At this point, Kusch begins to shift from imaginary construction to locus of enunciation, and his sensibility, honed by the place he is from, begins to change under the influence of the place from which he is speaking/writing.

América profunda is divided into two parts. The first is devoted to understanding a report by an Amerindian intellectual of Inca descent to the Spanish missionaries in charge of extirpating Amerindian idolatries during the early years of the seventeenth century. The second part, by contrast, is devoted to the historical and intellectual context of western Europe during the early modern period and the philosophical thinking that emerged from it. Kusch plays each part against the other and stresses the sense of *estar aquí* (to be here, to be at) that he finds in the report by the Andean intellectual, Pachacuti Yamki, whom Kusch credits with the reinvention of Andean traditions in colonial times. Kusch by no means assumes the "pure" survival of authentic remains of an Amerindian past. Since by "culture" he means a program for action rather than a collection of objects, what survives and remains from the Amerindian past are cognitive patterns of dealing with new situations, allowing for creativity, resistance, and survival very much shaped by the colonial difference. If *estar aquí* summarizes the remaining forces of an Amerindian past, *ser alguien* (to be someone) summarizes the worldly philosophical attitudes of merchants in the construction of a commercial world of objects. Both attitudes coexist and interact in America. This world of objects (in which human beings built nature) begins to be perceived as a replacement for, rather than an alternative to, a world of organisms (in which nonhuman beings built nature), and the "possession of objects" begins to be perceived as preferable to "participation and interaction with organisms." The coexistence—in Kusch's argument—of the notion "to be here" with that of "to be someone" corresponds to his earlier conception of the coexistence of the filthy with the clean.

At the end of his book, Kusch returns to his personal experience in Cuzco to describe the peculiarity of being in America, of an existence blending both European ways of doing things outside of Europe and Amerindian cognitive patterns, however disrupted by European people and institutions, in the remote West (or, as the Spaniards liked to call it, the "Indias Occidentales"; see fig. 2). This tension leads Kusch to explore "the wisdom of America," a notion based on his theory of "cultural phagocytosis" as a two-way process: while Western civilization was transformed at the borders by Amerindian traditions, those same transformation-producing traditions have been and continue to be relegated to a secondary (or tertiary) status by hegemonic promotion of the "civilizing process" during the colonial period, and of "progress and modernization" during the postcolonial period (Gyekye 1997, for Africa; Gargand Poinkh 1995, for India). More recently, the postcolonial intellectual has been able to choose between promoting civilization/progress/modernization or resisting it and dealing with the complexities of a groundless ground. Both options entail confronting the complex problems of Occidentalization: namely, the discontinuities of the European and the Amerindian classical (invented) traditions. Kusch's "phagocytosis" comes close to Ortiz's "transculturation," Santiago's "space-in-between," and my own notion of "border thinking."

In Kusch's formulation, imaginary constructions and loci of enunciation operate in a specific spatiotemporal context: the Andes, as constructed from and within a Western discursive formation at the margins of the West and on the groundless ground of immigrant families. Such a focus permits Kusch to evacuate the space traditionally occupied by centuries of intellectual colonization, leaving it to be filled by self-identifying agencies and by the constitution of new loci of enunciation emerging from the fragmented memories and ruins of ancient Amerindian civilizations, rather than filling it with his own anthropological discursive representations of the other. Although Kusch didn't live to see similar development in other writers and scholars (he died in 1979), the names and the texts of Domitila Barrios de Chungara and José María Arguedas, in the Andes, and Rigoberta Menchú, in Mesoamerica, can be added to the general project Kusch anticipated. Their discourses, like Kusch's, represent neither the other nor the community of the speaker; they are cultural interventions that stake their claims to new places from which to speak (e.g., local histories and critical claims to the particular) and, by so doing, contribute to the endorsement of a double consciousness, a border gnosis, restituting to the subaltern an epistemological potential of which they have been deprived: to know both the reason of the master and the reason of the slave, while the master only knows his own reason and the unreason of the slave. Rather than representations of other agencies or of preexisting communities, Kusch Menchú, etc. shall be conceived as performances inviting participation of members of an already existing community as well as those who wish to become members of an extended community composed of new loci of enunciation.

My interpretation of these discourses and how they should be theorized draws on the models (or examples, if you wish) on which Kusch based his theories. The most familiar of these is the distinction in Peru between the mountains and the coast, a geographical division that also operates sociologically, historically, and philosophically as a play of borderlands. In the mountains, the "to be here" principle of the Amerindian philosophy of life prevails. On the coast, "to be someone" is the driving force of the Peruvian middle class, which lives and practices Western ways of life and beliefs on the margins of the Western world (especially on the Pacific coast of Peru). Between the mountains and the coast lies the space of migration to the cities. Kusch articulates this distinction as follows:

> The deep sense of opposition between coast and mountains in Peru is a conjugation of two rhythms of life which embody two of the species' experiences, each of which struggles silently to prevail. But because the struggle is unequal in terms of the means utilized and the force of each side, the indigenous struggle has become encysted within the other [struggle]. It is from this perspective that we have countries like Bolivia and Peru or zones such as the Argentine North where, underneath the dynamic culture, the ancient stratum breathes like a cyst, with its ancient communal and collective breath. It is a substratum that remains ignored, and is registered only within the sphere of folklore or ethnography, but which offers its silent, measured resistance until it achieves success, no longer in the direct act of rubbing or contact between cultures, but in the qualities of weakness and fiction of *being* (identified), as its antagonist, which wants to reside on the coasts of America. . . . Undoubtedly, the indigenous culture constitutes a perfectly structured entelechy—as Spengler would say—to an extent much greater than that of its antagonist. And the solidity of this culture, its cohesion and persistence, is based on what used to be called *to be* (located), which lacks a transcendent reference to a world of essences and exists on that plane of mere existence within the realm of the species, which lives out its great history firmly committed to its "here and now" or, as we already stated, in that margin where the human ends and the divine wrath of the elements begins. And in this resides its definition as the culture of the mountains or of *being* (located) in opposition to its antagonist, the culture of the coast or, better still, that of the mere *to be* (identified), as simply *to be* someone. (Kusch 1963, 166–68)

A Hegelian synthesis would be expected at this point, following a philosophical analysis in which two poles of a cultural process have been identified. But if the synthesis is conceived hierarchically, as an elevation (*Aufhebung*) of one pole, which of these two poles would prevail? From a European perspective, "to be someone" would seem preferable, a sign of modernization and progress. An Ameri(can)indian perspective would lean instead toward "to be here," privileging a more satisfying way of life. But this position would still remain within a Hegelian framework, albeit one with inverted values. Kusch's theory of cultural phagocytosis is formulated as a means of superseding an inverted Hegelian dialectic:

> On the strictly cultural level, rather than on the level of civilization, it is only possible in America to speak of a probable dominion of the *to be* (located) over the *to be* (identified), because the *to be* (located), as a vision of the world, occurs in Europe as well. . . . For all of that, it isn't possible to speak of an elevation, but [to speak] instead—to the extent that it deals with a new establishment for the West—of a distention or, better yet, a phagocytosis of the *to be* (identified) by the *to be* (located), above all, as a *to be someone* phagocytosed by a *to be here*. (Kusch 1963, 171)

Once the terms of a dialectic had been established and the Hegelian model challenged, Kusch could introduce new approaches to and findings in European history similar to the traces of the challenges posed by Amerindian agencies to the promotion of Western civilization in the Americas. Such challenges were identified by philosophers and historiographers (e.g., Toynbee, Jaspers, Spengler) when they perceived the fall of Western civilization as a "cultural phagocytosis" (in Kusch's terms) of the individual, and the individualistic philosophy of "to be someone" as the rebellion of the masses or, as Kusch would say, by the multitudes transforming the notion of distinct individualities ("to be someone") into that of the "anonymous one" ("to be here") as well as the Western idea of "human communities" constructed from a conglomeration of distinct individualities.

I would like to compare Kusch's concept of phagocytosis with Frederick Douglass's narrative of slavery, in the interpretation provided by Paul Gilroy. Gilroy reads Douglass's narrative as an alternative to Hegel's master-slave dialectics and the way we can read Kusch today (see also pp. 110–111). This comparison is also relevant for the correlation between "indigenism" and "negritude" that I'll introduce later in this chapter. Here is Gilroy's reading of a particular passage of Douglass's narrative:

> In a rich account of the bitter trial of strength with Edward Covey, the slave breaker to whom he has been sent, Douglass can be read as if he is systematically reworking the encounter between master and slave in a striking manner which inverts Hegel's own allegorical scheme. It is the slave rather than the master who emerges from Douglass's account possessed of "consciousness that exists for itself," while this master becomes the representative of a "consciousness that is repressed within itself." Douglass's transformation of Hegel's metanarrative of power into a metanarrative of emancipation is all the more striking as it is also the occasion for an attempt to specify the difference between a pre-rational,

spiritual mode of African thought and his own compound outlook—an uneasy hybrid of the sacred and the secular, the African and the American, formed out of the debilitating experience of slavery and tailored to the requirements of abolitionisms. (Gilroy 1993, 61)

Douglass's reversal, in another way, creates at the same time an epistemic potential for the slave (the subaltern); while the slave knows both the reason of the master and the reason of the slave, the master only knows his own reason and the "unreason" of the slave (we could replace here master-slave with civilization-barbarism). "Phagocythosis" is precisely that moment in which the reason of the master is absorbed by the slave, and, as in the "Pontificial Mundo" of Guaman Poma (see my introduction), subaltern reason incorporates (phagocytes) another reason to his or her own. That potential, and that intellectual force, is the privilege and intellectual force of all kinds of border gnosis, from Douglass to Kusch, from Anzaldúa to Khatibi, from Ortiz to Hall. Similarly, we find it in the borders lived by Afro-Americans, Amerindians, Arabs, Jews, Chicanos, and others. I am not, of course, advocating an apartheid kind of epistemological privilege. I am suggesting that border gnosis, in its different manifestations, is the future planetary epistemological and critical localism.

The master-slave dialectics of Hegel is the past; the epistemology of the present is border gnosis. This epistemology, in its own successful expansion, has created the condition for the proliferation of border gnosis, new sensibilities and new grounds for action. Kusch's imaginary (re)construction of the idea of "community" goes beyond a celebration of "to be here," because he sees it not merely as a distinctive feature of Amerindian agencies, but, on the contrary, as the way in which Amerindians practiced a philosophy of life and philosophized a life practice that privileges interactions with "living organisms" (i.e., nature) over "constructed objects" (i.e., the commodification of nature). The lesson Kusch extrapolates from Santa Cruz Pachacuti, the Amerindian thinker of the late sixteenth and early seventeenth centuries, is the coexistence of order and chaos, in contrast to Western modes of thought, where the main drive is to control chaos and impose order (fig 10). The idea of community is akin to this general principle, with the life of the individual striving "to be someone," regulated so as to make him or her fit into a community that must accommodate the constructed objects of modernity. Thus, if "to be here" is the challenge that America (as a growing cultural phagocytosis with unbalanced power relationships) poses to Western civilization from its very margins, such a challenge is also part of a larger process in which the forces of "to be here" are fighting the hegemony of "to be someone," which Kusch sees not only in the fragments of the European Renaissance and Enlightenment, but also in the fragments of Marxism and psychoanalysis. Briefly, the notion of cultural phagocytosis (as the struggle

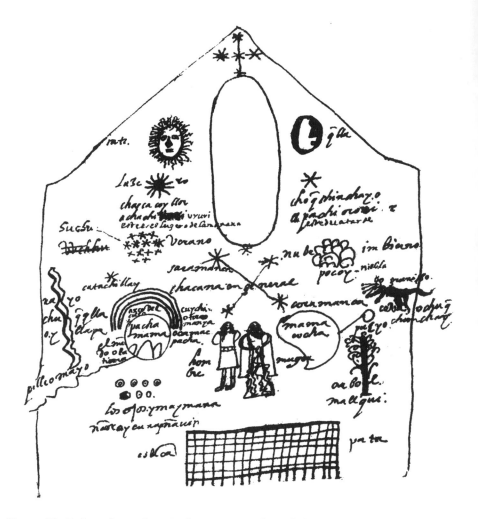

Figure 10. D. Joan Santa Cruz Pachacuti's cosmological diagram, presumably inscribed in the Temple of Coricancha, Cuzco. Pachacuti's diagram is dated toward the beginning of the seventeeth century. It was reproduced in *Relación de Antigüedades Peruanas* (Madrid 1789).

of a conscious self "to be here") becomes both a crucial key word (a type of border gnosis) and the springboard for a politics of cultural and social transformation, which he develops mainly in his last two books (Kusch 1976; 1978). The question is not to celebrate past glories but, rather, how they can be brought into a planetary present.

Most readings of Kusch (Roig 1993; Castro-Gómez 1996) stop here, in 1963, with *América profunda*. The next fifteen years are generally left out. But let's turn first to an earlier, transitional stage of Kusch's reflections on indigenous and popular cultures. His 1970 book, *El pensamiento indígena y popular en América* (Indigenous and popular thought in America), goes beyond the philosophical speculations of *América profunda* and moves toward articulating an ethnophilosophy grounded on countering modernity and searching for a politics of cultural transformation. The narrative of his personal experience of walking through the city streets of Cuzco, Peru, with which *América profunda* opens, is paralleled in *El pensamiento* by an ethnographic interview that Kusch and his assistants conducted with a father and son in the Bolivian countryside. The conversation revolves around the need for an electric water pump, suggested by the ethnographers as a means of improving productivity, but which arouses the silent opposition of the father and the more evasively expressed opposition of his son. This conversation becomes Kusch's paradigmatic example of the arguments against "progress" and "modernity as (Western) technology" in his later books. In *El pensamiento*, however, Kusch uses the interview to ask what it means to practice a philosophy of life in America, contrasting, as it were, his own philosophical reflections with the practical effects of the Amerindian father's silent opposition to the electric pump. How should that silence and opposition to modernization be read? What does it mean in the context of "thinking in America" or "thinking from America" (which, of course, is radically different from asking whether there is "an American way of thinking," a "Latin American thought," or, even worse, what "an American way of thinking" might be or look like)?

This is the moment in which Kusch's concern with the ideology of modernization and development, which were invading Latin America at the time and have created the conditions for the emergence of "dependency theory" and "internal colonialism," departs from his early preoccupation and opens up new perspectives toward understanding epistemological subalternity and contributes, without naming it such, to the decolonization of knowledge. Thus, we can explain Kusch's relevance for activists and intellectuals concerned with agricultural production in the Andes (Grillo 1993), his affinities with those who speak about "decolonization of the mind" (Thiong'o 1981) and with those who are working on the strategies of modernity in the construction of dominating knowledge and epistemology (Apffel-Marglin and Marglin 1990).

El pensamiento indígena y popular en América begins by questioning the practice of philosophy in America and the logic of displaced discursive practices. The suspicion that philosophical practices could not be both articulated in universal terms and locally instantiated (i.e., in a given historical, sociological, or personal dimension), which had been planted in *América profunda* and flowered in *El pensamiento*, is developed in *Esbozo de una antropología filosófica* (1978). Kusch argues that philosophy is not something one could practice in Greece or Germany and then export or apply to different parts of the world, including colonized areas like Asia, Africa, or America. Heidegger's *dasein* ("to be there"), for example, was not a technical term but a commonplace of popular German. By analyzing Heidegger's project etymologically, Kusch connects it with the decay of the German middle class during the early twentieth century. Thus, according to this argument, the circumstances under which "being" found itself in a situation of decay paralleled those under which bourgeois "feeling" arose in response to the crisis of the individual and as an attempt to resolve it. Assuming that Heidegger's philosophical project was grounded on a social crisis that could be particularly "felt" in Germany (and perhaps in other parts of Europe), Kusch concludes that American philosophical practices and projects would of necessity be different, since the American historical situation, sociological problems, and configurations of human sensibility were not those of Germany (or Europe) from *where* Heidegger was thinking (cf. Cornel West on the "American" evasion of philosophy in chapter 1 of this book).

Kusch addresses this issue more explicitly in the introduction to the third edition of *El pensamiento* (1977). If, as he argues, philosophy as practiced in Greece or Germany could not be exported or applied to other parts of the world, then the issue of "universals" should be examined from a different angle. For Kusch, it is in the self-awareness of certain living organisms (which at some point in the history of the West became self-conceived as "human beings") that the principle of minimal rationality (which, of course, he doesn't label as such, although it is implicit in what he calls "popular thought") is grounded and poses a challenge to the conversion of differences into values. The principle of minimal rationality, according to Kusch, is what allowed "universals" to be simultaneously conceived and repeatedly constituted in different regions and to challenge the conversion of differences into values and power by assigning universality to one region. That is, whatever was considered universal was conceived as such only from the privileged perspective of one (self-privileged) region.

Kusch's development of these ideas entails a departure from Heidegger's *dasein* or, in Kusch's terms, "the circumstances in which *dasein* is located," the place, in other words, of dwelling, thinking, and saying. In creating a parallel between Heidegger's conditions for thinking to his own place of thinking and saying, Kusch reads Heidegger's response to the crisis of a

German middle class in the process of decay. (To anticipate and counter a likely fervent reaction among Heideggerians to Kusch's or my own simplification here, I would urge us all to keep in mind that Kusch was concerned with theorizing the place of thinking and of saying, not with Heidegger's thought or work per se.) Kusch's explicit focus on the Argentinian middle class mirrors Heidegger's implicit one on the German (a focus made more evident by Victor Farías' *Heidegger et le nazisme* [see Farías 1987; Lacoue-Labarthe 1990]). The point in Kusch's reading of Heidegger's *dasein* is to put in relief the embodiment of a conceptual apparatus that looks disembodied and universal.

Heidegger's 1927 *Being and Time* is, in Kusch's view, a formidable effort to rethink centuries of Western philosophy from the perspective of the feelings engendered by "being there," that is, the place Heidegger was from (including his social class, ethnic group, education, etc.) and the place where he was then (as a philosopher in Germany between the wars, observing the rise of totalitarian regimes in Europe, and using vocabulary and expressions from the Black Forest region). Kusch's notion of cultural phagocytosis similarly emerged from his own awareness of past and present locations: as a philosopher, member of the Argentinian middle class, of German ancestry, in constant dialogue with Andean intellectuals of both the university and the indigenous communities (e.g., *yatiris*), as well as with the Andean people. These circumstances clearly informed Kusch's prefaces to the first (1970) and third (1977) editions of *El pensamiento*. His allusions in the 1977 preface to such events as the social movements sweeping Córdoba in May 1969, the killing of the leader of the General Confederation of Workers the following July, and the 1973 return of Juan Domingo Perón to the Pink House, connect the third edition to the first, where Kusch had laid the foundation for his theory of cultural phagocytosis. The search for "indigenous thought," says Kusch, reflects not a desire to see it excavated scientifically, but "the need to rescue a thinking style" native to ancient America (the Andes and Mesoamerica) and still practiced in rural areas as well as on the periphery of some urban communities (e.g., in Bolivia and on the outskirts of Buenos Aires, where thousands of people from Bolivia and northern Argentina had emigrated, attracted by the city's industrial modernization).

In other words, Kusch sees a need to reinscribe ancient/traditional Andean thought in the present as a cultural and political intervention and contribution to Argentina's social transformation. Finding such roots (or such ruins) would be equivalent to Heidegger's identification of *dasein* as a means by which to articulate the tensions in popular German—not in the technical vocabulary of philosophy, but in the linguistic "place of living"—as well as an equivalent to Heidegger's digging in the roots of Greek and Latin words to elaborate his own thinking. And so it was for Kusch, with one exception: since he sought his roots in popular Aymara and Quechua, what was at stake for him was not the dialectic between "high" and "low" (German), but rather the space in between the "major" colonizing languages and the "major" languages of the colonized people.

In *El pensamiento* (1970), Kusch compares Heidegger's *dasein* with the Aymara term *cancaña*, whose meaning could be rendered as "being as essence in process," and with *utcatha* (or *utatha*), which means "to be" in the sense of "to be here" (like the Spanish *estar*) or, perhaps better, "to be at home" (*uta*, home). These Aymara words are reminders of Hegel's (1955, 1:152) dictum, "Philosophy is being at home with the self, just like the homeliness of the Greek; it is man's being at home in his mind, at home with himself." They also reflect Heidegger's correlation between "dwelling" and "thinking." How can we account for these similarities if not in something similar to what Charles Taylor named "minimal rationalities," on the one hand, and something similar to what Foucault named "power and knowledge," on the other? Nevertheless, Kusch sees enormous differences between Hegel/Heidegger's metaphorical descriptions of thinking in terms of "being at home" or "dwelling" and similar concepts in Aymara—differences that Kusch attributes to "power and knowledge": the construction of knowledge by capitalist institutions under colonial conditions, two sides of the same coin. He relates the similarities, however, to the foundations of minimal rationality: the self-awareness of self-conscious beings who could understand and describe themselves in the process of understanding both the sky as a dome and their own ability to think of the sky as a dome (fig. 4; see also chapter 6). Furthermore, *utcatha* is related to *utcaña*, which means "seat of a chair" but also "mother," in the sense of "the womb from where women inseminate." Thus *utcatha*'s meaning of "to be here" has the complementary senses of a seat (on a chair), of shelter (in a house), and of germination (in a womb); hence knowledge and understanding are related to place and body (not to the mind). *Dasein* and *utcatha* become, in Kusch's argument, the reference points for two "thinking styles," both of which he is able to understand by working from the fragments of European civilization (in Argentina and the Andes) and from the ruins of Andean civilizations (the Quechua and Aymara languages).

While "America" as an imaginary construction is Kusch's main concern in *América profunda*, his focus shifts to the locus of enunciation and the question of philosophical practices at the margin(s) of Western civilization in *El pensamiento*. The risk Kusch took (and the price he paid in the marginalization of his own work) was to practice philosophy on and at the margins of philosophy as a discipline, thereby enacting its displacement from within. Kusch also had to confront a different problem, namely, how to get philosophically beyond the legacy of Greek philosophy, as constructed and practiced from the European Renaissance to contemporary Continental philosophy, and how to recognize philosophical thinking as such "beyond" that traditional frame. How was he to recognize, and believe in, the counterpart of the anonymous (at least in the recognized history of Western philosophy) Andean *yatiri*? How was he to extend the principle of minimal rationality to the point where intellectual success and influence became part of an economic and social structure that would rise above social control and domination, even when the successful and influential intellectual might not be directly responsible for the structure of domination?

In other words, how was Kusch to legitimize Andean "cosmology" as philosophy not only as a subject to study but also (like the history of philosophy itself) as a tradition from where to think? After all, should "philosophy" in America be constructed as a discipline and developed from the fragments of the European institutionalization but not from the ruins of ancient Andean and Mesoamerican civilizations as well? By bringing the Amerindian philosophical legacy to bear on the context of popular culture in Latin America, Kusch contributes to the historical construction of America (i.e., to the reinscription of the suppressed in the present), while at the same time he carves a locus of enunciation (i.e., a reallocation of colonialism's allocated cultures grounded on the movable grounds of border gnosis). That is, Kusch contributes to the displacement of a unified image of America, whether as an extension of Europe or as its opposite, as both an imaginary construction and locus of enunciation, by foregrounding the marginal survival of European fragments and Amerindian ruins. This double marginality of the Latin American intellectual is one of two fundamental lessons we can learn from Kusch, the other being how to transform losses into gains and to capitalize on our double marginality by making it a place from where to think and speak, a place where life depends on a continual cultural phagocytosis on a border gnosis evading, constantly, the pure reason of modernity. Beyond that place of double marginality, the voices of mutual "others" (Europe *or* Andean) can be heard as other voices (Europeans *and* Andeans; Kusch, Heidegger, and the Bolivian *yatiri*).

What is then at stake in Kusch's contribution? First, and beyond questionable dichotomies that could be reformulated today, is the fact that the "beginning" of "thinking" cannot be located in Greece and that, therefore, what is ultimately relevant is "thinking," not "philosophy." Second, the relationship between knowledge and interest can be located in what calls for thinking, and what calls for thinking cannot be detached from the needs thinking is calling for, in Greek, Aymara, Chinese, or Arabic. Third, "thinking" within the epistemological coloniality of power cannot be but border thinking, whether that border thinking is practiced by an Amerindian or a Creole from German descent. The Zapatistas, once again, taught us that translating European cosmologies, which Rama claims cannot be abandoned in America, into Amerindian cosmologies and vice versa has an epistemological potential similar to the one emerging out of the Afro-American intellectual production both in Anglo-America (e.g., Du Bois's "double conscious-ness") and the Caribbean (Glissant's "Creolité"). This is just to respond to what Rama sees as the alternatives to a Creole, European-bound, mentality. I return later to the Latino/as mind, which is still another story evolving in the Americas and transforming the Creole territorial idea and ideology of "Latin America."

Transculturation: Thinking About the Borders and Creolization

We are now in a position to go back to Rama's observation about the Afro-(Latin)-American possibilities of autonomous development "within the American continent." Rama was certainly thinking about "Latin America," otherwise, he would not have overlooked Anglo-America and the Carib-bean. Let's then begin by the distinction, equivalent to the one I introduced in the preceding section. Haitian poet and essayist, René Depestre, living in Cuba, published in 1969 a very important article on the problem of identity of the "Negro Man" in Caribbean literatures. Although he overlooked the gender question, contrary to Rama he asserted a strong presence of Afro-Caribbean literature and culture, particularly in the twentieth century. But, of course, Depestre was thinking in the French, English, and Spanish Carib-bean, while Rama was mainly thinking about Spanish American continental countries, plus Brazil. Depestre underlined the distinction between "Negri-tude" and "Negrism" and emphasized their differences. "Negrism," in Carib-bean letters, has been mainly an intellectual and literary movement by white men in support of the Afro component in Caribbean history. "Negritude" instead is a new consciousness among black people about the historical con-ditions of black people.

Depestre's clarification could be complemented, historically, with Frantz Fanon's brilliant and persuasive argument on the differences between West Indians and Africans. But, first, notice the interesting game of confronted mirrors in the geographical identification: Depestre talks, in Spanish, about the "Antillas" (French "Antilles"), and he includes French-, Spanish-, and English-speaking islands, in a way synonymous with "Insular Caribbean" (i.e., excluding continental Caribbean such as Florida, east of the northeast of Brazil, north of Venezuela, northeast of Colombia, the Atlantic coast of Central America). In a nutshell: the insular area where Spanish, French, Dutch, and English colonialism shaped the geopolitical, geohistorical, and epistemological configuration. The English translation of Fanon's analysis of the black Caribbean and Africans reads as a paradox: "West Indians and Africans." To name the black Caribbean "West Indians" is the sign of a gener-alized confusion that has been also expressed by Angel Rama in the article

I have been using as guide for the second part of this chapter. Rama stated, without any remorse or contrition, that:

> El grito de Frantz Fanon, "Abandonemos Europe," no es nada más que una frase. Imposible abandonar lo que ya está integrado, como estructura mental y jerarquía de valor, a la personalidad creadora. *Este martinicano carece de conciencia americana y afirma una improbada deserción, porque en definitiva, cuenta con el eventual respaldo de una tradición cultural no europea, que el asume racialmente: la africana negra. Juega la carta de la raza que le han impuesto los blancos europeos—la negritud—porque mejor o peor, ella comporta una tradición cultural autonoma.* (Rama [1965] 1993, 61)

> Frantz Fanon's cry, "Let's abandon Europe," is nothing but a sentence. It is impossible to abandon what is already ingrained in the creative personality of the Americas, in its mental structure and hierarchy of value. *This Martinican completely lacks American consciousness at the same time that he asserts a nonproved desertion because, in the last analysis, he counts on the support of a non-European cultural tradition that he assumes radically: the black African. He plays the role that has been imposed on him by white Europeans: Negritude. For better or worse, "negritude" implies an autonomous cultural tradition.*

One really doesn't know very well what to do with this observation—right in so many points, but with a tone that makes the reader think that there is something wrong with Fanon's lack of "(Latin) American consciousness." Certainly, Rama doesn't have Fanon's "black consciousness" either. What indeed Rama could have said is that Fanon doesn't have "a Latin American consciousness in the same way that a Creole Spanish speaker, working on Spanish colonial legacies and on the ideology of postindependence of Spanish speaking America, has." And that would have been all right. But the problem with Rama is that, in the article I am quoting, and it is only a sample of widely shared positions, "American consciousness" is confused with one of its historical manifestations: the "hegemonic" imaginary of the Creole intelligentsia within the subaltern location of Latin America in the order of the modern/colonial world system. The apparent oxymoron of the last sentence is necessary to capture the nonlinear complexity in the articulation of the modern/colonial world system imaginary.

But let's go back to the Martinican's analysis of the differences between West Indians and Africans. Fanon's thesis is basically the following: there was a changing mutual perception between West Indians and African blacks before 1939 and after 1939. Before 1939, blacks in Martinique did not consider themselves or act as blacks but, rather, as European:

> In every West Indian, before the war of 1939, there was not only the certainty of a superiority over the African, but the certainty of a fundamental difference.

> The African was a Negro and the West Indian a European. . . . The West Indian was not a Negro; he was a West Indian, that is to say, a quasi metropolitan. . . . The Negro, in short, was a man who inhabited Africa. (Fanon [1952] 1967, 20)

The change in attitude occurred at the confluence of two events: the return of Aimé Césaire and his celebration of "negritude" as something to be proud and not ashamed of and the fall of French colonialism in the context of World War II. Martinicans changed their attitude, and the pride imaginary of blackness replaced the previous erasure of the black West Indian in support of the European West Indian. Certainly, and as we saw in Depestre, it doesn't seem to be an "American consciousness" in Caribbean (particularly black Caribbean) intellectuals in the same way that there is a lack of "Caribbean consciousness" among Latin American (particularly Creole Latin American) intellectuals. Bilbao's original partition between "two races and two languages" in one continent seems to be breaking up with the already strong presence of the Afro-American (Caribbean and the continental United States) and the emergence of Amerindian intellectuals with a long tradition of expression through social uprising rather than in writing (I'll come back to this point in the conclusion to this chapter). What is more important, a new consciousness seems to be in the making at the intersection of European fragments in the Americas, and the displacement of Amerindian and Afro-American knowledge and cultural production that invite a view of the future at the opposite end of that anticipated by Rama: instead of being either predestined to die or to be satisfied with the insertion of the ruins of Afro-American and Amerindians into the fragments of the European mentality, border thinking is moving in a different direction: toward a new (epistemological) consciousness where their "culture" (and here "culture" excludes "knowledge") is being rearticulated as double consciousness, Creolité, or, briefly, as border thinking.

In Spanish America a true border thinking does not emerge until the work of José María Arguedas and Rigoberta Menchú (see chapter 5). The first, although Creole himself, was educated and lived among Quechua communities in Peru. Rigoberta Menchú spent twenty years of her life in a Maya-Quiché community in Guatemala. Arguedas spoke Spanish and Quechua, although Spanish was his first language. Rigoberta Menchú also spoke Spanish, but her first language is Maya-Quiché and she learned Spanish in her twenties (1984). Cuban anthropologist Fernando Ortiz (1881–1969) was a Cuban and Creole anthropologist who seriously believed in the principles of social science, although his creative bent allowed him to mix literature and social sciences in a very productive and seductive way (e.g., his *Cuban Counterpoint: Tobacco and Sugar*, [1940] 1995). In a sense, his concept of *transculturation* was and is an important step toward border thinking, although the borders that Ortiz erased exist in the object of study, not in the knowing subject. Although he indeed produced a transculturation of anthropological discourse by bringing together anthropology and literature, thereby producing anthropological knowledge in a geohistorical location that is supposed to be the location of anthropological knowledge but not of its knowing subject, he never brought transculturation to this level of self-reflection. Transculturation is out there—in the enunciated and not in the locus of enunciation. The fundamental difference between transculturation on the one hand and double consciousness, new mestiza consciousness, and Créolité on the other can be located precisely in the fact that the latter are all key words that question the universal location and the epistemological purity of the knowing subject (see chapter 7). Let me expand on this affirmation (for a more full-fledged introduction to Ortiz's *Cuban Counterpoint*, see Coronil 1995; see also pages 15 and 169).

Ortiz's concept of *transculturation* largely contributed to move the discourse on race to the discourse on culture. Mariátegui (1894–1930) had already taken an important step, in Peru, by linking the ethnoracial question to economy, as we will see later. It is very well known that *transculturation* was suggested as a better alternative to Bronislaw Malinowski's notion of *acculturation*, used by the Polish anthropologist who was educated and working in England, to account for cultural changes in areas of "cultural contact" (Malinowski 1943). While *acculturation* pointed toward cultural changes in only one direction, the *transculturation* corrective was meant to call attention to the complex and multidirectional processes in cultural transformation. Although both Malinowski and Ortiz were certainly aware of the relation between transculturation and colonialism, neither of them formulated it as a process in the imaginary of the modern world system and of modernity/coloniality, as I am trying to do in this book. Malinowski was operating within the contemporary effort to raise anthropology to a scientific level and to erase the political links between anthropology and colonialism in the nineteenth century. Ortiz was concerned with both Cuban and Caribbean history, as well as with anthropology. Malinowski assumed an epistemological position closer to Schiller's recommendation and Habermas's endorsement. Ortiz was, instead, a "Third World" anthropologist who, even when he believed in the scientific value of anthropology, maintained a visceral relation to Cuba and the Caribbean that was stronger than his intellectual relations with disciplinary norms and academic formation (Ortiz studied in France). Yet, Ortiz did not—and perhaps could not—think of cultural anthropology in terms of dominant and subaltern positions in the field of knowledge, those of doing anthropology *from* within imperial nations (like England in the 1930s) and *from* colonized countries (like Cuba in the same period, although of course, not by England). Coronil, instead, took that step and suggested that "what today is called 'cultural anthropology' may be more aptly addressed as 'transcultural anthropology' " (Coronil 1995, xlii).

"Transcultural anthropology," in other words, introduces transculturation to the locus of enunciation, border thinking in disciplinary practices, a double consciousness (so to speak), in the very heart of the discipline. That is to say, "transcultural human sciences" means to introduce border thinking to disciplinary formations instead of only having "transculturation" as a descriptive concept for the object of study. And that is precisely what I think Kusch taught us to do. More than producing a study of Aymara categories of thought, Kusch engaged himself in a thinking process from those categories, intersecting them with philosophical categories that have existed "since the time philosophy was born in Greece," as Habermas would like to say. But let's listen to Ortiz himself before pursuing the comparison with Kusch:

> I am of the opinion that the word *transculturation* better expresses the different phases of the process of transition from one culture to another because this does not consist merely in acquiring another culture, which is what the English word acculturation really implies, but the process also necessarily involves the loss or uprooting of a previous culture, which could be defined as deculturation. In addition it carries the idea of the consequent creation of new cultural phenomena, which could be called neoculturation. In the end, as the school of Malinowski's followers maintains, the result of every union of cultures is similar to that of the reproductive process between individuals: the offspring always has something of both parents but is always different from each of them. . . .
>
> The concept of transculturation is fundamental and indispensable for an understanding of the history of Cuba, and, for analogous reasons, of that of America in general. (Ortiz [1940] 1995, 102–3)

When introducing the concept of transculturation, Ortiz announces that he has a work in progress "dealing with the effect on Cuba of the transculturations of Indians, whites, Negroes, and Mongols." Clearly, Ortiz's concern is the "national" history of Cuba, which he was able to map as a complex, transcultured history instead of the homogenous imagined community. Even if colonialism could not be absent in a work such as the one carried through half a century of research, national history, rather than the location of Cuba's history in the larger picture of the modern world system, was at the center of his concern.

The advantage of the term transculturation over mestizaje is not only its power to move us away from racial consideration, but also its ability to invite a second move toward the "the social life of things." It allows for the detachment of specific cultural unities from specific communities of people, identified either in ethnic or national terms (e.g., Cubans, Indians, white, Negroes, and Mongols). Transculturation proved a useful concept to explain the long process of transculturation of tobacco, sugar, coffee, and tea, as well as the transculturation of the "blacks' drums" ("los tambores de los negros") (Ortiz [1940] 1995, 181–88). I quote in extenso two paragraphs, both crucial to understanding transculturation at large (beyond the history of Cuba) and its relevance for the understanding of the imaginary of the modern world system, modernity/coloniality, and the argument, made recently from Latin America, to think beyond Eurocentrism (Quijano 1992; Dussel 1998a), and beyond Occidentalism (Coronil 1995; Mignolo 1996e; 1997a). I have not seen these paragraphs commented on elsewhere, and even less underlined in their relevance for a critic of modernity from the perspective of coloniality. Allow me to repeat a quotation from page 15:

> Tobacco reached the Christian world along with the revolution of the Renaissance and the Reformation, when the Middle Ages were crumbling and the modern epoch, with its rationalism, was beginning. One might say that reason, starved and benumbed by theology, to revive and free itself, needed the help of some harmless stimulant that should not intoxicate it with enthusiasm and then stupefy it with illusions and bestiality, as happens with the old alcoholic drinks that lead to drunkenness. For this, to help sick reason, tobacco came from America. And with it chocolate. And from Abyssinia and Arabia, about the same time, came coffee. And tea made its appearance from the Far East.
>
> The coincidental appearance of these four exotic products in the Old World, all of them stimulants of the senses as well as of the spirit, is not without interest. It is as though they had been sent to Europe from the four corners of the earth by the devil to revive Europe when "the time came," when that continent was ready to save the spirituality of reason from burning itself out and give the senses their due once more. Europe was no longer able to satisfy its senses with spices or sugar, which, aside from being rare and, because of their costliness, the privilege of the few, exited without inspiring, strengthened without lifting the spirits. Nor were wines and liquors sufficient, either, for although they nourished daring and dreams, they were often the cause of degradation and derangement and never of thoughtfulness or good judgment. *Other spices and nectars were needed that should act as spurs of the senses and the mind. And the devil provided them, sending it for the mental jousts that initiated the modern age in Europe: the tobacco of the Antilles, the chocolate of Mexico, the coffee of Africa, and the tea of China. Nicotine, theobromine, caffeine, and theine—these four alkaloids were put at the service of humanity to make reason more alert.* (Ortiz [1940] 1995, 206–7; emphasis added)

Ortiz was mainly thinking from the experience of slavery and the African contingents in Caribbean local history. While Ortiz moved from race and culture toward the transculturation of objects and commodities, Mariátegui paid more attention to the economic arguments hidden under discourses. Let's listen to Mariátegui on the Indian question, formulated in economic rather than in racial terms (even when most of the time Mariátegui couldn't detach himself from the racial vocabulary of the late nineteenth century).

> The supposition that the Indian question is an ethnic problem is nourished by the oldest bag of tricks of imperialist ideas. The notion of inferior races helped the white West in its process of conquest and expansion. To believe that Indian emancipation will emerge from an active racial mixture is gullible and an antisociological idea that can only be sustained by a simple-minded importer of merino sheep. (Mariátegui [1924] 1991, 23; my translation)

Transculturation is precisely an attempt to respond to the need of border thinking, rather than the need to describe hybridity as a particularity of the object, thus maintaining the distinction between a "pure" knowing subject and a "homogeneous" epistemology that studies and celebrates the hybridity of the world. Furthermore, if transculturation was concocted by Ortiz in between his role as an anthropologist from the margins (like Darcy Ribeiro) and his national and populist bent, it is nonetheless crucial to keep in mind that Ortiz's transculturation is traversed by the colonial difference, even though it is not theorized as such by Ortiz himself. To recognize that the world is hybrid (Garcia-Canclini [1989] 1995), particularly as a postnational move showing the ideological underpinning of the homogeneity claimed and proclaimed by official discourse of nation building, changes the content of the conversation, not its terms. In order to change the terms of the conversation, it is necessary to move toward a border epistemology that is, at the same time, a "thinking in languages" (as Khatibi insisted) or a "bilanguaging love," as I argue in chapter 6.

CONCLUDING REMARKS

In this chapter I have tried to outline a map of the border of the empires whose tensions contributed to the fabrication of a homogeneous notion of Latin America in the colonial horizon of modernity. Similar to the situations in France and the United States today of massive migration, the homogeneity of the nation or of the subcontinent was necessary. These conflicting homogeneous entities (Latin America, France, the United States, etc.) as we know them today are part of the imaginary of the modern/colonial world system. They reveal and they occlude. They are also the grounding of a system of geopolitical values, of racial configurations, and of hierarchical structures of meaning and knowledge. To think "Latin America" otherwise, in its heterogeneity rather than in its homogeneity, in the local histories of changing global designs is not to question a particular form of identification (e.g., that of "Latin America") but all national/colonial forms of identification in the modern/colonial world system. These are precisely the forms of identification that contribute to the reproduction of the imaginary of the modern/colonial world system and the coloniality of power and knowledge implicit in the geopolitical articulation of the world.

In the next chapter I explore similar issues but focus on the structure of knowledge in relation to the geopolitical world order. What are the relations, in other words, between geohistorical locations and the production of knowledge? This will be the overarching question for the next chapter.

CHAPTER 4

Are Subaltern Studies Postmodern or Postcolonial? The Politics and Sensibilities of Geohistorical Locations

The five volumes of Subaltern Studies represent a formidable achievement in historical scholarship. They are an invitation to think anew the relation between history and anthropology *from a point of view that displaces the central position of the European anthropologist or historian as the subject of discourse and Indian society as its object. This does not mean a rejection of Western categories but signals the beginning of a new and autonomous relation to them.* As Gayatri Spivak has often pointed out, to deny that we write as people whose consciousness has been formed as colonial subjects is to deny our history. *However, the consciousness of ourselves as colonial subjects is itself modified by our own experience and by the relation we establish to our intellectual traditions.*
    (Das 1989; 310; emphasis added)

La restauración del orden cósmico—que la idea de un tiempo histórico lineal y progresivo rehusa comprender, a no ser como un "volver atrás la rueda de la historia"—puede ser aprehendida también con el concepto *nayrapacha*: pasado, pero no cualquier visión de pasado; más bien, "pasado-como-futuro," es decir, como una renovación del tiempo-espacio. Un pasado capaz de renovar el futuro, de revertir la situación vivida. No es esta la aspiración compartida actualmente por muchos movimientos indígenas de todas las latitudes que postulan la plena vigencia de la cultura de sus ancestros en el mundo contemporáneo? . . . Al confrontar la catástrofe del nazismo, Walter Benjamin escribió: "ni los muertos estarán a salvo del enemigo si este triunfa" (1969). *Esta visión de la historia, que escondida pervive en los resquicios del mundo occidental,* podría también iluminar la comprensión del *pacha*, y cruzar así, la brecha de lenguajes que continúa entrabando la acción histórica, pero también la interpretación de la rebeldía indígena, pasada o contemporánea.[1]
    (Rivera Cusicanqui 1993; emphasis added)

---

[1] The restoration of the cosmic order (that is rejected from the perspective of a progressive conception of historical time, except when it is taken as a "rotation backward of the wheel of

TRAVELING THEORIES, BUSINESS-CLASS INTELLECTUALS
WORKING IN THE THIRD WORLD, AND THE
IMPORTATION/EXPORTATION OF THEORIES AND KNOWLEDGE

Theories travel, I heard, and when they get places, they are transformed, transcultured. But what happens when theories travel through the colonial difference? How do they get transcultured? I also heard that when theories get to places where colonial legacies are still in the memories of scholars and intellectuals, traveling theories may be perceived as new forms of colonization, rather than as new tools to enlighten the intelligence of the theories' host or to reveal a reality that could not have been perceived without the theory's travel, or inviting a theory to stay just as it was going by. I have been persuaded by both arguments, especially when I heard them from colleagues and friends whose opinion I respect. For instance, I have heard in Argentina that cultural and postcolonial studies or theories are an exportation of North American intelligentsia, even though it has been said that postcolonial theories are an invention of Third World intellectuals in the U.S. academy (Dirlik 1994). However, I heard what I heard in Argentina from the same people (sometimes even the same person) who were, fifteen years ago, championing the importation of French theoreticians, British cultural studies, or Frankfurt critical theory, and are still holding such positions today. So, there is something beyond the fact that theories travel and are transcultured, and that there are people in the places where theories are received who suspect the fact that theories travel. The questions then shall be, Where are theories produced? Where do they come from? From the perspective of those hosts of traveling theories? What function or role did theory X play in the place where it emerged and what is the function or role that such a theory played in the place where it traveled or has been exported? The issue is, briefly, What is the ratio between geohistorical location and knowledge production? What are their local histories? And the question is being asked, here, in the geohistorical frame of modernity/coloniality, or of the site of epistemology in the modern world system, which is the same thing. But the question sets the stage, also, for an answer from a border

---

history") could be understood in the concept of *nayrapacha*. *Nayrapacha* means past, but not any vision of the past. It means specifically "past-as-future," that is to say, as a renovation of time-space. A particular past that could change or renew the future could reverse the lived situation. Isn't this conception and aspiration currently shared by many indigenous social movements everywhere who are theorizing the relevance of their ancestors' culture for and in the modern world? . . . Walter Benjamin, confronting the catastrophic reality of Nazism wrote, "not even the dead will be protected from the enemy if the enemy succeeds." *This conception of history, a history that is hidden but that survives in the fissures of the Western world*, could also illuminate the understanding of *pacha*. By so doing it would then be possible to cross the language gap that continues muddling historical action and the interpretation of indigenous rebellions, in the past as well as in the present.

perspective. As such, the answer could be that theories do indeed travel and get transcultured. They become objects. But can "thinking" travel? Border "thinking" (and not theory) is the issue; "thinking" from a border perspective becomes, then, the central issue—whether theories travel or not (on "traveling theories," see Coronil 1995, xxxvi ff., and his elaboration after Said 1983, 223–24, and Clifford 1989, 177–88).

Theories travel, certainly, and from all directions: from the left, from the right, and from the center. How are they rehearsed when they travel through the colonial difference? Are they just being rehearsed in a new scenario or do they face their limits in that new scenario? The answer in this book is a yes to the second possibility once the point of arrival is tainted by the colonial difference. It is also from the colonial difference, I have been and will continue to argue, that epistemologies from the limits of the colonial difference are emerging. I made this argument at the end of chapter 1, putting Khatibi and Derrida in dialogue. I add here a new example, *La crise des intellectuels arabes*, by Larui (1974). Larui hosted several traveling theories, across the Mediterranean. Some were liberals and were traveling through time, from the European Enlightenment. Others were Marxists and were traveling from the past and from the present. And others were not traveling—they were the theories that stayed put and were ingrained not in a particular geographic territory but in the Arabic language. The traveling theories were traveling from North to South. The languages in which they dressed and traveled were the colonial languages, chiefly French and German. When this happens there are several possibilities. One is to force the adaptation of the arriving theory, from the right or from the left, and propose civilization, modernization, and development or to propose resistance, revolution, and radical social transformation. And still another, provoked by the discomfort of the theories that stayed put and dressed in Arabic, is to close the doors and the eyes and to propose a defense of the dwelling place facing the "danger" brought by travelers. And still another is to think, critically, at the intersection of the dwelling place and the new travelers, from the right and from the left, and to look at all of them critically. That is, to think from the borders implies producing an epistemology that, as one of Larui's (1974) enthusiastic commentators put it (Djaït [1980] 1990, 195–205), neither reproduces the limits of Marxism beyond the colonial difference, nor reproduces the limits of an Arabic defense of tradition, a tradition that was created, precisely, by the colonial difference. The alternative is a double critique, to the travelers and to the homeowners: to travelers and homeowners in hegemonic positions from the perspective of travelers and homeowners in subaltern positions. That is, basically, the historical conditions of border thinking or border epismologies, emerging from a critical perspective on the coloniality of power and the colonial difference.

A TRIP TO THE UNDERGROUND

But sometimes theories do not travel; they stay put. And when this happens, the colonial difference makes them invisible to the mainstream and universal scope of theories than can travel and have passports to cross the colonial difference. There are always reasons to explain why things are the way they are and not different. I will not go into that terrain here, but will instead talk around theories, related to subalternism, that did not travel, or at least did not travel so much or that far. One of Enrique Dussel's many publications includes a small book with two articles, one by Dussel himself, which is the written version of a lecture delivered by him in 1971. Dussel's lecture was titled "Para una fundamentación filosófica de la liberación Latinoamericana"(For a philosophic argumentation of Latin/American liberation) and was delivered at the Universidad de Salvador, a Catholic university in Buenos Aires. The other contribution was by Argentinian philosopher Daniel Guillot on the evolution of Emmanuel Levinas's thinking. The book was published in 1975 by Editorial BONUM, an obscure publishing house in Buenos Aires. In 1994, Siglo Veintiuno Editores, one of the two major publishing houses in the Spanish-speaking world, with branches in Spain, Buenos Aires, Colombia, and elsewhere, published *Debate en torno a la ética del discurso de Apel. Diálogo filosófico Norte-Sur desde América Latina.* Enrique Dussel was the editor of the book and contributed with a fundamental article on "La razón del otro: la 'interpelación' como acto-de-habla" (The reason of the Other: "Interpellation" as speech act). This publishing house was also of a clearly leftist bent. The topics and concerns were the same we find in his lecture of 1971, published in 1975, although there were some important changes.

In 1971 Dussel, starting and departing from Levinas, conceived totality as composed by "the same" and "the other." Describing the totality formed by "the same" and "the other," Dussel called it "the Same." And we'll see soon why. Outside totality was the domain of "the other." The difference in Spanish was rendered between *lo otro*, which is the complementary class of "the same" and *el otro* relegated to the domain exterior to the system. I am tempted to translate this view today as a "interior" and "exterior" subalternities. Socially and ontologically, the exteriority is the domain of the homeless, unemployed, illegal aliens cast out from education, from the economy, and the laws that regulate the system. Metaphysically, "the other" is—from the perspective of the totality and the "same"—the unthinkable that Dussel urges us to think. "Philosophy in Latin America, and this is a first conclusion, should begin by making a critique of Totality as totality" (1975, 21). This conception is useful in the sense that the difference between interior and exterior subalternities is framed in legal and economic terms. Thus, it is indeed a class difference. However, the difference is not justified in terms of class but in terms of ethnicity, gender, sexuality, and sometimes nationality (i.e., if the nationality in question happens to be "against" democratic and Western nationalistic ideals). Nobody is cast out because he or she is poor. He or she becomes poor because he or she has been cast out. On the other hand, this difference allows us to understand that gender, ethnic, and sexual differences could be absorbed by the system and placed in the sphere of interior subalternity. This is visible today in the United States as far as Afro-Americans, women, Hispanics, and queers (although with sensible differences between these groups) are becoming accepted within the system as *lo otro*, complementary of the totality controlled by "the same."

Beyond the fact that Dussel used some questionable metaphors based on the structure of the Christian family to make his argument, he also underlined very important historical dimensions:

1. A critique of modern epistemology or modern thinking (*el pensar moderno*);

2. The coloniality of power introduced by Christianity in the "discovery" of America and in what Dussel (1996; 1998a) most recently identified as the modern world system. Dussel placed what is known today as Latin America in the exteriority of "the other" upon which the modern world system constituted itself;

3. Claims that looking at Latin America as "the other" explain the successive constructions of exteriorities in the colonial histories of the modern world system and, consequently, the similarity (beyond obvious differences in their local histories) among regions of the "Third World" (e.g., the Arabic world, black Africa, India, Southeast Asia, and China);

4. Consequently, and beyond the details of the geopolitical relations and the fact that these observations were made during the crucial years of the cold war, the geopolitical conclusions were that Europe, the United States, and the Soviet Union constitute "the geopolitical same" while the rest constitute "the geopolitical other." At this point the location of Latin America as "the other" is ambiguous. Dussel's argument tries to show the uniqueness of Latin America as the only geopolitical and subaltern unit—with the exception of Cuba—that cannot entertain a dialogue with Europe, the United States, and the Soviet Union at the same time, while all the other geopolitical units can, but this line of argumentation is unconvincing. However, I would like to retain from this issue Dussel's confrontation with Marxism in the modern world system as well as in Latin America.

His conceptualization of Totality in historical and socioeconomic and legal terms led Dussel, a serious scholar of Marx (Dussel 1985; 1988; 1990) to become a critic of Marx and of Marxism in Latin America. Marx's unquestionable contribution to the analysis of the functioning of capitalist economy should not be confused with Marx's sightless when it came to the location of "the other" (*el otro*) and the exteriority of the system. That is, Marx, according to Dussel, only thinks in terms of totality ("the same" and "the other," which is the working class) but is less aware of alterity, the exteriority of the system. Hence, Marx's thinking on these issues is located within modern epistemology and ontology. In his critical analysis about modern epistemology (*el pensar moderno*), that term to which he attributed the conceptualization of totality I described earlier, Dussel summarizes ideas well known today, although less familiar in 1971. Modern thought since Descartes, Dussel argues, presupposed an ontology of totality that, for reasons that are quite simple, had to include a metaphysic of alterity as negativity. The reason, he argues, can be found in the ontological break of modern thought with its Greek legacies. The modern concept of being is secular and is therefore built upon a negation of the other, which is identified with the God of Christian totality. The same, now, is the *ego*, an *ego* without God. Totality, according to Dussel, is no longer a *fysis* (in the sense of ancient Greek philosophy) but *ego*; there is no longer a physic but an *egotic* totality. To this egotic foundation of totality corresponds the Kantian *Ich denke* and Marx's *Ich arbeite*. Hegel, for whom Knowledge and Totality are the Absolute, installed himself, according to Dussel, at the crux of modern thought. Neither Nietzsche nor Marx could escape from the modern paradigm. Nietzsche's mystical experience, in the Alps, where he discovered that "All is one," trapped him in the idea of an eternal return to "the Same," a Totality moved by "a will to power," to which Dussel opposes the "dominated will." He concludes by saying that:

> A esta modernidad pertenece tanto el capitalismo liberal, y por lo tanto tambien el dependiente latinoamericano, como tambien el marxismo ortodoxo. Esto me parece fundamental en este momento presente de América Latina. Puedo decir que no son *radicalmente* opuestos siquiera, sino que son ontológicamente "lo Mismo." Esto, evidentemente, no lo aceptarían con ninguna facilidad muchos marxistas del tipo althuseriano, por ejemplo. (Dussel 1975, 21)

> To this modernity belongs both liberal capitalism, and consequently Latin American dependent capitalism, as well as orthodox Marxism. This premise is basic for me, at this particular junction of Latin American history. I can say that liberal capitalism and Marxism are not *radically* opposed but that they are indeed ontologically "the Same." This conclusion may not be easily accepted, I believe, by Althusserian-Marxists.

Dussel's view of the inadequacy of Marxism for Latin America is grounded in his analysis of modern thought and the place of Marxism in this paradigm—

mainly, in the fact that modern thought was oblivious of coloniality. "Latin America" in this case could be read as the unthinkable of modernity, or as only thinkable within modernity, but not as coloniality. In his own words,

> El marxismo es incompatible ontológicamente no sólo con la tradición Latino-americana sino con la meta-física de la Alteridad. No es puramente una inter-pretación económico socio-política, es tambien una ontología, y, como tal, es intrinsicamente incompatible con una metafísica de la Alteridad. No es incom-patible, en cambio, lo que podría llamarse *socialismo*; esto ya es otra cuestión. (Dussel 1975, 41)

> Marxism is ontologically incompatible not only with the Latin American tradi-tion but also with the metaphysic of alterity. Marxism is not only an economic and sociopolitic interpretation but, as such, is intrinsically incompatible with a metaphysic of Alterity. It is not incompatible, on the contrary, with something that could be called *socialism*. This is a different story.

Here, Dussel puts his finger on an issue and a possible debate within the left itself. First of all, Dussel's view of Marxism as ingrained in "modern think-ing" (*el pensar moderno*) and not alien to it, has been restated by others more recently (Immanuel Wallerstein recently did so in his discussions of the geoculture of the modern world system [1991a, 84–97]). But that is not all and perhaps not the most interesting aspect of Dussel's position. Of more interest for the argument of this chapter is the fact that it coincides with the positions defended by Aymara intellectual and activist Fausto Reinaga. What are the grounds from which Dussel is defending this argument? My sense is that it has to do with his view of the geopolitics of Christianity. Let me explain.

First, he offers an argument claiming a "philosophy of liberation" as a proposal from Latin America for Latin America. This simplistic formulation may not have as many adherents these days as it may have had in the 1970s. However, I think that the argument deserves to be revisited precisely in the context of Dussel's geopolitics of Christianity and in my own thinking of the articulation between local histories, colonial difference(s), and global designs. I can imagine that people of leftist persuasion would agree that global designs implemented by Washington or, in previous years, Moscow, were indeed new forms of coloniality of power and should not be tolerated from the perspective of local histories. We see later in this chapter a position close to this formulation defended by Nelly Richard, in Chile. On the other hand, there is an argument that, at another level, works in a different direc-tion: when global designs are from the intellectual Western avant-garde and not from "foreign" states, the situation changes. I have already given an example in the introduction to this book and the introduction to this chap-ter, invoking the reactions to the importation/exportation of cultural studies and postcolonial talk in and from Latin America. From a cosmopolitan perspective (and, of course, from the perspective of global designs), arguments against the exportation/importation of cultural studies or postcolonial discussions to Latin America are seen as risking essentialism, defending localism and authenticity, and so on. From a regional perspective, the situation would look different: a form of colonization from a "foreign" state or from a "foreign" cosmopolitan intellectual project.

But this is not exactly what Dussel had in mind when he proposed liberation philosophy as a local history project from the memory of that local history. Dussel compared Herbert Marcuse's project in the United States with philosophy of liberation in Latin American. He observed that the needs of a prosperous society and the model for a way out of it would be different from the needs in a pauperized society and the model for a way out of it. He also insisted on the differences between liberation philosophy in Europe or in the United States and in Latin America, the laboring class in the "center" and in the "periphery," the hourly salary of a poor German and a poor Bolivian ([1973] 1976, 164–70). From a planetary geopolitical perspective, Dussel perceived the United States, Europe, and the Soviet Union as the only three developed and industrialized countries in 1971. Latin America, the Islamic world, black Africa, Southeast Asia, India, and China were considered subdeveloped areas. Things have changed by now, and in chapter 7 I discuss the new world order proposed by Samuel Huntington (1996). However, the particularity of Latin America in this geopolitical order remains. Latin America, according to Dussel, is the only post-Christian geopolitical unit among the underdeveloped countries. Consequently, the future of Latin America cannot be projected without taking into serious consideration the legacy of a "colonial Christianity" (1973, 143). This is one of the reasons—and a reason Dussel explores in great detail—why Marxism doesn't fit in Latin America. The other is the Amerindian legacy. Although Dussel did not explore the history of Amerindian culture in the same detail he explored the history of Christianity in this period, Amerindian and Afro slavery were always mentioned as *el otro*, or the exterior subaltern in the process of colonization. In volume 2 of *Caminos de la liberación Latinoamericana* Dussel describes, in a paragraph, the overall historical frame of his theoretical investigation:

> The European expansion of the sixteenth century was not a harmless geopolitical fact but, rather, essentially an ethical fact for the Christian world, because there was to be a profound injustice within that expansion. When gold and silver were extracted from America and sent to Europe in quantities five times as great as the gold and ten times as great as the silver that existed in Europe, inflation ran rampant. Within the century many people became poor because ten pieces of silver came to be worth only one. The Arabs, without losing a thing

in that century, became poor because the quantity of gold and silver arriving in the Mediterranean basin was so great and its value fell so low. Their fall became evident at the battle of Lepanto, which marked the beginning of the disappearance of the Turks, not because they were less valiant but because inflation was wiping them out. To afford a warship or to pay an army, they had to pay double or more. But the Turks no longer had gold or silver, whereas the Spaniards and, little by little, the Genoese and Venetians were able to pay hard cash. They conquered the Atlantic, which now became the new center. In the North Atlantic are Russia, the United States, and Europe. Japan and Canada ought to be added also. This is the center, and all the rest is periphery. (Dussel [1973] 1976, 8)

Now, Dussel's view of the conquest and of *el pensar moderno* resonates, although indirectly, in Aymara intellectual and activist Fausto Reinaga. In 1970 he was stating blatantly, in the first sentence of his book *La revolución india* (1969), "I am neither a writer nor a 'mestizo' man of letters. I am an Indian. An Indian who thinks, produces ideas, that engender ideas." He began the introduction to his book by reinscribing the history of the modern/colonial world system from an Amerindian perspective. In *América India y Occidente* (Amerindian America and the West, 1974), he explains from his own perspective the limitations and the oppression enacted by *el pensar moderno*, to use Dussel's terminology. It would be difficult to render in a few lines a book that Reinaga himself describes by writing, rightly so, that "the thoughts in this book are singular. They do not have species, genre, or bibliographic genealogy in Western culture" (1974, 11). And it would be difficult to provide the reader with a view of Reinaga's thoughts beyond the political violence that nourished it, and which was provoked by the anguish and dangers of his own life. From his position, and in this book, he traced an intellectual and political map that echoes, once again, and from the perspective of an Amerindian intellectual instead of a philosopher of liberation, the memory and current situation of Amerindians in Latin America. The radicalism of his position requires more than a simple description. However, what is important to underline for my argument is the rereading of the Western history of ideas from an Amerindian perspective and the emergence, from this reading, of a space that had not and could not have been thought from that perspective. Reinaga fills the "unthinkable" of Amerindian history with the utopian reality of a society modeled upon Amerindian society. For Dussel, the "unthinkable" becomes the exterior other (*el otro*) rather than *lo otro* interior to the system. Radical subalternity is then the space of the "unthinkable" from the perspective of the modern/colonial world system and its own imaginary, even when that imaginary develops itself as a critique of domination (as in the case of Marx and Marxism in Latin America, which both Dussel and Reinaga discuss).

I close this section by bringing in Marxist perspectives in Latin America and confronting them with the colonial difference, an issue that was not an issue from the Marxist perspective until recently when intellectuals like Rivera Cusicanqui and, before her, Anibal Quijano, Roldolfo Stavenhaguen, and Pablo Gonzálo Casanova raised the issue in terms of internal colonialism and the coloniality of power. However, the colonial difference was not yet perceived by Marxist critical intellectuals like José Aricó and Juan Carlos Portantiero in their analyses of Marx and Gramsci in Latin America. This time the view is provided by Marxists themselves as they respond to criticism of Marx as a Eurocentric thinker, a debate that could be as easily located in the 1970s, the years in which Dussel and Reinaga were developing the arguments I just summarized. A key thinker in this domain was José Aricó. His book *Marx y América Latina* (1980), complemented by his book on Antonio Gramsci (1988), and Juan Carlos Portantiero's book on Gramsci (1977) are central texts on the subject. These three books are indeed part of the canon and the mainstream of leftist thinking between 1970 and 1990 not only in Argentina but in Latin America, a period that frames the exile and the return of Argentinian intellectuals. Colonial legacies and ethnic questions are not issues in this discussion. Carlos Franco, in the introduction to Aricó's (1980, 9) book on Marx, describes the heart of the problem as "el desencuentro de América Latina y el marxismo" (the discrepancy between Latin America and Marxism). This problem had already emerged with Juan Carlos Mariátegui when he tried to accommodate, within Marxism, the Amerindian question, as I have already explained in chapter 3 (see also Quijano 1981). Aricó's analytical rigor and careful reflection lead him to ask what it means to be a Marxist in Latin America. His question about the ratio between geopolitical location and production of knowledge is, indeed, a question about the intersection of local histories and global designs. Aricó's careful examination of Marx's text on the Americas, India, and Ireland justifies the limits denounced by Dussel and Reinaga, while at the same time retaining Marx's fundamental contributions in his analysis of the logic of capitalism. The same concerns would be later expressed by Andean sociologists and anthropologists like Rivera Cusicanqui and Xavier Albó (on which I comment later), underlining the tensions between class and ethnicity in the Andes.

Aricó provided indeed two incisive arguments and enlightening analyses to account for the discrepancy between Latin America and Marxism in which he gets close to the colonial difference. One is to locate a theoretical level to a problem (e.g., the discrepancy) that was discussed at the political level. For the second, Aricó identifies in Marx's writings the "origin" of the discrepancy and, consequently, suggests that the problem may not lie in Marxism (or any of its versions) but in Marx's writing itself (Franco 1980, 10). I briefly summarize the second point, which is more strictly related to my discussion here and in this chapter. The "origin" of the discrepancy, if I read Aricó correctly, is located in the unresolved tension in Marx's thinking between analytical categories and geopolitics. Aricó addresses here this fundamental question: why was Marx blind to Latin America? Why did he not only miss Bolivar's point and celebrate the U.S. expansion toward Latin America, but also not pay the Americas in general (and Latin America in particular) the same attention he paid Africa and Asia? Why was this so when in Europe the discussions about the nature of America, prompted by Buffon and l'Abbé Reinald in the eighteenth century and Humboldt at the beginning of the nineteenth century, were so prominent? One answer could start from the minor role Hegel gave to the Americas in his lessons of universal history: a promising future, but absent from the past and from the present. But above all, Aricó suggests, Latin America was unthinkable in the colonial horizon of modernity. In the eighteenth century the Latin and heavily Amerindian part of the Americas was clearly conceived not as *el otro* (or the radical other as Dussel pointed out) but as the "margins" of the same. Aricó will call this marginal position "exteriority":

> Condenada a un presente abierto sólo a la perspectiva inmediata de una repetición del camino recorrido por Europa, América interesaba únicamente en su relación externa con Europa. . . . "América" sólo existía en "Europa."

> Es esta indudablemente la visión que subyace en los textos de Marx y Engels sobre América Latina, textos que, volvemos a insistir, no fueron tan escasos como se creyó. A partir de ella América Latina era considerada en su exterioridad, en su condición de reflejo de Europa, porque su interioridad era inaprehensible, en cuanto que tal inexistente. (190, 99)

> America, condemned to an open present and to a repetition of a path shaped and accomplished by Europe, was of interest only in its external relation to Europe. . . . "America" only existed in "Europe."

> This is without a doubt the hidden vision in Marx and Engel's writings whose size is not as small as it was generally assumed. This vision made Latin America visible only in its exteriority, in its condition of a mirror of Europe. Its interiority was impossible to apprehend and, consequently, America was not existent.

Theories travel: some alone, some in company. When they arrive at places, their adaptation to the new environment may or may not be as easy as the enthusiasm of the moment of arrival may suggest. Other theories do not travel, or travel less and with more difficulties. Perhaps we need to think more about when and why a theory that was produced to account for a type of question, problem, and historical situation in a geopolitical and geohistorical location within a local history becomes a global design, is desired and invited to a new locale. Briefly, from the brilliant argument developed by Aricó (1980, 121–35) on Marx's difficulties in understanding Bolivar and independence in Latin America as a form of decolonization, it is possible to restate the theory in terms of Marx's awareness of colonialism and, at the same time, his blindness to the colonial difference. And there are two reasons for that. One can be traced back to the Enlightenment and consisted in the temporal colonization of the sixteenth century, erasing from the rising conception of modernity the fact that Spanish and Portuguese empires created the conditions for the very emergence of the European Enlightenment. The other was contemporary to Marx and entailed the heavy attention received by Asia and Africa due to the rise of England as a leading nation in the modern/colonial world. If America was conceived in the eighteenth century as the daughter and inheritor of Europe, that prospective future was only visible in "Anglo" America. "Latin" America suffered a second subalternization in the modern/colonial world imaginary, as a consequence of its colonial past in the hands of an empire in decay. One can say, then, that even if Marx was and still is a source and a foundation for the internal critique of capitalism, it was also difficult, if not impossible, for him to perceive the colonial difference and, therefore, the coloniality of power. The question is whether the colonial difference requires, as a precondition of its "intelligibility," the colonial experience rather than colonialism as an object of sociohistorical descriptions and explanation. I suspect that this may be the case and, if it is, it is also the condition for epistemological diversity as a universal project, or for "diversality," in Glissant's expression, as a universal project. (I return to this in chapters 6 and 7.) I believe that Latin American subaltern studies will have to deal with these issues at some point, both in terms of Marxism and in terms of Latin America, in relation to Latin American and area studies and to the geopolitics of knowledge, as I suggested in this previous section. In the following pages I discuss some particular issues surrounding the politics of knowledge and the geopolitics of the coloniality of power. The reader particularly interested in Latin American subaltern studies should compare the genealogy of theoretical and political reflections in Latin America with the genealogy of the Latin American Subaltern Studies Group in Anglo America (Beverley 1996).

Adapting and Housing Traveling Theories in/from the Third World

Theories traveling from the South have the colonial difference inscribed in their luggage, as we already saw in the case of Darcy Ribeiro. The South Asian Subaltern Studies Group has had a significant impact, since the early 1990s, among Latin Americanists in the United States and intellectuals and social scientists in Latin America. I'll organize the following comments on three different and interrelated experiences: First, the constitution of the Latin American Subaltern Studies Group, the publication of the "Founding Statement" (Beverley, Oviedo and Aronna 1995; see Beverley 1996 for a narrative of the group constitution), and the special volume of *Dispositio/n* 46; second, an influential article by historian and Latin Americanist Florencia Mallon (1994) and her book on peasants and the nation in nineteenth century Mexico and Peru (1995); and, third, an introduction to subaltern studies, published in Bolivia and edited by sociologist Silvia Rivera Cusicanqui and historian Rossana Barragán (1997). This volume contains translations of a dozen core articles by members of the South Asian Subaltern Studies Group, plus an introduction by the editors.

These three cases reveal a network of connections and hierarchies in the ratio between knowledge production and geohistorical locations. I insist that when I say geohistorical location I am not only talking about a particular geographical place but of a geographical place with a particular local history: La Paz, or Bolivia, is not Wisconsin or Pittsburgh. In La Paz, Spanish, Aymara, and Quechua become indispensable to understand both colonial and national histories, or the coloniality of power in the colonial and national history of Bolivia. Thus, while Rivera Cusicanqui and Barragán translated Spanish articles by members of the South Asian Subaltern Studies Group from English (for whom English is comparable with Spanish for Rivera Cusicanqui and Barragán as evinced in the parallel between "British India" and "Spanish America") into Spanish, the Latin American Subaltern Studies Group and Mallon published their works in English. English for the South Asian Studies Group is like Spanish for Rivera Cusicanqui and Barragán. However, I do not anticipate a translation of Bolivian intellectuals into English. Why not? Of course, Spanish and English do not have the same clout and power today in the domain of knowledge (see chapters 5 and 6 for a more detailed discussion of this topic). If indeed theories travel and get transcultured, it is necessary first to specify, historically, from where they depart and to where they go, how they travel, how they get transcultured, and the language in which traveling theories are fabricated, packaged, and transculturated. Coloniality of power and the colonial difference are unavoidable "inconveniences" of the trip.

To start with, the Latin American Subaltern Studies Group consists mainly of literary and cultural critics, although it includes one historian, one anthropologist, and one political scientist. In any event, historiography as a disciplinary formation was never a crucial issue in the "adaptation" of South Asian to Latin American Subaltern Studies. Judging by Beverley and Oviedo's (1993) introduction to a volume devoted to postmodernism in Latin America, the issue was postmodernism in Latin America, rather than postcolonial nationalism in India. And judging by Beverley's personal narrative about the coming into being of the group, the main disciplinary question was between cultural and subaltern studies. For Beverley (1996), the institutionalizaton of cultural studies in the United States prompted him to lean toward subaltern studies, where he found a more satisfactory connection between scholarly pursuit and the politics of knowledge. Florencia Mallon's concern, instead, is historiography as a discipline. As a historian she feels more at home since the South Asian Subaltern Studies Group not only consists of mainly historians, but it encompasses a group of historians brought together by the writing of India's history from a postcolonial and subaltern perspective. Again as a historian, Mallon (1994) looks with suspicion at the fact that a group of Latin Americanists in the United States with backgrounds of mainly literary and cultural criticism are also appropriating the contribution of the South Asian Group. What the Latin American Group and Mallon have in common is their finding a revelation in the South Asian Group. For the Latin American Group, the revelation solved the problem presented by the crisis of the left after 1989 and offered a new perspective from which to look at the significance of the three main Latin American revolutions of the twentieth century (Castro in Cuba, the Sandinistas in Nicaragua, and the Mexican Revolution at the beginning of the twentieth century). For Mallon, it offered, instead, a new departure for the historiography, in the United States, about Latin America.

The collection edited by Rivera Cusicanqui and Barragán brings a whole new dimension to the foreground. For Rivera Cusicanqui and Barragán, the South Asian Subaltern Studies Group was more than a "revelation" and a solution to a dead end. It was indeed a "revelation" of how close the concerns of the group were to their own, how many common interests existed between what it has been thinking and writing since 1982 and what Bolivian scholars where doing at more or less the same time without knowing each other. This was a "revelation" after the facts. I suspect that traveling theories in this case could have gone in two directions. However, English has priority in the market and in travel agencies for first class and faster travel. It was a happy encounter that produced Rivera Cusicanqui and Barragán's publication, and it was made possible by the fact that several years before the publication both editors had been in contact with the South Asian Subaltern Studies Group and participated in a workshop in India, at the same time that Indian scholars (e.g., Amin) visited Bolivia. So, scholars and intellectuals travel, too, like theories. And they relate in a different manner to the topics at hand. I am not suggesting that it is "bad" to be an Indian or Latin American scholar in the United States, or that it is "bad" to be a Third World scholar inventing postcolonial theory in the United States, or that it is "good" to stay in India or Bolivia and write in Hindi or Spanish or Aymara. I am just saying that knowledge production is not detached from the sensibilities of geohistorical location and that historical locations, in the modern/

colonial world, have been shaped by the coloniality of power. Scholarship, traveling theories, wandering and sedentary scholars, in the First or the Third World, cannot avoid the marks in their bodies imprinted by the coloniality of power, which, in the last analysis, orient their thinking. It is the coloniality of power that calls for "thinking" in and about the modern/colonial world system. And in that sense, "thinking" doesn't travel but operates at the intersection of memories and information, of past decisions, current events, and utopian hopes.

Rivera Cusicanqui and Barragán's edited translation, titled "Postcolonial Debates," took the contribution of the South Asian Subaltern Studies Group in a different direction from that announced by Beverley, Oviedo, and Aronna (1995) in their introduction: "There is something about the very idea of a Latin American postmodernism that makes one think of that condition of colonial or neocolonial dependency in which goods that have become shopworn or out of fashion in the metropolis are, like the marvels of the gypsies of *One Hundred Years of Solitude, exported to the periphery,* where they enjoy a profitable second life" (1995, 1; emphasis added). In spite of the cautious framing, the fact is that, for Beverley, one contribution of the Latin American Subaltern Studies Group was to introduce the postmodern dimension in subaltern studies. For Rivera Cusicanqui and Barragán, however, the postcolonial question remains central to subaltern studies. Thus, the title of my chapter. As such, my argument here is a continuation of the discussion on the postmodern and the postcolonial introduced in chapter 1 and, at the same time, a prolongation of the discussion on the intellectual history in Latin America, outlined in chapter 2. Briefly stated, the postmodern debate in Latin America was predominant in the countries of the Atlantic coast (Bahia in Brazil being an exception), with a low demographic presence of the Amerindian and Afro-American population. The postcolonial question, instead, is centered in countries with a dense Amerindian population (Bolivia, Peru, Ecuador, Guatemala, Mexico) as well as in the English and French Caribbean (Lamming, Glissant).

Let's move now to Florencia Mallon's arguments. As a Latin American scholar in the United States, Mallon enthusiastically endorsed the South Asian Subaltern Studies "model."

At the very beginning of her contribution to a special issue of *American Historical Review,* Mallon states that "Latin Americanists, often Eurocentric in our borrowing from other historical or theoretical traditions, have in this instance taken as a model a school born and bred in another part of the so-called Third World. What is afoot?"(1994, 1493). Mallon's cautious footnote alerts the reader to the fact that this is not the first time that "South-to-South" dialogue has occurred. She quotes several examples to indicate that in the particular field of "peasant studies" and "African diaspora," there has been dialogue between scholars studying Latin America and scholars studying South Asia and Africa. But where were those scholars, in the South or in the North? Mallon ends the footnote by noticing that despite those examples "the main point continues to be that Latin American history, as a field, has tended to connect more readily to historical and theoretical traditions based in Europe. In this sense, of course, it is quite similar to other historical fields, including those based in Europe or the United States, which are indeed a great deal less conversant across the 'South-North' divide than are scholars who work on so-called Third World areas" (1994, 1492).

What indeed is afoot in Mallon's statement regarding "South-South" and "South-North" dialogue among scholars working *on/in* "the so-called Third World"? There are two very puzzling issues here. (1) Why does Mallon remain silent about the dialogue between "North American" scholars for whom Latin America is a field of study, and "South American" scholars and intellectuals for whom Latin America is not just a field of study but a place of historical and political struggle? (2) Is Mallon assuming that Latin America is only a place to be studied and not a location for theoretical thinking and, by so doing, recasting the ideology of area studies in the vocabulary of subaltern studies? (Mignolo 1993a).

There is another difficult issue to deal with: the increasing tensions of a growing interconnected transnational world coexisting with the destructiveness of national and ethnic sensibilities and ideologies. On the one hand, then, it is advisable to look for transnational alliances and to build international communities that transcend the shortcomings of nationalism. On the other hand, acting at a transnational level could end up in an abstract demand for justice, which ignores regional interests and needs (a celebration of traveling theories and a reproduction of subalternization of knowledge). These are, in a nutshell, the two positions stated by Arjun Appadurai (1996) and Partha Chaterjee (1997). But they are also the two positions assumed at once by the Zapatistas: transnationalism as a way of empowering themselves for their confrontation with the state, and nationalism as a form of countering globalization (Subcomandante Marcos 1997b). Although the *local* is not necessarily the *national*, the tensions between the national and the transnational at the geohistorical level seem to mirror the demands between the epistemological and the emotional at the subjective level in/of subaltern consciousness (Sarkar 1989; Bhadra 1989). A corrective of Max Weber is necessary at this point. For Weber, the individual had to be taken into account in explaining social actions as long as Weber's individual was solely driven by rational actions. Subaltern studies introduced the level of *affective actions as a different kind of rationality.* Thus, while the national/transnational dilemma could be cast in a different paradigm, it needs to be rearticulated as one of the epistemological distinctions of the modern reason between rationality and sensibility (Das 1989, 317; Quijano 1992).

My discussion of the politics and sensibilities of geocultural locations takes into account the urgencies of the national and the transnational as well as the tensions between the "rationality of reason" and the "rationality of emotions and sensibilities." My main thesis here is that *if* subaltern studies in/of the Americas had the possibility of modeling its own space and surviving, then *it would have to derail the subalternization of cultures of scholarship enacted by Orientalism, first, and Latin America (area) studies, second.* Relevant for the following argument are two important points made by Das (1989): that "subaltern" *is not a category but rather a perspective*; and that the subaltern perspective is not engaged in understanding such and such social organization or social actions per se but in understanding its "contractual" relations under colonial rules and the "forms of domination belonging to the structures of modernity" (1989, 313). Stated in this way, the current version of Latin American subaltern studies is within the framework traced by Darcy Ribeiro (see the epigraph to this chapter) in his view of colonization as subalternization of people and cultures. Since one of the main concerns of subaltern studies as a perspective is countering modernity and displaying the idea that modernity is a European phenomenon, the postmodern or the postcolonial are indeed linked to this assumption. Instead, a "transmodern" perspective as proposed by Dussel ([1993] 1995) is conceived as a planetary phenomenon "beyond Eurocentrism." From this perspective, the "adoption" of South Asian subaltern to Latin American studies, two issues are central: the differences between Indian colonial history (under British colonialism) and the colonial history of the Americas (Latin/ Anglo-America and the Caribbean), including successive colonial and imperial legacies; and the differences between India, a *country* of 800 million people, and Latin America, an undefined group of countries and a subcontinent (see chapter 2).

Inside Third World Theories

Gyan Prakash (editor of the special issue of the *American Historical Review* devoted to subaltern studies) entitled his introduction "Writing Post-Orientalist Histories of the Third World: Perspectives from Indian Historiography" (1990). In that article Prakash extended Indian historiography to the "Third World" and compared historians of India (such as Romila Thapar, Bernard Cohn, and Nicholas Dirks) with the subaltern studies group. And he concluded:

> This historiography's (Thapar, Cohn, Dirks) *critical focus on epistemological procedures* makes it somewhat different from the Subaltern Studies, which *targets the colonial or nationalist will*. While the former (Thapar, Cohn, Dirks) analyzes

power relations in the context of academic disciplines and institutions, the latter sees itself disrupting and derailing the will of the powerful. (Prakash 1990, 402; emphasis added)

Prakash compared these two kinds of historiographies ("post-Orientalists") with Indology and area studies in Europe and North America and concluded that Indology and area studies are two scholarly practices insuring the continuity of an Orientalist discourse that maintains the distinctions East/West, First/Third World, and reinforces national origins. Prakash perceives in the historiography of India practiced by subalternist historians an identification with the subordinated subject position, which becomes acute in formulating "critical third-world perspectives" and in recasting the geohistorical categories founded and implemented by Indology and area studies: "From the perspective of Subaltern Studies, Indian historians have obviously developed and embraced the victim's subject-position more readily; but because the experience and expression of subordination are discursively formulated, we are led back to the processes and forces that organize the subordinate's subject position" (Prakash 1990, 403). Instead, post-Orientalist historiographies (like Cohn, Thapar, Dirks) show that "The third world, far from being confined to its assigned space, has penetrated the inner sanctum of the first world in the process of being "third-worlded"—arousing, inciting, and affiliating with the subordinated others in the first world" (Prakash 1990, 442).

The location has been moved from "nationalism" to socioeconomic arrangements (e.g., Third World). Who are the enemies and the allies? How are the forces being realigned? What new alliances are at stake? One group of enemies, which we have already seen, is constituted by the continuity of Orientalism (e.g., Indology, area studies) and nationalist historiography (whose practitioners have contemporary beliefs in "solidly grounded existence and identities"). Derrida, Foucault, and Said are quoted as foundation or warranty for the predicament that the two sets of enemies are forces to be superseded and to which task post-Orientalist historiographies are contributing. If "solidly grounded existence and identities" should be questioned (if not just declared lost), and national origins replaced by subordinated subject positions, then what is left is a displacement from political identification at a national level, to identification with subject positions at a global capitalist-economy level.

The politics and sensibilities of geocultural locations bring together theories and human agency in a complementary fashion. Asking about the location of theories implies, first, historicizing any claim about the universality of reason and certain "forms" of knowledge and not others relegated to object (primitive, barbarian, oriental "knowledge") and, second, analyzing the belief that theoretical thinking is unattached to linguistic and geohistorical locations (see chapter 5). Furthermore, emphasis on loci of enunciation and the location of theories reveals constantly that the ground for theories is not a universal subject placed in the local history of the West, but that theoretical production and the self-definition of theories is located in specific languages and local histories. It is the local (i.e., local histories) that calls for thinking, not the universal ground of the "human" mind translated into a local concept of reason that became one of the crucial concepts of the modern/colonial world imaginary.

As we all know, Michel Foucault (1969) mapped the archaeology of the "human sciences" in Western civilization. More recently Immanuel Wallerstein added some observations linking the emergence of the social sciences with colonial expansion in the modern world-system. Wallerstein departs from the premise (sustained by many) that there are universal truths about human behavior that hold across all time and space. He goes on to forewarn us about this idea by revealing the complicities between knowledge and colonial power:

> The minute you say that (that there are universal truths across time and space), it becomes no different whether you study Germany in the present or India in the fifth century B.C., because you are looking for universal truths. Since the data on Germany in the present is 5,000 times better—harder is the word— than the data on India in 5,000 B.C., we study Germany in the present to arrive at our generalizations. . . . At least 95 percent of all scholars and all scholarship from the period 1850 to 1914, and probably even to 1945, originates in five countries: France, Great Britain, the Germanies, the Italies, and the United States. There is a smattering elsewhere, but basically not only does the scholarship come out of these five countries, but most of the scholarship by most scholars is about their own country. So most of the scholarship is about these five countries. . . .
>
> That leads to the second cleavage. The fact is that the five countries were not the entire world and there was some vague awareness in the scholarly community that there was a world beyond the five countries. What they did in our view was simply to invite two other disciplines to study the rest of the world. The first and most obvious is anthropology, which was invented to study the primitive world. The primitive world was defined in a very simple way: in practice, as the colonies of the five countries. . . . These groups were presumed to be unchanging and timeless. (Wallerstein 1996, 3)

The second discipline, which preceded anthropology, was Oriental studies, covering everything that was not Europe, the five countries of scholarship, and their respective colonies. Oriental studies (as we know after Said 1978 and more recently after Khatibi [1976] 1983) took care of civilizations that had writing and religion but that were left out of European modernity; civilizations that, like the primitives, were conceived as frozen and ahistoric.

In that distribution of knowledge, ancient Andean and Mesoamerican civilizations were left out, since they had been obscured by the ambiguous place of Ibero-America in the nineteenth-century distribution of knowledge. But above all, they belonged to the "New" and not to the "Old" World, where the Orient was located. What's more, the "New World," after all, was in the west, not in the east. A group of independent nations, which broke their ties with Spain and Portugal, were no longer the colonies of the five countries (as a matter of fact, Spain and Portugal were not among the five countries), and the Aztec, Maya, and Inca so-called empires were disconnected from nineteenth-century Latin America and—for several reasons—not paired with the Islamic world, China, or India. Thus, the interest in Mesoamerica and the Andes was, first, a concern of European scholars who turned their eyes west instead of east; and in the twentieth century, a disciplinary configuration (parallel to Oriental studies) emerged mainly in the United States rather than in Europe, as interest in things Latin American grew in this country (Coe 1992). On the other hand, pre-Columbian (Mesoamerican and Andean) studies was quickly complemented by the emergence of what is today Latin American studies, although the history is very complex (Cline 1966; Berger 1993; Lambert 1990). Born in the 1920s as a scholarly enterprise supporting U.S. interests in Latin America, the field became a house for scholars of leftist persuasions after the Cuban Revolution, as Mallon's article and the "Founding Statement" indicate.

Now, if the politics of location make us aware that there is no universal macrotheory for everything imaginable under that theory, or that theories of class cannot account for ethnic issues (or vice versa), that psychoanalysis may not work for a *caste* society in Calcutta since it was created to deal with the problem of *class* society in Europe at the turn of the century (Nandy 1995, 81–144), the sensibilities of location make us aware of the emotional foregrounding (ethnic, national, cosmopolitan, sexual, class) of the human agency in theory building, at least in the social sciences and the humanities. Sensibilities are not essential and are not inscribed in one's birth, but are formed and transformed in the family, the school (for those who have access to it), and society, acquired and lost, in the course of a life span. As recent events in postpartition India, Ireland, and ex-Yugoslavia reveal, the sensibilities of geohistorical locations have to do with a sense of territoriality (which is never lost—and should not be confused with "national identity"—either in exile or in a cosmopolitan sensibility), and includes language, food, smells, landscape, climate, and all those basic signs that link the body to one or several places (see chapter 6). That nationalist ideologies transformed these experiences into forms of coercion and violence should not obscure the fact of the mutual inscriptions of the body and geohistorical locations. Cosmopolitanism and exile, allow me to repeat, are not an admonition to the sensibility of historical location; they are particular configurations of it: they are a warning to the sensibility of "national" (as *a* particular manifestation of the geocultural) locations. The fact that we are living more and more in exile in a growing cosmopolis does not mean that sensibilities are lost. Once again, the sensibilities of geohistorical locations are not essential features of national identities; national identities are just one historical kind of sensibility.

From the Latin American Archive

Colombian Germán Colmenares is perhaps, among modern historians and critics of historiography, one of the most lucid thinkers of the limits of historiography in Latin America. Colmenares's writings published almost a century and a half after the decolonization of Colombia (roughly between 1968 and 1997) were caught between the limits of traditional historiography in Latin America and the new perspectives being opened up in France by the Ecoles des Annales and in England by the New Left (E. P. Thompson). Later on (toward 1980) Colmenares (1987) incorporated in his work Hayden White's reflections on historiographical narratives. But he remained within historical criticism of nineteenth-century historiography. I surmise that the limits of Colmenares's reflections were due to the heavy tradition imposed by the national imaginary. During the same period (between 1964 and 1990), new perspectives were coming from intellectuals living in between and, paradoxically, in reverse—that is, U.S. scholars working in Latin America rather than the opposite, as is the case today.

Richard Morse was a controversial figure in Latin American Studies in the 1960s and 1970s, and his writing remained influential until the 1990s. His poignant criticism against Latin Americanism is perhaps one of the reasons for his marginal situation today in the circles of Latin American scholars working in North America. Morse enters the picture here because, among other reasons, he is a historian and, I should add, a trilingual and tricultural historian. He has not only studied Latin American histories and cultures, but he has also devoted much time to "thinking" *about* and *from* Latin America, next to Latin American intellectuals from Brazil to Mexico.[2] Morse

---

[2] Why am I underlining "Spanish-/Portuguese-speaking countries"? Because Spanish and Portuguese are languages that fell off the bandwagon of modernity and became subaltern languages of scholarship among the major languages of modernity and colonialism (English, German, French, Spanish, Portuguese, Italian, see chapters 5 and 7).

is a paradigmatic example to caution the underlying assumptions of (Latin American) area studies and its aftermath, Latin American subaltern studies.

In 1964, the year in which the Latin American Studies Association was in its inception, Morse was forcefully criticizing North American Latin Americanists. He perceived a lack of critical perspective among Latin Americanists on the differences between the two Americas. He noted how much of those silenced differences were pungent for Latin American studies as a North American invention that placed Latin America as a *field* of studies, but not as a place where theories and ideas were produced. This difference can be articulated more clearly if we consider literature and philosophy *in* Latin America and compare them to the social sciences and Latin American studies *in* the United States. While the social sciences in the U.S. and European universities are *about* Latin America (i.e., as a field of study), literature and philosophy *in* Latin America are not *about* Latin America but, I would venture to say, *from* Latin America. This *thinking from* literature and philosophy is deeply rooted in the Spanish and Portuguese languages as well as in colonial legacies. This is a "privilege" and a "need" compelled by the colonial difference. Morse criticized Latin Americanists in North America for lacking an awareness of the fundamental colonial differences between the two Americas:

> Here my purpose is to suggest, as clinically as possible, that the defects of Latin American studies in the United States are largely attributable to the fundamental alienation between the two Americas. By alienation I do not gently mean unfortunate misunderstanding that might be remedied by a bit more knowledge and good will. What concerns me is the fact that for many of our Latin Americanists the intensive study of their subject kindles their subconscious hostility to it. The heart of the matter is that here are two cultures whose historic spiritual trajectories are not merely different—this would not produce backlash when the attempt is made to "understand"—but diametrically opposed. (Morse [1964] 1989, 170)

Morse's observation was made in 1964, and I have not the slightest intention of pretending that this diagnosis could be applied *mutatis mutandis* to the "founding statement" of the Latin American Subaltern Studies Group or to Mallon's enthusiastic endorsement of Indian subaltern studies. The general problem, however, persists. I do claim that the differences between the two Americas that Morse points out are very important to reflect on the *location* of areas *to be studied* and on the cultures of scholarship *from where to study*; to reflect also in the *location* of the agency and locus of enunciation from where imaginary constructions (e.g., the result of scholarly studies or intellectual reflections) are produced (see chapter 2); to reflect on the implications and consequences of *being from* and *being at* (Gilroy 1990–91) in the academic, epistemological, and political investments of agencies of scholarship.

Another important aspect of Morse's observation that should be explored is the languaging (rather than language) differences between the two Americas[3] as they impinge on the cultures of scholarship. First, as I already mentioned, Spanish and Portuguese became subaltern languages in the colonial reconfiguration of modernity. Second, Indian subaltern studies are cast in the language of the British Empire. What should be explored, then, is the language and the languaging aspects of subaltern studies in/of India and subaltern studies in/of the United States or in/of Latin America. Morse's observation should be translated into the realm of language and languaging (see chapter 6) in order to locate the difference between the two Americas: English as the hegemonic language and the languaging of scholarship, and Spanish and Portuguese (and we could include the French of Martinique or the English of Jamaica) as subaltern languages and languaging (see chapter 7) of cultures to be studied (see chapter 4).

Morse perceived the need and has greatly contributed to building intellectual genealogies in Spanish and Portuguese, and has worked toward the restitution of intellectual production in these languages, which have been relegated to a subaltern position by the scholarly production in French, English, or German: the languages of modernity, modern colonialisms, and the cultures of scholarship (Wallerstein 1996). It is not by chance (as I noted earlier) that the configurations of the human sciences and the study of civilization flourished in the nineteenth century, while area studies took over after World War II when the United States supplanted the hegemony of modern Europe (England, Germany, France) and put a premium on the studies of the Third World. The distribution of the world in three ranked areas after World War II is contemporaneous with the foundation of the Latin American Studies Association.

The current discussion on subaltern studies (Beverley et al., Mallon) and postcoloniality (Seed, Prakash) contributes nonetheless to keeping alive a theoretical and epistemological dimension that Morse alluded to as a lack in Latin American studies. It is perhaps this dimension that would allow for a metatheoretical perspective bringing together Latin Americanists in the United States fascinated by Indian subaltern studies, and previous theoretical contributions by scholars and intellectuals in Latin America deeply concerned with the situation of their countries, the continent, and the exploitation of subaltern communities. I avoid a detailed discussion of these contributions; and, although just mentioning them could be problematic, I take the risk: Darcy Ribeiro's rethinking of the civilizing process and colonial strategies to locate languages, cultures, peoples in subaltern positions (see

---

[3] A more detailed argument on the concept of "languaging" appears in chapter 6.

chapter 7); the dependency theory of Prebisch, Cardoso, Faleto, and others as a theoretical answer from Latin America to the raising of transnational corporations and globalization in the 1970s; internal colonialism, as introduced by González Casanova (1968) and Stavenhagen (1965; 1990) in Mexico in the 1970s (and still alive in Albó and Barrios [1993] in Bolivia) (also Apel 1996, 172–76; Dussel 1996b, 217–19; Rivera Cusicanqui 1993) to account for emerging Amerindian social movements at the confluence of class and ethnic conflicts. This is another example of the colonizing bent of subaltern studies, both in the version of the founding statement as well as in Mallon's article, in which—furthermore—the already strong presence of Gramsci in Latin America was blatantly ignored (Aricó 1988).

Gender, Disciplinary Formations, Subaltern Positions

At this point an interesting issue arises: the fact that the intellectual genealogy of theoretical thinking in/from Latin America may look like a masculine one (see also chapter 2). Is it a gender issue that prevents Seed and Mallon from establishing alliances, for instance, with the Latin American thinkers that Morse incorporates in his discourse? The answer may be yes if we think about the particular examples exploited by Morse, but it would be difficult to maintain that only men in Latin America are thinking in/from a geohistorical location (see chapters 1 and 2), as Bolivian sociologist and activist Silvia Rivera Cusicanqui and Chilean literary critic Nelly Richard, who locates herself as "a Latin American" (Richard 1995, 219), illustrate.

Let me begin with Nelly Richard, a Chilean scholar of French origin whose work has been included in the reprint of Beverley, Oviedo, and Aronna (1995). Richard, in a well-known article formulated in a postmodern theoretical framework, indirectly addressed the question of "subaltern cultures" (1995). Ribeiro (1968) was concerned with a similar problem, although cast in an anthropological and evolutionary vocabulary of the time. However, the issue of subaltern cultural areas as a consequence of several layers of colonization, the hegemony of an unilinear historical time identified with Europe as the pinnacle of civilization, the need to introduce diverse historical rhythms by denying the denial of coevalness, and so forth—all that was already discussed by Ribeiro. Nevertheless, an empty space remains between Richard and Ribeiro, a space of neglect produced by the very hegemony that both of them are fighting against.

Richard builds her argument by matching up postmodern theorizing with the Latin American condition: Latin American marginality and the postmodern defense of the margins, the crisis of authority and the metanarrative of the crisis, the theory of decentering and the center function of this theory as a symbol of cultural prestige, and the rhetoric and the politics of difference.

Richard addresses an issue that, in her view, "structured the behavior of the Latin American periphery faced with the universalizing paradigm of the center: dependency and imitation as colonialized inflections, but also parody and recycling as decolonizing strategies" (1995, 219). The meaning of "peripheral" is analogous to the meaning of "subaltern," if we allow the term to refer to "cultures" and languages and not just to social classes or communities—that is, everything that lies in a relational space will be located in "an inferior rank."

In her article entitled, "Postmodernism in the Periphery," Richard points out the need to counter the process of subalternization:

> By creating the possibility of a critical rereading of modernity, postmodernism offers us the chance to reconsider all that was "left unsaid" and to inject its areas of opacity and resistance with the potential for new, as yet undiscovered, meanings. In the Latin American context, this review of modernity allows us, once again, to pose the question of our own identity, *that of individuals born of and into the dialectic mixture of the different languages surrounding us, which have practically fused to produce a cultural identity experienced as a series of collisions. This identity can be understood as an unstable product of modernity's tropes which involve a continuous regrouping, distorting and transforming of imported models, according to the specific pressures pertaining to the critical reinsertion of these models into local networks.* (Richard 1987–88, 469; emphasis added)

I raise the question of cultural identity in Latin America, not because I am expecting to solve the problem and tell you what that identity is, but to underline the need of geohistorical identifications persistent in critical theory as well as in philosophy and literature. We also have seen it in Albó, who begins and closes his articles with his own "experience of a series of collisions" with the name "Indies," "New World," "America," "Latin America," and "Abya-Yala," a name used by the Cuna Indians of Panama as a mythical location (and we could add "Tawantinsuyu" and "Anahuac," the name used by the Incas and the Aztecs to name the(ir) worlds). What interests me, in other words, are the politics and sensibilities of geohistorical locations (Mignolo 1995b; 1997a) in the production, exportation, and importation of knowledge. Thus, if the subalternization of Amerindian languages and ethnic cultures has been a constant issue in Latin America since the 1970s, why is this legacy being forgotten and recast in the discourse of Indian subaltern studies? Are we facing new forms of academic colonialisms under the belief of a new and liberating discourse? Finally, are Indian subaltern studies relevant for intellectuals living and thinking in/from Latin America, or are they a particular need for Latin Americanists in the United States?

INTERNAL COLONIALISM AND SUBALTERN STUDIES

I would like to state at the outset that internal colonialism is the reformulation of the colonial difference within the formation of the modern nation-state after decolonization (the category will have a different.meaning in nineteenth-century France, for instance, than in nineteenth-century Mexico); and that the term begins to lose its historical meaning at the current stage of global coloniality in which the demise of the nation-state is replaced by a form of coloniality not anchored in nation-state territories. If internal colonialism may not have today the relevance it had in the past 180 years, the colonial difference survives with all its force as it is being rearticulated in the new global forms of coloniality of power. I commented earlier in this chapter on the difference between subaltern studies in India, aiming at "derailing and disturbing the will of the powerful," and academic historiography of India in the United States, producing radical transformation in history as a discipline. In the 1960s, Morse expected two similar courses of action from Latin Americanists: more awareness of the differences between the society in which knowledge is produced (the United States) and the society that is taken as a field of knowledge (Latin America); and intellectual recognition, a more productive dialogue, and the construction of theoretical genealogies linking the "study" *of* Latin America *from* the United States with the "reflections" *on* Latin America *in* Latin America. Neither Morse nor Prakash bring the question of geohistorical identification into the discussion, but I introduce it here as a new aspect to those highlighted by both of them. The following questions to subaltern studies in/of the Americas could be asked:

1. Would Latin American subaltern studies aim to transform historiography as an academic practice and introduce a new dimension in the history of Latin American studies, or would it also aim at "disturbing and derailing the will of the powerful"?

2. If instead of Latin American subaltern studies the question is subaltern studies in/of the Americas, how would the field of study (i.e., imaginary constructions) and disciplinary practices (i.e., loci of enunciation) be conceived, given the divide in the Americas due to the diversity of colonial experiences and the hierarchy of power established by internal colonial and imperial conflicts?

3. How would the question of geocultural identification be dealt with in Latin American cultural studies or subaltern studies in/of the Americas? I am not thinking of geohistorical identification as something to be analyzed and studied but rather to be reflected upon: how does geocultural identification impinge on Latin American scholars in the United States, and on Latin American scholars in Latin America;

or in Latin American scholars in between the United States and Latin America, in whichever direction you would like to conceive the "in between"?

I am not in a position to answer these questions here. I would just add a new example to elucidate what I have in mind by asking such questions. I will also deliver what I promised by commenting on Rivera Cusicanqui's contribution to the understanding of "subaltern" communities in Bolivia.

Xavier Albó, a Bolivian anthropologist of Spanish (Catalan) origin, recently edited and published in La Paz two volumes on *Violencias encubiertas en Bolivia* (Albó and Barrios 1993), with the participation of several Bolivian social scientists. The two volumes are the result of a series of meetings (Bogotá 1989, 1990; Lima 1990) called by the Asociación Peruana de Estudios e Investigación para la Paz (APEP), with the intent of looking for scholars' and social scientists' contributions to building democracy and peace in the Andes. The first chapter (about 140 pages) of Albó's edited volume was written by Rivera Cusicanqui and entitled "The Roots: Colonizers and Colonizeds." Since the two volumes were published in 1993, one could think that the title reflects a lack of awareness or ignorance of the fact that in other circles the dichotomy "colonizercolonized" is either suspect or superseded; or one could wonder why Indian subaltern studies are not used as a banner to solve the problems of progressive scholars in Bolivia after the end of the cold war. One could be disappointed when Rivera Cusicanqui introduces on the first page the concept of "internal colonialism," ignoring the myriad "post" concepts that have been produced in the past ten or more years. There is no mention of "subaltern," "postmodernism" or "postcolonialism" in a study of Bolivia in which Amerindian social movements that are built and enacted not just as social classes (i.e., peasants) but as ethnopolitical communities are being highlighted constantly. That is perhaps why "internal colonialism" could be more appropriate in Rivera's reflection, since "internal colonialism" has a strong ethnic emphasis that "subaltern" locates in social classes. Of course, it is not that "ethnicity" should be substituted for "social classes," for, as Albó points out,

> We do not doubt the importance and necessity of continuing to do analysis based on the social classes and their interaction; it is essential from every point of view. But we should also seriously question ourselves about the exclusivity of such analysis. . . . The other dimensions of the popular movement come into consideration, such as ethnic, or racial, identity in the case of African Americans, as well as Indian and mixed race groups; different cultural expressions, for example, in the area of popular religion or language; relations between the countryside and the city or between the capital and the urban periphery and

regionalisms; the growing women's movement, in which all of these elements coexist. (Albó 1995, 20)[4]

It is clear to me that Albó's and Rivera's implicit proposals are no less powerful and masterful than any of Guha's or Indian subaltern studies' pieces. They are very similar indeed: powerful and disturbing pieces of writing with a will toward social transformation, toward linking scholarship and radical politics that also work, although indirectly, toward disciplinary scholarly transformations.

There is a central thesis in Rivera's argument:

> La hipótesis central que orienta el conjunto del trabajo, es que en la contemporaneidad boliviana opera, en forma subyacente, un modo de dominación sustentado en un horizonte colonial de larga duración, al cual se han articulado—pero sin superarlo ni modificarlo completamente—los ciclos mas recientes del liberalismo y el populismo. Estos horizontes recientes han conseguido tan solo refuncionalizar las estructuras coloniales de larga duración, convirtiéndolas en modalidades de colonialismo interno que continuan siendo cruciales a la hora de explicar la estratificación interna de la sociedad boliviana, sus contradicciones sociales fundamentales y los mecanismos específicos de exclusión-segregación que caracterizan a la estructura política y estatal del país y que están en la base de las formas de violencia estructural mas profundas y latentes. (Rivera Cusicanqui 1993, 31)

> The central thesis of this argument is that in contemporaneous Bolivia, a form of domination grounded in a colonial horizon of long duration is at work, although underground and invisibly. To this horizon has been added—but without totally superseding or modifying it—the most recent cycles of liberalism and populism. These more recent horizons were only able to rework the colonial structures of long duration by converting them into modalities of internal colonialism, and these older structures remain crucial when an explanation of the internal stratification of Bolivian society is needed, and when the fundamental social contradictions have to be explained, when particular mechanisms of exclusion and segregation, distinct from the political and state structures of the country, need to be revealed, since they are the very foundation of the most pervasive forms of structural violence.

In the first chapter, entitled "Pachacuti: Los horizontes históricos del colonialismo interno," Rivera outlines the coexistence of layers of historical memories in the present: the colonial cycle (1532–1820); the liberal cycle (1820–1952); the populist cycle (1952 to the present). Once again, these

---

[4] The relevance of ethnic conflicts does not need to be argued in light of contemporary world history. Comprehensive summaries and analysis can be found in Horowitz (1985) and Stavenhagen (1990).

are not successive stages of progressive unilinear historical events, but coexisting temporalities that produce and explain structural violence in Bolivia.
But why "Pachacuti" and not simply "Los horizontes históricos del colonialismo interno"? Because the Aymara concept "Pachacuti" (literally, *teoría del
vuelco*, metaphorically, "catastrophe theory") is stated as a category of
thought that coexists and interacts with the Western notion of "revolution."
It is not a question here (neither Rivera Cusicanqui's nor mine) of *traditionally* defending a notion of tradition (see the epigraph by Rivera at the beginning of this article). I have no intention of asserting the real and authentic
meanings and values of either the Aymara notion of "Pachacuti" or the Marxist notion of "revolution." I would borrow Anthony Giddens's notion of
"post-traditional social orders" to frame what the merging of "Pachacuti"
and "revolution" may mean in the Andes. For Giddens a "post-traditional
social order" is not one in which tradition disappears—far from it. It is one
in which traditions change their status. Traditions have to explain themselves, to become open to interrogation or discourse (Giddens 1994: 5). A
conceptualization of social transformation complicitous with social movements and of what Albó (1994) calls, in another article, "the bold alliances
between Aymaras and Neoliberals in Bolivia" accounts for the current composition of Bolivian state leadership until 1997: a vice-president, Victor
Hugo Cárdenas, of Aymara descent with a long experience of participation
in Amerindian popular social movements (Rivera Cusicanqui 1990).

But what remains as a not well-known foundational statement for Andean
subaltern studies, grounded in the tension between colonial legacies and cultures of scholarship, is Rivera's "Sendas y senderos de la ciencia
social Andina" (1992). Rivera Cusicanqui's interpretation of the crisis in
the social sciences in the Andes in 1992 is supported by ten years of research and publication. First, her research focuses on the peasant movements in Colombia (1984), where the analysis is carried on in terms of
"campesinado" as a social class. In 1984, however, with the publication of
Oprimidos pero no vencidos (1984), a distinction emerges between "campe-
sino-*aymara*" or "campesino-*quecha*" on the one hand, and "campesino" on
the other. Whereas the first two strongly indicate the tensions between ethnic and class relations, bringing to the foreground Spanish colonial legacies
entrenched with later colonial expansion and the growing strength of the
capitalistic system, the second indicates social configurations with less ethnic frictions. Thus, from this moment on, Rivera Cusicanqui's emphasis on
the complexity of ethnic/class relations authorizes her to criticize Andean
social sciences for their blindness to ethnic issues and colonial legacies in
their interpretation and understanding of Andean social, cultural, and
historical issues. It is not by chance that in the South-South Exchange
Programme for Research on the History of Development, Rivera Cusicanqui

was invited to join the South-South Exchange Programme Committee. What this recognition amounts to, according to Rivera Cusicanqui, is "that the subaltern studies groups in India are doing something similar to what we have been doing in the Andes at least since the 70s" when a handful of Argentinian (see Tandeter 1976) historians began to look at the economic history of Potosi—the idea of "feudalism" or "capitalism"—in order to understand what it may mean in Latin America and in the colonial period. Rather than borrowing a European or a Third World model to understand Andean society, the movement went in the opposite direction: to look at the problem first rather than at the model. Or, even better, to provide an understanding of colonial domination from its living experience, so as to counter the living experiences of the colonial metropolitan centers upon which experience theories of "feudalism" and "capitalism" have been generated.

SUBALTERNITY AND THE COLONIAL DIFFERENCE: BETWEEN THE POSTCOLONIAL AND THE POSTMODERN

There is another point, mentioned earlier, that I would like to elaborate on in connection with the idea of posttraditional social orders: are subaltern studies postcolonial or postmodern? First, the collection of articles edited by Beverley et al. (1995, 95) links subaltern studies with postmodernism. Second, Florencia Mallon (1994) inserted "postcolonial" in the subtitle of her book on Mexican peasant history. Third, subaltern studies in India are linked to postcolonial studies rather than to the postmodern paradigm, as Prakash's (1994) article makes clear. Finally, while Albó and Rivera Cusicanqui, in Bolivia, seem to be working in a conceptual paradigm more akin to the postcolonial, Richard, in Chile, clearly links her reflections to the postmodern (although her discourse at times resonates with sentences written in the late 1950s and early 1960s by Césaire and Fanon). What is at stake in these ambiguities?

My tentative answer is that in Latin America (as well as in certain areas of Asia and Africa) the postmodern and the postcolonial-Occidental are two faces of the same coin, locating imaginary constructions and loci of enunciation in different aspects of modernity, colonization, and imperial world orders. For example, the nineteenth-century intellectuals of the Southern Cone politically embraced the civilizing mission (Sarmiento, Bello) (see chapter 8) while modern technology (the frontiers, the railroad) was being exported to the Southern Cone and was part of the emergence of new colonialisms (Britain, France) and the fading away of the old ones (Spain, Portugal). Instead, for intellectuals in the Andes, Mexico, and Guatemala, the

legacies of the sixteenth century promoted the notion of "internal colonialism" and postcolonial paradigms were more appropriated than postmodern
ones. In the Andes and Mesoamerica (Mexico and Guatemala), the early
colonial coexisted with the early modern (at its inception), the modern with
the colonial, the postmodern with the postcolonial. Thus, we should remember here that the introduction of "post-Occidentalism" (Fernández Retamar
[1974] 1995) in this context is just a local reflection of colonialism in Latin
America.

Post-Occidentalism could help in superseding the dichotomy postmod-
ern/postcolonial, which sounds like a reinscription of the classical dichotomy between the fragments of marginal European institutions and the ruins
of ancient Mesoamerican and Andean civilizations. Perhaps we should think
more in terms of globalization and in civilizing processes in which the entire
planet is participating—in the diversification of temporalities brought about
by an increasing move to deny the denial of coevalness (which was one of
the most effective strategies of modernity to justify coloniality; see chapter
8) and to diversify our intellectual investments and avoid master models.
Modernity cannot be understood without coloniality; coloniality cannot be
understood without modernity. If, as Ribeiro (1968) taught us, the last stage
of the civilizing process (i.e., the early modern and early colonial periods)
consisted in a massive "subalternization of cultures" that became—by the
sheer effect of the discursive practices of modernity—the non-West, then
"subaltern studies" may have as one of its horizons the rearticulation of the
notion of civilizing processes, no longer conceived as subalternization of
cultures but as a plurilogic and pluritopic process contributing to a planet
in which similarities-in-difference could replace the idea of similarities-and-
differences, manipulated by colonial and imperial discourses. While similar-
ities-and-differences is the conceptual framework in which the very idea of
Western civilization has been constructed (relegating the differences to the
barbarian, the savages, the cannibals, the primitives, the underdeveloped,
etc.), similarities-in-difference calls instead for a relocation of languages,
peoples, and cultures where the differences are looked at, not just in one
direction (the direction of the restricted notion of civilizing processes as the
triumphal march of modernity), but in all possible directions and regional
temporalities. *The* civilizing process is the triumphal march of the human
species, of a variety of civilizing processes, and *not just* the global spread of
European/Western civilizations under the banner of progress, civility, and
development.

Subaltern studies in/of the Americas, in this context, becomes a reflection
on the construction of subalternity since the early stages of globalization,
on the diverse temporalities of the Americas due to the diversity of Amerindian civilizations, and on European colonialism. Once the United States
took a leading position in Western expansion and the previous Christian

and civilizing missions were recast in terms of development and modernization, not only were South America and the Caribbean relocated in different
temporalities, but they (South America and the Caribbean) also became
"fields of studies," and North America the site of a branch of scholarship
identified as "Latin American studies." But now, in a world where the civilizing processes move in all possible directions, Subaltern Studies could contribute to decolonize scholarship, by critically reflecting on their own production and reproduction of knowledge and by avoiding the reinscription
of the strategies of subalternization. In "posttraditional social orders," the
traditional defense of traditions should be constantly contested at all levels,
including the cultures of scholarship and the parochial defense of disciplinarity, even under new paradigms. Brand new traditions are the needs of the
times. The postmodern and the postcolonial should be superseded and
shelved as concepts belonging to the legacies of colonial and imperial discourses (West-East; First-Third Worlds; developed-underdeveloped, etc.):
"Posttraditional cultures of scholarship" would be part of a process of social
transformation of traditional epistemologies (mainly where the politics and
ethics of Latin American areas of study are concerned) and of contentious
discussion on the legitimacy of the postmodern and the postcolonial. The
social sciences and Western philosophy are reaching the limits of the colonial difference.

THE COLONIAL DIFFERENCE IN CHAKRABARTY'S DILEMMA

It has recently been said in praise of the postcolonial project of *Subaltern Studies*
that it demonstrates, "perhaps for the first time since colonization," that "Indians are showing sustained signs of reappropriating the capacity to represent
themselves within the discipline of history." As a historian who is a member of
the *Subaltern Studies* collective, I find the congratulations contained in this re-
mark gratifying but premature. . . . I have a more perverse proposition to argue.
It is that insofar as the academic discourse of history—that is, "history" as discourse produced at the institutional site of the university—is concerned, "Europe" remains the sovereign, theoretical subject of all histories, including the
ones we call "Indian," "Chinese," "Kenyan" and so on. *In this sense, "Indian"
history itself is in a position of subalternity; one can only articulate subaltern subject
positions in the name of history.* (Chakrabarty 1992a, 1)

The entire question of disciplinary, interdisciplinary, and perhaps transdici-
plinary knowledge is at stake in Chakrabarty's observation that as far as
subaltern studies (in India and about India) remain within the realm of
history (as discipline), they are subaltern not only because of their concern
with subalternity, but because their own disciplinary practice, as disciplinary

practice, is subaltern. One example he provides to understand better the subalternity of "Indian" historiography is the following:

> That Europe works as a silent referent in historical knowledge itself becomes obvious in a highly ordinary way. There are at least two everyday subalternities of non-Western, third-world histories. Third-world historians feel a need to refer to works in European history; historians of Europe do not feel any need to reciprocate. . . . "They" produce their work in relative ignorance of non-Western histories, and this does not seem to affect the quality of their work. This is a gesture, however, that "we" cannot return. We cannot even afford an equality or symmetry of ignorance at this level without taking the risk of appearing "old fashioned" or "outdated." (Chakrabarty 1992a, 2)

If such is the dilemma, what is the solution? Chakrabarty proposes "provincializing Europe." What does this mean? First, I would like to examine what it doesn't mean. "Provincializing Europe" is not a project of pure rejection of "modernity, liberal values, universals, reasons, grand narratives, totalizing explanations, and so on" (Chakrabarty 1992a, 20); it doesn't mean either a project in support of cultural relativism, in the sense that all of the preceding are culture-specific and belong to Europe only (20), which will lead to support a nativist, nationalist, or atavistic project, which is not the solution either (21). What "provincializing Europe" means, basically, is "the recognition that Europe's acquisition of the adjective *modern* for itself is a piece of global history of which an integral part is the story of European imperialism"; and "the understanding that this equation of a certain version of Europe with 'modernity' is not the work of Europeans alone; third world nationalisms, as modernizing ideologies *par excellence*, have been equal partners in the process" (21). This equation was particularly strong in nineteenth-century Latin America with postcolonial intellectuals such as Domingo F. Sarmiento in Argentina for whom, as for many others (and rightly so), the future was to follow the lead of modern Europe. That Sarmiento in Argentina coexisted with Bilbao in Chile, who opposed French and U.S. imperialism, is an equation that can be observed in post–World War II decolonizing movements, to which Chakrabarty is referring.

Since Chakrabarty's argument is built on the very idea that modernity is founded on narratives of *transition* (in which, as in Garciá-Canclini, the modern presupposes the traditional, which became the necessary exteriority on which the interior of *modernity* is being defined), he puts great emphasis on the narratives about the "nation" and "citizenship" as the sites where the project of "provincializing Europe" may take place. He focuses on narratives that "celebrate the advent of the modern state and the idea of citizenship" and at the same time plays them down. Chakrabarty states that the idea of citizenship is the repression and violence that are instrumental in the victory of the modern as is the persuasive power of its rhetorical strategies. . . . Nowhere is this irony more visible—the undemocratic foundations of "democracy"—than in the history of modern medicine, public health, and personal hygiene, the discourses which have been central in locating the body of the modern at the intersection of the public and the private. . . . The triumph of this discourse, however, has always been dependent on the mobilization, on its behalf, of effective means of physical coercion. (Chakrabarty 1992a, 21)

"Provincializing Europe" is, in the last analysis, a historiography that through writing and the intersection of both sides of modernity (how the Third World contributes to modernity at the same time that modernity produces the Third World or, equivalently, inside and outside modernity) spatializes time and avoids narratives of transition, progress, development, and point of arrivals. But if history, as a discipline, cannot do it or if history, as a discipline, kills itself by producing narratives beyond the timing of "reason" and "temporality," this is precisely what "provincializing Europe" means: "the politics of despair will require of such history that it lays bare to its readers the reasons why such predicament is necessarily inescapable. This is a history that will attempt the impossible: *to look toward its own death by tracing that which resists and escapes the best human effort at translation across cultural and other semiotic systems, so that the world may once again be imagined as radically heterogeneous.* This, as I have said, is impossible within the knowledge protocols of academic history, for the globality of academia is not independent of the globality that the European modern has created"(Chakrabarty 1992a, 23; 1992b; emphasis added). If, then, Chakrabarty's dilemma is the fact that to write history implies remaining under European disciplinary hegemony, his proposal to go beyond it is to "provincialize Europe," and doing so implies, at its turn, going beyond the disciplines and producing a trans- instead of an interdisciplinary knowledge. Thus the role Chakrabarty attributes to *translation* in his project, the death of history and the beginning of translation as a new form of knowledge that displaces the hegemonic and subaltern locations of disciplinary knowledge. In other words, how to provincialize Europe as a historian when historiography is declared to be bound to Europe is Chakrabarty's dilemma.

In 1982 Edouard Glissant suggested a way out of this type of dilemma. His advantage was being outside the field of historiography, and writing from the perspective of literature and philosophical practices from the colonial experience. In other words, Glissant gets close to what I understand Chakrabarty as wanting to do (provincializing Europe) because Glissant speaks from a decentered disciplinary position. Or from "literature" (and not from "Literature," which is an institutional and canonized form that contributes to the very idea of "modernity"), which is not only a transdisciplinary practice in Glissants' definition, but also a transmodern one: a practice from the colonial horizon of modernity. History, with a capital "H," "is a totality that excludes other histories that do not fit into that of the West. . . . This ethnocentric principle unites the mechanism of the Historical process (the Christian God, the proletariat of industrialized nations) with the soul of the West. The hierarchical system instituted by Hegel (ahistory, prehistory, History) corresponds clearly with the literary ideology of the time. . . . And the last Western attempt to conceptualize a History, that of Toynbee, will organize the Total System based on a discriminatory sequence (great civilizations, great states, great religions) indispensable in such projects" (Glissant [1981] 1989, 76). And he concludes:

> Only technical hegemony (that is, the acquired capacity to subjugate nature and consequently to intoxicate any possible culture with the knowledge created from this subjugation and which is suited to it) still permits the West, which has known the anxieties resulting from a challenged legitimacy, to continue to exercise its sovereignty which is no longer by right but by circumstances. As it abandons right for circumstances, the West dismantles its vision of History (with a capital H) and its conception of sacred Literature. (Glissant [1981] 1989, 76)

Anthropologist and historian Fernando Coronil, also a member of the Latin American Subaltern Studies Group, objected to Chakrabarty's formulation:

> The argument that "a third-world historian is condemned to knowing Europe as the home of the modern" reveals but also confirms Europe's ideological role as the indispensable key to the inner reality of the third world. While Chakrabarty analyzes the effectivity of this ideological division between Europe and its Others, one wonders whether the acceptance of this division at the same time risks reinscribing a notion of Europe as civilized . . . and of the third world as savage. (Coronil 1997, 14)

At this point Coronil (1995) sends the reader to his introduction to Fernando Ortiz's *Cuban Conterpoint* where he uses Ortiz's concept of transculturation to problematize the separation between First and Third Worlds and to question the notion of Europe as the home of theory. Let's then take a closer look at Coronil's proposal on these two issues, since we are here at the heart of the subalternization of knowledge, which is the main topic of this book. And furthermore, Coronil makes these two points on the basis of Ortiz's 1940 work as a Cuban anthropologist confronting the authority of Malinowski, a Polish anthropologist invested with the authority of British anthropology, which, as the case may be, brings a striking parallel with the case of History, as a discipline, in which Chakrabarty grounds his argument.

Coronil is perhaps closer to Chakrabarty than he himself believes. But there is more. In the same year that Chakrabarty published this article on history, Enrique Dussel published an article entitled "Eurocentrism and Modernity" ([1993] 1995), which I discussed in chapter 2 and which opens with the following assertion:

> Modernity is, for many (for Jürgen Habermas or Charles Taylor, for example), an essentially or exclusively European phenomenon. In these lectures, I will argue that modernity is in fact a European phenomenon, but one constituted in a dialectical relation with a non-European alterity that is its ultimate content. Modernity appears when Europe affirms itself as the "center" of a *World* History that it inaugurates; the "periphery" that surrounds this center is consequently part of its self-definition. (Dussel [1993] 1995, 65)

Chakrabarty, Coronil, and Dussel seem to agree on this: modernity is not necessarily and only European or Western; Europe is not the home of knowledge because knowledge is produced everywhere. *However*, for many, as Dussel says, the fact is that Europe is modernity and, as such, the home of theory. As for Chakrabarty, once he recognizes the problem, he proposes "provincializing Europe" as a project to work toward the subalternization of knowledge. Dussel, in the same vein, proposes a *transmodern* project, which, like that of Chakrabarty, will work at the intersection and the planetary contribution in the making of modernity without ignoring the relation of power or, as Quijano will say, the coloniality of power. Coronil, for his part, will end up suggesting a *transcultural* anthropology that looks complementary to Chakrabarty's and Dussel's projects. Coronil does indeed a wonderful job in contextualizing the complexity and richness of Ortiz's concept of transculturation, particularly in the way Ortiz defines and enacts transculturation not only in terms of cultural exchange among human beings but in those of commodities such as tobacco and sugar:

> By casting commodities as the main actors of his historical narrative, Ortiz at once displaces the conventional focus on human historical protagonists and revalorizes historical agency. . . . Thus historical agency comes to include the generative conditions of agency itself. As a critique of reification, Ortiz's counterfetishism questions both conservative interpretations that reduce history to the actions of external forces, and humanists and liberal conceptions that ascribe historical agency exclusively to people. . . . Transculturation thus breathes life into reified categories, bringing into the open concealed exchanges among peoples and releasing histories buried within fixed identities. (Coronil 1995, xxix–xxx)

Thus conceived, *transculturation* shall be at the center of any subaltern studies project, particularly in the way that Ortiz, in his analysis, also breaks away from the limitations that anthropology, as a discipline, embodies, like history in Chakrabarty's analysis: perhaps Ortiz's *Cuban Counterpoint* could be read as an attempt toward the death of anthropology "by tracing that which resists and escapes the best human effort at *translation across cultural and other semiotic systems*" (Chakrabarty 1992a, 23; 1993). I suspect that Coronil has discovered, in the work of Ortiz, in his transcultural anthropology, that *knowledge works as translation and translation works as knowledge*, that is, *trans-* rather than *inter*disciplinary, undermining disciplinary foundations of knowledge (history or anthropology) as disciplines. *Translation*, contrary to disciplines, doesn't have a "home." When Coronil observes that Ortiz, "by examining how cultures shape each other contrapuntally . . . shows the extent to which their fixed and separate boundaries are the artifice of unequal power relations," he is suggesting that a contrapuntal perspective may allow us to understand how the three-world schema is underwritten by fetishized geohistorical categories which conceal their genesis in inequality and domination. More importantly, this perspective may help develop nonimperial categories which caution rather than confirm the work of domination (Coronil 1995, xli). Contrapuntual analysis, the "method" of a transcultural anthropology, is, in my view, complementary to "translation" beyond the discipline of history in Chakrabarty, and a companion to Dussel's transmodernity as a critic epistemology and disciplinary foundation. All of these projects are different (albeit complementary) answers to the undeniable subalternization of knowledge in the modern/colonial world that prompted Chakrabarty's dilemma as well as Coronil's reaction to it. *Transculturation*, in other words, could be conceived as a particular kind of border thinking, and border thinking is, in my argument, the basic need for subaltern epistemology and for thinking beyond the dichotomies produced by "Occidentalism" as the overarching imaginary of the modern/colonial world system, an imaginary that magnified the achievements of "modernity" (for reasons that are clear in the arguments of Dussel, Chakrabarty, Quijano, and Coronil) and played down its darker side, "coloniality." Quijano's restitution of coloniality from the underground of the imaginary of modernity (and its critic, postmodernity) is indeed an important contribution to provincializing Europe, envisioning transdisciplinary (e.g., transcultural anthropology as one case in point) and transmodernity.

Quijano's articulation of "coloniality and modernity/rationality" provides a description and an explanation to what, for Chakrabarty, is the starting point of his argument: the hegemonic site of modern epistemology in Europe (West, or the Atlantic world) and the double operation in the subalternization of knowledge associated with such a hegemony: (1) the transformation of other forms of knowledge in objects of study (some examples of this include Amerindian gnoseology observed and described by Spanish missionaries, in the sixteenth century as an affirmation of Occidentalism; Orientalism, in the eighteenth and nineteenth centuries, once Occidentalism was already established; and area studies, in the twentieth century, which contributed to the consolidation of the social sciences); and (2) the port of departure for traveling theories and disciplinary formations. For instance, one of the recommendations for the future of social sciences provided by the report of the Gulbenkian Commission on the restructuring of the social sciences starts from the recognition of three antinomies, in their very foundation, that should be superseded:

> The classification of the social sciences was constructed around two antinomies which no longer command the wide support they once enjoyed: the antinomy between past and present, and the antinomy between idiographic and nomotethetic disciplines. A third antinomy, that *between the civilized and the barbaric world*, has few defenders anymore, *but in practice still inhabits the mentalities of many scholars.* (Wallerstein et al. 1996, 95; emphasis added)

I'll come back to this last point in chapter 7. For the time being I would like to emphasize, first, that, if not in terms of "civilized" and "barbaric" worlds, Chakrabarty's dilemma is a reaction to the fact that such a distinction between "serious" and "interesting" forms of knowledge "inhabits the mentalities of many scholars." Second, and indirectly related, is the fact of practicing sociology, say, in Africa or in Latin America. Paulin J. Hountonkji ([1993] 1988, 345–64) analyzed the difficulties of everyday life, in relation to research, not only in the social sciences, but in the medical sciences (above all) as well. Corruption in government and lack of information, through books or technology, are other encumbrances to pursuing research "successfully" as it could be done in Paris, Bordeaux, New York, or Durham. The fact is, then, that epistemological canons are not dissociated from social and economic organization, and it is a trap to pretend and aim, in Third World countries or countries that are still paying the consequences of colonial legacies, at practicing social sciences in the same way as in Germany or the United States. Nevertheless, and in spite of difficult material conditions, the call for thinking is always there. Thus, the piercing issue here is to move beyond a culture of scholarship, in which social and economic structures of subordination and domination are imbedded, to the basic fact that thinking is at the same time universal and local: thinking is universal in the very simple sense that it is a component of certain species of living organisms and it is local in the sense that there is no thinking in a vacuum, that thinking (like eating or evacuating, which is also a universal of certain species of living organisms) responds to material and local needs. Thus, this conception of thinking, at the same time local and universal, is a way of conceptualizing from the epistemological perspective of border thinking, and not from the perspective of the distinction between body and soul (or mind) according to which "mind" is universal and that "mind" in modern epistemology was appropriated and universalized by the very concept of reason.

This pattern, by the way, emerged in parallel to an economic rationality that today we call capitalism and with the three main languages of modern scholarship: English, French, and German. Traveling theories, in other words, have to go through translation. The need of translation is already embedded in a structure of power that is not only related to the "grammar" of a given language but also to its history and its site in the modern/colonial world system. Why aren't Spanish and Portuguese, for instance, power languages in modern cultures of scholarship? Why is modern scholarship translated, in general, from English to Arabic but not vice versa? Why is there no prominent contribution from Arab philosophy or sociology to international and planetary scholarship? These are simple questions, often forgotten, that had to do with Chakrabarty's dilemma and Coronil's distinction between canon and theories. Canons, in literature or in scholarly disciplines, provide the points of reference, the foundation, and the form of control in literary studies as well as other scholarly disciplines, in the human as well as in the natural sciences (Mignolo 1989b). And in that sense, Coronil is right to say that canons, and not theories, are imperial attributes (1995, xlii). However, theories can be canonized and, as such, become carriers of the imperial virus. As far as theories have to be expressed in certain languages, the virus is unavoidable. Perhaps a "transcultural disciplinary practice" and a project of "provincializing Europe" would be to push the virus to the extreme: as far as theories, canonical or not, are expressed in colonial languages, "transcultural thinking" (e.g., border thinking) would make it possible to interfere with and intervene in such theories with categories of thinking that have been suppressed in languages that have been suppressed: thus, the relevance of Kusch's contribution, and the undeniable fact that the Zapatistas's theoretical revolution (Mignolo 1997d; forthcoming) emerges from the intervention of Amerindian categories of thought (Tojolabal, Tzotzil, etc.) into Marxist categories translated from German into Spanish.

But let's go back to Quijano's description and explanation of why Europe has been equated with modernity and with the "home" of knowledge and theories. Let's insist, first, that for Quijano "coloniality" does not belong so much to historical periods or particular forms of domination (Spanish or English colonialism; or late capital formation identified at the beginning of the twentieth century as imperialism, both in the form of British and later on U.S. or Soviet imperialisms), as to what he calls the "imaginary" of the repressive side of modernity. Like Chakrabarty, Quijano is careful to point out that it is not a question of denying the brighter side of modernity both in its European as well as planetary manifestation, but of not forgetting its darker side. For instance, in relation to the concept of "totality" Quijano observes:

No es necesario, sin embargo, recusar toda idea de totalidad para desprenderse de las ideas e imágines con las cuales se elaboró esa categoría dentro de la modernidad europea. Lo que hay que hacer es algo muy distinto: liberar la producción del conocimiento, de la reflexión y de la comunicación, de los baches de la racionalidad/modernidad europeas. (Quijano 1992, 446)

It is not necessary to reject every idea of totality in order to get rid of the images and ideas in which the concept of totality was brewed with European modernity. What it is necessary to do is something quite different: to liberate production of knowledge from the forms of reflection and communication, as well as from the crumbles of European modernity/rationality.

Quijano's project is described, by himself, as an intellectual decolonization which I perceive as equivalent to Chakrabarty's "provincializing Europe," Coronil's "transcultural disciplines," or Dussel's "transmodernity." And when I say "equivalent," I mean that each project could and should be translated into the other, as different forms of border thinking (which, of course, is also mutually translatable); but also that they cannot and should not be subsumed into a universal concept, unattached to any local history. To "provincialize Europe" is to take it as one more local history, without forgetting (how could one?) its hegemonic role in the modern/colonial world system. What I am trying to avoid is positing one of these concepts as a master one, as an empty signifier containing and accommodating all the rest. To do so would imply maintaining the terms of the conversation, a concept of totality (named by an empty signifier) that will contain the rest but which will maintain the control and allow for a position of power to those who align themselves with it. When Quijano proposes to maintain the concept of totality as a heterogeneous and not homogenous totality, it would also be necessary to imagine such heterogeneous totality with several heads, not with just one. One head governing a heterogeneous totality is expressed in the idea of an empty signifier, which will maintain all the problems that multiculturalism presents today. A totality that is at the same time heterogeneous and multiheaded needs border thinking as a guiding epistemology, and a series of metaphors that will replace the hegemonic image of the human body describing social totality and positing the head as the governing center. Quijano analyzes this image both in relation to the structure of the nation-state and of the coloniality of power: the imaginary dividing the planet between pagans and Christians, barbarians and civilized men, underdeveloped and developed nations.

Quijano's analysis of how the idea of modernity being European constitutes itself and how the idea of modernity as a European phenomenon was linked to epistemology and the coloniality of power is indeed very helpful. His point of reference is the current epistemological crisis founded in the structural relation between a knowing subject and an object to be known (e.g., see also Rorty 1982 for a similar critique coming from a different perspective and with a different project). This antinomy should be listed as a fourth one, and perhaps the one that provides the grounding for the other one, in Wallerstein et al.'s analysis I commented on earlier. But, be that as it may, there are two thorny issues in Quijano's analysis that provide a new departure from existing and well-known criticisms of the same problem.

The first issue involves the correlation of knowing subject/known object, which in its emergence was an emancipatory epistemological move away from beliefs in and the authority of God in Christian theology; and also a liberation of the individual from social hierarchical and rigid religious structures as they were in "pre"-modern Europe. However that liberation went together with the formation of economic relations, the consolidation of urban life, and an economic class associated with the "burgh." The installation of the knowing subject as final authority cut off the possibility of conceiving knowledge as an intersubjective enterprise and, thus, the object became not only different but exterior to the subject. The object was also defined by its property: exteriority and intrinsic properties differentiate the object from the knowing subject. This is well known, and it is also attributed to Descartes, whose philosophy established the grounds for such an epistemological foundation and the concept of reason in which the knowing subject grounds his or her knowledge. However, the paradigms of rationality and of humans as rational beings were already established in the sixteenth and the seventeenth century, by missionaries like Bartolomé de las Casas (Dominican) and José de Acosta (Jesuit) in their investigations of the history and nature of the Amerindian, as well as for the theologians of the School of Salamanca (most of them Dominican) when discussing the "rights of the people" and whether the Indian could be enslaved (cf., Pagden 1982, 142–97).

Now, according to the second issue, the emergence of a knowing subject is correlative, Quijano stresses, with the emergence of the idea of private property, which is also the correlation between an individual and something else, the object called "property": "The same mental pattern underlines both ideas, knowledge and property, and both correspond with the emergence of the modern society" (1992, 442). But what has not been emphasized enough is that in the rise of the individual, as economic and epistemological subject, the process was not only articulated as "emancipation" from social restriction within the very European, Christian, and self-defined Occident, but by suppressing all other forms of society and of persons precisely during the period in which the idea of a Christian and western Europe was being articulated in its difference with pagans, infidels, and barbarians outside Europe and either in the margin of the West (like the Amerindians in the Indias Occidentales); or in the other two continents, Asia and Africa (the lands of Ham and Shem). Quijano states:

The radical absence of the "other" not only postulates an isolated social existence in general. It also negates the very idea of social totality. As has been demonstrated by European colonial practices, the economic and epistemological paradigm makes it possible to obliterate every reference to any other possible "subject" outside of the European context, that is, to make invisible the colonial order as part of the totality, at the very moment in which the very idea of Europe is in the process of constituting itself in relation to the rest of the world in colonization. The very idea of "Europe" and "Occident" is already a recognition of identity and, therefore, of the difference with other cultural experiences. (Quijano 1992, 442)

Quijano concludes that with this paradigm in gestation, in which cultural differences were translated into hierarchical arrangements, and reason was the primary criteria for subject formation, "only Europe is rational and can have subjects. Other cultures are not rational" (1992, 443). Briefly, in Quijano's account of things (e.g., the crisis of modernity and its epistemology), what is relevant is the correlation between epistemology and economics, on the one hand, and, within the local history of Europe itself, epistemology and colonization, on the other hand, in the constitution of Europe as a geopolitical and economic entity from which the rest of the world is measured, studied, and classified. Such a picture, in other words, is a picture of the coloniality of power and knowledge, which, Quijano claims, is still at work beyond the changing faces of old colonialism, modern imperialism, and postmodern globalization. This is also the frame in which subalternization of knowledge and Chakrabarty's dilemma originate. This is also the frame in which border thinking, in its different forms, which means also an actualization of different local histories in which they are emerging, brings a different image of totality: not a homogenous totality, neither a heterogeneous one with one head, but a fragmentation of colonial local histories in which global designs, including epistemological ones, are constantly being remade. If such a picture could have in place a "before" (during the five hundred years of the formation and consolidation of the modern world system), it is only in the past decades that a strong consciousness of the crisis of modernity and the epistemological potential of border thinking is becoming conceptualized as such and worked out, not as marginal or degraded forms of knowledge but as the very potential of the border epistemology emerging from the colonial difference.

CONCLUDING REMARKS

In this chapter South Asian subaltern studies as well as their adaptation by Latin Americanist historian Florencia Mallon and by the Latin American

Subaltern Studies Group were discussed and questions about the correlation between geohistorical location and production of knowledge were asked. One of my concerns was how travelling theories "cross" the colonial difference. In this regard, it is important to keep in mind the differences between the original project of South Asian Subaltern Studies Group formulated in terms of querying the "historic failure of the nation to come to its own" and of making clear that "it is the study of this failure which constitutes the central problematic of the historiography of colonial India" (Guha 1988, 43). Although one can say that it is this problematic that engages Mallon's (1994) and the Latin American Group's adaptation, in both cases there is a lack of attention to the fact that Latin America is not a country, like postpartition India, and that the many countries of Latin America (mainly Spanish American countries in both cases [Mallon and the Latin American Group]), obtained their independence at the beginning of the nineteenth century and not in 1947, a date very close to all the members of the South Asian Group. Second, I reviewed several critical contributions in Latin America and in the United States, in the past thirty years or so, akin to those of the South Asian Subaltern Studies Group (as it is clear in the recent translation in Spanish, published in Bolivia, and edited by Rivera Cusicanqui and Barragán), ignored by Mallon, and while included in Beverley, Oviedo, and Aronna's anthology, *Postmodernism in Latin America* (1995) were not recognized in its historicity. Even less recognized were the *colonial* dimension in Latin American history (Rivera Cusicanqui 1992) and the coloniality of power introduced by Quijano. The persistence of the coloniality of power that prompted Chakrabarty's dilemma is being reproduced in Latin American Subaltern Studies. Thinking from the "method" of a "model" prevails over thinking from the "problem."

The following chapter begins where this one left off: the coloniality of power and knowledge in relation to national values and national and colonial languages as foundations and warranties of scholarship, in which modernity/rationality (Quijano) and the foundation of the social sciences (Wallerstein et al.) were grounded. Following the argument in this chapter, I explore possibilities opened by the crisis of national language as complementary alternatives to "provincializing Europe" (Chakrabarty), "transcultural and transdisciplinary knowledge" (Dussel and Coronil), and "decolonization of knowledge" (Quijano). In chapter 5 the focus is on languages and literatures, in chapter 6, on languages and epistemologies.

Part Three

SUBALTERNITY AND THE COLONIAL
DIFFERENCE: LANGUAGES, LITERATURES,
AND KNOWLEDGES

CHAPTER 5

"An Other Tongue": Linguistics Maps, Literary Geographies, Cultural Landscapes

THE FIRST VERSION of this chapter[1] was read at a conference on theoretical issues in Hispanic Studies, in November 1994. I remember, and I was not surprised, that one of the questions raised at the conference was why I chose to include Michele Cliff, a Jamaican author writing in English, in my argument. When I submitted the paper for its publication in the conference proceedings, one of the referees suggested I add examples like Augusto Roa-Bastos from Paraguay or Miguel Angel Asturias from Guatemala, since most of their work deals with issues relevant for my argument, Roa Bastos working within the tension of Spanish and Guarani and Asturias between Spanish and Mayan roots languages. The referee was certainly right in his or her observation, but that was not the point, since Roa Bastos or Asturias would have been useful to restate the case in different local histories of Spanish colonization in Spanish America that in my talk were discussed through José M. Arguedas (from Peru). I could, of course, have mentioned similar cases (like Asturias and Roa Bastos), but repetition of the same was not (and is not) my point. I was trying to think coloniality and the Americas and move away from the remains of nineteenth-century ideology, expressed by Francisco Bilbao, about the "two languages and two races" in the Americas, as I discussed in chapter 3. Nationalist ideology about language and literature is so pervasive that even progressive literary and cultural critics could be blind to it. Thus, how was it possible in a conference on Hispanic (and in the best of possible worlds) Latin American literatures and cultures, to have as main examples of my argument Frantz Fanon, from Martinique; Michele Cliff, from Jamaica; Gloria Anzaldúa, a Chicana from the United States, and José Maria Arguedas, from Peru? Since I did not accept the referee's recommendation (because it would twist my argument into a terrain my argument was contrasting), I declined the invitation to publish my talk at the conference as a paper in the proceedings. Soon after that event, I was asked for a contribution for a

---

[1] The part of the title in quotation marks comes from Alfred Arteaga's *An Other Tongue: Nation and Ethnicity in the Linguistic Borderlands* (1994). The reader may have already noted the parallel with Khatibi's "an other thinking," which explored in chapter 1.

special issue of *Modern Language Quarterly* (Mignolo 1996d) devoted to "regionalism in Latin America." I thought that my talk on "linguistic maps and literary geographies" was appropriate for the occasion. This time, the referee only requested I move Arguedas to the front of the article, since in the original version it was the very last example. I accepted this suggestion and the article was published (1996d), although I recognized that the "Spanish" unconscious in Latin America was behind the request and not all that Arguedas had done to bring Quechua back after centuries of "Spanish" (American) repression. This anecdote is a good example of how the coloniality of power works within us, hiding the colonial difference under and spot lighting the values of national languages and a national conception of subcontinental Latin America. This chapter intends to delve into the coloniality of power and highlight the colonial difference in the work of language, literature, and their contribution to a domain of culture tangential to cultural industries.

While the process just outlined was taking place, I read Alfred Arteaga's interesting collection entitled *An Other Tongue: Nation and Ethnicity in the Linguistic Borderlands* (1994), and more recently, Rosario Ferré's novel in English, *The House in the Lagoon* (1996), Gustávo Pérez-Firmat's *Next Year in Cuba* (1995), and Ariel Dorfman's memoir, also in English, *Heading South, Looking North* (1998). These readings allowed me to expand on my argument. But what is my argument? In chapter 3, I made a part of it pointing out how the images of the two Americas and the overlap between Anglo and Latin America came into being. Basically, independence from Spain and from England, which was a particular case of decolonization, was followed by a process of nation building in a new imperial order. One of the strong weapons in building homogeneous imagined communities was the belief in a national language, which was tied up with national literature and contributed, in the domain of language, to the national culture. Furthermore, the complicity between language, literature, culture, and nation was also related to geopolitical order and geographical frontiers. Language and literature were part of a state ideology, supported by its organic intellectuals (Poblete 1997); this ideology was at the foundation of departments of languages and literatures, national or foreign, in countries around the world. My argument, then, is that history, and particularly the past twenty years, is transforming national geopolitical configurations built mainly during the nineteenth century at the intersection of nations that were empires (England) or strong domains (France), on the one hand, and nations struggling against old colonialism (Spain, Portugal) and negotiating with new nations (England, Spain, Portugal), on the other. Instead of assuming the unity of a Spanish American literature and culture, based on Spanish language, I look at the Americas, including the Caribbean, in the history of the modern/colonial world system and in the colonial horizons of modernity. Thus, this chapter presupposes a point of departure that I already made in chapter 2, but that I repeat here for the readers' convenience:

> The modern world-system was born in the long sixteenth century. The Americas as a geosocial construct were born in the long sixteenth century. The creation of this geosocial entity, the Americas, was the constitutive act of the modern world-system. The Americas were not incorporated into an already existing capitalist world-economy. There could not have been capitalist world-economy without the Americas. (Quijano and Wallerstein 1992, 549)

The aim of this chapter is to set the stage for thinking about languages (and, of course, their implications for literature, cultures of scholarship, linguistic policy, education, etc.) in a transnational world, against the scenario of national ideologies linking language, literature, culture, and territory in one homogeneous whole. I assume that theoretical models dealing with languages have been built in complicity with colonial expansion. The linguistic and philosophical models of the twentieth century, and most remarkably those popularized in the 1960s and 1970s, are of little use for dealing with the transnational dimension of plurilanguaging, since they appear in academic discourse as a universal-speaking subject. Plurilanguaging better captures a situation that has been defined from the perspective of national ideologies in the opposition between "foreign languages" (mainly in First World countries) and "bilingual education" (mainly in Third World countries). The speaking subject, curiously enough, was modeled on the experiences and the idea of national languages that were, at the same time, imperial languages. My argument implies the legacies of the early modern and colonial periods (modernity and coloniality) and joins forces with efforts to demodernize and decolonize scholarship, along with discourses in the public sphere that emerged in postmodern and postcolonial theorizing after World War II. In this genealogy, modernity and coloniality presuppose the coexistence of the modern state and imperial domains in a way that was not yet articulated in the early modern period under the Spanish and Portuguese empires. It is precisely in comparing language practices and public policy in the early modern period (sixteenth, seventeenth centuries) with the current stage of global coloniality that we witness a significant switch in the way languages are conceptualized in relation to both colonial control and national ideologies, on the one hand, to knowledge and reason, on the other. These are indeed two sides of the same coin. What we are witnessing now, as the arguments that follow illustrate, is a relocation of languages and cultures made possible by the very process of global interconnection.

It is worth noting, parallel to what I just wrote, that the early colonial process designed to "modernize," Christianize, and civilize the world was transformed in the last quarter of the twentieth century into a process with an aim to "marketize" the world and no longer to civilize or Christianize it. Coloniality continues to be, in this global domain, an unnamed, unspoken driving force of modernization and the market. Paradoxically, the emphasis on consumerism, commodities, and increasing marketplaces plays against the control imposed by early Christian and civilian programs. In the first place, non-Western languages such as Quechua and minority Western languages such as Catalan are reemerging from the forceful repression they were subjected to during the national period in Latin America as well as in Europe. Second, Western languages such as Spanish, French, and English are being fractured by emergent languaging practices in formerly colonial domains. Finally, the processes resulting from the internal hierarchy within Western expansion and from the relegation of Spanish to second-class languaging rank (as it was considered inadequate for philosophical and scientific languaging) find their way of intervention prompted by migratory movements from areas colonized by the Spanish and British empires and their national configurations during and after the nineteenth century. If a word is needed to identify the locus of these phenomena and processes, it is "transculturation" (see my introduction). Transculturation subsumes the emphasis placed on borders, migrations, plurilanguaging, and multiculturing and the increasing need to conceptualize transnational and transimperial languages, literacies, and literatures. Border thinking shall help us to think languages otherwise (see also the introduction and chapter 6). Transculturation, in other words, infects the locus of enunciation, and not just as a social phenomenon allowing for the celebration of the "impure" in the social world from a "pure" perspective couched in a national language and in "scientific" epistemology.

Sociohistorical transformations demand disciplinary modifications as well. The challenges presented to language and literary scholarship by transnational and transimperial languaging processes are epistemologically and pedagogically serious, for they impinge on the very conception of the humanities as a site of research and teaching. This is particularly the case when reevaluations are viewed from the perspective of nations with colonial legacies rather than from the perspective of the European modernity. Such challenges alter the commonly held belief that linguistic and literary studies deal only with texts and literary authors, with canon formation and transformation, and with aesthetic judgments and textual interpretations. Transnational languaging processes demand theories and philosophies of human symbolic production predicated on languaging and transnational and transimperial categories, on a new philology grounded on border thinking that could replace and displace "the" classical tradition in which philology and philosophy were housed in classical (Greek, Latin) and modern/colonial languages (English, French, German). The clouding of national frontiers also demands rethinking disciplinary boundaries, if not undoing them. In the past ten years, a substantial exchange has taken place among literary theorists, critics, and social scientists, chiefly in the fields of anthropology and history. Transimperial, transcolonial, and transnational (and by *trans* I mean beyond national languages and literatures as well as beyond comparative studies that presuppose national languages and literatures) cultural studies could serve as a new inter- and transdisciplinary space of reflection, in which issues emerging from Western expansion and global interconnections since the end of the fifteenth century might be discussed and linguistic and literary studies redefined. Literacy, the missing and complicitous word between languages and literatures, and languaging, a concept difficult to grasp in the Western denotative philosophy of language, are moving to the forefront of this transdisciplinary discourse. In the early modern world, languages were attached to territories, and nations were characterized by the "natural" links between them.

THE PROBLEM: "WHAT ARE NATIONAL LANGUAGES GOOD FOR" IN A TRANSNATIONAL WORLD?

Coulmas (1988, 10–11) formulated the problem and the complicity between language, nation, and state as follows:

> Stressing the identity of language and nation is one thing, but demanding political autonomy for a linguistically defined group is, of course, something quite different. Languages have always been used to establish or claim a sphere of influence. As imperial languages they have been imposed on dominated ethnic groups by whoever had the power to do so. A uniform code has more often than not been regarded as a matter of administrative convenience for governing a country of empire. However, ideologizing language is a different matter; and if language can be employed as a symbol of nationality by a dominant group, dominated groups may, of course, exert the same logic and make political claims based on their linguistic identity. *Thus, while the idea of a national language and its political enforcement may be said to function as a cohesive force, the reverse is also true. Language may be as disruptive a force as any culture marker, and it is clear that the national language-ideology has bred intra-communal strife and, in a sense, created minorities in many countries that have established themselves as states in modern times.* (Coulmas 1988, 11; emphasis added)

After World War II, languages and territories were redefined when area studies emerged as a consequence of the hierarchical division into First, Second, and Third Worlds. And after the 1970s, massive migration brought a new way of backing up the "natural" belief in the links between languages and territories. In contrast, area studies was a distribution of scientific labor among scholars located in the First World that was meant to secure (both in terms of war and in terms of production of knowledge) its primacy in the order of economy as well as of knowledge. From this perspective, languages needed to be attached to "cultures" and "territories." Thus, insofar as the configuration of area studies coincided with the latest period of globalization (1945–89), it brought into the foreground a new meaning for the expression "understanding other/foreign languages and cultures." A fundamental problem then becomes "understanding diversity and subaltern languages and knowledges," where "understanding" is used both as a gerund and as an adjective. When it is employed as an adjective, "understanding diversity" becomes part of the paradigm in which we encounter expressions such as ethnic diversity or cultural diversity. In such cases, "understanding diversity" can be read as equivalent to "diversity of understanding," provided that we can make sense of expressions such as ethnicity of understanding and cultures of understanding. And by this I mean two things: understanding global diversality, to which universalism belongs as one particular and diverse cultural entity; and understanding diversity beyond the national/imperial language ideologies. I first comment on particular cases (Arguedas, Cliff, Becker, Anzaldúa) before coming back to languaging and diversity/diversality.

THEORIES ARE WHERE YOU CAN FIND THEM

What is permitted in literature is not allowed in cultures of scholarship. Cultures of scholarship (which I discuss in the next chapter) could make of hybridity an interesting topic of study, but the discourse reporting the finding cannot be hybrid itself! You cannot, for example, be a sociologist and publish an article in a prestigious and refereed sociological journal (or any other discipline for that matter) and write like Anzaldúa wrote *Borderlands/ La frontera* (1987). "Indigeous sociology," for instance, would most likely be written in English but not in an "Indigenous" Language. Disciplinary language should be as pure as the blood of early Christians in Spain. Languaging shall be controlled by rules, and one must respect grammatical structure, discourse coherence, and argumentative logic. All this is certainly fine. But it is neither the only way nor the best way to produce, transplant, and transform knowledge. The problem is that the restrictive rules operating in cultures of scholarship are based on the belief that literature is fine, but doesn't constitute serious knowledge; and that is a consequence of both the imperial difference (e.g., science vs. literature) and the colonial difference (e.g., literature vs. folklore). Glissant, for instance, as writer and essayist, writes about the Caribbean and Creolité in an argument that, although keeping French language as a "vehicle," is an argument in "Creolization": bilanguaging in Creole, incorporating French into it, instead of translating Creole into French! Anzaldúa can write about the border and new mestiza consciousness, by appropriating English and Spanish and producing border knowledge and border thinking.

Anthropologist and cultural critic Nestor García Canclini ([1989] 1995) describes the hybridity of the border, but without engaging himself in border thinking. The hybridity of Tijuana in García Canclini's argument is rendered in a discourse that is not hybrid itself, that maintains the homogeneity of language and rules established in cultures of scholarship. In the following section I attempt to bring another view of literature, looking at it from the perspective of the theoretical knowledge that it generates. My discussion is intended to create, through border thinking (e.g., thinking in between human sciences and literature), a frame in which literary practice will not be conceived as an object of study (aesthetic, linguistic, or sociological) but as production of theoretical knowledge; not as "representation" of something, society or ideas, but as a reflection its own way about issues of human and historical concern, including language, of course; not necessarily the grammar or the phonetic, but the politics of language as far as literary practices have been, in the modern/colonial world system, linked in different ways to the coloniality of power in its colonial as well as national versions, and as far as canon formation and national and Western values have been woven together to produce the linguistic maps, the historical geographies, and the cultural landscapes of the modern/colonial world system within its internal logic (e.g., imperial conflicts) as well as in their external borders (e.g., conflicts with "other" cultures; the colonial difference).

The Uncoupling of Languaging from National Literature

José María Arguedas's introduction to his *Tupac Amaryu Kamaq Taytanchisman*, (1962) is titled "I Do Not Regret Writing in Quechua," and it is devoted to explaining his decision. Anticipating objections from "quechólogos," who would like to preserve the purity of the Quechua language, Arguedas says that he has used Castilian words with Quechua declension as well as Castilian words written as the Indians and "mestizos" pronounce them. He notes that in his text there is just one Quechua word that belongs to a sophisticated register of Quechua and that there are also words taken from the Huancaconchucos dialect. Despite these few obstacles, Arguedas states that the book of poems is accessible to the Quechua-speaking population in the linguistic map of Runasimi, from the Department of Huancavelica to Puno, Peru, to the entire Quechua zone in Bolivia. Furthermore, he believes that the book he has written in Quechua could be well understood in Ecuador.

Arguedas also mentions that the Haylli-Taki was originally written in the Quechua he speaks, his native language, Chanca. After writing the book of poems, he translated it into Castilian. In the introduction he notes that an "impulso ineludible" forced him to write the poems in Quechua:

> A medida que iba desarrollando el tema, mi convicción de que el quechua es un idioma más poderoso que el castellano para la expresión de muchos trances del espíritu y, sobre todo, del ánimo, se fue acrecentando, inspirándome y enardeciéndome. Palabras del quechua contienen con una densidad incomparables la materia del hombre y de la naturaleza y el vínculo intenso que por fortuna aún existe entre lo uno y lo otro. El indígena peruano está abrigado, consolado, iluminado, bendecido por la naturaleza: su odio y su amor, cuando son desencadenados, se precipitan, por eso, con toda esa materia, y también su lenguaje.

While I was developing my subject matter, my conviction that Quechua is a language better suited and more powerful than Castilian to express critical moments of the soul *trances del espiritu* and, above all, critical moments of mind, was growing on me; becoming a source of inspiration and of growing excitement. Quechua words embrace the human and natural dimension in a density without parallel and, above all, the Quechua words also embrace the relationships that fortunately still exist between humanity and nature. Peruvian indigenous people are sheltered, comforted, brightened, blessed by nature: when their hate and love are unleashed, they hastily move toward grasping humanity and nature, with a force that also includes their language.

> Sin embargo, aunque quisiera pedir perdón por haberme atrevido a escribir en quechua, no sólo no me arrepiento de ello, sino que ruego a quienes tienen un dominio mayor que el mío sobre este idioma, escriban. Debemos acrecentar nuestra literatura quechua, especialmente en el lenguaje que habla el pueblo; aunque el otro, el señorial y erudito, debiera ser cultivado con la misma dedicación. *Demostremos que el quechua actual es un idioma en el que se puede escribir tan bella y conmmovedoramente como en cualquiera de las otras lenguas perfeccionadas por siglos de tradición literaria. El quechua es también un idioma milenario.* (emphasis added)

Nevertheless, and even if I would like to excuse myself for daring to write in Quechua, I have to confess that I am not regretting it at all; on the contrary, I would even go further and to beseech those who have a better command of Quechua than mine to write themselves. We must enhance our Quechua literature, particularly in the language spoken by the people without forgetting the other Quechua, the erudite and noble Quechua, that must also be cultivated with the same intensity. *We will probe that current Quechua is a language in which it is possible to write with the same beauty and moving effect possible to achieve in any other language that has been improved through centuries of literary tradition. Quechua too is a millenarian language.* (Arguedas 1962, 5)

In Latin America different manifestations of the tensions between linguistic maps, literary geographies, and cultural landscapes can be linked with the dismissal of Amerindian languages under colonial and Western expansion. It will be helpful for the reader not familiar with Arguedas's life and interlanguage trajectory, the color of his skin, and the memories and experiences inscribed "under" it to read a little of his narration of those experiences:

> My mother died when I was two and a half. My father married a second time—
> a woman who had three sons . . . [and] who owned half the town; she had many
> indigenous servants, as well as the traditional contempt and ignorance of what
> an Indian was, and because she despised and hated me as much as [her] Indians,
> she decided that I was to live with them in the kitchen, eat and sleep there.
> (Arguedas 1972, 247; translated and quoted by Sandoval 1998, xxii)

Arguedas's need and decision to write in Quechua, to translate his poem into Spanish and to write a justification comparing Quechua with Spanish, clearly articulate such tensions. He has struggled both with the millenarian forces and the memories of a language grounded in the body of those living and dying in the linguistic map and literary geography of Runasimi (to whom he addresses his poems), and with the centennial and institutional forces of a transplanted language grounded in the body and memories of Castilians living and dying in Spain, as well as in a New World constructed on the ruins of Runasimi.

There are other linguistic experiences complementing those of Arguedas and foreshadowing the question of language and colonialism, an area in which linguistic maps, literary geographies, and cultural landscapes collide and in which social and cultural transformations reinforce each other. Let us now compare the Andes with the Caribbean and with the Mexican-U.S. border by bringing into the discussion a Jamaican, Michelle Cliff (1995) and a Mexican American writer, Gloria Anzaldúa (1987).

Cliff, who underlines the differences between metropolitan English and the colonial English of the West Indies, is more concerned with the political and cultural dimensions of language than with matters of accent or lexicon. Of the several types of Creole languages in the Caribbean, I would like to remind the reader of the main varieties: the Creole of French lexicon spoken in French Guyana, Martinique, Guadeloupe, and Haiti; "Papiamentu," the Creole language of Castilian and Portuguese lexicon spoken in the Dutch Caribbean; and the English Creole spoken in Barbados, Jamaica, Trinidad, Tobago, and elsewhere (Citarella 1989). Cliff refers to this last variety in her text.

The daughter of an affluent family, Cliff pursued graduate studies at the Warburg Institute in London. Her dissertation on game playing in the Italian Renaissance took her to Siena, Florence, and Urbino, a journey that ended with her participation in the feminist movement and in her recovery of an identity she had learned to despise. I will let Cliff speak for herself by quoting extensively from the preface to *The Land of Look Behind*:

> I originated in the Caribbean, specifically on the island of Jamaica, and although I have lived in the United States and in England, I travel as a Jamaican. It is Jamaica that forms my writing for the most part, and which has formed, for the most part, myself. Even though I often feel what Derek Walcott expresses in his poem "The Schooner Flight": "I had no nation now but the imagination." It is a complicated business. Jamaica is a place halfway between Africa and England, to put it simply, although historically one culture (guess which one) has been esteemed and the other denigrated (both are understatements), at least among those who control the culture and politics of the island, the Afro-Saxons. As a child among these people, indeed of these people, as one of them, I received the message of anglocentrism, of white supremacy, and I internalized it. As a writer, as a human being, I have had to accept that reality and deal with its effect on me, as well as finding what has been lost to me from the darker side, and what may be hidden, to be dredged from memory and dream. And it is there to be dredged. As my writing delved longer and deeper into this part of myself, I began to dream and imagine. . . .
>
> One of the effects of assimilation, indoctrination, passing into the anglocentrism of the British West Indian culture is that you believe absolutely in the hegemony of the King's English and in the form in which it is meant to be expressed. Or else your writing is not literature; it is folklore, and folklore can never be art. Read some poetry by West Indian writers—some, not all—and you will see what I mean. You have to dissect stanza after extraordinarily Anglican stanza for Afro-Caribbean truth; you may never find the latter. But this has been our education. The Anglican ideal—Milton, Wordsworth, Keats—was held before us with an assurance that we were unable, and would never be enabled, to compose a work of similar correctness. No reggae spoken here. (Cliff 1985, 12–13)

Cliff makes it clear that colonial literature will always be viewed as inferior when confronted with the practice defined and exemplified by the metropolitan literary canon. The same language, the same syntactic rules, but the game played under different conditions results in diverse verbal practices: folklore is not literature, just as myth is not history. In both cases, the "wisdom of the people" was invented to distinguish "taste and knowledge of genius and educated few," establishing a hierarchy of cultural practices parallel to economic and political regulations and government.

It is *languaging*, thinking and writing between languages, that Arguedas and Cliff allow us to emphasize, moving away from the idea that language is a fact (e.g., a system of syntactic, semantic, and phonetic rules), and moving toward the idea that speech and writing are strategies for orienting and manipulating social domains of interaction. Both Arguedas's and Cliff's linguistic conceptualization and literary practices create fractures within languages (Spanish in Spain and in Peru; English in Jamaica) and between languages (Spanish on the Iberian Peninsula in contact with Spanish "dialects" and in the Andes in contact with "Amerindian languages"; English in England, and in the Caribbean, in contact with Creole languages), revealing the colonial aspects of linguistic, literary, and cultural landscapes. The very concept of literature presupposes the official language of a nation/empire and the transmission of the cultural literacy built into them. Therefore, it is not sufficient to recognize the links between the emergence of comparative literature as a field of studies and literature's complicity with imperial expansion and nation building, with all the complexities entailed in the process: English nation building and empire building in the nineteenth century was not the same as nation building in Argentina during the same period. Nor is it adequate to denounce the pretended universality of a European observer who does not recognize the regionality of other literatures (Said 1993). It is the very concept of literature, like the philosophical and political conceptualization of language, that should be displaced from the idea of objects (e.g., grammar of the language, literary works, and natural history) to the idea of languaging as cultural practice and power struggle. Furthermore, colonial expansion and colonial legacies in the modern world system and in the double side of modernity/coloniality have created the conditions, on the one hand, for languaging across the colonial difference and, on the other,' for inventing a discourse about languages that places the languaging of colonial powers above other linguistic and cultural practices.

Let me further explore the question of languaging and colonialism by moving to Anzaldúa's *Borderlands*. To read *Borderlands* is to read three languages and three literatures concurrently, which is also a new way of languaging. It would be helpful to bear in mind Alton Becker's articulation of the idea of languaging, based on his experience of dealing with Burmese and English:

> *Entering another culture, another history of interactions, we face what is basically a problem of memory.* Learning a new way of languaging is not learning a new code, into which the units of my domain of discourse are re-encoded, although the process may begin that way; and if the new way of languaging shares a history with my own, the exuberances and deficiencies may not get in the way of simple interactions. However, at some point the silences do get in the way and the wording out gets slow and hard. *A new code would not be so hard and painful to learn; a new way of being in the world is.* (Becker 1991, 227; emphasis added)

I quote Becker not as a linguistic authority (even if he is) but next to the writers, Arguedas, Cliff, and Anzaldúa: theorizing is a way of languaging, just as languaging implies its own theory; theorizing languages within social structures of domination is dealing with the "natural" plurilingual conditions of the human world "artificially" suppressed by the monolingual ideology and monotopic hermeneutics of modernity and nationalism. In *Borderlands/La Frontera*, Anzaldúa remaps linguistic and literary practices, articulating three linguistic memories (Spanish, English, and Nahuatl). Chapter 6, for example, is titled "Tlilli, Tlapalli: The Path of the Red and Black Ink." Here, Anzaldúa provides an explanation of the title:

> For the ancient Aztecs, in tlilli, in tlapalli, la tinta negra y roja de sus códices (the black and red ink painted on codices) were the colors symbolizing escritura y sabiduria (writing and wisdom). . . . An image is a bridge between evoked emotion and conscious knowledge; words are cables that hold up the bridge. Images are more direct, more immediate than words, and closer to the unconscious. Picture language precedes thinking in words; the metaphorical mind precedes analytical consciousness. . . .
>
> I write the myth in me, the myths I am, the myths I want to become. The word, the image and the feeling have a palatable energy, a kind of power.
> Con imágenes domo mi miedo, cruzo los abismos que tengo por dentro. Con palabras me hago piedra, pájaro, puente de serpientes arrastrando a ras del suelo todo lo que soy, todo lo que algún día seré.
> Los que están mirando (leyendo),
> los que cuentan (o refieren lo que leen).
> Los que vuelven ruidosamente las hojas de los códices
> la tinta negra y roja (la sabiduría)
> y lo pintado,
> ellos nos llevan nos guián,
>   nos dicen el camino.
>
> With images I tame my fear, crossing my innermost abyss
> With words I become stone, bird, bridge of snakes dragging along
>   to the ground level all that I am, all that some day I will be.
> Those who are looking at (reading),
> Those who are always telling (or narrating what they read).
> Those who noisily unfold the leaves of the codices
>   the black and the red ink (wisdom),
>   and that which is painted,
> They are who carry us and guide us
>   they show us the way.
>
> (*Anzaldúa, 1987*)

These two paragraphs show the juxtaposition of several memories. The Spanish quotation in verse form comes from the *Colloquios y doctrina christiana*, a dialogue between the first twelve Franciscan friars and representatives of the Mexican nobility, who arrived in Mexico in 1524 after the fall of

Mexico-Tenochtitlan. The dialogue was recorded in Nahuatl, collected and then translated into Spanish by Bernardino de Sahagún around 1565. Originally, this quotation, which reports the answers of the Mexican nobility to the Franciscan presentation, requesting that they adopt the Christian doctrine, was in Nahuatl. The excerpt quoted by Anzaldúa narrates the moment in which the Mexican noblemen refer to the Tlamatinime (the wise men, those who can read the black and the red ink written in the codices). Anzaldúa's languaging entangles Spanish, English, and Nahuatl (the first two with a strong "literary" tradition kept alive after the conquest; the third, which was and still is an oral way of languaging, was disrupted during and marginalized after the conquest), and her languaging invokes two kinds of writing: the alphabetic writing of the metropolitan center and the pictographic writing of pre-Columbian Mexican (as well as Mesoamerican) civilizations.

But there are still other configurations removing the deep belief in the natural family ties between language and territories (Mignolo 1989a). I urge the reader to remember that I am not questioning the importance of "being born" in a language, as Cuban writer Edmundo Desnoes (1994) puts it and, I would add, to "live in" one or more languages, as many writers in the past (Nabokov, Beckett, Conrad) and Latino/a writers today (Anzaldúa, Moraga, Hijuelos, Labiera, etc.) know so well. On the contrary, this was one of my assumptions when I argued in favor of the logic and sensibilities of geohistorical locations, conceiving exile also as a location. You may or may not have a "mother tongue" as Derrida argues (see chapter 1), but you cannot avoid "being born" in one or more language(s), to have them inscribed in your body, as I argue in the next chapter. National ideologies were successful in naturalizing one language, defending its purity, linking it to a territory, and building monotopic sensibilities that supported influential conclusions in linguistics as a science and in a long Western philosophy of language tradition (Aarsleff 1982). I have been arguing that the current stage of globalization is daily questioning—through the expansion of capital, new financial circuits, technoglobalism, and massive migrations—national ideals and principles about the purity of language, the homogeneity of literature, and the distinctiveness of national cultures.

The Cuban Journal *Temas* (10 [1997]), a Cuban publication on matters of culture, ideology, and society, devoted a significant portion of a recent issue to the question of cultural production in Spanish and English. Ambrosio Fornet, whose intellectual integrity I highly respect and whose critical work I admire, gets himself into a difficult position in trying to find the criteria under which one can decide what counts as Cuban literature after 1959, when a significant production in the United States is written in English or Spanish and some times in both (Aparicio 1996; 1997). One of the brisk points of the argument is the unconscious coupling of language and territory, of Spanish and "Cubanity." The same issue that, in the nineteenth century, energized intellectuals in the South and in the North to conceive the two Americas in terms of two languages, without questioning the fact that such a link between language and territory and such a conflict between English and Spanish was set up prior to independence in the imperial conflicts between England and Spain, of which the defeat of the *Armada Invencible*, in 1588, was a significant point in the reordering of the modern world system and in the ways languages, subcontinental cultures, and nations were tied up together. There is more than Cuba and the United States involved in the language/literature issue Fornet is discussing, as there is more than the question between Mexico and the United States, when it comes to the same issue, among Chicano/as. There are the imperial conflicts between Spain and England since the seventeenth century, and those between Spain and the United States articulated in different manners in 1848 (with Mexico) and 1898 (with Cuba and Puerto Rico). The first fissure of the modern/colonial world system was brought about by the conflicts between Spain and England, when the field of forces and the content of its imaginary began to change. The second grew around a powerful and complex rearticulation of the modern/colonial world system. These imperial conflicts involved an empire in decay and another in ascent. But above all, they were also between an English-speaking country formed after its independence in the late eighteenth century, and two Spanish-speaking countries that were, at the end of the nineteenth century, still fighting for an independence that other Spanish-speaking countries had already obtained almost a century before. It was, in other words, a substantial displacement of the field of forces to the Western Hemisphere, a notion that came together with the Americas gaining independence and fighting for their place in the imaginary of the modern/colonial world order.

I would like to insist on Ambrosio Fornet's concern with the "Cubanity" of a certain kind of literature written in English and in the United States. As he himself recognizes, the question is a national question, and a national question from the perspective of a nation under siege after 1989. Fornet maintains that it is not the place of birth of a writer that makes him or her of one particular "nationality" but rather it is the language that he or she inhabits that gives the writer a place of belonging. The main issue remains the location of the writer within a given group of people identifying themselves with a national formation. But, basically, the entire issue and all the problems Fornet runs into are due to the fact that he maintains the links between language, territory, literature, and (national) culture. In other words, Fornet is addressing the problem of the canon, the canon of national literatures. However, while such issues would have been quickly resolved fifty years ago, within the unproblematic criteria of the national language and the homogeneous history of the nation, after the 1970s, social and historical transformations revealed the limits of such criteria.

But let's go back to Fornet's main line of argumentation. First of all, Fornet assumes the monolanguaging principle and argues that bilingual writers have indeed a "choice" between languages and the possibility to decide which one fits better their needs (1997, 5). However, Fornet insists, while this scenario is viable theoretically in practice, the writer cannot always take advantage of the possibilities of one language without sacrificing the other. He is right to stress that bilingualism is never symmetric, but he is wrong in assuming that bilanguaging has to be symmetric. The asymmetry of languages is not a question of a person knowing one better than the other, but it is a question of power within the diachronic internal structures of the modern world system and of its historical external borders (the colonial difference). I have addressed this issue in the first chapter when discussing Khatibi's position vis-à-vis Arabic and French, within the historical background of the early modern period when Arabic was displaced toward the exterior margin of an emerging new commercial circuit (which will become what today we name modern world system) linked with Spanish, Latin, and Christianity. In the case of Arguedas, the asymmetry between Spanish and Quechua is obvious, as it is obvious and necessary to remember that it is the coloniality of power and knowledge in the modern world system that created such a situation. Now the question is not to maintain the purity of both languages, being aware of their asymmetry: accepting that Quechua, for example, is better for poetry and Spanish for narrative, but that when it comes to theory and production of knowledge, Spanish is to English, French, or German what Quechua is to Spanish. The question is how to "infect" both, Spanish and Quechua (and in the case of Latino/as, Spanish and English), by injecting Quechua into Spanish and Spanish into English, as the case may be. Bilanguaging, in other words, is not precisely bilingualism where both languages are maintained in their purity but at the same time in their asymmetry. Bilanguaging, as in Arguedas, Anzaldúa, Cliff, "Creolité" (as we will see later), or the bilanguaging of the Zapatistas who write in Spanish inserting structures and concepts of Amerindian languages, is not a grammatical but a political concern as far as the focus of bilanguaging itself is redressing the asymmetry of languages and denouncing the coloniality of power and knowledge.

I hope it is clear that I am not trying to argue with Fornet, nor do I intend to intervene in the debate his article addresses. I found both the debate and Fornet's article of a crucial significance and my intention here is to look at the issue from the perspective of coloniality of power rather than from a national belonging—to look at the issues in the conflictive history of the modern world system (in the making and remaking of its interior and exterior borders) and the possibility of transcending and displacing the values attached to the purity of the language and the subsequent problems that such an assumption implies. Let me quote Fornet to understand better in what terms the problem is being framed, and how much this frame has to do with the national ideology that is limited to account for a social and historical move toward transnational configurations. Once again, it is not a question of being for or against the nation; it is a question of critically examining that the national values placed on languages and literatures no longer correspond with the transnational experience of a significant part of the population as well as with the translanguage experience in countries like Bolivia, where the important pattern is not current migration but colonization in the sixteenth century, which sets the conflictive stage between language and territory:

> Una ensayista ha descrito asi a los dos principales contendientes: los defensores del inglés desdeñan la posición marginal que ocupa el español en la sociedad y tratan, por consiguiente, de insertarse en el mainstream por la vía del idioma, como han hecho o tratado de hacer numerosos escritores chicanos, puertorriqueños y, en general, "latinos." Los defensores del español, en cambio, han "sacralizado su idioma y califican de herejía cualquier transgresión lingüística." (Fornet 1997, 8)

> A female essayist described the position of the two contenders in the following manner: those who defend English despise Spanish and the marginal position it occupies. Consequently, they try to situate themselves in the mainstream by the medium of language and they use English. We have seen this move enacted by many Chicano, Puerto Rican, and, in general "Latino" writers. Those who defend Spanish have, instead, revered the purity of their language and qualify as heresy "any linguistic transgression."

The defense of the purity of language should be contextualized, since the fact is that those who defend the purity of Spanish in the United States do not necessarily share the same ideology as the Spanish Academy in Madrid when it comes to linguistic politics. Fornet observes that the language question is the terrain where cultural power is at stake. But who is fighting for cultural power? Cubans themselves, according to Fornet, since those "who write in English are excluded and marginalized from anthologies and studies on Cuban culture in exile." However, Fornet insists on "nationality as literary category" and the role of the state in protecting national authors. He adds that, in principle, "a national author is, simply, the natural or the one who was naturalized and therefore has the right to be recognized and promoted by the system" (1997, 9). In other words, once "nationality" is recognized as a category, all kinds of tricks have to be invented in order to decide who is in and who is out. For that reason, I prefer the general notion of "local histories." The "nation" in such a conceptualization is a particular version of local history. Certainly, it is historically potent as has been implanted in the imaginary of the modern/colonial world system and exported beyond its limits in such a way that it has become difficult to imagine a social organization beyond the nation. I would like now to pursue this discussion bringing to it an example from Puerto Rico and another from Chile. These two examples will help us in placing the question of language, literature, and nation at a different level and, also, to compare particular local histories (such as Cuba, Puerto Rico, and Chile) in which such relations acquire a different configuration.

Now think about new developments that are taking place in the domain of literature practiced by members of the Creole population in Spanish speaking-countries that are changing the image of the "continental divide" and, consequently, literary geographies. By "Creole" I mean here the population of European descent and cultural affiliation or, if you wish, the "natives" originated by colonization, those who achieved independence and took power after it. Rosario Ferré, a well-known writer and member of a wealthy and politically influential family in Puerto Rico, wrote her last two novels (*The House in the Lagoon*, 1995; *Eccentric Neighborhoods*, 1998) in Puerto Rico, but in English. Let's read two paragraphs of the first novel:

> Puerto Rico was often in the news at the time; it was described by the press as an exotic, far-off possession, where there was a dire need for public works. The island had been a colony of Spain for four hundred years and, as William Randolph Hearst's newspapers often pointed out, was mired in poverty. This situation more than justified the United States taking over the island after the Spanish-American War. Ninety percent of the population was illiterate, and bilharzia and hookworm were rampant . A roster of projects was to be undertaken by the federal government to better the lot of the inhabitants. (Ferré 1995, 42)

> In Puerto Rico *we*'re all passionate about politics. *We* have three parties and three colors *we* identify with: Statehood and the New Progressive Party are blue, Commonwealth and the Popular Party are red; and Independence is green. Politics is like religion; you are either for Statehood or for Independence, you can't be for both. Someone has to be saved, someone must burn in hell, and if you're for Commonwealth you're floating in limbo. (Ferré 1995, 42; emphasis added)

Let's suppose that the novel was written by, say, Rebecca James, a Bostonian who married a Puerto Rican and became engaged in the history of the island. It would be a different read, whether Rebecca James "believed" or not what she said about politics in Puerto Rico and whether Rebecca is engaged in politics as we know Ferré is. But Rebecca James, unlike Rosario Ferré, would not have the "memories in Spanish" about the history and passions of the islands, and neither would she be writing memories in Spanish in the English language. There are plenty of interesting issues to discuss here, which I will not indulge in. I am interested in only one of them, which I put in the following formula: next semester I will teach a seminar, graduate or undergraduate, it doesn't matter, on Spanish or Latin American literature, whichever your prefer. My reading list will be the two novels by Ferré, in

English, plus Ariel Dorfman's *Heading South, Looking North* (1998), originally written in English, and Gustávo Pérez-Firmat's *Next Year in Cuba*
(1995), written also in English. As you can see, these texts "represent" three
Spanish American countries: Chile, Cuba, and Puerto Rico. Now, should I
teach this seminar in English or in Spanish? And how will I justify my seminar? By saying, for instance, that the "new Spanish or Latin American literature" is written in English? Or should I just forget about this and only choose
literature written in Spanish, even if that literature is written in the United
States, as we already have two of the recent recipients of the Casa de las
Américas (Cuba) award in the short-story category and one, Lourdes Fernández de Castro (1998), in the artistic and literary essays category?

Ferré's situation is different from both Dorfman and Pérez-Firmat, for she
is writing in English in Puerto Rico, while Dorfman and Pérez-Firmat are
writing in English in the United States. The geopolitical configuration of the
story of the three countries is also quite different as Chile, for instance, is
not historically tied to the United States as are Puerto Rico and Cuba. However, all of them are writing "Spanish memories" in "English language" and
so breaking away from the natural links between language and territory. The
three of them, furthermore, are different in this respect from the Chicano/a
writer for whom memories are both in Spanish and English and for whom
the question of belonging to a nation is, if not as clear-cut, at least more
complicated. Alfred Arteaga, in the introduction to the collection of essays
edited by him, *An Other Tongue* (1994), explaining his view on the relation
of language, subjectivity, and nation, observes:

> These matters of subjectification affect me personally in the manner in which I
> conceive myself in regard to *nation* and *ethnos*. I define myself as a Chicano. I
> was born in California and am a citizen of the United States, but my relation to
> that nation is problematic. U.S. Anglo-American nationalists define their nation
> to the exclusion of my people. Today in California, for example, the male Repub-
> lican governor and the two female Democratic Senators, collude in generating
> anti-immigrant (i.e., Mexican in the United States) hysteria: that I am rendered
> alien by U.S. jingoism remains a quotidian fact. My nation is not Mexico, yet I
> am ethnically Mexican and racially mestizo. But my people exist in the border-
> lands that traverse the national frontiers of the United States and Mexico. *It is
> obvious for us here that the language we speak both reflects and determines our
> position in relation to the two nations.* . . . Being Chicano in California at the end
> of the twentieth century means being constantly a subjected Other within the
> discourses of race, ethnos, and nation in a racist, ethnocentric, and nationalist
> society. (Arteaga 1994, 4)

Not long ago I heard a colleague from the Southern Cone objecting to
arguments similar to Arteaga's I have been making elsewhere. He bluntly
stated that the Latino/a and Chicano/a issues were a U.S. problem not

"ours." The "ours" referred to his concept of "Our America," by which he meant Spanish- and (perhaps including Brazil) Portuguese-speaking America. But again, he was conflating language and territoriality. For if it is true that the Latino/a question may not be a particular issue for Uruguay, Argentina, or Chile as particular nations, at the same time it cannot be concluded from here that it is not a "Spanish or Latin American" problem. The Latino/a question involves both "Spanish" language and "Latinidad" as a geopolitical and imperial conflict articulated in the nineteenth century at the crossroads of South America, Spanish, French, and U.S. imperial interests. The national paradigm is prevalent both in Fornet and in my colleague from the Southern Cone, but while for Fornet, Cubans/Latino/as in the United States is a problem, it is not so for my colleague in Uruguay, perhaps due to the fact that there is no massive migration from Uruguay to the United States.

I have been arguing that the strong links between language, literature, culture, and territory construed as a neutral configuration in the nineteenth century are being constantly uncoupled by social transformations as well as cultural practices. Recent decisions in the state of California against bilingual education speak for themselves. Maintaining the links between language, literature, culture, and territory implies reproducing imperial allocations of cultural configurations, and, in the case of "Latin America," remaining locked and attached to a form of identification that coincides with the organization imposed by the imperial world order. Similar problems are encountered in Bolivia or Peru, when it comes to Aymara/Quechua and Spanish, instead of Spanish and English. Border thinking in the colonial horizon of modernity could contribute to understanding and acting on colonial legacies entrenched in current everyday "cross-cultural" conflicts. Where do we act? In education, in the media, in all possible spaces where and when "culture" becomes a question of power, domination, and liberation. The fact, for instance, that in the United States "bilingual education" implies Spanish/English and not, for instance, English/French or English/German is also a fact loaded with the history of imperial conflict and the repressive imaginary of modernity/coloniality in the domain of language, "culture," and knowledge. But let's take the argument further and look at "Creolité" in this context.

Languaging beyond Nation-States

The scenario I have just sketched is embedded in a larger picture where colonial legacies and current globalizing processes meet, which I introduced in the first part of this chapter. The growing process of economic and technological global integration and some of its consequences (massive migrations) are forcing us to rethink the relationships between (national) languages and territories. The rearticulation of the status of nations, as a result of the global flow of economic integration, is forming a world of connected languaging and shifting identities. As people become polyglots, their sense of history, nationality and race become as entangled as their languaging. Border zones, diaspora, and postcolonial relations are daily phenomena of contemporary life.

How migration modifies languaging is related to its geopolitical direction. While migrations during the nineteenth century moved from Europe toward Africa, Asia, and the Americas, at the end of the twentieth century they moved in opposite directions. Thus, migratory movements are disarticulating the idea of national languaging and, indirectly, of national literacies and literatures in Europe as well as in the United States. On the other hand, the rise of indigenous communities and their participation in the public sphere (such as the recent events in Chiapas, or the cultural politics of the state in Bolivia) complement migratory movements in their challenge to the idea of national languaging and to the one-to-one relationship between language and territory. The notion of homogeneous national cultures and the consensual transmission of historical and literary traditions, as well as of unadulterated ethnic communities, are in the process of profound revisions and redefinitions. We need to think seriously about the processes by which languaging and the allocation of meaning to groups of people presumed to have common features (e.g., "ethnic culture," "national culture," etc.) are being relocated and how linguistic maps, literary geographies, and cultural landscapes are being repainted.

The current process of globalization is not a new phenomenon, although the way in which it is taking place is without precedent. On a larger scale, globalization at the end of the twentieth century (mainly occurring through transnational corporations, the media, and technology) is the most recent configuration of a process that can be traced back to the 1500s, with the beginning of transatlantic exploration and the consolidation of Western hegemony. Paradoxically, the early modern and early colonial periods (roughly 1500–1700, with the predominance of the Spanish and Portuguese empires), as well as the modern and colonial periods (roughly 1700–1945, with the predominance of the British Empire and French and German colonialism), were the periods when the consolidations of national languages took place concurrently with migrations promoted by transatlantic exploration and improved means of transportation. This progress created the conditions necessary to undermine the purity of a language that unified a nation. The construction of the first giant steamer (between 1852 and 1857) made possible transatlantic migrations unimaginable until then. Millions of people migrated from Europe to the Americas between 1860 and 1914, complicating the linguistic colonial map and placing increasing demands on national literary geographies. In Argentina, for example, intellectuals were uneasy at the end of the nineteenth and the beginning of the twentieth centuries, when the national and linguistic community was shaken up by massive Italian immigration (Conde 1988). Migrations of people and the internationalization of capitals during the second half of the nineteenth century impinged on the spread of print culture and general education, emphasized by nation builders in both Americas. Thus, by the end of the nineteenth century, Amerindian legacies were becoming museum relics, more a reality of the past than a critical force of the present. Nahuatl, among others, became a language (i.e., an object) of the past, rather than a languaging activity of millions of people, suppressed by national languag(ing)es.

Migratory factors introduced an element of disorder in the otherwise quiet horizon of linguistic, literary, and territorial homogeneity. While Arguedas's landscape presents the conflict between languaging practices prior to Spanish colonizing migrations and the introduction of new practices brought by the colonizing migratory movements, Cliff and Anzaldúa draw a different map: that of reverse migration, the migration from colonial territories relabeled Third World (after 1945) toward the First World (Cliff to Europe; Anzaldúa's ancestors to the United States). One could say that Arguedas, on the one hand, and Cliff and Anzaldúa on the other, are the end of the spectrum whose chronological beginning I locate around 1500. Arguedas experienced the legacies of the linguistic conflict created by migrations from the metropolitan centers to the colonial domains, and the fractures of local languages introduced by colonial ones. For Cliff and Anzaldúa, in contrast, languaging practices fracture the colonial language. In Cliff's texts, these fractures result from the linguistic transformation of imperial languaging practices in colonial domains. In the case of Anzaldúa, such fractures occur due to the languaging practices of two displaced linguistic communities: Nahuatl, displaced by the Spanish expansion, and Spanish, displaced by the increasing hegemony of the colonial languages of the modern period (English, German, and French).

Anzaldúa's observations about the future geographies of languaging practices are relevant to my argument: "By the end of this century, Spanish speakers will comprise the biggest minority group in the United States, a country where students in high schools and colleges are encouraged to take French classes because French is considered more 'cultured.' But for a language to remain alive, it must be used. By the end of this century English, not Spanish, will be the mother tongue of most Chicanos and Latinos." Cherríe Moraga's *The Last Generation* (1993) articulates a similar idea: English, not Spanish, will be the languaging practice of Chicano/as and Latino/as. I am not in a position either to mistrust or to contradict such predictions. I would, however, like to present some doubts based on other experiences. These doubts support the implicit desire expressed by Anzaldúa and Moraga to derail the process that they both predict. Anzaldúa's fear, for instance, that English will become the national languaging of Chicano/as and that French will be the foreign languaging of distinction may not look the same in 1994 as it looked in 1987. I have two reasons to cast these doubts: one is the decreasing number of students taking French at the college level in recent years; the other is the increasing interest in *la Francophone*, with the changing linguistic maps and literary geographies of French outside France and the increasing awareness in social and academic discourse of the relationship between language and race. Francophone languaging has as much in common with French languaging in France as Hispanic languaging in the United States has with Castilian languaging in Spain: the same *languages* allow quite different languaging priorities, feelings, and knowledge.

Frantz Fanon's ([1952] 1967) reflections on the colonial legacies and linguistic politics of French outside France and the complicities between linguistic ideology and race are relevant to this discussion. If nineteenth-century Europe invented the concept of race and this concept bridged the gap between seventeenth-century "purity of blood" and twentieth-century "color of your skin," then the place of linguistic ideology in the modern/colonial world system imaginary has been effortlessly traced. The method of classifying animal species provided the basis for the hypothesis that the "human races" were founded on an inheritance that transcended social evolution (von Humboldt 1988). At the same time, the new science of linguistics found its inspiration for classifying languages in the method of the biological sciences, associating, by the same token, the supposedly unique character of peoples with the characteristics of their languages. The gaps between Indo-European and Semitic (Hebrew and Arabic) languages were constructed as linguistic oppositions with racial implications. This statement is familiar to those educated in Spanish colonial discourse with the evaluation of Amerindian languages by Spanish missionaries and men of letters. Ernst Renan (1863), for example, talked about the monstrous and backward character of Semitic languages, as opposed to the perfection of European languages, in a way that echoed early Spanish missionaries and men of letters. Today the belief in a hierarchy of human intelligence based on languaging-as-ethnicity is alive and well, even in academic circles, although it is not always expressed as such.

Fanon's first chapter of *White Masks, Black Skins* ([1952] 1967), an indirect response to Renan, is titled "The Negro and Language." He states: "I ascribe a basic importance to the phenomenon of language. That is why I find it necessary to begin with this subject, which should provide us with one of the elements in the colored man's comprehension of the dimension of the other. For it is implicit that to speak is to exist absolutely for the other" (17). Fanon's speculations revolve around the black people in the French Antilles with respect to the metropolitan language and, further, with respect to the distinctions among languages between those of Martinicans and Guadeloupians in the Caribbean and those of Antilleans and Senegalese in the context of African diaspora. Colonial mimicry consisted, in the first context, of achieving white status by speaking good French. In the second, Martinicans felt that they were "better" than Guadeloupians and blacks in the Antilles and "better" than Senegalese, owing to the ways in which they related to the French language. This is why Fanon states at the beginning that "the Black man has two dimensions. One with his fellows, the other with the White man." Thus, Anzaldúa's fear that French distinction will prevail over Spanish subalternity in the United States may have an interesting turn if we consider the growing force of French out of France (i.e., the so-called *Francophone*, although France itself is also a Francophone country!), similar to Spanish out of Spain and to English out of England and the United States. In any event, the modern aura of territorial French is being paralleled by Francophone linguistic maps, literary geographies, and cultural landscapes.

CRÉOLITÉ AND BORDER THINKING

When it comes to "Créolité" the colonial difference doesn't need to be emphasized. It is the foundation of "Creole thinking" and of "thinking in Creole." There is a question of gender, however, that I bypass here, but the interested reader can consult the articles of Maryse Condé and James Arnold (Arnold 1995; Condé 1998). My focus will be on language, ethnicity and the geopolitics of the insular Caribbean at the crossroads of imperial conflicts—that is, where the internal and the external borders of the modern/colonial world have been articulated over the centuries, from the early Spanish colonialism to the late intervention of the United States, going by the British, French, and Dutch interventions in the Caribbean Basin.

The meaning of "Creole" in the French and English Caribbean differs from the meaning of the same word in the Spanish Caribbean island as well as in the mainland. In an interesting sense, the difference in meaning is at the intersection of the first and second phase of the modern world system: the "Creole" engendered by Spanish and the "Creole" engendered by English and French colonialisms. Furthermore, in Spanish "Creole" refers to a particular group of people of European descent, who speak Spanish. In the French and English Caribbean, "Creole" is a language. As is obvious in this case, those two stages are not "one after the other," when the second replaces the first. But they coexisted and coexist. "Creoles" in Bolivia and Mexico are the "mestizos" in power. Whatever their blood proportion, culturally they have adopted the Western cosmology. More than racially characterized, "Creoles" are marginal Westerners in Spanish America, rooted in the Spanish language and memories but uprooted from Europe, they are defined by the national ideology they built for themselves. The "Creoles" in the Caribbean are instead descended from the slaves and, contrary to their Spanish counterparts, did not enjoy power. On the other hand, "Creole" in the Caribbean is the name of a subaltern language equivalent to Aymara in Bolivia. Whether Creole emerged as a transformation of French, in the islands, by the very French who were living far away from the metropolis and was learned and adapted by the slaves, or whether it is a transformation of French by the slaves themselves, negotiating their first language with French is irrelevant here. The main question is that there isn't an equivalent to French or English Creole in Spanish. Contrary to the cases that we have seen so far of two distinct and different languages in relation to one another (e.g., Spanish and English or Spanish and Aymara), "Creole" in the Caribbean is both the matrix language and the language to which it is related. But in any case, "Creole" was until recently considered an inferior dialect, and not a language (see chapter 6 on the relation of language, dialect, nationalism, and coloniality).

The three authors of *Éloge de la créolité* (In praise of Creoleness) (1993), Bernabé, Chamoiseau, and Confiant, have made distinctions between Creolité, Negritude, Americanité, and Antillanité. These distinctions uncouple, on the one hand, language from ethnicity and, on the other, language from territoriality. The first (uncoupling language from ethnicity) was mainly an operation of colonial expansion, the second (uncoupling language from territory), of state building. Créolité, on the other hand, is not presented in a progressive manner, as a new concept that would supplant the previous one, but as a concept that integrates them in their difference between themselves and in their difference with Creoleness. Negritude, introduced by Aime Cessaire, was a restitution of African blackness in confrontation with European whiteness, a georacial articulation. By Americanité, the authors of *Éloge* refer to all immigrants, in the entire Americas, from Argentina to New England, including the Caribbean. I will quote in extenso their own definition of Americanness and Caribbeanness.

These distinctions have very serious implications for the geohistorical discussion of chapter 2. The ontological dimension of and the natural correlation between language, territory, and race assumed by nineteenth century intellectuals divided the Americas between the Spanish and the Anglos and left the Caribbean out of the picture. Spanish-speaking countries (Santo Domingo, Puerto Rico, and Cuba) were naturally attached to the territorial imagery of Spanish America. However, Barbados or Jamaica could not have been attached to the national imaginary of the United States in the same way, just because their official language was English. On the other hand, and since the dominant ideologies in nineteenth-century America were those built by intellectuals from the countries gaining independence from England and Spain, the French Caribbean was still more isolated, even while being "Latin"! A good case in point is the fact that the Haitian Revolution was forgotten, at least until the 1970s. The Haitian Revolution remained not only isolated from France, but also from the ideologues of independence in Spanish- and Anglo-speaking continental countries. Of course, Canada should be brought into the picture, particularly now that NAFTA has re-articulated North America in a way that could not have been anticipated by Bilbao or Jefferson. The foundation of the geopolitical imaginary of the modern/colonial world system and the place of the Americas in it goes back to the sixteenth century. In the nineteenth century, however, it began to be organized by an "American"-born intelligentsia, expressing itself in English and Spanish. The time of the Caribbean has now arrived with the emergence of a black intelligentsia. But that is not all, because the voices of Amerindian intellectuals that we have been hearing since the 1970s are also complicating the picture presented and defended from the perspective of Spanish American Creoles: the "absence" of Amerindians, generally located in the Pacific coast during the period dominated by the Atlantic imaginary, should be added to the "absence" of the Caribbean.

But let's return to Creoleness and the Caribbean. I will now spend more time exploring the epistemological potential of Creoleness as a particular form of border thinking, arising from a particular local history of the modern world system, traversing the three phases: from the early slave trade under the Spanish Empire, to its continuation under French colonialism and the repercussions of the U.S. presence in the Caribbean in the long twentieth century (i.e., since 1898). Here are the distinctions between Americanness and Carribeanness:

> First, the sociohistorical processes that produced Americanization are different in nature from those which were at work in Creolization. Indeed, Americaniza-tion and its corollary, *the feeling of Americanness*, describe the progressive adap-tation, and with no real interaction with other cultures, of Western populations in a world they baptized new. Thus the Anglo-Saxons who formed the thirteen colonies, embryo of the future American state, displayed their culture in a new environment, almost barren, if we consider the fact that the native Indians, who were imprisoned in reservations or massacred, did not virtually influence their initial culture. . . . Just as the Italians who emigrated massively to Argentina during the nineteenth century, or the Hindus who replaced the black slaves in the plantations of Trinidad, adapted their original culture to new realities with-out completely modifying them. *Americaness is, therefore, in many respects, a migrant culture, in a splendid isolation.* (Bernabé et al. 1993, 92–93)

Creoles, Caribbeanness, and Creoleness are still categories that overlap but which belong to different levels. Being or defining oneself as Creole means identifying a group of people, differentiating them from others. Thus, to say that "neither Europeans, nor Africans, nor Asians, we proclaim ourselves

Creoles" (1993, 75) is an identification in relation to a territory, and to the historical processes that created that territory. But, above all, it is defined by an "interior attitude," by a mode of being rather than by a way of looking. "Creoleness" is defined by describing such mode of being that is, in the particular local history in which it is defined and conceived, first and foremost an outcome of French colonization in the extended Caribbean, including Louisiana, where Caribbeanness and Americanness overlap:

> We might find them (Caribbeanness and Americanness) juxtaposed or interpenetrated within the same country: thus in the U.S.A., Louisiana and Mississippi are predominantly Creole, whereas New England, which was initially inhabited by Anglo-Saxons only, is just American. After the abolition of slavery, however, and the rise of black people in the North, and during the twentieth-century arrival of Italians, Greeks, Chinese, and Puerto-Ricans, one might rightly think that the conditions are ripe for a process of Creolization to start presently in New England. (Bernabé et al. 1993, 93)

Thus, if Creoleness is defined from the mode of being engendered by French colonization in the Caribbean, it is also projected beyond it to characterize Creoleness as a world experience. The "periphery in Creolization" according to Finnish anthropologist Ulf Hannerz (1987a; 1987b; 1991) characterized the current phenomena of mixing languages and knowledges as consequences of decolonization, increasing migrations, and the growing extension of the media to places where people do not migrate. Hannerz described a sociohistorical scenario starting from a metaphor with a well-defined historical and geopolitical location: French colonialism. The same can be done with other metaphors of the same kind, such as borderlands (as I have been using them as a starting point), double consciousness, transculturation. However, it is important to distinguish the dimension in which "Creolization" is used by Hannerz and how it is used by the black Caribbean intellectuals. "Creolization" for Hannerz is similar to transculturation for Ortiz: it is a description of mixed "genes" and "memes" in social history, but not a mixture of the anthropological loci of enunciation from which Creolization or transculturation or hybridity in other occasions are described. Ortiz employed the term to describe the nation. Hannerz, fifty years later, uses his to describe a world phenomenon.

For Caribbean intellectuals, however, Creoleness is also something that happens to them that is engrained in their own being and in their own thinking. It is, in other words, a phenomenon engrained in thinking itself. It is a particular case of "border thinking," similar in its logic but different in its history from the Chicano/a experience in the geohistorical borderlands. It differs similarly from the double consciousness of slave legacies in the United States, and still more from "an other thinking" claimed by Khatibi at the intersection of French and Arabic, with the old memories of Spanish conflicts with the Moors. Creoleness, instead, describes a territorial and geo-historical location. As such, it is defined as the "only process of Americaniza-tion of Europeans, Africans, and Asians in the Caribbean Archipelago" (Ber-nabé et al. 1993, 93). More specifically, Creoleness is defined as a mode of being connected to economy, and more specifically to plantation economy from the experience of French colonialism in the Caribbean, applicable to similar experiences around the world: "European and African in the small Caribbean islands; Europeans, Africans and Indians in the Mascarene is-lands; European and Asian in certain areas of the Philippines or in Hawaii; Arabs and black Africans in Zanzibar" are all historical experiences creating the condition of a mode of being defined as "Creoleness" that is not attached to a territory and to a language but, rather, to disperse an interconnected territoriality: "Generally resting upon a plantation economy, *these popula-tions are called to invent the new cultural designs allowing for a relative cohabi-tation between them*" (Bernabé et al. [1989] 1993, 92).

The crossing of peoples, territories, nationalities, memories, religions all come back to language as a basic component of "Creoleness": "Our pri-mary richness, we the Creole writers, is to be able to speak several languages: Creole, French, English, Portuguese, Spanish, etc." (Bernabé et al. 1993, 104). Like "an other thinking" in Khatibi, Creoleness is a way of think-ing in languages, beyond of course the monotopic purity of the national languages (e.g., "all who come to this country have to speak X, because X is *the language of this country*," a statement that has currency in several parts of the world today, particularly in the core nations of the modern world system). But, of course, Creole language is what defines a mode of being. However, the program and project of Creoleness is not only to rec-ognize and celebrate Creole as a language different from French, but to write and think in Creole appropriating French—hence, the epistemological potential of border thinking as a subaltern perspective in Creoleness. Think-ing and writing in Creole no longer implies maintaining the same prin-ciple of purity and coherence of French as a hegemonic and colonial lan-guage; although it may imply isolation because of the limited number of speakers of Creole in relation to French. But to think and write in Creole, from Creole, appropriating French, means to "use" a vehicular language, like French, thus encroaching a mode of being into a dominant one but from the perspective of the subaltern. That is, in general, what border thinking as an epistemological perspective is all about. Thus, as far as Creoleness is a mode of being, of thinking and writing in a subaltern language, from the subaltern perspective and using and appropriating a hegemonic language—all this is not only limited to a particular local history but is similar to several local histories made at the intersection with global designs, the coloniality of power, and the expansion of the modern world system. As such, Cre-oleness offers a different take on "universality" and it opens up the dimension of "diversality" as the authors of *Éloge* define themselves the domain of conviviality and hospitality.

The major claims of *Éloge* are programmatic as they define not only a new aesthetic, but an aesthetic that is also an epistemology. First, the very foundation of Creoleness demands a complexity in thinking parallel to the complexity of Creoleness as a phenomenon ("Exploring our Creoleness must be done in a thought as complete as Creoleness itself"; Bernabé et al. 1993, 90). There is a significant and illustrative difference here between, as I pointed out in chapter 3, *studying* hybridity as a complex phenomenon from an interdisciplinary perspective (e.g., cultural studies)—which maintains, however, the epistemological principle of the social sciences, presupposing the universality of the observer—and *thinking* it as an epistemology that overflows its disciplinary definition. In the latter, Creoleness is conceived and formulated as "an annihilation of false universality, of monolingualism, and of purity" (1993, 90). Thus, the possibility and the necessity of producing knowledge without maintaining disciplinary principles and a monolinguism of the hegemonic languages of knowledge (e.g., English or French) is what Creoleness (as Anzaldúa's "new mestiza consciousness") proposes. For that reason, the authors of *Éloge* limited their proposal (at the time of its writing) to art, but with the conviction that it should eventually go beyond it. For, indeed, how does one define and practice a complex epistemology that is beyond its disciplinary normativity ("The need for clarification based on two or three laws of normality made us consider ourselves as abnormal beings"; Bernabé et al. 1993, 90)? Art allows for that abnormality: "That is why it seems that, for the moment, *full knowledge of Creoleness will be reserved for Art*, for Art absolutely. . . . But it goes without saying that Creoleness is inclined to irrigate all the nervures of our reality in order to become gradually its main principle" (Bernabé et al. 1993, 90).

Creoleness helps in expanding several points I have been making earlier. First of all, Creoleness as a particular mode of being in relation to a particular language formation (Creole) implies to "inhabit the language," not just to be "born in a language." This statement doesn't contradict Desnoes's argument, on which I commented earlier, only his conceptualization. What Desnoes said about Spanish obviously encompasses more than being born in it; it means inhabiting the language. Consequently, this inhabiting a language is not limited to Creoleness; but it is from the experience of Creoleness that the very notion of inhabiting a language was forged. Philosophy of language, as constructed in the Western tradition, from Plato to Wittgenstein, underlines the relationship between language and the world, meaning and significance, and its inner logic, the grammatical structure (Taylor 1985, 1:213–92). "Being born" and "inhabiting a language" were never part of that tradition (with exceptions such as Heidegger and Levinas), especially since the seventeenth century, when a paradigm of scientific and disciplinary knowledge was founded on the distinction between primary and secondary qualities. Primary qualities belonged to the object, while secondary to the subject: "Only in the experience of creatures endowed with the particular form of sensibility we call sight can things be coloured" (Taylor 1985, 1:46). In such an epistemology there is no room for the notion of being born and inhabiting a language as a source of knowledge. This, I submit, is the difficulty that Derrida has in dealing with Khatibi. While "an other thinking" in Khatibi (like "Creoleness" for the authors of *Éloge*) is an epistemology founded in the "inhabitation" of a language (Creole or Arabic) in tension with a colonial language (French in both cases), for Derrida that experience of "inhabiting" a language seems to be alien as he plays his game as a critic of the Western philosophical tradition I just mentioned, within it—that is, inhabiting a philosophical tradition that has difficulty in accepting a reflection on language based on the principle of a language being inhabited.

Second, Creoleness invites going back to "Chakrabarty's dilemma" and the question of history and subaltern studies. Literary Creoleness takes the place of historiography, since historiography, as a disciplinary practice, cannot reach the source of Creoleness. "Our history (or more precisely our histories)," state the authors of *Éloge*, "is shipwrecked in colonial history." This formulation, like several others from *Éloge*, owes much to Glissant. In this case, the debt is to Glissant's distinction between Literature and literature; History and history, established in his *Le discours Antillais* ([1981] 1989, 61–77). As writers of literature, the authors of *Éloge* claim damages for the silences of official history. "What we believe to be Caribbean history," they go on, "is just the history of the colonization of the Caribbean" Bernabé et al. (1993, 98). What is missing is "the opaque resistance of the Maroon allied in their disobedience. The new heroism of those who stood up against the hell of slavery, displaying some obscure codes of survival, some indecipherable qualities of resistance, the incomprehensible variety of compromises, the unexpected syntheses of life" (1993, 98). Now, such a formulation most likely would be approved by disciplinary term historian and practitioners, but perhaps not accepted as a disciplinary formulation of the problem. If this is the case, then Chakrabarty is right: history as a discipline is European history as far as memory retrieved by literature is not of epistemological value. But the prosecution against colonial history by the authors of *Éloge* continues:

> So that our history (or our histories) is not totally accessible to historians. Their methodology restricts them to the sole of colonial chronicle. Our chronicle is behind the dates, behind known facts: *we are Words behind writing*. Only poetic knowledge, fictional knowledge, literary knowledge, in short, artistic knowledge can discover us, understand us, and bring us, evanescent, back to the resuscitation of consciousness. (Bernabé 1993, 99)

Creoleness offers another "methodology," thinking at the crossroads and in the borders of colonial history which, like French language for Creole, cannot be avoided but must be appropriated and then turned inside out, so to speak. What is not in the records, which would not be readily accepted from a normative historiographic perspective, has to be constructed otherwise. Glissant proposed sceneries as a method, and the authors of *Éloge*, following Glissant, "silence" as destination:

> When applied to our histories (to this sand-memory fluttering about the scenery, the land, in the fragments of old black people's heads, made of emotional richness, of sensations, of intuitions) interior vision and the acceptance of our Creoleness will allow us to invest *these impenetrable areas of silence where screams were lost.* (Bernabé 1993, 99)

Creoleness transcends the distinction between history and literature, a distinction readily accepted from the perspective of the social sciences, insofar as literature is literature and not history. Creoleness, however, cautions such a distinction, which is ingrained in territorial epistemology. *Éloge* explicitly addressed this issue: "Creoleness is an annhihilation of false universality, of monolingualism, and of purity" (Bernabé 1993, 90), a configuration in which literature *and* history can be acceptable. "History" as a discipline is "universal" not because of its topic necessarily, but because of its very foundation, as in Chakrabarty's dilemma. The authors of *Éloge* propose Creoleness as "liberation," in this case from historiography, from universality, and from purity. Updating memory, beyond the *universality* of the historiography of colonial history, leads to *global diversality* as a desire and as a political project; and *global diversality*, conceived from border thinking and Creoleness, leads to a desire and a project of conviviality and hospitality beyond the frontiers established by universalism, purity, and monolingualism—a totality that's not a *uni-verse* but a *global di-verse*. This position is summarized in the following paragraph, of singular relevance for my argument:

> Our primary diversity will be part of world diversity, recognized and accepted as permanent our Creoleness will have to recover itself, structure itself, and preserve itself, while changing and absorbing. *It will have to survive in Diversity.* Applying this double move will automatically favor our creative vitality. *It will also prevent us from returning to the totalitarian order of the old world, fixed by the temptation of the unified and definitive.* (Bernabé 1993, 115)

Global diversality as a desire and a political project resembles what Latin American theologian of liberation, Hans Hinkelammert (1996, 238), called "fragmentation as a universal project." "Fragmentation" has a postmodern ring to it, although Hinkelammert's argument, and its historical horizon grounded in coloniality, is indeed closer to Creoleness than it is to postmodern thinkers. Hinkelammert's concern is with the need for a "new logic" that will take us away from the "abstract universal," which is the logic of universalism, of purism, of monolingualism. For Hinkelammert, an other logic cannot be an other or opposite abstract universalism (e.g., the logic of the neoliberal world or of a utopian neosocialism) but a "logic of the plural" (1996, 238). He conceived plurilogic (Hinkelammert's version of *global diversality*) as *fragmentation*; "fragmentation/pluralization as a project implies a universal answer. Fragmentation cannot be fragmentary" but plural (1996, 238) and decentered. While for the authors of *Éloge* French as language and culture is the agent of enacting monism and universalism, for Hinkelammert it is the global logic of capitalism at the end of the twentieth century. Creolness as the logic of diversality and fragmentation as a universal project of pluralization are responses in search of an other logic and an other thinking that cannot be other than border thinking from the perspective of the subaltern as I have been trying to argue from Khatibi's "an other thinking," Du Bois's "double consciousness," the authors of *Éloge* (Bernabé, Chamoiseau, Confiant), as well as Glissant's "Créolité/Diversality," Anzaldua's "new mestiza consciousness," Hinkelammer "fragmentation/plurality." When looked at individually, each concept emerges as a response from a subaltern position—from very specific local histories—to global designs as agency of subalternization. And each concept doesn't rise as an opposition from victimization, but all enact a position of "celebration" (e.g., in praise of Creoleness), of an other logic articulated from the perspective and the experience of subalternity, and incorporating hegemonic knowledge into it.

CONCLUDING REMARKS

Let me conclude by coming back to the diversity of understanding, connecting it with *global diversality and colonial difference*. Insofar as linguistic maps are attached not only to literary geographies but also to the production and distrbution of knowledge, changing linguistic cartographies implies a reordering of epistemology. "Serious" knowledge and "serious" literary production have been enacted since the sixteenth century in the colonial languages of modernity and their classical foundations (Greek and Latin). Global interconnections are now bringing us back to the relevance of millennial languaging (such as in Chinese, Arabic, Hindi, and Hebrew) once relegated to second-class status (during the early modern and the modern periods to a critical examination of the "purity of languages"; and to the relevance of languages suppressed under the banners of the nation, such as Quechua and Aymara in Bolivia and Peru, and Nahuatl and Maya in Mexico and Central

America. Thus languages, languaging, and diversity of understanding go hand in hand with subaltern knowledge and with understanding diversity as global diversality rather than as "difference" within the "universal."

In this chapter, I have explored the implications of national ideologies in the domain of languages and literatures intermixed with the colonial difference. I have asked the question, What are national languages good for in a transnational world? National ideologies, in the modern/colonial world system, had different moments and profiles. "Nation" in the sixteenth century didn't have the same meaning as "nation" after American independence and the French Revolution. "Nation" as a decolonization project after World War II doesn't have the same meaning as "nation" and "republic" at the beginning of the nineteenth century, when "independences" became the first wave of decolonizing projects. But "nation," from the early *Orbis Universalis Christianus* to the secular version of "reason" as human liberation from "his self-imposed nonage" in Kant's known expression [1790], 1973), changed its meaning as well as social configuration. While Kant's motto in itself is appropriate for the emergence of subaltern discourses and interpretations that we have seen in this chapter (and, as such, a "great" contribution of the Enlightenment) the connection between a philosophical statement and the preexisting Christian ideology linking, in the history of colonization from the sixteenth to the eighteenth centuries, the pagans with the barbarians, and the barbarians with the Amerindians, and the African with the slave brought into the picture the notion of the "civilizing mission."

Without Kant knowing or planning it, the formidable recommendation "Have the courage to use your own understanding" (Kant, [1790] 1973) became the privilege of the few who assigned to themselves the humanitarian task of civilizing other people and telling them how to have the courage to use their own understanding. Michel-Rolph Trouillot's analysis of the Haitian Revolution as a direct consequence of the blindness of the Enlightened mentality shows that the courage and the vision of those Haitians who carried the Haitian Revolution in using their own understanding was not recognized. The Haitian Revolution, unlike independence in the Americas and the French Revolution, was an achievement by people whose "human" status was not clearly recognized by American and French revolutionaries. Afro-Americans or Amerindians (as in the case of the failed uprising of Tupac Amaru in the second half of the eighteenth century, in Peru) were not in the picture of the Enlightenment idea of "man" and "citizen." Afro-Americans' and Amerindians' independence was tied up with decolonization, while the achievement of independence by "early Americans" in the North or "Creoles" in the South was just that, independence of people of European descent from their European forefathers. Universality of human reason became the justification for cultural differentiation, which in the case of the Americas had its foundation in the early configuration of Amerindians, Afro-American, and European communities. Language was intrinsically related to community formation and to geopolitical configurations.

The successful silencing of the Haitian Revolution in the history of the Americas ended up in the two dominant geopolitical and linguistic ideologies, Spanish America and Anglo-America, with Brazil as a supporter cast when "latinity" was necessary in the imperial conflicts emerging in 1848. Amerindians and Afro-American communities, in other words, have been out of the picture in the making of the "two Americas." The Haitian Revolution is a moment within the history of the modern/colonial world system and of the reconfiguration of modernity/coloniality, as important in the history of the modern world as are the Anglo American independence, the French Revolution, and the independence of Latin American countries. And the Haitian Revolution is crucial also for envisioning a new scenario of geopolitical configurations and for understanding the function of languages for political interventions and for building communities. "An other tongue" is the necessary condition for "an other thinking" and for the possibility of moving beyond the defense of national languages and national ideologies—both of which have been operating in complicity with imperial powers and imperial conflicts (as the silence of the Haitian Revolution clearly shows in the construction of the imaginary of the "Americas").

The emergence of "Latinos" in the United States complicates the picture further, particularly in the three moments of national and imperial power that created the conditions of its emergence: 1848 (Mexico-U.S. border); 1898 (Spain-U.S. War, Cuba, Puerto Rico late independence), and 1959 (the Cuban Revolution). If 1848 was a signal that the continental divide was a dream from the perspective of global designs, 1898 and 1959 broke away also with the continental divide and brought the Caribbean in the picture and, with it, the French and British Caribbean. Although territorial configurations were complementary of imperial languages and linguistic (colonial and national) maps as the foundations of literary geographies and cultural landscapes, at this moment history is demanding "an other tongue" and "an other thinking" built over the colonial difference rather than on national and imperial territories.

In the next chapter, I pursue a similar discussion but at the level of language and epistemology, instead of language and literature/culture.

CHAPTER 6

Bilanguaging Love: Thinking in between Languages

> Menardo *had loved* [emphasis added] the stories his grandfather
> told him about the old man who drank stinking beer and talked
> *with* [emphasis in original] the ancestors. Menardo *had loved*
> [added] the stories right up until the sixth grade when one of the
> teaching Brothers *had given them a long lecture* [added] about
> pagan people and pagan stories.
> (Leslie Marmon Silko, *Almanac of the Dead*)

LIVES ON the border (De Vos 1994) are conceived and experienced in and from different perspectives: either as the authenticity of the native cultures being harassed by globalization or as the authenticity of the North Atlantic (or Western) culture either in danger or still in its triumphal planetary march. The celebration of bi or pluri languaging is precisely the celebration of the crack in the global process between local histories and global designs, between "mundialización" and globalization, from languages to social movements, and a critique of the idea that civilization is linked to the "purity" of colonial and national monolanguaging. Thus, in this chapter, I return to the distinction between globalization and "mundialización" that I introduced at the beginning of these meditations and query the classical distinction between expert and nonexpert knowledges.

I would like to explore further the colonial epistemic difference thinking through the possibility of a bilingual or bilanguaging (as I will explain in this chapter) epistemology. Reason and knowledge, in the modern world, presupposed the purity and the grammar of a language and, without mentioning it, epistemology became entangled with national ideologies. Latin was the language of knowledge and wisdom, since the Renaissance. Scientific achievements in a secularized world were related to a given country and to a given language. Philosophy was also regional and "Continental" philosophy became the paradigm of philosophical practice, backed up by its

This chapter evolved in a graduate seminar, cotaught with Miriam Cooke, during the spring of 1995 (at Duke University), entitled, "Linguistic Maps, Literary Geography, Cultural Landscapes." I owe much of my argument and examples to Miriam Cooke and to the graduate students in the seminar (K. Barnes, J. Baskin, J. Beasley-Murray, D. Carson, C. Chia, T. Devine, A. Curtis, G. Dobbins, F. Gómez, A. Karim, P. Mishra, I. Nwankwo, C. Parra, A. Prabhu, A. Sommer, W. Villalba).

invented Greek predecessors. Subalternization of knowledge was not only possible because a given concept of "reason" became hegemonic and the point of reference to evaluate other logics and ways of thinking at the same time that hegemonic languages (see chapter 7) were imposed upon others. In the process of spreading Christianity or the civilizing mission and the corresponding languages of these global designs, the transformations of local histories (both the hegemonic and the subaltern) took place and "mundialización" emerged as the other side of globalization, parallel to the two sides of modernity/coloniality. The slash between globalization/mundialización (which I leave here in Spanish and without quotation marks) and between modernity/coloniality is then the signpost of the border spaces created, through several centuries of religious, economic, and epistemic Western expansion, all over the planet. For a long period of time, subaltern knowledges and languages were taken for granted. Even those who lead the way in subaltern local histories believed in the superiority of Western epistemology, in the Americas as well as in Asia or Africa. Today, or in the past half a century with the growing influence of the second wave of decolonization after World War II (the first wave took place between 1776 and 1821, roughly, in the British colonies of North America, in the French colony of Haiti in the Caribbean, and in several Spanish speaking countries including (Argentina, Chile, Peru, and Mexico), new forms of knowledge revealing the limits of modern Western epistemology are emerging in the borderlands of globalization/mundialización, modernity/coloniality, borders inhabited by the colonial difference. Border thinking demands a bilanguaging rather than a territorial epistemology, which supported ancient religions and science, its secular Western version, as well as economic planning and social organization. This chapter explores this possibility.

Items, the organ of the Social Science Research Council, published a shorter version of the lecture that Immanuel Wallerstein delivered at Stanford University to mark the publication of *Open the Social Sciences*. He observed that "[a]t least 95 percent of all scholars and all scholarship from the period 1850 to 1914, and probably even to 1945, originates in five countries: France, Great Britain, the Germanies, the Italies, and the United States. There is a smattering elsewhere, but basically, not only does the scholarship come out of these five countries, but most of the scholarship by most scholars is about their own country" (1996a, 3). In a previous publication (1996) Wallerstein had already anticipated the point I just quoted, although he had also included the languages of scholarship. He had said on this occasion, after referring to the geohistorical locations of the social sciences, "Five countries, four languages. The geopolitics of the time placed at least three of these languages—English, French and German—on a par in terms of prestige and influence (that is, the number of non-native speakers who had learned the language as the primary second languages)" (1996; 2). Further

down, after reviewing the changes the social sciences went through in
the past 150 years, Wallerstein observed that "Meanwhile, however, scholarly demography changed. The numbers of Spanish-speaking scholars
grew steadily, and they have increasingly laid claim by amending its statutes
in 1994, making Spanish the third official language of the association"
(1996, 3).

In this chapter I attempt to connect the politics of languages and cultures
I have explored in the previous one with the politics of language and knowledge. The colonial difference and the coloniality of power is here located at
the core of gnoseology, epistemology and hermeneutics, the nomothetic and
ideographic sciences (Wallerstein 1991b, 237–56). What are the epistemological implications of the fact that "five countries, four languages" saturate
academic production, although the "geopolitics of the time placed three of
these languages—English, French and German—on a par in terms of prestige and influence"? I look at the larger picture of the epistemological consequences of the geopolitics of language distribution in the modern world
system in chapter 7. Here, I concentrate on exploring the limits of the
politics of knowledge articulated around language, and the main colonial languages of the modern world system, as indicated in Wallerstein's observations.

Consequently, my interest here is on language and on signs and memories
inscribed in the body rather than signs inscribed on paper. I have explored elsewhere (Boone and Mignolo 1994; Mignolo 1995a) the question of
writing and knowledge and I do not repeat the argument here. Instead, I
pursue the effort, introduced in the previous chapter, of thinking beyond
language. I elaborate further on the idea of languaging, that moment between speech and writing, before and after language, that languages make
possible. Instead of language and knowledge, I talk here about languaging
and knowing. I hope that this exploration allows me to convince you of the
validity of knowledge beyond the "three prestigious languages"—knowledge that the "three languages" in complicity with modern epistemology
and the modern concept of reason, contributed to suppress. Languaging is
not used to single out bi- or plurilanguaging situations. On the contrary
bilanguaging reveals the ideology of monolanguaging (and particularly the
idea of national languages in the imaginary of the modern states), that is, of
speaking, writing, thinking *within* a single language controlled by grammar,
in a way similar to a constitution's control over the state (Von der Valde
1997). Antonio de Nebrija at the end of the fifteenth century wrote the first
grammar of one of the languages of the modern world system (Spanish),
and clearly linked grammar to colonization (Mignolo 1992b; 1992c 1996).
While Nebrija's strange attractors enabled him to order the chaos of everyday languaging, Anzaldúa found herself in a situation in which everyday
bilanguaging in the borderlands brought to life the dissipative structures

making of language an object no longer controlled and wrapped up in a grammar, but languaging (bilanguaging) imbedded in her body. While Nebrija contributed, at the very inception of the modern world system, the ability to imagine language as a structured object and a national symbol, Anzaldúa contributed, at the dawn of the system, the ability to reveal languaging behind languages and bilanguaging as a fundamental condition of border thinking. In other words, while the imaginary of the modern world system focused on frontiers, structures, and the nation-state as a space within frontiers with a national language, languaging and bilanguaging, as a condition of border thinking from the colonial difference, open up to a postnational imaginary. Consequently, border thinking is post-Occidental in the larger picture of the modern world system and postcolonial in the history of the politics of language of modernity/coloniality.

In the preface to *Borderlands/La frontera* (1998), Anzaldúa states:

> The switching of "codes" in this book from English to Castillian Spanish to the North Mexican dialect to Tex-Mex to a sprinkling of Nahuatl to a mixture of all of these, reflects my language, a new language—the language of the Borderlands. There, at the juncture of cultures, languages cross-pollinate and are revitalized; they die and are born. Presently this infant language, this bastard language, Chicano Spanish, is not approved by any society. But we Chicanos no longer feel that we need to beg entrance, that we need always to make the first overture—to translate to Anglos, Mexicans and Latinos, apology blurting out of our mouths with every step. Today we ask to be met halfway. This book is our invitation to you—from the new mestiza. (Anzaldúa 1987, preface)

I would add that this chapter, and the book I am writing, is taking up that invitation and aims at thinking knowledge and epistemology from languaging and bilanguaging, and touching upon their consequences for public policy and education. Indeed, and as I have discussed in the previous chapter, my own argument—here, in this book—is a double articulation of my early sensibility formed in Latin American Spanish and the arrival of English late in my life. I would say, then, with Umberto Maturana and Francisco Varela (1987), and following up on Anzaldúa's invitation, that a significant number of human beings, or, if you prefer, living organisms, operate in language; and I would add that language is not an object, something that human beings have, but an ongoing process that only exists in languaging (Maturana and Varela 1987, 206–15). Martin Heidegger ([1957] 1977; [1954] 1977) used to say that language is the home of Being. One might say, rather, that language is the home of Languaging. Being is a concept entrenched with a denotative philosophy of language that isolates the notion of "idea" as the result of thinking according to the singularization of "personhood" and of "self." Languaging, however, locates interaction among individuals, among human beings instead of in preexisting ideas. It is precisely at the intersection between person, self, humans, living organisms—or what have you—where languaging is located as the condition of the possibility of language. Richard Rorty's dictum—that while the philosophical paradigmatic concept in the nineteenth century was "idea," in the twentieth century it is "text" (1982, 90–109)—could be superseded (or at least challenged), by introducing the concept of "languaging." The possibility of conceiving and asking for thinking beyond thoughts and languaging, indeed beyond language, discloses the recursive capacity of languaging: languaging in language allows us to describe ourselves interacting as well as to describe the descriptions of our interactions.

National languages came forth in languaging, in complicity with the state and with institutions regulating the uses and abuses of language. Coloniality of power and the colonial difference were and are at work in all those parts of the planet where nation building (in nineteenth-century Latin America or mid-twentieth-century Asia and Africa) was coupled with the colonial difference. One wonders how the idea of one language, one territory became so successful that it displaced the natural diversity of plurilanguaging (or, at a more perceptible level, of plurilingualism). How was it that literacy and written grammars traced the frontiers between languages and controlled the natural flow of languaging without the policing of written grammars and natural politics of language? However, around 1970 signs that national languages were not as natural as they were presumed to be began to manifest themselves and call attention to the diversity of language in a given national territory. Not surprisingly, these signs were coming from the so-called Third World, at a time when social movements were paralleled by a rethinking of bilingual education within the camp of linguistic policy and by a surge of sociolinguistic research on bilingualism and subaltern languages (e.g., Labov's [1872] work on "black English"). It was also during the 1970s that the Chicano movement began to make its mark on the U.S. public sphere, bringing to life and articulating a process and a practice I would call bilanguaging (I explain later why this was not just bilingual).

It was also in the 1970s that the idea of the Third World's inability to put forth convincing ideologies articulating linguistic pluralism with nationalism was advanced. This occurred as the conflicts between imperial and indigenous languages presented an obstacle to the process of decolonization. On the other hand, it appeared that colonial powers were not ready to relinquish the national ideology of languages nor the idea of cultures associated with them. The massive display put forth by the Spanish government before, during, and after 1992 to claim the glory of the "discovery" of America is still vivid in our memory. Spain continues still today its efforts to "sell" Spanish culture through U.S. universities, a luxury that is not allowed to

Bolivia, for instance. We are currently witnessing the flow of French francs to the United States and Latin America in order to keep alive the legacies of French culture in the Americas and around the world, a luxury that is not allowed to Martinique, Guadeloupe, or Morocco, for instance. Meanwhile, American English is becoming more and more the language of international transactions and, paradoxically, is challenging the linguistic unity of the European community, where American English overshadows English's legacy as the language of the British Empire. It is not just the grammar of the language that is at stake, but the geopolitics of language: global designs drawing linguistic maps, literary and epistemological cartographies. A curious paradox is that as English becomes more detached from its own territory, its grounding is superseded by a transnational dimension. Finally, English becomes a language that allows for national, transnational and intranational identities and identifications. Globalization made possible both massive migrations and the visibility of local social movements. By the same token, it made possible the resurgence of indigenous languages suppressed by colonial and imperial expansion and by the surge of fractured imperial languages within and outside national territories (see chapter 4). This situation invites us to wonder how in the nineteenth century the links between languages and territories were described and how "languaging in natural and imperial languages" became a natural terrain of national and imperial (cultural) conflicts.

Such a task could be pursued on several fronts. I would like to focus on the very foundation of a philosophy of language, which was also an explanation of the nature of language, as well as a justification to use language as an object of desire and an instrument of colonial or national domination. The former scenario may be seen from the perspective of groups on the receiving end of colonial expansion who perceived languages according to the perspective of imperial ideology and assumed that the language of the empire was/is preferable to their own native ones. Or, in the case of Spanish or English in the Americas, the imperial version could be preferable to the local one. This was the debate between Andres Bello (a Venezuelan living in Chile) and Argentinian Domingo F. Sarmiento in the first half of the nineteenth century (Ramos 1989). The use of language, as an instrument of domination, constructs it as an object of desire since education and literacy in the colonies are based on the model and history of the empire. The paradox that decolonization after World War II went hand in hand with nation building, when nation building was part of the very process of modernity, can be understood from the perspective of literacy and the transmission of European national ideals to the colonies. If then reconceptualizing languages and their complicity with the nation could be pursued on several fronts, I would try—as I said—to look at the foundations (which were not there, but posited as such) of a philosophy that is both a conceptualization of the nature of language and a conceptualization of the complicities between language, empires, and nations. My rethinking will also be an attempt at an undoing and at a projective reconfiguration.

A BORDER TONGUE, A BORDER THINKING

The question is, How shall I proceed in this rethinking and undoing? From "where" will I rethink? From the legacies of the very foundations I am trying to undo? Is it enough to describe the heterogeneity or hybridity of the enunciated, maintaining at the same time the homogeneity and purity of enunciation? Would it be possible to build on a foundation that is not the foundation that allowed for the justification of national imperial languages and their complicity with knowledge? Perhaps one could begin from the centers, which became margins due to the hegemony of major languages linked with territories and with nations. We should perhaps begin to think from border languages instead of from national languages. So, I begin with two chapters of Gloria Anzaldúa's *Borderlands/La frontera* (1987), "How to Tame a Wild Tongue" and "Tlilli, Tlapalli[:] The Path of the Red and Black Ink":

> I have been accused by various Latinos and Latinas. Chicano Spanish is considered by the purist and by most Latinos deficient, a mutilation of Spanish. . . .
>   But Chicano Spanish is a border tongue which developed naturally. Change, evolution, enriquecimiento de palabras nuevas por invencion o adoption have created variants of Chicano Spanish, un nuevo lenguaje. Un lenguaje que corresponde a un modo de vivir. Chicano Spanish is not incorrect, it is a living language. (Anzaldúa 1987, 55)

Anzaldúa's observation resonates, unwillingly perhaps, in the history of Castilian, which arose from border languaging by Latin, spoken in the northern part of the peninsula, and by Arabic, spoken in the central and southern regions. It also resonates in the history of Castilian, from Antonio de Nebrija to Anzaldúa herself, passing through Andres Bello, in Spanish America—the ideologue of Spanish language for the independent colonies of America (see Ramos 1989; Cussen 1992).

In 1492—the year of the final victory by the Kingdom of Castile against the Moors—when Nebrija told Queen Isabella of Spain that languages were the empire's companion, he answered the queen's question about the purpose of a grammar of a vernacular language. About three hundred years later, when European romantic intellectuals reacted against the search for language universals (à la Leibniz) and brought the discussion back home to the region and to the people, they anticipated a philosophy of language linked to public policy and to nation building (Aarsleff 1982, 146–209). Toward the end of the nineteenth century, this philosophy would create the strong conviction that there is a one-to-one relationship between languages and territories, and that there is a one-to-one relationship between the people speaking a given language and their sense of identification with themselves and their territory (Hobsbawn 1990, 14–45). The idea of linking languages and territories was not a new one introduced by the philosophy of the Enlightenment. Rather, it had already been clearly articulated a century after Nebrija, when José Aldrete in Castile wrote the first history of the Castilian language in 1601 (Mignolo 1992b; 1995a, 29–67). These were the heydays of the Castilian Empire in the (West) Indies, an empire that extended from the Caribbean to the Philippines and to the Pacific Islands. It was indeed in the history of the language that its complicity with territory was explored by Aldrete. In approximately one hundred years, Castile had extended its domain across the Atlantic and the Pacific, had created a grammar for the language of the kingdom that extended beyond the Iberian Peninsula in Europe, and had produced a history of the language linked to a geography located at the center of the kingdom (Mignolo 1992b; 1992c).

To understand Nebrija's implications for cultures of scholarship, it is necessary to understand that his argument rested on a philosophy of language whose roots could be traced back, on one hand, to Saint Augustine and the merging of Platonic and Christian tradition in order to solve the problem of a unified language needed to counteract the plurality of existing tongues and, on the other, to Valla's (1406–57) *Linguae latinae elegantiorum libri sex*, written to save Christian Rome from linguistic and cultural illiteracy ("barbarus").

In Spain, and some forty years after Nebrija composed his grammar, Luis Vives (familiar with Saint Augustine's work and responsible for the critical edition of his works orchestrated by Desiderio Erasmus) was delineating *la questione de la lingua* in terms of the contrast between the primordial language spoken by Adam and the Tower of Babel as the event that initiated linguistic diversity (Vives 1964). Saint Augustine's strong belief in one original language comes from the Scriptures and also from his Platonic theoretical framework. As a Neoplatonic and Christian, Saint Augustine's reading of the Holy Book assumed the metaphysical principles of an original unity from which the plurality and multiplicity of things could be accounted for. The original and unified language, according to Saint Augustine, need not and could not be named because it was not necessary to distinguish it from other human languages. It could be called human language or human locution (*De civitate Dei* 16.11.1). However, the human language was not enough to keep human beings happy and away from transgressing the law, as expressed in the project of building a tower to reach heaven. The division of languages that caused the division of people and communities reached the number seventy-two and each of them was identified with a particular name. It was at this point that it became necessary to find a name for the primordial language in order to distinguish it from the rest. Saint Augustine had good reasons to believe that the original (primordial) language was Hebrew.

While Vives was acquainted with Saint Augustine and was developing a philosophy of language that would be used, directly or indirectly, by the missionaries colonizing native languages, Nebrija was somehow rewriting Valla's program outlined in the preface to his *Linguae latinae elegantiorum* ([1442?] 1952). Valla realized that rebuilding an empire was not a goal that could be reached by means of arms. Instead, he intended to achieve it by the expedient of letters. By contrasting the Latin used by his ancestors with the expansion of the Roman Empire, and by underlying the strength of the language as a unifying force over the geographical conquests, Valla foresaw the Roman recovery of its lost power and, as a consequence, predicted the central role that Italy was assigned to play in the future. Certainly, in 1492 it was difficult for Nebrija to anticipate much about the future colonization of the New World. It should have been clear to him, however, that Castile had an opportunity to take the place of the Roman Empire. If the preface to his *Gramática Castellana* was indeed a rewriting of Valla's preface, the historical conditions had changed: while Valla was attempting to save an already established empire in decadence, Nebrija was predicting the construction of a new one.

There are other issues that deserve to be compared. Valla's fight against the barbarians, his belief that the history of civilization is the history of language (in anticipation of Vico), and the strong connections he perceived between language and empire are issues that are repeated by Nebrija. There are, however, some significant differences: Nebrija visualized the center of the empire in Castile instead of Italy and Castilian as the language of the empire instead of Latin. It naturally follows that grammars of native Amerindian languages have been written mainly in Castilian using Nebrija's Latin (not Castilian) grammar as a model. It is also interesting to note that histories of the New World have been mainly written in Castilian. From these differences follow the tension between Latin as the language of learning, and Castilian as the language of politics and conversion. The time had arrived to move from writing grammars of native languages to writing histories of natives' memories.

The first histories of Amerindian cultures known in Europe were written by members of the culture that introduced Western literacy to the natives (Mignolo 1981; 1982). In the process, the native methods of recording the past and transmitting it to future generations suffered the consequences of literacy both in the form of learning a new form of writing and reading and of being narrated (perhaps without knowing it) by those who were introducing the alphabet (Scharlau and Monzel 1987; Mignolo 1989a; 1992a; 1992b; Boone and Mignolo 1994). Spanish historiographers acted in the belief that the alphabet was a necessary condition of historiographical writing. They recognized that Amerindians had means of recording the past (either by oral narratives or in picto-ideographic writing), although the Spaniards did not acknowledge that it was the Amerindian equivalent to historiographical writing. Once they concluded that the Amerindians did not have historiography, they appointed themselves to write and put into a coherent form the narratives that, according to the Spanish historiographers, the Amerindians told in a thoroughly incoherent manner. When a situation such as this arises in which the act of writing the history of a community means both suppressing the possibility that community may be heard and not trusting the voice of the "others," we are witnessing a good example of the colonization of discursive genres (or types). The case seems to be similar to that of writing grammars. While in one case, grammars take the place of the native implicit organization of languages, writing histories takes the place of native explicit organization of past oral expression and nonalphabetic forms of writing. In the first case, an implicit knowledge is ignored; in the second, an explicit knowledge is being rewritten.

Knowing this story, it is surprising to read Fichte's address to the German nation (Fichte [1808] 1922; Balibar 1994, 61–84) and to ponder the implications of his distinction between dead and living languages. Dead languages for Fichte were not languages no longer spoken during his time but rather tongues cut-off—that is, languages with broken and mixed traditions. French, for instance, was cut off from its Latin roots before becoming a language in its own right, and English became a mixed language following the Norman conquest. In contrast, German was the only language through which a continuous link with the past could be traced back to immemorial times. German was a living language and only living languages could express the soul of the nation. It is also surprising, although perhaps unwarranted, that Spanish was not among Fichte's concerns. By not discussing Spanish and Portuguese—and with Italian in the background of a glorious Renaissance memory—the question was divided among German, English, and French, the three languages of modernity and imperial expansion since the eighteenth century that Wallerstein associated with the emergence of the social sciences. These were the languages of the "heart" of Europe in Hegel's lessons on universal history, delivered more or less during the same years that Fichte addressed the German nation regarding the question of language. Spain, at that time, was receding behind the picture of European modernity, the emergence of new nations and new empires. Castilian, like Portuguese and Italian, was becoming a subaltern language within imperial conflicts and the building of new linguistic and cultural hegemonies. (I return later to this historical moment, which I will identify as the first demotion of the Spanish language in the construction of European modernity.)

Almost two centuries after Fichte, the articulation of living and dead tongues was reversed, and cutoff tongues were given the status of living ones:

> Chicano Spanish is not incorrect, it is a living language, for a people who are neither Spanish nor live in a country in which Spanish is the first language; for a people who live in a country in which English is the reigning tongue but who are not Anglo; for a people who cannot entirely identify with either standard (formal, Castillian) Spanish nor standard English, what recourse is left to them but to create their language? A language to which they can connect their identity, one capable of communicating the realities and values true to themselves— a language with terms that are neither espanol ni ingles, but both. We speak a patois, a forked tongue, a variation of two languages. (Anzaldúa 1987, 55)

The similarities between Anzaldúa and Fichte are obvious: they both talk from the inscription of language in their bodies, from languaging in language toward an emerging German nation-state and an emerging Chicano community. They are both concerned about borders, although from quite different perspectives and interests. Fichte looks at borders as the walls that protect the inside from foreign dangers (Balibar 1994). Anzaldúa looks at borders as the places where the distinction between the inside and the foreign collapse; the borders themselves become the location of thinking and releasing the fears constructed by national intellectuals toward what may come from the outside. Historically, however, the differences are enormous: Germany became the language of a powerful nation-state toward the end of the nineteenth century; Spanish in the United States became the language of ethnic minorities and endured a third historical demotion. The second demotion, which I do not discuss here, occurred after World War II when the world was divided into three ranked areas and Spanish became the language of a significant portion of the Third World.

I now make a brief reference to text and textile and bring in Anzaldúa's chapter on Aztec writing, "Tlilli, Tlapalli" (see chapter 5). Benedict Anderson [1983] 1991, in his classic book, pays a significant amount of attention to the role of the printing press in building national communities. The printing press was also instrumental before the nineteenth century in the process of colonial expansion, from territorial control to literacy and education. The notion of "text" became more and more limited to alphabetic literacy and the book, and certain books containing national narratives became national icons. All other written forms were automatically relegated to the realm of folklore, the subaltern dimension of nation-states' concept of culture. Anzaldúa's "In Tlilli, Tlapalli[:] The Path of the Red and Black Ink" brings to the surface a dimension of "text and nation" that was suppressed twice: once by the early colonial system of education and then by the nation builders' conviction that the nation and civility were partially founded in alphabetic literacy. The rearticulation of language and writing by the nation-state achieved a double subalternization of writing: first, by promoting alphabetic writing to the pinnacle of civility and, second, by maintaining a gender division in writing practices. "Men of letters" were in control of the literacy within the state apparatus; "textile" remained in the hands of women and in the realm of folklore. By bringing back "the path of the red and the black ink," the ancient writing systems, Anzaldúa refurbishes the conceptualization of writing and text, and opens up the doors to rethink the complicities among texts, nations, empires, and cultures of scholarship.

EPISTEMOLOGY AND IMPERIAL/NATIONAL LANGUAGES

From the conflicts among the imperial languages and between imperial and subaltern languages, I now move to cultures of scholarship, which are also cultures in conflict. I explore two aspects: the complicities between imperial languages and structures of knowledge; and the difficulty, if not impossibility, of certain languages becoming languages of scholarship. Hierarchies are established in language. Looking at languaging instead of at languages may allow us to see behind the scenes and to conceive knowledge beyond disciplinary boundaries and across discursive genres associated with national and imperial linguistic hierarchies and subsequent structures of knowledge.

There is a splendid moment in Pierre Bourdieu's "Thinking about Limits" (1992), in which he places himself in a disciplinary-theoretical as well as a language genealogy. As a sociologist interested in education, Bourdieu understands the paradox implied in the process itself: "if we are not educated, we *cannot think much at all*, yet if we are educated we risk being dominated by ready-made thoughts." Can we really not think much at all if we are not educated? Is it only education that calls for thinking? Or is education a manipulation of thinking? In order to address these questions, let us look at languages and education in colonial expansion and nation-building strategies. Let us concentrate on colonial legacies, national languages, and disciplinary foundations in the educational system that teaches us (i.e., those of us who have access to such education) how to think. Let us also follow Bourdieu in his journey of self-disciplinary location.

The epistemological tradition in which Bourdieu began to work, he confesses, was for him "like the air that we breathe," which is to say that it went unnoticed. He recognizes that his is a very local tradition tied up with a number of French names: Koyré, Bachelard, Canghilhem, and, if we go back a little, Duhem. Bourdieu further explains:

> One should study the historical reasons for its existence, since it was not at all
> a *national miracle*, but no doubt *related to favourable conditions* within the struc-

ture of the education system [emphasis added]. This historical tradition of epistemology very strongly linked reflection on science with the history of science.
Differently from the neo-positivist *Anglo-Saxon* tradition, it was from the history
of science that it isolated the principles of knowledge and scientific thoughts.
(Bourdieu 1992, 41)

Cultures of scholarship are cast in terms of textual national legacies, for it
is in and by texts that the educational system, in modern and Western Europe (the Europe of Hegel and Fichte), is structured and that science is
articulated, packaged, transmitted, and exported.

But let me explore further the equation texts-nations-cultures of scholarship. In an effort to elucidate the theoretical frame of his own thinking,
Bourdieu honestly pursues a comparison (this time) with the German philosophical tradition. The comparison is necessary in order to justify the trans-
ferability of scientific thinking from the science of nature to the human
sciences, a that which is more difficult to take in the German philosophical
legacy because—according to Bourdieu—the distinction between "Erklaren-
Verstehen" (explanation-understanding) builds a wall between the natural
and the human sciences. French legacies, he concludes,

propos[e], then, a reflection which is much more general, from which I have
drawn an epistemological program that can be summed up in one statement:
"The scientific fact is conquered, constructed, confirmed." The conquest of the
given is a central concept in Bachelar's thought, and he sums it up in the term
epistemological break. Why is this phase of scientific research important, and
why does it separate, as seems to me to be the case, the tradition I represent
from the dominant Anglo-Saxon tradition? It is because to say that the scientific
fact has to be fought for is radically to defy, in this regard, all of the givens that
social scientific researchers find before them. (Bourdieu 1992, 43)

This brief description of Bourdieu's self-location within the theoretical
and epistemological parameters of the human sciences and linguistic/textual
national traditions is not intended to describe my own theoretical premises.
I am interested in the underlying links between scientific texts and nations,
between languages and cultures of scholarship. How should we think from
models and theories provided by Chicano/a thinkers, such as Gloria Anzaldúa or Cherrie Moraga, among others? How should we operate in language
from the edges of what disciplinary self-descriptions placed as the exterior
of a disciplinary interior? How should we erase the disciplinary distinctions
between external narrative forms, such as the myth, and internal narrative
forms, such as history? How should we rearticulate them in the sphere of
human languaging, beyond discursive genres framed in imperial languages
and epistemological structures of domination? There is one point on which
I concur with Bourdieu, however, and I take it as a theoretical premise: "if

the state is so difficult to think, it is because we are the state's thinkers, and because the state is in the head of the thinkers. Put like that, this has the feel of a phrase that still floats too much in the air, but one can see for example in Durkheim's texts all that his thinking on the state owed to the fact that he was a functionary of the state" (1992:40). Thus, if the state is complicitous with the production and distribution of knowledge, can theoretical and scientific thinking be produced at the margin of the major national languages, entrenched within colonial expansion since the eighteenth century? Can the state think from the colonial difference? In principle, no, because coloniality of power is embedded in the state and as such it *reproduces* the colonial difference and represses the possibilities of *thinking from* it.

CULTURES OF SCHOLARSHIP, NATIONAL LANGUAGES, TRANSNATIONAL KNOWLEDGE

A question that we might ask at this point is what happens with national languages and cultures of scholarship in a transnational world? How should we move away from the "natural" connections between structures of knowledge and national-imperial languages, as Wallerstein has pointed out? One obvious answer is implied in my previous discussion on Bourdieu: national languages linked to modern European nations and colonialism (English, French, German) after the eighteenth century persist as the main languages of culture of scholarship; knowledge, and forms of knowledge are exported like any other commodity, and imperial languages are the mediators in these kinds of transactions, from models for economic restructuration to theories of historical narratives, ethical arguments, and philosophies of languages. Another possible answer would be related to the description, analysis, explanation, and understanding of language turmoil engendered by massive migrations to imperial centers, on the one hand, and by the consequences of decolonization, on the other. What these social transformations engendered was not a new form of science or of philosophical thinking, but "literature" produced either in the ex-colonies or at the margins of metropolitan centers receiving massive migratory movements. The consequences of such a double movement (e.g., [a] exportation of knowledge and patterns of scholarship to ex-colonies; [b] decolonization and massive migrations from ex-colonies to metropolitan and industrial centers) are obvious: the so-called Third World (external or internal to so-called First World nations) is supposed to produce "culture" while the First World is supposed to produce scholarship and science: a distribution of scientific labor that contributed to maintaining the hierarchy of languages implanted by previous colonialisms (see chapter 1).

Such a distribution of scientific labor could be rethought from the bilanguage literature of frontiers and borderlands. Nonetheless, in order to do so it is necessary to reconceptualize literature and scholarship and see them both as different agencies of languaging. In the context of the state, its citizens are encouraged to abide by rules that make monolanguaging hegemonic (Fishman 1996, 3–16) and bilanguaging a subaltern language interaction. Therefore, disciplinary foundations are legalized in the realm of monolanguaging, but banned in the realm of bilanguaging. Can bilanguaging then be taken as a theoretical foundation and Anzaldúa as an intellectual reference of knowledge and understanding, in a way similar to Bourdieu's appeal to French and French intellectuals in his disciplinary and sociological practice? Can bilanguaging and border thinking (as well as Khatibi's "an other thinking" and Du Bois's "double consciousness") be the foundation of an epistemology that bypasses epistemological grounding in national and imperial languages?

In order to foresee this perspective it is necessary to accept that languaging, like thinking, is beyond language and thought; languaging is the moment in which "a living language" (as Anzaldúa puts it) describes itself as a way of life ("un modo de vivir") at the intersection of two (or more) languages. At this point, the differences between the bilingual and the bilanguage/bilanguaging, between linguistic policy and languaging become apparent: bilingualism is not a way of life but a skill. If bilanguaging were not a life-style, if it were not existentially and politically dramatic but rather a skill, we would not be able to understand José Maria Arguedas in Peru, who killed himself in the tension of bilanguaging. Nor would we understand Gloria Anzaldúa in the United States, whose seductive force is the force of bilanguaging as living-between-languages and not just a bilingual aesthetic exercise. Indeed Frantz Fanon's analysis of the displacement of French in the Caribbean and Africa, deeply entrenched in racial tensions, is an exemplary instance of bilanguaging in the same language, as is the "Creole epistemology" emerging from the Caribbean thinkers I commented upon in the previous chapter.

Furthermore, the reason that I prefer bilanguaging and bilanguagism rather than bilingualism is because I am trying to draw in something that is beyond sound, syntax, and lexicon, and beyond the need of having two languages (as Fanon's example testifies, bilanguaging as a form of life is possible in the fractures of an hegemonic [national or imperial] language): the law that instills fear and shame among those who do not master the master language. "Chicanas who grew up speaking Chicano Spanish have internalized the belief that we speak poor Spanish. It is illegitimate, a bastard language," observers Anzaldúa (1987, 58). And she adds: "Chicanas feel uncomfortable talking in Spanish to Latinas, afraid of their censure. Their language was not outlawed in their countries. They had a whole lifetime of being immersed in their native tongue; generations, centuries in which Spanish was a first language, taught in school, heard on radio and TV, and read in newspapers" (Anzaldúa 1987, 58).

Languaging should take us not to the soul of the people reflected in language (as Fichte would like to have it), but to what makes language possible: without languaging, no language is possible. Languaging is not a replacement of Humboldt's *energeia* but rather a "way of life," engaging needs and desires to enact the politics and ethics of liberation. Now, since languaging is interacting *in* language and language is what allows for describing and conceiving languaging, bilanguaging then would be precisely that way of life between languages: a dialogical, ethic, aesthetic, and political process of social transformation rather than energeia emanating from an isolated speaker.

LANGUAGING, EDUCATION, AND CRITICAL THINKING

I would like to pursue this line of thought by introducing Paulo Freire's *Pedagogy of the Oppressed* ([1972] 1993) in this section and by discussing Cherríe Moraga's *The Last Generation* (1993) in the next one.

Freire's notion of *dialogical thinking* allows me to elucidate one aspect of languaging beyond Humboldt's *energeia* and to explore border thinking at another level. His dialogical thinking is more than an analytical concept: it is also a means for action and liberation. Liberation from what? one may ask. From social and economic oppression, but also and mainly as intellectual decolonization: not the universal emancipation of "them," in the Enlightenment project, but its complement, "liberation" from coloniality, the darker side of modernity. Although literacy is the main agency of dialogical thinking and human liberation, Freire does not explicitly explore language as an issue related to both national domination and human liberation. However, his take on dialogical thinking shows the way to a displacement of hegemonic notions of disciplinary or scholarly knowledge. Freire talks about thinking *with* instead of thinking *for* or thinking *about* people. His dialogical thinking as an educational project authorizes a recasting of Bourdieu's framing of his own scientific tradition in order to analyze educational systems and national languages.

Bourdieu maintains a legacy in which science and scholarship are monological: it is a *thinking about* rather than a thinking with. The goal of science and scholarship is to conquer the facts, whether perceived as human nature or natural nature. Consequently, if the thinkers of the human sciences are the thinkers of the state, there is a close link between the human sciences and the impossibility of *thinking with*. If the nation-state and (to paraphrase Freire) the dominant elites were to think *with* the people, the contradiction would be superseded and domination would end. Instead, scholarly thinking and studies *about* the nation and languages may prevent citizens from thinking about the nation by themselves. If this is the case, we need a different kind of thinking in the realm of linguistic policy and educational projects. Languaging should be brought into the picture; and bilanguaging, as a way of knowing and of living emerging from the detritus of colonial and national expansion, could contribute in the struggle to reconvert subaltern memories from places of nostalgia to places of celebration.

Bilanguaging and dialogical thinking, as practices as well as conceptualizations of such practices, should also contribute to the transformation of the human sciences into forms of knowing that outdo the humanitarian generosity of hegemonic power, and that recast cultures of scholarship by the recognition of diversity of knowledge which outshines monothinking and monolanguaging. Freire's dialogical thinking forms a network with my own concept of bilanguaging and with Abdelkebir Khatibi's "une pensée autre" (an other thinking), placed at the intersection of the so-called Western rationality and its exterior, the ways of thinking that were presumed to be, at some point, integrated and transformed into rationality (Khatibi [1983] 1990, 63–112). Moreover, his double critique is located at the intersection of Western and Islamic legacies. If Freire's dialogical thinking engages literacy and moves toward "conscientization" as a form of liberation, Khatibi's double critique pursues intellectual and scholarly decolonization. It is a third place, a third word, which is also a delinking from Western reason and a critique of its adaptation to Maghrebian *sociologie*. This effort is made possible, according to Khatibi, by departing from Western critiques of science, technology, and metaphysics (Nietzsche, Heidegger, Derrida) and by relocating it in "our bilanguage situation" (57; Khatibi uses the term *bilingüe*, but his thoughts are beyond the realm of the bilingual proper). The bilanguage situation Khatibi alludes to is part of two forms of metaphysics, indeed a bimetaphysics, both Western and Islamic. Khatibi's dramatic search is the instability of walking on the frontiers, the frontiers of bilanguaging, which represent the unavoidable inscription of colonial legacies that displace the deconstruction of Western metaphysics from within its boundaries toward a decolonizing effort: deconstruction becomes decolonization in the fractured space of bilanguage and bilanguaging.

My own situation is quite different from that of Khatibi. The double forms of metaphysics for someone born and educated in Argentina (or in Latin America, for that matter) have a different configuration. The detritus of Western reason is certainly there, as in Maghreb, but Islamic legacies are alien. Amerindian legacies do not have a common Greek heritage, unlike Islam and the constitution of the West. Bilanguage and bicultural situations in the Americas are alien to the transfiguration of the ancient Greek thinking machine in the Arabic world and in Western Christianity.

BORDER THINKING, BICULTURAL MIND—DOUBLE CONSCIOUSNESS

Similar to those found in Khatibi are the politics and ethics of bilanguaging in Chicano and Chicana intellectuals, such as Gloria Anzaldúa, Cherrie Moraga, Ramón Saldívar, and Norma Alarcon. In her latest book (*The Last Generation*, 1993) Moraga introduces the notion of "bicultural mind," which I perceive as a member of the same family as Anzaldúa's "New Mestiza," Khatibi's notion of "an other thinking." The discursive genealogy created by Moraga is a genealogy building on dual memories, memories articulated in two or more languages, rather than by means of a disciplinary tradition. It constructs knowledge, although nondisciplinary knowledge: a knowledge that is, like bilanguaging, a life-style and struggle for liberation, not from the darker tyranny of theological thinking (how the Renaissance and the Enlightenment justified knowledge) but, paradoxically, from the control of reason as the disciplinary grammar of knowledge in cultures of scholarship. Can such knowledge be produced within disciplinary (e.g., human sciences) frameworks? Can disciplines operate in a space of dual epistemologies? Would it be possible to think at the bilanguage intersection of Quechua and Spanish, for example, or Nahuatl and English? Can bilanguaging from the spaces of languages inscribed in different epistemologies (for instance, French and Arabic, or Spanish and Quechua), epistemologies that emerge from the fractures of the languages of "scientific" and "philosophical" knowledge in Western modernity and its aftermath around the world, generate new ways of knowing? The answer is simply yes, although difficult to accept in a world where hegemonic epistemology has the convincing power of technology supported by an ideology where achievement is measured by the amount of objects produced, consumed, accumulated, and sold. Furthermore, given the complicities between nation-state, languages, disciplinary configuration, and consumerism, bilanguaging epistemologies run the same risk as other cultural productions accepted as "folklore," "magic," "mysticism," and the like. I would like to insist, however, that bilanguaging in certain situations and in certain colonial legacies could lead the way toward a radical epistemological transformation.

The "bicultural mind" (in my terminology the "bilanguaging mind") is the "mind" inscribed in and produced by colonial conditions, although diverse colonial legacies engender dissimilar "bicultural minds." Consequently, bilanguaging and nations will be shaped by the place that the nation occupies in relation to colonial and imperial structures. The local is inscribed in the global. Moraga theorizes the double bind between the local and the global in the domain of the people, the body, and sexuality: "it is historically evident that the female body, like the Chicano people, has been colonized. And any movement to decolonize them must be culturally and sexually specific" (Moraga 1993, 149). The articulation of the local and the global is inscribed in a particular colonial legacy: the Spanish colonization of America (with an accent), and the U.S. imperial moves toward Mexico and Latin America. Moraga exploits the date that she finished the book, 1992, five hundred years after the recognized cultural beginning of globalization as Western expansion. That is, one side of Moraga's constructed colonial legacy is not located in the legacies of the European Enlightenment and in North Atlantic modernity, but in the early modern and early colonial period and the expansion of the Spanish Empire. As a matter of fact, modernity and colonization after the eighteenth century, if not irrelevant, are quite secondary in Moraga's wounds:

> Chicano Nation is a mestizo nation conceived in a double-rape: first, by the Spanish and then by the Gringo. In the mid-19th century, Anglo-America took possession of one-third of Mexico's territory. A new English-speaking oppressor assumed control over the Spanish, Mestizo, and Indian people inhabiting those lands. There was no disallowing that the United States had stolen Aztlan from Mexico, but it had been initially stolen from the Indians by the Spanish some 300 years earlier. (Moraga 1993, 153–54)

Now, what does this double rape mean in terms of languages and languaging? First, it signifies the rearticulation of Amerindian languages by the Spanish colonial system of education and, by the same token, the subalternization of Amerindian languages in relation to Spanish. Second, it is the system of the rearticulation of colonial languages themselves (Spanish, Portuguese, Italian, French, German, English), the growing influence of the languages attached to the second wave of colonial expansion (German, French, English), and, above all, the hegemonic role of English during the third wave of globalization, from 1945 to the present. Spanish is both a hegemonic language allowing for the subalternization of Amerindian languages and a subaltern language of North Atlantic modernity. And I would add, it is three times subaltern. Spanish was first displaced toward a subaltern position within the European community itself during the seventeenth century when Seville was replaced by Amsterdam as the center of global transaction, and when French, German, and English became the languages of reason and science. In other words, these became the languages of disciplinary configurations implied in Bourdieu's genealogy of sociological scientific practices. Second, after World War II and the division of the world into three ranked areas, Spanish became the language of a significant portion of the Third World, Hispanic America. Spanish was devalued a third time when it became the language of Latino communities in the United States.

Let me explore this issue further. Moraga states that she finished *The Last Generation* in 1992. The introduction is dated December 31, 1992. She makes explicit the significance of this date: five hundred years after Columbus arrived to the lands that would be later called America, and she writes America with an accent on the *e*. The second date is 1524, the date after the fall of Mexico-Tenochtitlan and the arrival of the twelve Franciscans—requested by Cortes to Charles I of Spain and Charles V of Europe, who then forwarded the request to the pope. The conflicts of languages, cultures, and knowledge are clearly articulated in this encounter between the Tlamatinime and the twelve Franciscans. The link here is between Moraga, the Chicanos (instead of the sociologists), and the anonymous Tlamatinime (instead of Bachelard, Koyré, Canghilhem):

> I write with the same knowledge, the same sadness, recognizing the full impact of the colonial "experiment" on the lives of Chicanos, mestizos and Native Americans. Our codices—dead leaves unwritten—lie smoldering in the ashes of disregard, censure, and erasure. *The Last Generation* emerges from those ashes. I write against time, out of a sense of urgency that Chicanos are a disappearing tribe, out of a sense of this disappearance in my own familia. (Moraga 1993, 2)

Aztlán as a place, and the anonymous *tlamatinime* as a social role set the stage for the most relevant chapter of the book: "Queer Aztlan: Re-formation of Chicano Tribe," in which Moraga discusses at length the idea of the nation and makes a move toward a new formation, a re-formation, of Chicano Tribe. This reformulation is being thought out at the same time that the nation-states of three countries (Mexico, the United States and Canada) were working on a territorial re-formation by regional integration (NAFTA). Moraga complements and dialogues with Leslie Marmon Silko's *Almanac of the Dead* (1991), particularly with the "five hundred year map" that Silko includes at the beginning of her novel (see fig. 1).

Bilanguaging acquires a new dimension, not just the dimension of the linguistic per se, or of dialogical thinking, but languaging in the sphere of sexuality, race, and human interactions. Bi-languaging is no longer idiomatic (Spanish, English) but is also ethnic, sexual, and gendered. Spanish and English "recede" as national languages, as the language of a nation called "Queer Aztlan" arises. After all, both are imperial languages, and Queer Aztlan proposes a different articulation of the nation in the last analysis, and whether English or Spanish would be irrelevant, on the one hand, because both are hegemonic languages of the empire and the nation, or, on the other hand, because they are unavoidable due to globalization and the consolidation of hegemonic languages, is a moot point. If English is the unavoidable choice because Queer Aztlan is a subaltern nation, it has its advantages: the possibility of fracturing the configuration of the hegemonic languages. Bilanguaging could be understood here as the displacement of hegemonic and imperial languages (Spanish, English) and their relocation into the perspective of Amerindian languages. In order to do so, it is necessary to think languaging beyond languages: the moment "before" language (not, of course, in a history of language from the paleolithic to the present, but in everyday linguistic practices), when the discursive alienation of what (in language) we call "consciousness" has not yet been articulated in the discursive structure of power; and the moment "after" language, when languaging (and, in this case, bilanguaging) becomes a process of "conscientization" (à la Freire) as liberation of colonial and national (official, hegemonic) discourses and epistemologies. Both moments of languaging ("before" and "after" language) allow Moraga to reconceptualize territoriality. The idea of "land" counters the national concept of "territory," as mapped by the nation-state. In the domain of languaging before language, "land" is inscribed in the primal domain of interaction of people among themselves and with the world; in the domain of languaging after language, "land" is reinscribed in the movement of conscientization and the articulation of new communities, beyond (national) languages. But, of course, this perspective will not be readily accepted in educational institutions (from the state to university and from the university to elementary and secondary education), dominated by the belief on a monotopic and pure epistemology supported by the text, be it sacred or secular.

Moraga departs from the fact that "the primary struggle for Native peoples across the globe is the struggle for land" (1983, 168). She adds: "Increasingly, the struggles of this planet are not for "nation-states," but for nations of people, bound together by spirit, land, language, history and blood. . . . Chicanos are also a nation of people, internally colonized, within the borders of the U.S. nation-state" (1993, 168–69).

In a global world, "land" becomes the metaphor for particular locations in space, for "places" that should be reconquered from the dispossessions enacted by colonial and national powers:

> Land remains the common ground for all radical action. But land is more than the rocks and trees, the animal, and plant life that make up the territory of Aztlan or Navajo Nation or Maya Mesoamerica. For immigrant and native alike, land is also the factories where we work, the water our children drink, and the housing project where we live. For women, lesbians, and gay men, land is that physical mass called our bodies. Throughout "las Americas," all these "lands" remain under occupation by an Anglo-centric, patriarchal, imperialist United States. (Moraga 1993, 173)

Caught between two colonial legacies, fearing equally the "Hispanization" and "Anglanization" of the Chicanos, loving equally English and Spanish as displaced and fractured colonial languages, with a certain nostalgia for the Spanish storytelling of her ancestors, Moraga's emphasis on "land" is indeed a retribalization and an effort of *concientisazao*, which moves away from both Spanish as the official language of Mexico and from English as the official language of the United States. Moraga reclaims Amerindian lega-

cies from today's United States, to today's Central America as she assumes
Ward Churchill's (1992) definition of "Indigenista" as someone who "takes
the rights of indigenous people as the highest priority," stating that "many
Chicanos would by this definition consider themselves Indigenists" (Moraga
1993, 165). Her statement is based on the fact that since the early 1970s
(and the date here is important in relation to the indigenous movement
in Latin America), "Chicanos have worked in coalition with other Native
American tribes and have participated in inter-tribal gatherings, political-
prisoner campaigns, land rights struggles, and religious ceremonies" (165).
Why this new tribalism? Is this new tribalism a search for the restitution of
authenticity that will disengage the possibility of decolonization (in Khatibi's sense)? Moraga suggests that " 'Tribe,' " based on the traditional models of Native Americans, is an alternative socioeconomic structure that holds
considerable appeal for those of us who recognize the weaknesses of the
isolated patriarchal capitalist family structure" (1993, 166).

   The risk of romanticizing tribalism is inscribed in the very structure of
hegemonic power and subaltern knowledge, and Moraga is aware of this.
"Original" tribal models have been corrupted by five hundred years of interaction with colonial and national institutions; there is no return to the "authentic," but there is a utopian effort to rescue Amerindian memories from
the dark rooms of national museums and to place them in a social space
where new communities could begin to be imagined. In Leslie Marmon
Silko's novel, tribalism is reinscribed (e.g., see part 6, "One World, Many
Tribes") in the dialectics between local territorial memories and global marketing. Current reservations and the problems therein are consequences of
a colonial model invented to disempower native peoples, causing high rates
of alcoholism, domestic violence, and so on. In Mesoamerica and the Andes,
Amerindian languages and knowledge have been kept aside as curious remains of glorious ancient civilizations. The defense of the tribal model is
necessary, then, as a conceptual tool, as a model of oppositional practices,
and as new forms of building imagined communities by restitution of what
colonialisms and nation-states have suppressed:

> In essence, however, the tribal model is a form of community-building that can
> accommodate socialism, feminism, and environmental protection. In an ideal
> world, tribal members are responsive and responsible to one another and the
> natural environment. Cooperation is rewarded over competition. Acts of vio-
> lence against women and children do not occur in secret and perpetrators are
> held accountable to the rest of the community. "Familia" is not dependent upon
> male-dominance and heterosexual coupling. Elders are respected and women's
> leadership is fostered, not feared. (Moraga 1993, 166–67)

Languages (Spanish/English) have been displaced and relocated in the
sphere of languaging. Languaging is the locus where "conscientization"

takes place, and this particular form of conscientization struggles with the tensions, on the one hand, between colonial and national dominating forms of consciousness and, on the other, between repressed and subjugated tribal forms of consciousness. Bilanguaging then becomes an act of love and a longing for surpassing the system of values as a form of domination.

Moraga ends her book with an urge toward love and transcendence, toward a new America "where the only 'discovery' to be made is the rediscovery of ourselves as members of the global community" (174). I understand her "ourselves" to be restricted both to the Chicano movement, or, at least, that aspect of the Chicano movement with which Moraga identifies, and to all oppressed communities in the world. That urge is articulated in the relocation of the law as language and text (colonial or national) into the law as languaging (perhaps the model for the educational system superseding the educational project): "We must submit to a higher 'natural' authority, as we invent new ways of making culture, making tribe, to survive and flourish as members of the world community in the next millennium" (1993, 174).

There is a danger here—to fall into the trap that links racial considerations in claiming identity with the remains of fascist ideology. To counter this danger there will be a tendency from leftist intellectuals to move toward class considerations and be linked with socialism and Marxism instead. Now, I would be attentive here to Venezuela's liberal thinker Carlos Rangel when he underlines following Hayek's argument (Hayek 1944) the fact that fascism and socialism are not necessarily opposites. Based on the experience of Stalinism and the Soviet Union, and also from a Third World perspective that was allien to Hayek, Rangel observes that

> Marxist-Leninist socialism and fascism are not essential contraries and antagonistic poles, as they themselves perhaps believed and insistently asserted (succeeding in persuading a whole generation), but rather enemy brothers. Fascism has the same statist ardor of Marxist socialism and is likewise antiliberal and therefore anticapitalist. Far from being the last shot of moribund bourgeois liberalism, it conceives itself as, and in fact is a political philosophy of the socialist family. ([1982] 1986, 6)

The point I am stressing here, and it is the point of the book, is that abstract universals (Christianity, liberal-fascism, or Marxist-socialism) taken at their extreme became authoritarian and repressive; and that, taken to their extreme, (neo)liberalism and (neo)Marxism (as civilizational projects) have the limits of abstract universals and "enemy brothers." I have been making this point also in Latin America, referring to (neo)Zapatism as the emergence of a border epistemology that announces diversity as universal projects instead of as a new abstract universal to provide an alternative to the previous ones (e.g., democracy or socialism). My point in this book, following Franz Hinkelammert (1996, 236–50), is that a new abstract universal won't do. Diversity as a universal project (or "diversality" in Glissant's [1998] formulation) is the future road, and the "diversality" requires a new epistemology, border epistemology. I have been looking for those traces in Moraga's book with no intention of promoting essential identities based on racial underpinnings.

COLONIAL DIFFERENCES; BILANGUAGING LOVE

My intention at this point is not to draw a picture or guess what an education system emerging from this process would look like. I'm concerned with *bringing* coloniality of power to the foreground and in *thinking from* the colonial difference. I am, however, in a position to say that bilanguaging and educational projects become necessary subjects of discussion for public policy, for conscientization in bilingual education, for contributing to building new communities, and for exploring new epistemological avenues in cultures of scholarship. Bilanguaging as a way of living in languages in a transnational world, as an educational and epistemological project, rests on the critique of reason, of disciplinary structures, and cultures of scholarship complicitous with national and imperial languages. Freire's distinction between *systematic education* (or Bourdieu's system of education) and *educational projects* is helpful here: *educational projects* (and, I will add, all kinds of intellectual projects including social movements) are continuous processes of resistance and, as Freire would say, of *concientisaçao*, parallel and in opposition to the *systematic* education of the colonial administration or of nation-state builders; these are systems in which violence is instilled by the agencies of economic, linguistic, and religious or cultural domination. Love is the necessary corrective to the violence of systems of control and oppression; bilanguaging love is the final utopic horizon for the liberation of human beings involved in structures of domination and subordination beyond their control.

While the nation-state promotes love toward national languages, bilanguaging love arises from and in the peripheries of national languages and in transnational experiences. Bilanguaging is a kind of love closer to the one envisioned by Freire for the pedagogy of the oppressed, than to the love of national languages promoted by nation-states:

> For the oppressors, however, it is always the oppressed . . . who are disaffected, who are "violent," "barbaric," "wicked," or "ferocious," when they react to the violence of the oppressors. Yet it is—paradoxical though it may seem—precisely in the response of the oppressed to the violence of the oppressors that a gesture of love may be found. Consciously or unconsciously, the act of rebellion by the oppressed . . . can initiate love. Whereas the violence of the oppressors prevents

the oppressed from being fully human, the response of the latter to this violence
is grounded in the desire to pursue the right to be human. (Freire [1972] 1993,
38)

Such is the kind of love I am trying to articulate with the notion of bilanguaging love: love for being between languages, love for the disarticulation of
the colonial language and for the subaltern ones, love for the impurity of
national languages, and love as the necessary corrective to the "generosity"
of hegemonic power that institutionalizes violence; this love is for all that
is disavowed by cultures of scholarship complicitous with colonial legacies
and national hegemonies. Finally, this love is a restitution of the secondary
qualities (e.g., passions, emotions, feelings) and of the impurity of language
that have been banned from education and epistemology since the very inception of early colonization and modern rationality. Beyond this general
longing toward emancipation, bilanguaging love is a move toward the decolonization of languages as first enacted by colonial expansion and then by
nation builders and their institutionalization of national languages. Perhaps
what I am trying to articulate here is Heidegger's concept of "care" as the
structural whole of existence, as the plentiful ways in which history is inscribed in one's body through birth, life, projects, inclinations—as one's
concern for other people as well as the awareness of one's proper being.
There is, however, a crucial difference between "bilanguaging love" and Heidegger's notion of "care": the inscriptions of signs in the body with which I
am concerned, the body in history and the body in which history has been
inscribed, are the inscriptions from colonial legacies and imperial structures
of domination and subordination. There is a discontinuity between "care"
and "bilanguaging love" (a classical tradition, Mignolo 1992b), an irretrievable break between Heidegger, on the one hand, and Anzaldúa, Khatibi,
Moraga, my own discourse, on the other—an irretrievable break that im-
pinges on the conception of nation and ethnicity within the legacies of the
classical tradition (e.g., Heidegger) as well as within the legacies of the colonial traditions and current imperial subordination (Anzaldúa, Moraga, Khatibi, Freire).[1]

CONCLUDING REMARKS

Richard Lee (1996) has drawn a useful scenario of the structures of knowledge in the twentieth century in two stages: 1945 to 1967–73 and from this
later date to 1990. The first period has been marked by 1945 and the atomic

---

[1] I am thankful to Homi Bhabha for pressing this issue and forcing me to state more clearly
my perception of the discontinuity between Heidegger's "care" and my own conception of
"(bi)languaging love."

bomb, which sealed the hegemony of the United States at the same time that it impinged on the articulation and the direction of knowledge production, both as a reorganization of the disciplines and as the creation of "area studies" attached to the Department of Defense. The consequences of this reorganization of the production, transformation, and transmission of knowledge intervened in the already established distinction between hermeneutics and epistemology, the humanities and the sciences, which had been established since the late nineteenth century, by Wilhelm Dilthey. This distinction was reconverted into the "two cultures" (Snow 1959) and materialized in the domain of literature and the humanities (philosophy, art history), on the one hand, and the natural sciences, on the other. However, the social sciences took a leading role in the period analyzed by Lee, and became closely related to "area studies." Although the community of social scientists was divided in its support and criticism of area studies, the fact is that the humanities were outcasts in this new distribution of knowledge. While "Occidentalism" encroached on the *studia humanitatis* (including men of letters and missionaries), and later "Orientalism" encroached on the humanities in the new secular order of knowledge, "area studies" became a province of the social sciences and the social sciences modeled on the legacies of nineteenth-century positivism. Lee describes different moments of reaction to that legacy (i.e., phenomenology, existentialism, avant garde art) in the period from 1945 to 1973 and elaborates in greater detail three critical aspects in the second period, 1973–90. These three aspects are:

1. The ambiguity of the idea of progress linked to the confidence in science, technology as warranty of progress, modernization and development.

2. The attack on classical sciences (e.g., Cartesian rationality and Newtonian physics) and the emergence of chaos theory and its influence in the social sciences and the humanities.

3. The collapse, as a consequence, of disciplinary boundaries and the emergence of cultural studies.

Now, a quick reflection on all these developments and transformations in the period analyzed by Lee indicates that all of them, without exception and including the arts, took place in the interior of the modern world system. As far as languages are concerned, they happened in the three major languages of the second and third phases of the system: English, French, and German. In this chapter, and in this book more generally, I attempted to bring to the foreground the internal epistemological conflicts (e.g., why, for instance, Spanish, Portuguese, and Italian are basically out of the picture) as well as the external epistemological conflicts (why Arabic, Aymara, or Chinese are not epistemically sustainable). Although I have focused on the Americas (e.g., Latin Americans and Amerindians, Afro-Caribbeans, and

Latinos in the United States), the discussion of Khatibi's "an other thinking" and his critique of sociology and "Orientalism" intended to open up a space of exploration beyond my competence. The process of decolonization in the period analyzed by Lee brings to the foreground the crucial question of suppressed memories and knowledges. Massive migrations introduce the question of plurilanguaging in a transnational world and the emergence of a postnational ideology and imaginary. The second period analyzed by Lee brought about the rise and demise of "area studies." And with it the sheer consciousness that the "Third World" not only produces culture to be studied, but knowledge that needs to be "sustained." Otherwise, the coloniality of power will be reproduced and the "crisis" of knowledge will be resolved within the same core that produced it. These are pointed instances of the complicity between the structure of knowledge and the modern world system. They reveal the quiet complicity between structure of knowledge, culture of scholarship, and the three major languages of the modern world system (as I have argued with the example of Bourdieu). However, we may be witnessing the moment in which the expansion of capitalism to East, South, and Southeast Asia will generate an imaginary beyond the modern world system as we conceived it until today.

Thus, the main argument of this chapter focused on current disarticulations of one of the major beliefs in the imaginary of the modern/colonial world system: the complicity between language, literature/culture, and nation. If such disarticulation is taking place for various historical reasons, including massive migrations from the former Third World to the industrialized North Atlantic countries, and technoglobalism, there have been—since the 1970s—a number of literary experiences and practices responding to such disarticulation. At the same time, and since the 1970s (as Hall has argued), one of the major cultural revolutions of our time has been the coming into being of communities claiming they write to participate in the making of planetary civilization.

Cultures of scholarship are in the process of being rethought and relocated. The colonial difference cannot be avoided, as Chakrabarty's dilemma clearly shows (see chapter 4). In this process we (scholars, social scientists or humanists) are being invited to look for models and genealogies beyond the colonial languages of the modern period (English, French, German as we have seen in Bourdieu's linguistic and epistemic genealogy) and their authoritative foundations (Greek and Latin), in "our" local insertions in the global system. In my case, such genealogies (à la Bourdieu) emerge from all those, in what Moraga calls the Américas (with an accent on the *e*), who feel that educational projects and epistemological foundations should not only be bilingual (which just scratches the surface of the problem) but also bilanguage (living and dying in the tensions of conflictive languaging, like Arguedas in Peru). Surmounting the epistemological colonial difference and solving Chakrabarty's dilemma may require, among other things, to relate research and teaching with specific projects having as their final destination the rearticulation of values beyond the colonial difference. If cultural critique is no longer or not always effective because the market value transforms culture into commodities (Horkheimer and Adorno [1944] 1995 120–67), one of the places of thinking in the humanities may very well be in the critique of values that keep on reproducing the coloniality of power—a paradoxical critique that has to assume its own status of commodity in its attempt to assure its political intervention from the colonial difference (e.g., from a subaltern position). Bilanguaging would then be the movable ground on which educational projects and the decolonization of scholarship can be located; where the complicity between colonial languages and scholarship could be rethought; where Babel may not be as bad as the ideologues of unification and the purity of blood, language, and thought it was.

In the next chapter I return to the particular issue I discussed here, from the larger perspective of globalization, coloniality, and the relocation of languages and knowledges.

Globalization, Mundialización: Civilizing Processes and the Relocation of Languages and Knowledges

THAT "civilization" is somewhat related to "globalization" and "modern/colonial world system" is obvious. How it is related it not obvious. I submit that the colonial difference is one of the missing links between civilization, globalization, and modern/colonial world system. The attention Wallerstein devoted to "civilization" (Wallerstein 1992) is indeed important although limited to the logic of the modern world system and oblivious of the colonial difference. In this chapter I attempt to remap the concept of civilization and to make the colonial difference visible in the crack between globalization and "mundialización" (Ortiz [1994] 1997; Glissant ([1990] 1997; 1998), and between civilization and culture (Béji 1997). "Globalization" and "civilization," the reader may remember, were introduced within the scope of global designs and local histories *in* which they are produced and from where they are enacted. "Mundialización" and "culture" instead, are the local histories *in* which global designs are enacted or where they have to be adapted, adopted, transformed, and rearticulated. Both local histories are mediated by the structure of power—more specifically, by the coloniality of power that articulates the colonial differences between local histories projecting and exporting global desgins and local histories importing and transforming them. The colonial difference brings the concept of civilization back to the modern/colonial world system where the notion was invented and where it serves as a powerful tool in rebuilding its imaginary.

To start with, while the term "globalization" suggests a process, "civilization" suggest an achievement. For that reason, Norbert Elias was forced to talk about "civilization process" to underline the becoming rather than the being of civilization/s. On the other hand, the idea of a "civilization process" was formulated as a field to be analyzed and as such was implicitly distinguished from "civilizing mission," which had a different pedigree: a goal and an objective of colonial expansion. "Globalization," instead and in a transnational lingo, is conceived as the last of three stages of global transformation since 1945: development and modernization after the end of World War II; the raising of the transnational corporation and the demise of the state after the world crisis of 1968 (Czechoslovakia, Mexico, France, the United States) and finally, the fall of the Berlin wall and the collapse of the Soviet Union. In a more sociohistorical vocabulary, "globalization" could be linked to U.S. sociologist Immanuel Wallerstein's modern world system (1974) and to its geoculture (1950; 1991a), and, of course, to German sociologist Norbert Elias' "civilization process" (1937); and finally, to a particular moment of the general process of civilization studied by Brazilian anthropologist Darcy Ribeiro (1968; [1969] 1978): the moment in which a new type of mercantilism based on slavery emerges, with the "discovery" of America, and it is attached to a Christian mission. Thus, in this book I am using globalization in two complementary ways: as a reference to the past half century and as a reference to the past five hundred years of the modern world system. In those five hundred years I conceive of four coexisting moments that, for obvious discursive and chronological reasons, I have to list one after the other: Christianity, Civilizing Mission, Development, and Global Market. Each moment corresponds to a particular global design and, certainly, originates different local histories responding to the same global designs.

In Spanish, Portuguese, and French a distinction is made between "globalizacion/globalizacao/globalizacion" and "mundialización/mundializaçao/mundialization." As I mentioned in the introduction to this book, the distinction was introduced, independently from each other, by Brazilian sociologist and cultural critic Renato Ortiz and by Martinican philosopher, essayist, and writer Edouard Glissant. The distinction is relevant at various levels. First, it reinscribes the divide between Latin and Anglo America I discussed in chapter 3. Second, it rearticulates the colonial difference in a new form of coloniality of power no longer located in one nation-state or a group of nation-states but as a transnational and transstate global coloniality. It makes sense, in this argument, to see neoliberalism as a new form of civilization and not just a new economic organization. "Globalization" becomes then an image of a a new civilizing design. Finally, his distinction between "mundialización" and "globalizacion" is nothing other than the new form in which coloniality of power is inscribed at the time of global coloniality and the colonial difference rearticulated. Local histories (mundialización) and global designs (globalización) situate the colonial differences at the intersections of both within the dense history and memories of the modern/colonial world system. But there is more. The parallels I established, in the introduction to this book, between "mundialización/globalización" in Ortiz's and Glissant's terminology and "culture/civilization" in Béji' words brings together the complicity between "civilization" and "globalization." The latter is the resemantization of the former in the transition from the hegemony of the British Empire to the U.S. leadership and the emergence of the transnational corporation. It makes sense from this perspective to say and insist that neoliberalism is not just an economic and financial question but a new civilizing design. Finally, the distinction between "mundialización" and "globalizacion" is nothing else than the new form in which coloniality of power is inscribed at the time of global coloniality and the colonial difference rearticulated.

The borders between globalization and "mundialización" and of civilization and culture, in Béji's (1997) conceptualization, provide an ample terrain to undo the map traced during the cold war by area studies. Huntington's (1996) description of the reorganization of the world order after the end of the cold war provides a useful tool to think of "civilizations" around new axes. However, the mixture of criteria leading nine different civilizations in the post-1990 world (fig. 9, pp. 36 supra) can be taken as a pedagogically useful gadget but not as a historically serious classification. Islamic, Hindu, and Buddhist civilizations seem to be recognized along religious boundaries; Latin American and African, along subcontinental lines since the Africa Huntington is speaking of is sub-Saharan Africa. North Africa does not belong to Africa, in this map, but to Islam. Japanese civilization is recognized by national formation criteria. Sinic is more complex since it involves historical, national, and political criteria. And finally Western is recognized by the cosmographic partition of the globe, mixed with the modern/colonial East/West distinction. But Western, furthermore, is recognized in its historical formation as the Christian world, but the Christian world limited to Europe. That is to say, Huntington provides a remaking of Europe as it was originally traced in the Christian T/O map when Europe was identified with Western Christianity and the land of Japhet.

The first drive toward globalization and the constitution of the modern/colonial world system was under the impetus of the *Orbis Universalis Christianus*, which was consolidated with the defeat of the Moors, the expulsion of the Jews, and the "discovery" of America. The second moment replaced the hegemony of the Christian mission with the civilizing mission, when a new type of mercantilism developed in Amsterdam and prepared the ground for the emergence of France and England as new imperial powers. If the civilizing mission was the secular version of the Christian one, the religious version didn't vanish but coexisted with the former, playing a secondary role. Since the end of the nineteenth century until World War II, the civilizing mission in its European version was remade in the United States in its rise to world power, and was rearticulated with the Manifest Destiny. After World War II it was development and modernization that took the lead and relegated the civilizing mission to a secondary place. And finally, efficiency and expanding markets took the lead and placed development and modernization as a necessary condition for the final goals of transnational capitalism. But, I repeat, Christian mission and civilizing mission are not ideas of the past, although they may not have the same force that they had in the sixteenth and the nineteenth centuries respectively. What I am arguing for here is the coexistence of successive global designs that are part of the imaginary of the modern/colonial world system. Changing global designs transforms the structure of the coloniality of power within the imperial conflict and the logic of the modern world system. Successive global designs rearticulated the system, reorganized the structure of power, redrew the interior borders, and traced new exterior ones. Asia and Africa, for instance, colonized by France and England at the end of the eighteenth and the beginning of the nineteenth centuries, established a new world order in relation to previous colonial relations between France and England in North America and the Caribbean. For that reason, Jamaica is not India and Martinique is not Algeria. Finally, new forms of nonterritorial colonialism emerged with the leadership of the United States, along with colonialism without a colonizing nation, or global coloniality (which we are witnessing at the end of the twentieth century).

"Civilization" as a term came forth late in the imaginary of the modern/colonial world system. In the sixteenth century the word didn't have the same meaning that it acquired in the late nineteenth century (Bull and Watson 1984; Gong 1984). The Christian mission was predicated on the conversion of the planet to Christianity, while the civilizing mission was entrenched with the secular concept of reason, with the rights of men and of citizens. Civilization understood as civilizing mission then has a double edge. Bull (1984) reports that intellectuals and government officers from China and Persia showed a great indignation for what they considered European arrogance in presenting to them the standards of civilization. But, in other parts of the world, such as Latin America, "civilization" was the major ideological goal of postindependence Argentina, and embraced later on all over Latin America. In 1845, Domingo Faustino Sarmiento published an authoritative book that canonized the great conflict of Latin American history: the conflict between civilization and barbarism. This formulation explains why independence in nineteenth century Latin America was not decolonization and why a project like the one defended by Sarmiento (who became president of the Argentinian Republic in 1872–78) could be better characterized as internal colonialism.

The situation was no less clear in Colombia. The civilizing mission in peripheral nation-building (or, if you do not like the metaphor, it can be restated: "nation-building processes in which their agents did not have much say in the imperial decisions that, in the nineteenth century, were distributing the world among themselves") was in tension with laissez-faire principles and at odds with the location of an emerging country such as Colombia in the international concert of nations (Rojas de Ferro 1995, 150–73). In nations that, if not peripheral, were also not at the heart of the industrial revolution, the civilizing mission had to cope with the international distribution of labor implemented by the very principles of the civilizing mission. That is to say, in order to civilize the world, it was necessary to accept first that the world needed to be civilized and that those who so proclaimed had the right model (e.g., the right global design) of civilization. Well, countries like Colombia in the nineteenth century were not among those countries represented in the fabric of civilizing models. On the contrary, Colombians in their own country were in charge of criticizing themselves in the name of a civilizing mission, which was a global design coming from a different local history. Florentino González, a leading figure in the liberal reforms, illustrates in his early discourses (1849) how internal colonialism worked in the name of expanding the civilizing mission:

> Granadins cannot compete in manufacturing with Europeans and Americans. . . . Europe, with an intelligent population, possessing steam technology, already skilful in the art of manufacturing, achieves the mission of transforming raw material within the industrial world. We must accomplish our mission, and we cannot have doubts about it, when we look at the prodigality of natural resources with which Providence has endowed our land. (Quoted by Rojas de Ferro, 1995, 62)

Rojas de Ferro's (1995) analysis for nineteenth-century Colombia complements Coronil's (1997) later observations on the international distribution of nature, in his study of Venezuela's political and economic configuration since 1930. Civilization goes together with technology and urbanization, and the areas of the world that need to be civilized were those which had their reaches in their land, and their land populated by "uncivilized" people. As Rojas de Ferro points out, the gap in technology mentioned in Florentino González's quotation is not enough to explain the lack of innovation in textile production in postindependence Colombia. That is, the phenomenon cannot be totally explained in terms of technology. Rather, Rojas de Ferro asserts, the answer should be sought in the "uncivilized" character "attributed to those engaged in textile and manual production: *mestizos*, Indians, blacks and women. Their identities were defined in terms of 'passionate' attributes which precluded a channelling of resources that would increase their productive capacities. They were perceived as 'barbarians' in need of civilization before they could be incorporated into the productive world. The international division of labour wherein Europe and North America specialized in manufacturing and Nueva Granada in agriculture furthered the belief in the 'uncivilized' local character of Neo-Granadins" (Rojas de Ferro 1995, 162). The colonial difference was working at its best in the very mind of progressive liberals in nineteenth-century Colombian nation building. The coloniality of power was making its way by shaping a new form of colonialism: internal colonialism in peripheral, postindependence countries during the nineteenth and the first half of the twentieth centuries.

But let's pause for a moment and go back to the sixteenth century to the encounter of an emerging new imaginary that reconverted and created a new frame to link languages, knowledge, and the limits of humanity.

LANGUAGES AND THE BOUNDARIES OF HUMANITY

A few decades before the advent of an unknown continent (from the perspective of European observers) and unknown people inhabiting it, geographical boundaries coincided with the boundaries of the humanity. Outlandish creatures with two heads, three arms, and the like were supposed to inhabit those regions beyond known geographical boundaries. The limits of geography coincided with the limits of humanity. In a matter of two or three decades, however, both boundaries (of the world and of humanity) began to be transformed radically. The outlandish creatures once inhabiting the unknown corners of the world were replaced by the savages (or cannibals) inhabiting the New World. The imaginary of the modern world system was on its way. Geographical boundaries and the boundaries of humanity in Christian cosmology were relocated by both the transformation of knowledge generated through cross-cultural interactions among people who until then had been unaware of one another, as well as by the growing awareness of the earth's expansion beyond the limits of the known. The cannibals and the savages were located in a space that began to be conceived as a New World.

Toward the end of the nineteenth century, however, spatial boundaries were transformed into chronological ones. In the early modern/colonial period (sixteenth century), a transformation took place between geographical and human boundaries; at the end of the nineteenth century, savages and cannibals in space were converted into primitives and exotic Orientals in time. While the sixteenth century was the scene of a heated debate about the boundaries of humanity—having Las Casas, Sepúlveda, and Vitoria as main characters in that controversy—toward the nineteenth century the question was no longer whether primitives or Orientals were human but, rather, how far removed from the present and civilized stage of humanity they were. Joseph François Lafitau (1681–1746) (*Moeurs des savages américains comparées aux moeurs des premiers temps*, 1724) has been credited as being one of the landmark thinkers in this process of converting the savages/cannibals into primitives/Orientals and in relocating them in a chronological scale as opposed to a geographical distance. The "denial of coevalness" (Fabian 1983; Mignolo 1995) was the end result of relocating people in a chronological hierarchy rather than in geographical places. The relocation of languages, peoples, and knowledges in time rather than in space, found its most systematic formulation in Hegel's *Philosophy of History* (1822), which remained uncontested until the past fifty years when intellectuals engaged with the movements of liberation and decolonization put pressure on its assumptions.

From Lafitau to Hegel the temporal paradigm was put in place, and a turning point took place in the imaginary of the modern/colonial world system, which Johannes Fabian (1983) aptly described by the expression "denial of coevalness." The denial of coevalness as a turning point in the modern/colonial world imaginary marks the difference between the spatial view of the early Christianizing mission of the Spanish Empire, and the early imperial moves by France and England in the Caribbean and in today's Canada. In the case of France, intellectuals and historians realized that France lost the opportunity to lead the way in the New World and now they had to follow the lead of the Spanish and Portuguese, not only in today's Canada but also in Florida, Louisiana, and Brazil (Lancelot Voisin, and Henri 1582). Regarding the Dutch and the English in the Caribbean, after a century or more of pillaging Spain, they began to settle in the Caribbean after 1620. Wallerstein (1980, 3–9) had noted a significant shift in the economy of the modern world system between the periods 1500–1650 and 1600–1750 (the date overlap is deliberate). He remarks, "the core of the European world-economy was by 1600 firmly located in the northwest Europe, that is, in Holland and Zeeland; in London, the Home Counties, and East Anglia; and in northern and western France" (1980, 37). However, the overall imaginary was still dominated by Christianity. The external borders of the system were not perceived as the space of the "primitives" but of the "pagans" and "infidels." "Civilization" was not yet a key word in locating people within and outside the system. "Civilization" entered together with the emergence of the secular state, with the change of intellectual spirit introduced by the Enlightenment. The passionate defense of "progress" and the compulsion to demote "tradition" were characteristic of this spirit. Although the debate between "les anciens et les modernes" preceded the Enlightenment, it was for the philosophical mind of the period that "modernity" and "tradition" became mutual enemies and that the French Revolution was converted into the paradigm of the imaginary of the *modern* world system. It was, in other words, the hegemonic self-description of the world system that made of the Enlightenment and the French Revolution the ultimate reference point of modernity. Wallerstein falls into the trap of "modernity's" self-description (or the autopoietic imaginary of the modern world system, to follow Maturana and Varela [1984] and Lhumann [1990, 1–20]) when, as I noted in a previous chapter, he states that the geoculture of the world system came into existence in the eighteenth century. I quote Wallerstein again: "In the case of the modern world-system, it seems to me that its geoculture emerged with the French Revolution and then began to lose its widespread acceptance with the world revolution of 1968" (1995, 163).

Wallerstein, halfway between the reproduction of the modern world system's self description, pretending to be its observer at the same time, buys into the myth of modernity and the tyranny of time in the imagination of world history from the interior of the modern world system (e.g., Hegel's universal history). Alain Tourain, instead, sees in the French Revolution the consolidation of the "West,"

> first European and then American, has maintained for centuries that modernization is nothing other than modernity at work, that its purpose has not been the effective mobilization of resources but the replacement of custom by reason. Modernization must be therefore endogenous, and the role of the state or of intellectuals should be limited to the removal of obstacles to the exercise of reason. (Tourain 1992, 128)

Space was dominant in the imaginary of the previous stage of colonial expansion (sixteenth and seventeenth centuries) driven by the exploration of the world and the making of world maps. Time, since the end of the eighteenth century, reordered universal history and became the "essence" of modernity: Heidegger was concerned with being and time, and not space; Proust was looking for *un temp perdu* and not, instead, for an unknown space. The linear time of universal history became, furthermore, entrenched with the very idea of the civilizing mission: to be civilized is to be modern, and to be modern means to be in the present. Thus, the denial of coevalness became one of the most powerful strategies for the coloniality of power in the subalternization of languages, knowgledes, and cultures.

If the first drive toward globalization in the constitution of the modern world system imaginary was the *Orbis Universalis Christianus*, the second and its legal heir was the *Standard of Civilization*, which linked secularization with a new global design. When Wallerstein affirms that in "the case of the modern world-system, it seems to me its geoculture emerged with the French Revolution" (1995, 1163), he is ignoring:

1. The potent reconversion, in the sixteenth century, of the *Orbis Universalis Christianus* into a new version of universal law that will accommodate the people of the New World into the Christian community, achieved by the international debates of the School of Salamanca.

2. The fact that from the sixteenth to the eighteenth century, Christianity remained the overarching imaginary of the modern/colonial world system (Christianity, the Occident, and Europe being one and the same thing).

3. The fact that secularization is indeed related to the French Revolution but it emerged independently of it and followed its paths parallel to it (Gong 1984).

Gong, in a study of the raising of the "standards" of civilization and the family of nations at the end of the nineteenth century, showed its connection with the emergence of an interstate system and its consequences, the need to put in place a code of international law. He went back to the eighteenth century to trace the movement from the Christian mission to the civilizing mission, showing, at the same time, how the latter presupposed and had been built on the former. In this schematic but useful history, Gong observes how the consolidation of the idea of Europe takes places as a replacement of the idea of Christendom, and consolidates not only as a geographic but as a political idea. The secular tendency of the Enlightenment "was reflected in the new types of cartography, as European explorers encountered and mapped the non-European world" (Gong 1984, 46). Gong describes several trends in the eighteenth and nineteenth centuries consolidating the idea of civilization and of the civilizing mission (including the Darwinian notion of survival and advancement of civilization, Compte's historical stages of knowledge, Gobineau's statement on the inequality of human races, etc.). But let me insist on one that is the most relevant for my argument: the secularization of European society. Gong observes:

> The trend toward secularization is clearly related, though in complex ways, to the distant origins of modern sciences, the beginnings of the idea of progress, the first historical criticisms of the Biblical records, the discovery of the true nature of other great religions and cultures of the world, in short, to many of the same influences which contributed to the emergence of the standard of "civilization." These influences called into question the Christian elements initially implicit in the identification of the international society with Christendom and contributed to a shift toward a standard based on the notion of a more general and abstract modern "civilization."
>
> *One element of the Christian tradition which the trend toward secularization not only maintained but intensified was the universality manifest in the biblical injunction to take the good news to every nation. Christianity's universalist aspirations were easily transformed into notions of a universal civilization which could progress by adhering to scientific principles. Progress toward civilization would come as the universal laws of physics, chemistry, and biology were applied, despite the myriad surface manifestations of the different cultures.*
>
> Thus the "civilizing" mission was born. It remained a moral crusade, with all the self-confidence and zeal that many thought the Christian reformers were losing in the face of a secular science challenge. (Gong 1984, 51; emphasis added)

The Christian mission did not go away in the eighteenth century; it was outcast, displaced, and reconverted into the secular civilizing mission. The formalization of the "standard of civilization" at the beginning of the twentieth century was indeed a crucial moment for two main reasons:

1. The acceptance of Japan (non-Christian, non-European) in the family of nations fulfilling the standard of civilization.

2. The acceptance of the United States (Christian but non-European) in the family of nations fulfilling the standard of civilization.

At the same time, new tensions emerged and old ones were intensified, involving non-European countries such as Russia, China, the Ottoman Empire, Persia, among others, tensions that lasted until World War II when a switch in power and the world order transformed the "standard of civilization" in a historical institution. The decolonization movement contributed to clarify that the standard of civilization were an aggressive political move from the European and colonizer country, backing a local ideal into the universal claims of early Christianity reconverted into local histories of sciences as the universal savior. Progress, then, was the ally of civilization to align the planet in a linear hierarchical organization, and it replaced the spatial and planetary salvation mission (not engrained in the idea of progress) of Christianity dominant at least until mid-eighteenth century, both in the Catholic and the Protestant world. The conceptualization of language and knowledge was dependent on the general ideology of the civilizing mission and the standard of civilization. The current stage of globalization has market power as its final goal. This goal can dispense with the values attributed to civilization, since the goal toward expanding the market doesn't contemplate the conversion of people to Christianity or to citizenship. Although the market's objectives cannot be detached from the ideology of development and modernization (Escobar 1995), they are spatial rather than temporal. The question is to expand the number of consumers all over the planet rather than to move toward a final destination set up by the standard of civilization created in a local history (Europe) and projected as a global design. Thus the market is creating the conditions for the restitution of space and for facilitating the intellectual task of denying the denial of coevalness (Fabian 1983), the secret and natural weapon of the civilizing mission and of the standard of civilization during the second phase of modernity/coloniality. "Civilization" is becoming, as Darcy Ribeiro resolutely claimed at the end of the 1960s, a planetary affair decided at the planetary scale rather than a global design from a particular local history: the history and the imaginary of the modern world system.

LINGUISTICS MAPS AND THE LOCATION OF KNOWLEDGE IN THE GLOBAL ORDER

Let's now examine how the links between languages and the boundaries of humanity shaped the idea of literature, cultures of scholarship, and civilization in European modernity. Modernity, the period of globalization that today is witnessing a radical transformation, is characterized and framed by a par-

ticular articulation of languages (English, French, German, Italian), literatures of these languages (with their legacy in Greek and Latin), and cultures
of scholarship mainly in English, French, and German. Italian remains the
foundation for Renaissance studies and maintains its clout for its close relation with Latin. Wallerstein has noted—as I already mentioned in previous
chapters—about cultures of scholarship that

> [a]t least 95 percent of all scholars and all scholarship from the period of 1850
> to 1914, and probably even to 1945, originates in five countries: France, Great
> Britain, the Germanies, the Italies, and the United States. There is a smattering
> elsewhere, but basically not only does the scholarship come out of these five
> countries, but most of the scholarship by most scholars is about their own coun-
> try. . . . This is partly pragmatic, partly social pressure, and partly ideological:
> *these are the important countries, this is what matters, this is what we should study
> in order to learn how the world operates.* (Wallerstein 1996, 3)

In other words, the languages and the scholarship of the countries came
from where the civilizing mission spread. Notice that Spain and Portugal are
no longer part of the languages and scholarship of the modern European
world.

Let's press this issue further by exploring once more the conversion of
the human differences in space into the human differences in time, and by
introducing two new players to the game: languages and literacies, on the
one hand, and the links between the boundaries of humanity, linguistic
maps, and the processes of civilization, on the other. The complicities between languages and the boundaries of humanity have been clear since the
beginning of Western expansion in the early modern period (Mignolo
1992c). If we dig into the archives, we can find similar examples in which
languages were taken as one of the foundations upon which to enact identity
politics; language served to define the boundaries of a community by distin-
guishing it from other communities. The connivance between certain languages, alphabetic writing, and the boundaries of humanity was not new in
the Renaissance/early modern period (Curtius 1929; Mignolo 1992c). What
was new was the planetary proportion and the long duration in which such
complicities began to be articulated.

The linguistic map shown in figure 11 gives you a better idea of the correlation between geographical locations and theoretical production. First, you
can see the correlation between geocultural and geolinguistic location of
modernity (white on the map) and the geocultural domains where European
modernity was not relevant or was received (willingly or not) as a foreign
element to be incorporated or resisted from the perspective of vernacular
languages and cultures. Second, you can see (horizontal lines) that the ma-
jority of the planet (with the exception of European countries) comprises
geohistorical cultural areas with more than ten languages each. Although

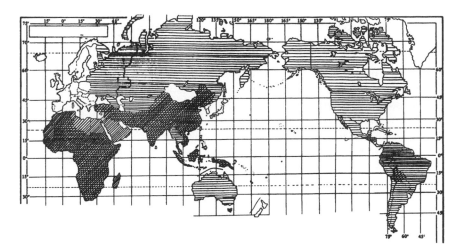

Figure 11. This lingustic map of the world has been drawn from the perspective introduced by Mateo Ricci, an Italian Jesuit in China, in the sixteeth century (see Mignolo
1995a, chap. 5). The Pacific is at the center of the map and the Americas are on the
left. An intriguing reversal and complication of the modern/colonial world imaginary
that divided the planet between West and East (Occidentalism and Orientalism); and
between North and South. Curiously enough, Europe is the only area of the planet
with less than ten languages! (From Florian Coulmas, ed. 1985. *Linguistic Minorities
and Literacy: Language Policy Issues in Developing Countries*. Berlin: Mouton Publishers. Used by permission of Mouton De Gruyter.)

this situation is in the process of being corrected, the fact remains that if
European countries were not counted as countries with more than ten languages, it was because imperial and national languages were the only ones
to count as such; the rest were counted as dialects. The discourse of the
civilizing mission was double-sided: one of nation building, the other for
colonial expansion. The map also shows (diagonal lines) that in most areas
of the world (with the exception of European countries), more than 40 percent of the population is illiterate. All sorts of conclusions can be drawn
from this statistic. One of them could entail, for instance, celebration of the
low illiteracy rate in European countries and the linking of this achievement
with the natural intellectual development of the people living in that particular area of the planet, where the agents and the agency of the civilizing
mission were located. On the other hand, one could link lower linguistic
diversity and lower illiteracy rates in Europe to the process of colonial and
global expansion since 1500. This date could also be used to locate the
process in which intellectuals living in the part of the planet that began to
be self-constructed as Europe, and as a territory where human civilization
attained its highest mark, put a heavy premium on the "letter" as a distinc-

tive sign of the concept of "civilization" that Renaissance and Enlightenment intellectuals forged for themselves: Guizot, for instance, apparently believed and explicitly stated that "civilization" was a pure European phenomena ([1828–1830] 1868).

Turning now to the complementary statistics in figure 12, we can see that there are about one hundred languages accounting for 95 percent of the world population. Of these one hundred, 75 percent of the world population speaks twelve. Of those twelve, six are colonial and, therefore, the languages of European modernity. Their ranking by quantity of speakers is the following: English, Spanish, German, Portuguese, French, Italian. Chinese is the most spoken language on the planet, above English. Although English enjoys the power of being accompanied and supported by the geohistorical location of capitalism during the period of the British Empire and, in the past half-century, in the United States. Spanish, although displaced as a relevant language of modernity (dominated by French, German, and English), has more speakers than French and German. Russian, the second displaced language from the European modernity, managed, nevertheless, to have a marginal presence through literature and has more speakers than German. Hindi is between Russian and German. Finally, Japanese, Arabic, and Bengali are languages whose number of speakers exceeds that of Portuguese, French, and Italian. But that is not all. Globalization and the enactment of the civilizing mission through the agency of colonial languages made it possible for these languages to be spoken far beyond their place of "origin." Thus, the delinking between languages and territories, the double-sided politic of languages (one for the nation, one for the colonies), and, finally, the increasing massive migrations made possible by the very industrial revolution and the means of transportation, reveal the splendors and miseries of the colonial languages: on the one hand, the story of their planetary scope; on the other, the story of their impossible control by their respective academies of national languages. In the meantime, the three languages of high modernity (English, German, French) remain the hegemonic languages of scholarship and world literature (Bourdieu 1991, 37–65; Mannheim 1990, 1–112). Certainly, well-established languages such as Chinese, Japanese, Arabic, or Hebrew were not suppressed by modern colonial languages, as was the case of less established ones like Quechua, Aymara, or Nahuatl, which suffered the impact of Latin and Spanish, supported by the infrastructure of what Darcy Ribeiro called "mercantile empires with a salvation mission" to distinguish Spanish (as well as Portuguese and Russian) empire(s) from "colonial-capitalistic mercantilism" (Holland and England, seventeenth century) and from the "industrial imperialism" enacted by England in the nineteenth century and the United States in the second half of the twentieth century.

Let's now turn toward Huntington's comment on language and civilization in this global era (see tables 1 and 2). Huntington's main argument is

Languages and World Population

Chinese
English
Spanish } 45 %
Russian
Hindi   } 60 %
German
Japanese
Arabic
Bengali
Portuguese
French
Italian

25 languages account for 75 % of the world's population.
± 100 languages account for 95 % of the world's population.

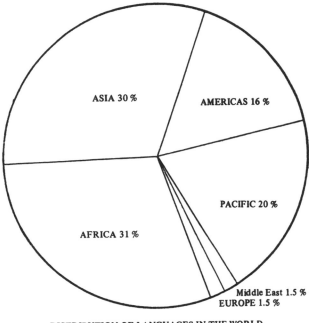

DISTRIBUTION OF LANGUAGES IN THE WORLD
BY CONTINENT (slightly adapted from Grimes 1978)

Figure 12. In relation to figure 10, Europe accounts for 1.5 of the languages of the world. However, cultures of scholarship in the modern/colonial world have been dominated by European languages (see also chapter 6). (From Florian Coulmas, ed. 1985. *Linguistic Minorities and Literacy: Language Policy Issues in Developing Countries*. Berlin: Mouton Publishers. Used by permission of Mouton De Gruyter.)

SPEAKERS OF MAJOR LANGUAGES
(Percentages of World Population*)

Year Language	1958	1970	1980	1992
Arabic	2.7	2.9	3.3	3.5
Bengali	2.7	2.9	3.2	3.2
English	9.8	9.1	8.7	7.6
Hindi	5.2	5.3	5.3	6.4
Mandarin	15.6	16.6	15.8	15.2
Russian	5.5	5.6	6.0	4.9
Spanish	5.0	5.2	5.5	6.1

* Total number of people speaking languages spoken by 1 million or more people

Source: Percentages calculated from data compiled by Professor Sidney S. Culbert, Department of Psychology, University of Washington, Seattle, on the number of people speaking languages spoken by 1 million people or more and reported annually in the *World Almanac and Book of Facts*. His estimates include both "mother-tongue" and "nonmother tongue" speakers and are derived from national censuses, sample surveys of the population, surveys of radio and television broadcasts; population growth data, secondary studies, and other sources.

Table 1. Two of the seven most spoken languages are the languages of the first and last colonial empires of the modern/colonial world system. The remaining five remind us of the colonial difference in language and knoweldge. (From Samuel P. Huntington. 1996. *The Class of Civilizations and the Remaking of the World Order*. Used by permission of Simon and Schuster.)

to disprove that English is (becoming) a universal language, the language of a unified civilization. He is right to say that when a Korean businessman and a Chinese banker speak in English they are not carrying in that conversation the weight of English/American civilization. Furthermore, there are far more speakers of Mandarin than English speakers. As a matter of fact, the totality of speakers of languages spoken in China is almost equal to the totality of speakers of colonial languages (see table 2). If we add to this the number of speakers of Hindi, Russian, Bengali, and Arabic, the number of speakers of noncolonial languages largely outweighs the number of speakers of colonial languages.

But the question is not so much the number of speakers as it is the hegemonic power of colonial languages in the domain of knowledge, intellectual production, and cultures of scholarship. In the domain of literature, for instance, one can write in English and still add to it the density of Spanish/Latin American memories, as Latino/as are doing in this country. English in postpartition India doesn't carry the same memory as national English in Britain; in the same way that English spoken in England by Third World immigrants doesn't carry the same cultural and ideological weight as the King's English. In other words, what the current stage of globalization is enacting is (unconsciously) the uncoupling of the "natural" link between

SPEAKERS OF PRINCIPAL CHINESE
AND WESTERN LANGUAGES

	1958		1992	
Language	No. of Speakers (in millions)	Percentage of World	No. of Speakers (in millions)	Percentage of World
Mandarin	444	15.6	907	15.2
Cantonese	43	1.5	65	1.1
Wu	39	1.4	64	1.1
Min	36	1.3	50	0.8
Hakka	19	0.7	33	0.6
Chinese Languages	581	20.5	1119	18.8
English	278	9.8	456	7.6
Spanish	142	5.0	362	6.1
Portuguese	74	2.6	177	3.0
German	120	4.2	119	2.0
French	70	2.5	123	2.1
Western Languages	684	24.1	1237	20.8
World Total	2845	44.5	5979	39.4

Source: Percentages calculated from language data compiled by Professor Sidney S. Culbert, Department of Psychology, University of Washington, Seattle, and reported in the *World Almanac and Book of Facts* for 1959 and 1993.

Table 2. The amount of speakers of Chinese languages equals, practically, the amount of speakers of Western (modern/colonial world system) languages. Hegemonic cultures of scholarship and, therefore, an image of civilization linked to knowledge, science and epistemology, have been articulated in the Western languages. (*The Clash of Civilizations and the Remaking of the World Order.* Used by permission of Simon and Schuster.)

languages and nations, languages and national memories, languages and national literature. Thus, it is creating the condition for and enacting the relocation of languages and the fracture of cultures. Indeed, the very concept of culture (and civilization in Huntington's perspective) is difficult to sustain as homogenous spaces for people of common interests, goals, memories, languages, and beliefs. It is true, as Huntington underlines, that after decolonization "native" languages are gaining ground as they are linked either to state politics or to social movements and in literature. Cultures of scholarship are also being relocated. Thus, if English is becoming the universal language of scholarship, English is not carrying with it the conceptual weight and value of Western scholarship. My contention is that something similar to what happens in literature is happening in cultures of scholarship: a border gnoseology is emerging at the intersection of Western epistemology and non-Western knowledge, characterized as "wisdom" by the former.

TABLE 3
Speakers of World Languages (in millions)

Language	Native Speakers	Total Speakers
Mandarin	853	999
English	330*	487
Hindi	348	457
Spanish	346	401
Russian	168	280
Arabic	195	230
Bengali	197	204
Portuguese	173	186
German	98	124
French	74	126

* Notice also that the number of "native speakers" of English is lower than the number of "native speakers" of Hindi. However, English surpasses Hindi in the "total number of speakers."

Source: World Almanac and Book of Facts (1997).

Let's, look finally, at the previous statistics from a different angle focussing on the number of "native speakers" and on those who learned a language through a process of "second/third language" acquisition. This difference is important not only for any particular language, but for the discussion on "English only" as well. The difference may be difficult to quantify but it is not less visible. Examples include learning a "foreign" language in the school or other institution in the "native" country; learning a "foreign" language as an immigrant in the country in which a "foreign" language is being learned; a combination of both as it is accomplished in "study abroad programs." The difference is important not so much because of the national values embedded today in a given language, but because of the fact that the language is the body and the sensibility (as I discussed in the previous chapter on the notion of "languaging"), national or otherwise. It is of course possible to think of alternative scenarios, transnational in nature, where from the beginning "native speakers" will no longer be exposed to a "mother tongue" but to a diversity of languaging without any umbilical cord attached to the mother or the mother country. But still in that scenario and for the near future, the question of language and the colonial difference will still be in place. Some languages will be hegemonic, others will be subaltern; still other hegemonic languages in a given context or local history will be at the same time subaltern in relation to global designs and their implementation.

Table 3 provides statistics on world languages. Proportionally, the difference between "native" and the total number of speakers is larger for English than for Mandarin. The 150 million "foreign" speakers of English is almost half of the number of "native" speakers. For Mandarin, instead, the 166 million difference between "native" and "foreign" is about a fifth of the former. Another interesting statistic involves Russian. The spread between "native" and "foreign" is larger here than in English; however, there are fewer total Russian speakers and the Russian language does not enjoy the hegemonic position that English does. The third interesting observation that can be made on this chart is that three of the modern/colonial languages (Portuguese, German, and French) are significantly smaller in number of speakers than the other seven languages in the chart, only two of them (English and Spanish) being modern/colonial languages. These statistics are complementary to the diagram in figure 12, in which European languages cover 1.5 percent of the total languages and speakers of the world, which is statistically similar to the 1.5 percent attributed to the Middle East. Thus, the colonial difference is clearly exposed in these statistics and the coloniality of power is openly revealed in the epistemological connection between particular languages and the structure of knowledge. Language rights are not just another item claiming the erasure of the colonial difference. Language rights disclose the epistemological colonial difference and the overarching structure of knowledge created and reproduced in the very creation and reproduction of the modern/colonial world system. Here the ratio between language and civilization is not related to the number of "speakers" but to the number of "readers." The question is not just how many speakers of a given language there are, but what is the rate of literacy in a given language and what is the ratio between languages in a given country and the language of the media. What are the languages of publication and distribution of knowledge?

GLOBAL LANGUAGE RIGHTS AND THE RELOCATION OF KNOWLEDGES

In June 1996 a World Conference on Language Rights took place in Barcelona, Spain, and more than one hundred nongovernmental organizations attended. One of the main goals of the conference was to approve a universal declaration of language rights, intended to be a complimentary resolution to the declaration of human rights. The final goal was to have this declaration approved by UNESCO (UNESCO 1998). The conference was presided by Rigoberta Manchú, the well-known Maya-Quiché intellectual and activist from Guatemala. This event, I submit, was the consequence of a radical transformation of those colonial beliefs that linked languages with the boundaries of the humanity from the early stages of modernity and globalization (Heath 1972; Skutnabb-Kangas and Phillipson 1995). Toward the 1970s the power of national states began to be eroded by the configuration of transnational economic alliances (the years of the Organization of Petroleum Exporting Countries, of Japan entering the world market, the consolidation of the transnational corporations). The weakening of the state was counter-balanced by the strengthening of communities that had been repressed precisely during the years of nation building and state consolidation. Asia and Africa were the locations of decolonization movements. Latin Americans experienced a revival of indigenous movements for their rights, their lands, their languages. Rigoberta Menchú emerged from these processes, as did the social movements in the Chiapas. What all this amounts to, among other important consequences, is the clear and forceful articulation of a politics and philosophy of language that supplants the (al)location to which minor languages had been attributed by the philosophy of language underlying the civilizing mission and the politics of language enacted by the state both within the nation and in the colonies (Bonfil Batalla 1982; Van Cott 1994).

But let me take a step back here and follow up the question of the standard of civilization as described by Gong. What happened to the standard of civilization after World War II? Indeed, the very idea was questioned before that moment within Europe itself and from countries with longer memories and achievements, like China or Persia. Indeed, Oswald Spengler ([1926–28], 1950) was already an alert to the enthusiastic view of European civilization which World War I indirectly questioned. World War II brought another perspective into consideration, and when countries from Asia and Africa who experienced European colonialism criticized international law linked to the standard of civilization and to the family of nations. "What was initially feared," Gong observed following R. P. Anand (1966), "as Afro-Asian rejection of international law *in toto* turned out to be a rejection of those aspects of it tainted by the colonial past" (Gong 1984, 90). The standards of civilization and the civilizing mission began again to be reconverted, this time under a new leader of the world order. No longer England and France, no longer the ideals of the French Revolution collapsing in the two successive wars of the modern world system, but the United States and a displacement of Eurocentrism toward the more encompassing Western civilization ideals. And they were reconverted in two directions.

The first change established "human rights" as new international standards (of which the United States became the champion, as witnessed today with the 1998 visit of President Clinton to China) and the United Nations as an international forum to avoid international discrimination instead of control of arrival to the standard of civilization. However, and once again, the "Universal Declaration of Human Rights" was pronounced by the protagonist of a local history projecting global designs. One could wonder whether China's resistance to it is due to a difference in perspective or because China had no say in what was called a "Universal Declaration." In other words, it may very well be the case that the tradition of the Christian mission and civilizing mission produced the right standards for the "Declaration of Human Rights" with universal values based on a local history. Or it may very well be that that is not the case, and any "universal" declaration cannot be other than a consensual agreement based on different standards and legacies of civilization (Islam, China, indigenous communities around the world, etc.). Certainly, it could be difficult and "dangerous" from a managerial perspective of democracy. It may very well be, in other words, that the old Western standards of civilization are alive, although unspoken, under the "Universal Declaration of Human Rights."

The second candidate to a successor of the standard of civilization, according to Gong (1984, 92), is the "standard of modernity," which manifests itself under different masks. The vindication of the universalism of science was a successful imaginary construction, pretending that science was not bound to cosmology, and hid the possibility of seeing "science" as a new form of it. As the vindication of quality of life related to health and using practical science as a source of improvements, and as a vindication of urban cultures as the standard of the cosmopolitanism, the norms and values of the global village reach a universal or global cultural standards.

With this transitional history in mind, I would like to go back to the question of the relocation of languages and knowledge in the current stage of globalization. The emergence of new local actors with an international agenda is obvious today. These new social actors are, at once, contesting the idea that global designs can only emerge from one particular local history and resetting the rules of the game. The inequality in power, however, is still evident. Indigenous movements in Latin America are a case in point.

In Latin America, the increasing influence and internationalization of indigenous organizations had a remarkable impact on the politics of language and education. The rise of what began to be called "new ethnicity" (Hall 1991a; 1991b) did not emerge all at once, of course. Behind this development there was a long tradition of rebellions, resistances, and adaptations controlled either by colonial or national powers (or both), and omitted in the teaching of national histories, cultures, and national literary practices (Heath 1972). Spanish, a subaltern language in the European modernity, became the official and hegemonic language in areas with a dense Amerindian population like the Andes (Bolivia, Peru, Ecuador) and Mesoamerica (Mexico, Guatemala). From the point of view of the Amerindian population, languages were critical in maintaining a sense of continuity from colonial times through the nation-building period, and up to the end of the twentieth century. The changes witnessed in the 1970s, the emergence of a new Amerindian consciousness, were propelled by Amerindians who had been employed by the state, either as community development workers or as schoolteachers. They were looking not only for a new Amerindian identity but also for the chance to put pressure on those in positions of power and in government in order to influence the future of Amerindian polity. On the other hand, technological globalization contributed to the process, since indigenous activists and their international supporters could be linked through the web of transnational information networks. One of the paradoxes of globalization is that it allows subaltern communities within the nation-state to create transnational alliances beyond the state to fight for their own social and human rights (Skutnabb-Kangas and Phillipson 1995). The right to have and use languages located in a subaltern position by the discourse of the civilizing mission and the public policy of the state, are part of the restitutions claimed under language and human rights. That is, the links between languages and the boundary of the humanities are entering into a process of disintegration whose consequences we may not yet foresee. Parallel to social movements and the premium placed on the language issue was the emergence of intellectuals of Amerindian descent for whom their "mother tongue" was naturally an Amerindian language (Aymara, Quechua, Maya, Nahuatl). The emergence of a new community of intellectuals in the cultural landscape of Latin America fits Gramsci's description of the "organic intellectual," although not necessarily in complicity with the state: "Every social group, coming into existence on the original terrain of an essential function in the world of economic production, creates together with itself, organically, one or more strata of intellectuals which give it homogeneity and an awareness of its own function not only in the economic but also in the social and political fields" (Gramsci [1944] 1992). For historical reasons, related to the history of colonialism itself, intellectuals of Amerindian descent in Latin America do not have the influence in the public spheres that Afro-American or Latin intellectuals have in the United States. One area where they have been active and influential is education and in contesting the state ideology regarding language and memories[1] (Hobsbawm 1990). More than a restitution of an authentic past, the intellectual articulation of history and education shall be understood in the process of nation building and colonial and imperial world order. To make a long story short, at the end of the nineteenth century, when the institutionalization of national languages was at its height (Gong 1984; Robertson 1992) and the cannibals of the early colonial period were converted into the primitives of the era of colonial expansion, and the standard of civilization was also stipulated among the major European powers, the civilizing mission and the concept of "civility" became a regulative principle in interstate, imperial, and neocolonial discourses in the Americas.

A case in point is the notion of "frontier" at the end of the nineteenth century in the United States as well as in Argentina: the "frontier" was the movable (westward) landmark of the march of the civilizing mission, the

---

[1] Intellectuals of indigenous descent have been active, mainly in Bolivia, Ecuador, and Guatemala, both as scholars and political leaders. Victor Hugo-Cárdenas, the former vice-president of Bolivia, is a case in point. Joanne Rappaport (1990) studied the life and deeds of several intellectuals of indigenous descent. Historian Roberto Choque is one distinguished figure currently in Bolivia, together with Humberto Mamani, Esteban Ticona, and others (1992). In the Islamic world, a similar concern is being explored by scholars and intellectuals of Islamic/ Muslim descent. See Ahmed and Sardar (1990, 194–212).

line dividing civilization from barbarism. The "frontier," however, was not only geographic but epistemologic as well: the location of the primitive and the barbarian was the "vacant land," from the point of view of economy, and the "empty space" of thinking, theory, and intellectual production. As Barrán (1990) persuasively states it: "The subjugation of the 'barbarian' sensibility was simplified by the fact that it [the barbarian sensibility] was ill-adapted to theorize itself, since theory was precisely its negation. That absence of self-theoretical reflection did not make possible the formation of a 'barbarian' counterculture, consciously programmed. Theory and pre-elaborated plans were, instead, the essence of 'civilization' and their agents were the intellectuals of the new society." Thus, the organic intellectuals of the Amerindian social movements (as well as Latino, Afro-American, and women) are precisely the primary agents of the moment in which "barbarism" appropriates the theoretical practices and elaborated projects, engulfing and superseding the discourse of the civilizing mission and its theoretical foundations. The "frontier of civilization" in the late nineteenth century has become the "borderland" of the end of the twentieth century. "Borderlands" (Anzaldúa 1987), contrary to "frontiers," are no longer the lines where civilization and barbarism meet and divide, but the location where a new consciousness, a border gnosis, emerges from the repression subjected by the civilizing mission.

The conceptualization of knowledge in terms of "frontiers" obeys the same logic as the spatial frontier where civilization was supposed to end and barbarism begins: a space to be conquered. In fact, Lynn White Jr. published an influential book in 1956 titled *Frontiers of Knowledge in the Study of Man* under such presuppositions. The frontiers of knowledge are the limits to which different disciplines have arrived at the moment the book was written, and the book was written under the presupposition that knowledge was limited to the disciplines. The book was organized accordingly: genetics, psychology, cultural anthropology, archaeology, history, sociology, geography, economy, history of science, philosophy, and so on. The book concluded by indicating the common changes in different disciplinary fields. A common ground was a change in the concept of personhood and, therefore, the object of study was being redefined in terms of people, of patterns of cultures, of action and interaction between people, and no longer the study of man. It is worthwhile to remember White's conclusions on the changing frontiers of knowledge at the very inception of the (epistemological) cold war. White's first conclusion is the changes in the Occidental canon of knowledge. The assumption that "civilization" is naturally Western civilization and that history is a linear succession of events that begins somewhere in Troy and arrives to North America, in the modern times, is no longer sustainable. In that pattern, man was Euro-American man and the rest were "natives." The "Western canon" observes White, has been replaced by a "universal (or global) canon." In it, Peru and Mexico (and by this he means

from ancient Inca and Aztec civilizations to today), Islam, ancient and contemporary India and China, among others, are no longer a window case of
curiosities but events in the planetary making of civilization.

And yet . . . things have changed in the order of the known, not in the
production of knowledge. The world has expanded, civilization is no longer
Western but planetary, but the disciplinary organization and norms remain
within the parameter of Western knowledge, as I have been discussing in
chapter 1 (cf. the case of African or Latin American "philosophy"). But how
can a change in the "Western canon of knowledge" be conceived? How can
we think beyond the disciplines, to promote a "transdisciplinary" thinking
that will cut across the niche of the disciplines include in White's book? *Open
the Social Sciences*, the Report of the Gulbenkian Foundation I mentioned
several times in this book, mentions "cultural studies" as a challenge and as
a possibility to transcend disciplinary boundaries. The discussion of "tradition," "consensus," and "democracy" in African philosophy (Wiredu 1997;
Eze 1997c), Kusch's restitution of an indigenous category of thoughts to intervene in philosophical and epistemological debates of the 1960s and 1970s
(in chapter 3), Rivera Cusicanqui's discussion of "liberal" and "ayllu democracy" in Bolivia (Rivera-Cusicanqui 1990), or the Zapatistas's theoretical revolution (Mignolo 1997d) are cases in which the "frontiers" of knowledge are
no longer located on the known but in the production of knowledge itself.

But let me offer a more concrete example of what I have in mind. You
may remember the narrative of the water pump and the attitude of the
Aymara county man that Kusch offered in one of his books and that I commented upon on chapter 3. The implications of Kusch's narrative are several:
the subalternization of indigenous knowledge by the knowledge constructed
around technology; the conflict of knowledge between the philosopher-an-
thropologist and the Aymara peasant; and, finally, the question of develop-
mental philosophy (Escobar 1995), in the 1960s. The emblematic situation
described by Kusch at the end of the 1960s are still being seriously considered in projects and discussion on sustainable development and alternatives
to development instead of alternative developments. The Proyecto Andino
de Tecnologías Campesinas (PRATECT) is a case in point. Rengifo Vásquez
(1991; 1998a; 1998b) has made a strong case for decolonization of knowledge in the area of rural development. His reflections (for which incidentally
Kusch offers theoretical support) parallel those pursued in different areas
and in different countries. Ramachandra Guha (1996) has explored the consequences of subalternization of peasant knowledge in India, during the
nineteenth century, as a consequence of the introduction of British irrigation
technology and then reproduced in the United States at the beginning of the
twentieth century. Gustavo Esteva (1996) has pursued the same concerns
through the life story of four Mexican peasants very similar to the situation
described by Kusch. The bottom line in all these analyses and narratives is

the conflict between "indigenous" and "modern" knowledge. The conflict, in other words, is in the very fact of thinking that there is an "indigenous" knowledge opposed to "modern" forms of knowledges, in this case, actualized by technology—when, indeed, the opposition is set up in and by the epistemological descriptions of what technology can do for you, descriptions that are cast in the frame of modernization and development.

But let me pause here to clarify my reference to a controversial example such as PRATEC. PRATEC promoted the most insidious criticism from well-respected Peruvian anthropologists and intellectuals to the most enthusiastic endorsement from non-Peruvian, U.S.-based anthropologists (Apffel-Marglin 1998, 1–30). It is not my intention here to mediate between both positions but, rather, to underline what in my view the contribution of the PRATEC is, despite the cogent criticism advanced by de Gregory and the excessive enthusiasm manifested by Appfel-Marglin. I like to think of PRATEC in parallel with the "Culture of Transience" project initiated by P. K. Garg and I. J. Parikh in India (Garg and Parikh 1995, 172–211). Global designs, be they Christian, (neo)liberal, or (neo)Marxist, were conceived and enacted from a particular local history generally identified as "the West" and, in this book, as the making and remaking of the modern/colonial world system. One can also talk about several local histories—for instance, Spanish colonialism in the Americas was not the same as British colonialism in India or U.S. colonialism in Puerto Rico. However, there are some common threads linking the Spanish, British, and U.S. approaches to life, society, and the world. At the same time, there was in the sixteenth-century Andes or in eighteenth-century India a different local history with a different ethos. It would be also possible to look at the differences between Aymara and Quechua, or between Hindi and Bengali speakers and world view. But it would be also possible to find a similar ethos linking the concept of life, society, and world among Aymara and Quechua or among Hindi and Bengali, as well as between Spanish and English speakers. Now, the Spanish and English speakers have been in contact with Aymara and Quechua speakers, on the one hand, and with Hindi and Bengali, on the other. But Aymara and Quechua speakers had never been in contact with Hindi and Bengali people. Furthermore, the contact between Spanish and Aymara/Quechua speakers, on the one hand, and English and Bengali/Hindi, on the other, were contacts defined by the coloniality of power and by the colonial difference. And it is the colonial difference that defines the external borders of the modern/colonial world system.

A "culture of transience" is one necessary corrective to globalization from the point of view of "mundialización" to globalization. The choices are not many. Once it is recognized that cultural homogeneity under Western global designs is as counterproductive as fundamentalist resistance justified in local history, a culture of transience is necessary. But it would also be counterproductive to move into a transience where the coloniality of power is maintained and the transition is only governed by global designs. It makes more sense to think that the culture of transience will be governed by local histories, the desubalternization of local knowledge, and an epistemological decolonization as a radical critique of the "beneficial for all" assumptions governing global designs, from a right- or left-wing perspective. It is at this intersection that the PRATEC project cannot be dismissed. What cannot be dismissed is, to start with, the restitution of Amerindian philosophy of life and conceptualization of society—neither with the intention of achieving an archaeological reconstruction of the "original" or the "authentic," nor with the academic and philological intention of producing knowledge to enlarge the museum but, rather, as an epistemic and political intervention in the colonial difference. Without this kind of possibility that can be practiced around the world and in/on the external borders of the modern/colonial world system, the only alternative left is a constant rereading of the great thinkers of the West in search of new ways to imagine the future. The increasing interest in Spinoza, in the past five years, is one example that can be explained by the need to look for new paths of knowledge and being unable to think from the colonial difference, from those knowledges and forms of knowing not attached to the name of a person but to the human epistemic energy and the political force of the colonial difference. PRATEC, with all its limitations, opens up the possibility of thinking from the ruins of Amerindian culture and of inscribing border thinking at the heart of the colonial epistemic difference. As Kusch did (Mignolo 1995b).

Arturo Escobar (1997) offers a way out that is akin with my own conception of border thinking. First, Escobar (1995) insists on looking for alternatives *to* development instead of alternative developments. Second, he lays out three different regimes of "knowledges" about or for the production of nature: organic, capitalist, and technonature:

> Broadly speaking, organic nature represents those modes that are not strictly modern; from the perspective of the anthropology of local knowledge, they may be characterized in terms of the relative indissociability of the biophysical, human, and spiritual worlds, vernacular social relations, nonmodern circuits of knowledge, and forms of meanings—uses of nature that do not spell the sytematic destruction of nature. Capitalized nature, on the contrary, is based on the separation of the human and natural worlds, and capitalist and patriarchal social relations. From the perspective of historical materialism, it appears as produced through the mediation of labor. Technonature, finally, is nature produced by new forms of technosciences, particularly those based on molecular technologies. As argued in poststructuralist and feminist studies of science and technology, it appears as produced more by technoscientific intervention than by labor-based

production of value. But meanings, labor, and technoscience are important to
all three regimes. (Escobar 1997, 221)

These three regimes of knowledges set the stage for what Escobar calls "cultural politics" and defines as "the process enacted when social actors shaped
by or embodying different cultural meanings and practices come into conflict with each other. The notion of cultural politics assumes that cultural
meanings and practices—particularly those theorized as marginal, oppositional, minority, residual, emergent, alternative, dissident, and the like, all
of them conceived in relation to a given dominant cultural order—can be
the source of processes that must be accepted as political" (Escobar 1997,
203). Cultural politics thus defined presupposes a different epistemology,
forms of knowledge that will articulate the three regimes: organic, capitalist,
and technonature. These regimes are not arranged in chronological order in
such a way that the newcomer displaced the previous one. These were precisely the strategies of knowledge of nature associated with capitalism, displacing to the realm of the magic or primitive the form of knowledge that
Escobar calls "organic" and that was relegated to the colonized areas and to
the Third World. But the new epistemology needed to articulate organic
knowledge with techononature as a political move toward the celebration
of life, countering capitalist mode of production as a drive toward death,
may not come from a "postmodern" way of thinking but, rather, from those
in the external borders of the modern/colonial world system. It is the coloniality of power that seems to be at stake in the "cultural politics" claimed by
Escobar, both understood as decolonization as a form of deconstruction and
in the form of border epistemologies that will transcend at once disciplinary
norms and regimes and bridge the gap between organic and techononature
forms of knowledge. In other words, they will transcend the opposition
between organic as primitive and capitalist and technonature as "civilized"
forms of knowledge and will, also, bring in fruitful dialogue, social movements and academic intellectuals in the domain of cultural politics.

　　Border thinking is not a counterculture, but the denial of the denial of
"barbarism"; not a Hegelian synthesis, but the absorption of the "civilizing"
principles into the "civilization of barbarism": a "phagocytosis" of civilization by the barbarian (as Argentinian philosopher Rodolfo Kusch will have
it), rather than the barbarian bending and entering civilization. It is also an
act of "anthropofagia," as Brazilian writer Mario de Andrade and Brazilian
poet and literary critic Haroldo de Campos word it. What we are facing here
are no longer spaces in between or hybridity, in the convivial images of
contact zones, but the forces of "barbarian" theorizing and rationality, to
which this chapter would like to contribute, integrating and superseding
the restrictive logic behind the idea of "civilization" by giving rise to what
the civilizing mission suppressed: the self-appropriation of all the good quali-

ties that were denied to the barbarians. "Border thinking" in all its complexity (geohistorical, sexual, racial, national, diasporic and exile, etc.) is a way of thinking that emerges as a response to the conditions of everyday life created by economic globalization and the new faces of the colonial difference.

HEGEMONIC LANGUAGES AND THE LOCATION OF KNOWLEDGES

At this point I would like to return to Wallerstein's (1996) observation about cultures of scholarship between 1850 and 1945, to the distribution of the scientific labor at the moment of high modernity and capitalist global expansion, and to pursue its transformation after 1945, when the center of cultures of scholarship began to be relocated in the United States. Let's remember also that the first is the period dominated by the civilizing mission and the standards of civilization, and the second by human rights and modernization. But before looking at the transformation of scholarly labor after 1945, let's briefly bring Elias into the picture to establish the links between the two periods just mentioned. According to his neo-Marxist model, there is a moment in the evolution of the human species in which the "warrior" and the "man of wisdom" emerged as particular social roles (Elias 1987; Mennell 1990, 359–72; Robertson 1992, 211–28, Kilminster 1998, 257–83). This moment is also, according to Elias, when the community became organized and survived on food surplus instead of on production and preservation. If we now make a quantum leap and link the simple version of the model to the danger of nuclear war (Elias's later concern) and to cultures of scholarship, we are forced to face once again the complicity between the "civilizing mission" articulated in colonial discourse and the "civilizing process(es)" articulated as an object of study of the human sciences in collusion with the ideology of the "civilizing mission"—that is, a configuration of knowledge whose power consisted in denying epistemological possibilities to the barbarians. Cultures of scholarship were precisely what people outside Europe either lacked (like the Aztecs or the Incas), or if they happened to possess them (like China, India, or the Islamic world), they became an object of study (e.g., the rise of "Orientalism"). Over the five hundred years of Western expansion and the creation of colleges and universities in colonized areas since the beginning of the sixteenth century, this belief became so strong as to make people doubt their own wisdom, when that wisdom was not articulated in Western educational institutions and languages. When comparative studies of civilization became a prestigious discipline within European research institutions, a distinction was made between civilizations that were converted into objects of study and civilizations that had the necessary frame of mind and cultures of scholarship to be the place from where to study other civilizations. Cultures of scholarship after World War II were recast under these legacies, although they adapted to the new needs of the third stage of globalization.

At the inception of what I have called the third stage of globalization (since 1945), decolonization went hand in hand with the cold war and the division of the world into three ranked areas (First, Second, and Third Worlds). Such a geohistorical division also implied a division of scientific and scholarly labor, as I have already noticed. Once countries were located as being (a) technologically advanced and free of ideological constraints; (b) technologically advanced but encumbered by an ideological elite, preventing utilitarian thinking; and (c) traditionally, economically, and technologically underdeveloped, with a traditional mentality obscuring the possibility of utilitarian and scientific thinking, the loci of scientific and scholarly enunciation were also established. The map of scholarly production between 1850 and 1945 traced by Wallerstein had scholarship located in Europe and the rest of the world was either the scene of interesting human achievements to study and understand, but frozen in time and antimodern, or of cultures where the civilizing mission had precisely the mission to civilize. The first was the province of civilizational studies (e.g., Orientalism), the second the province of anthropology. The dominant colonial cultures of scholarship were in France, England, and Germany. After 1945 the previous landscape was redressed slightly.

Once the new world order was accepted, the distribution of scientific labor was reorganized accordingly. "Culture," and no longer "civilization," was the term used to locate a huge area of the planet within the premodern, that is, the Third World. We are getting here, from a different angle, to a crucial point of this book, which I have been making throughout: the genealogy from comparative ethnology in the sixteenth century (Pagden); Orientalism in the eighteenth and nineteenth centuries (Said); anthropology in the nineteenth and twentieth centuries; to the social sciences and area studies after 1950. Border gnosis emerges as a displacement of this genealogy and as an effort toward the restitution of *location* as a geopolitical and epistemological configuration of knowledge production. To understand what I am driving at, think of the exportation of the social sciences to the Third World, to which the Gulbenkian Report (Wallerstein et al. 1996) looks critically. And think again about "Chakrabarty's dilemma." What is at stake in these cases is the limits of the social sciences, and cultures of scholarship, to fulfill the needs of local histories at the receiving end of global designs, be they economic or intellectual, from the right to the left. "Chakrabarty's dilemma" makes clear that cultures of scholarship cannot be "exported" and "adapted" to a new situation without taking into account the colonial difference and the subalternization of knowledge. What cultures of scholarship export is mainly a "method," since the problems they deal with are problems related to their own place of origin. What border thinking from the colonial difference shall contribute would be to place the "problem" engrained in the colonial difference (the local problem) before the "method." Starting from the problem instead of starting from the method, assuming the colonial difference as conceptual geneology instead of the geneology of the social sciences (or culture of scholarship in general), would release knowledge from the norms of the disciplines. But, above all, it will make visible that knowledge production from the colonial difference will have to deal with the "silences" of history and the "difference" of coloniality, that is to say the colonial difference. Border thinking then emerges, historically, at the end of the cold war as a critic of the scientific distribution of the planet. And it emerges, logically and conceptually, from the perception of knowledges and languages placed in a subaltern position in the exercise of the coloniality of power.

The humanities were not alien to such a distribution of labor, although they did not occupy a central place in it. To take just one example: the study of languages and literatures was cast within the same epistemological frame. The languages of literature were mainly the colonial languages of the modern period with their distinguished legacies: Greek and Latin. Literary studies remained within that tradition. Literature in the modern period was increasingly cast as "national literature" and, of course, written in a national language. Literary studies (in their historicophilogical foundation before 1945) as well as in their structuralist and poststructuralist formulations of the 1970s, focused on the literature of the five countries of scholarship mentioned by Wallerstein. "Other literatures" were considered part and parcel of civilization rather than literary studies. I am sure we all noticed that Spain was not among the five countries of modern scholarship. And, of course, Spanish did not count as a language of scholarship. This imperial rift of the modern period put Spain and Spanish in an ambiguous place between "Eastern civilizations" and "modern Europe." When it comes to Latin America, the location of Spain between the Arabic world of North Africa and the European world of western Europe becomes further complicated because of the relations during the modern period between Spanish and Amerindian languages, and by the fact that Andean and Mesoamerican civilizations were not part of European civilizational studies in the nineteenth century (Coe 1992). "Civilizations" were in the East. Latin America became, by the nineteenth century, an extension and surrogate of Europe. Latin America was, then, of particular interest to understanding the question of languages, literatures, and literary studies in the changing distribution of scientific labor and cultural practices since 1850. Spanish language, in Latin America, was twice subaltern: it was no longer the Spanish of Spain, which itself became marginal to European modernity beginning in the seventeenth century. On the other hand, Amerindian languages in their complex and rich relations between the oral and the written (Boone and Mignolo 1994) were not part of reflections on languages and literatures, but of pre-Columbian Studies (a particular version of civilizational studies framed within the history and legacies of Spanish colonialism), of folklore and ethnohistory, or, more recently, of colonial cultural studies (Mignolo 1992a; 1992c; 1992d). In summary: languages and literary studies were maintained within the epistemological framework of cultural practice and scholarship of North Atlantic modernity and the cultural configuration shaped by the idea of civilization and the civilizing mission, together with the process of economic globalization.

The position I have been articulating throughout this book (as well as in my previous one; see Mignolo 1995a) almost naturally moves toward a conceptualization of the world order close to the one painted by Samuel P. Huntington (1996): "The most important groupings of states are no longer the three blocs of the cold war but rather the world's seven or eight major civilizations" (Huntington, 1996: 21). We can, of course, dispute Huntington's categorization and listing of the so-called "seven or eight" civilizations (Western, Latin America, African, Islamic, Sinic, Hindu, Orthodox, Buddhist, Japanese) and even more so their territorial locations, but this is not the point I would like to pursue here. What I am more interested in is the following:

> Non-Western societies, particularly in East Asia, are developing their economic wealth and creating the basis for enhanced military power and political influence. As their power and self-confidence increase, non-Western societies increasingly assert their own cultural values and reject those "imposed" on them by the West. The "international system of the twenty-first century," Henry Kissinger has noted, ". . . will contain at least six major powers—the United States, Europe, China, Japan, Russia and probably India—as well as a multiplicity of medium-sized and smaller countries." (Huntington 1996, 28)

If, following Huntington, Kissinger's six major powers belong to five different civilizations, and there are important Islamic states whose strategic locations, large populations, and/or oil resources make them influential in world affairs, and, furthermore, in this new world order local politics is becoming the politics of ethnicity and global politics is the politics of civilization, what would be the rearticulation of the social sciences and the humanities? Would the social sciences, art, and literature maintain the same focus and central position they occupied in the modern/colonial world system (western Europe, Russia, and the United States), or will they be decentralized in the same way capitalism is being decentered? What would be the relationship and the complicities between cultures of scholarship and "artistic" production within the six major powers rearticulating the three-world order of the cold war period? Would social scientists and art and literary theorists maintain their disincorporated belief in the disincorporated and universal status of scientific and scholarly knowledge in such a way that, say, the social sciences and art in India in the twenty-first century will maintain and import the Western classical tradition in art and cultures of scholarship? Shall we believe in the report of the Gulbenkian Foundation that the universality of the social sciences, although tempered by the interdisciplinary contribution of cultural studies, will be at the same time incorporated in the distinctiveness in each of the "seven or eight civilizations" Huntington is talking about, or they will maintain a universal configuration beyond each "civilization"?

BORDER THINKING AGAIN

I have suggested that the economic conditions created by globalization contributed to the rise of "barbarian theorizing" (e.g., border gnosis, double consciousness) not as an opposition to "civilian [in their double meaning of civilization and citizenship] theorizing" but as a displacement and departure. The comparison between Norbert Elias's and Darcy Ribeiro's study of civilization processes could be helpful in this regard. There are three aspects of the comparison I would like to highlight. First, while Elias conceives the civilization process as a particular European phenomena of the past five hundred years, Ribeiro conceives it as a long, diverse, and complex set of processes of the human species. Second, while Elias focuses on the civilizing process, which is at the same time the consolidation of (western) Europe as a world hegemonic power, Ribeiro looks at Europe as a recent outcome of human civilizing processes that were preceded by previous hegemonic power and will also be transformed and dissolved in a future governed by what Ribeiro calls "the thermonuclear revolution and future societies." Third, while both Elias and Ribeiro are still prisoners of the temporal arrangement of human histories implanted in modernity, Ribeiro's concern with colonization and European expansion allows him to open the doors for a spatial conceptualization of civilization processes and of local histories arranged around successive and surviving centers of world hegemony. Fourth, and finally, the fact that Ribeiro's geocultural focus and concerns are the Americas and not Europe (as in the case of Elias's) makes it impossible for him not to analyze the process of European civilization as a process of subalternization of world cultures: "Nothing in the world," Ribeiro states, "was left out by the forces liberated by the European expansion. In it we detect the foundation of the reorganization of nature, whose flora and fauna were normalized all over the planet. It [European colonial expansion] is the main agency for the disappearance of thousands of ethnic communities, for racial mixtures and for the linguistic and cultural extension of European people. In the process of this expansion, modern technologies as well as forms of social organization and bodies of cultural values relevant in and for Europe were disseminated and generalized. The outcome of this process is the modern world, unified by commerce and communication, activated by the same technology, inspired by a basic and common system of values" (Ribeiro and Gómes 1996, 41–52). This, in a nutshell, is Ribeiro's view of what Elias called "civilizing process."

Now, what is relevant in this comparison to understand "barbarian theorizing" as border gnosis and as epistemology emerging from the conditions created by the last and perhaps more radical stage of globalization is the possibility (for someone like Ribeiro) of theorizing from the border (border as threshold and liminality, as two sides connected by a bridge, as a geographical and epistemological location): that is, of having both the formation in "civilized theorizing" and the experience of someone who lives and experiences, including the training in "civilized theorizing," in communities that have been precisely subalternized and placed in the margins by the very concept and expansion of European civilization. Thus, an *anthropologador*: someone who was trained as an anthropologist while at the same time was part of the "other." The common knowledge that Ribeiro is a "Third World theoretician," implied by Meggers (1991) in her introduction to the first edition of *O processo civiliçatório*, was clearly stated by Sonntag in his preface to the German edition: "The sheer fact of there being a theory *from/of* the Third World *for* the Third World makes the censured ones those who continue to believe that the belly of the world is someplace in between Vienna, Berlin, Bonn, Moscow, Washington or Rome. The fact that Ribeiro doesn't attribute to the First World a relevant role in the formation of 'future societies'. . . implies clearly a challenge which has to be confronted by critical theory of the developed world [e.g., 'civilian theorizing'], immediately and seriously, if it doesn't want to run the risk of disappearing" ([1969] 1978, 216). The only change I would make to this paragraph is that Ribeiro's theory of the "civilizing process" is certainly a theory *from/of* the Third World, *but not only for the Third World*. Sonntag, with plenty of goodwill, maintains the regional scope of Third World theorizing for the Third World, as a kind of "barbarian" counterculture to which still First World theorizing has to react and accommodate itself. Third World theorizing is also *for* the First World in the sense that critical theory is subsumed and incorporated in a new geocultural and epistemological location.

CONCLUDING REMARKS

In summary, it is my contention that globalization is creating the conditions for the spatialization of the civilizational processes and, by so doing, denying the denial of coevalness as one of the main epistemological strategies of colonial/imperial expansion. This process is creating the conditions for "barbarian theorizing": theorizing from/of the Third World (the expression used metaphorically here) for the (First/Third) entire planet. This chapter identifies some of the instances (social movements and language rights, emergence of new sites of thinking in between disciplines and in between languages, e.g., the self-restitution of barbarism as a theoretical locus, and a progressive force offering valuable correctives to the abuses of post-Enlightenment reason, science, and disciplinarity), in which the denial of the denial of coevalness materializes itself by redressing and implementing long-lasting forces, sensibilities, and rationalities repressed by the one-sided ideology of the "civilizing mission/process," and its complicity in the subalternization of knowledges and cultural production throughout the planet. Remapping new world order implies remapping cultures of scholarship and the scholarly loci of enunciation from where the world has been mapped. The crisis of "area studies" is the crisis of old borders, be they nation borders or civilization borders. It is also the crisis of the distinction between hegemonic (discipline-based knowledges) and subaltern (area-based knowledges), as if discipline-based knowledges are geographically disincorporated. Border thinking allows us to remap cultures of scholarship in terms of "area-based disciplinary knowledge," bringing together and erasing the borders between knowing *about* and knowing *from*. Border gnosis will help in imagining a world without rigid frontiers (national or civilizational) or a world in which *civilizations* will have to defend *their unity and their purity*; that knowledge, in the last analysis, did not begin with the Greeks but simply with life.

In the last analysis, border thinking is located at the intersection of local histories enacting global designs and local histories dealing with them. That is why border thinking can only be so from a subaltern perspective, since the enactment of global designs is driven by the desire for homogeneity and the implicit need of hegemony. Marxism provided an alternative to the hegemonic force and ideology of liberalism. But it was also a global design—oppositional and alternative, but global design nonetheless. Border thinking points toward a different kind of hegemony, a multiple one, as in a New medievalism (Tanaka 1997) in which a world of multiple centers would be dominated by none. In other words, diversity as a universal project allows us to imagine alternatives to universalism. The "West and the rest" in Huntington's phrase provides the model to overcome, as the "rest" becomes the sites where border thinking emerges in its diversity, where "mundialización" creates new local histories remaking and readapting Western global designs (Christian, liberal, and neoliberal development, modernization and market, Marxist-Socialists ascendance of the working class) and transforming local (European) histories from where such designs emerged. Globalization/ "mundialización" is reenacting old local histories and projecting them toward a future in which border thinking will be prominent in creating what

Glissant (1998) calls "La diversalité de la mondialization" interacting with the "homogeneity of globalization."

The fall of communism and the crisis of Marxism may be a way of understanding the "end of history" not in the sense that Francis Fukuyama (1992) understands it but as the "end" of the modern/colonial world system as reconverted in the nineteenth century. The fall of communism does not imply the victory of (neo)liberalism but the symptom of the crisis of the philosophical and epistemological principles that subtended both, liberalism and Marxism, as two sides of the same coin. In this sense, the crisis is the crisis of the modern/colonial modern world system and not of one of its aspects. Leonard Woolf could say in 1928 that between 1800 and 1900 "Europe passed through a revolution that was both internal and external" and that "this tremendous change in the internal constitution of Europe and in the fabric of its civilization was accompanied . . . by an equally important change in relation of Europe to the rest of the world" (Woolf 1928, 7–8). Samir Amin, at the end of the twentieth century, would say instead that "Never more than today has humanity shared the feeling that the Earth is one and indivisible and that all peoples of the planet belong to a sole system, notwithstanding the extremely divergent positions they occupy within it: an integrated natural system, as illustrated by ecological interdependence; an integrated economic system to the extent that the Eastern bloc countries have abandoned their tradition of relative autarky; even an integrated cultural system following the extraordinary intensification of communications which has resulted in the most advanced forms of Western technology being transferred to the most remote village of the planet" (Amin 1996, 10; 1995a; 1995b; González Casanova 1996, 10). "Interdependence" may be the word that summarizes the break away from the idea of *totality* and brings about the idea of *networks* whose articulation will require epistemological principles I called in this book "border thinking" and "border gnosis," as a rearticulation of the colonial difference: "diversality as a universal project," which means that people and communities have the right to be different precisely because "we" are all equals.

An Other Tongue, An Other Thinking,
An Other Logic

I

In chapter 2 I attempted to delineate the notion of post-Occidental reason and to locate it at the borders of modernity/coloniality. The argument kept in its horizon the internal borders of the modern/colonial world system, the historical density of its making (Arrighi 1994), and the diversity of the borders, becoming more complex due to the historical diversity at the intersection of the local histories of imperial powers and those local histories upon which the coloniality of power, in its constant reconversion, was exercised. Nation building, both in the nineteenth century in the Americas (see chapter 3) and in the twentieth century in Africa (Mandani 1996) and Asia (Chaterjee 1993) was a reconversion of the coloniality of power from its exercise in the colonial state to its new form under the nation-state. It is precisely that reconversion that could be properly described as "internal colonialism." Internal colonialism is the coloniality of power imbedded in nation-state building after decolonization.

The argument in chapters 5 and 6 looked at the colonial difference in language, literature, and epistemology. Starting from chapter 2, chapter 6 took the argument a step further. That is, while in chapter 2 a distinction was made between the postmodern and the postcolonial-Occidental, in chapter 6 an effort was made to imagine possible scenarios for an epistemology that is no longer trapped and forced to "begin" from its modern articulation, with its back to the colonial difference. One could naturally link Benedict Spinoza to the colonization of the Americas, tracing through him the transformation of the ethicoreligious imaginary from José de Acosta at the end of the sixteenth century (MacCormack 1991, 434–55). It was natural that Spinoza would be more aware of religious colonialism and a critic of modern imagination and that he could be taken as a paradigmatic case of radical critic to modern epistemology and politics (Balibar 1985). But, still, thinking from the colonial difference implies thinking from an other place, imagining an other language, arguing from an other logic. The canonical thinkers of the Western canon can no longer provide a starting point for the epistemology that the colonial difference requires.

Let me add a new scenario. In chapter 2 I distinguished postmodern from post-Occidental thinking as a critique of modernity from the interior borders (postmodernism) and from the exterior borders of the modern/colonial world (post-Occidentalism). This observation could be extended to deconstruction (which I explore in chapter 1) and to world system analysis, which is implied in several of my arguments but is never directly addressed. World system analysis is indeed a critique of Eurocentrism (Wallerstein 1997), but a Eurocentric critique of Eurocentrism, like postmodern theories and deconstruction are. In his presidential address to the Fourteenth World Congress of Sociology, Wallerstein identified six challenges to the social sciences, with four of them more directed in particular to sociology (Wallerstein 1998a). Two of the challenges are relevant to my argument. One comes from the external borders of the world/colonial system (Abdel-Malek 1981) and could be added to the many instances on which I build my argument. I would like to devote a paragraph here to the challenge of feminist theory. Evelyn Fox Keller, trained as a mathematical biophysicist, Donna J. Haraway, trained as a hominid biologist, and Vandana Shiva (Shiva 1994; Shiva and Mies, 1993), trained in theoretical physics are Wallerstein's examples (1998a, 38). There is a remarkable difference between the epistemological critique one encounters in Fox Keller and Donna Haraway, on the one hand, and on Vandana Shiva, on the other. As Wallerstein himself observes, "Vandana Shiva's critique is focused less on scientific methods proper than on the political implications that are drawn from science's position in the cultural hierarchy. She speaks as a woman of the South, and thus her critique rejoins that of Abdel-Malek" (1998a, 42). That is, Abdel-Malek and Vandana Shiva are critiquing epistemology, in the social and natural sciences, from the colonial epistemic difference and the experience of subaltern knowledges. Let me complement Wallerstein's examples, which he doesn't push to the limits, with one of my own: Paula Moya's criticism of postmodern feminist perspective (and, more specifically, of Donna Haraway's appropriation of Chicana's discourse) from a Chicana perspective:

> Within the field of U.S. literary and cultural studies, the institutionalization of a discourse of postmodernism has spawned an approach to difference that ironically erases the distinctiveness and relationality of difference itself. Typically, postmodernist theorists either *internalize* difference so that the individual is herself seen as "fragmented" and "contradictory" . . . or they attempt to "subvert" difference by showing that "difference" is merely a discursive illusion. . . . In either case, postmodernists reinscribe, albeit unintentionally, a kind of universalizing sameness (we are all marginal now!) that their celebration of "difference" had tried so hard to avoid. (Moya 1997, 126)

Moya complements her own observation with one from Linda Alcoff (Alcoff 1995), where she observes that "the rising influence of postmodernism has had a noticeable debilitating effect on the project of empowering women as knowledge producers, producing a flurry of critical attacks on unproblematized accounts of experience and on identity politics." And Moya adds to this observation that "such critical attacks have served, in conventional theoretical wisdom, to delegitimize *all* accounts of experience and to undermine *all* forms of identity politics—unproblematized or not" (Moya 1997, 127). I am aligning these examples with those of Vandana Shiva and Abdel-Malek as far as they are generated from the colonial difference. Postmodern criticism of modernity as well as world system analysis is generated from the interior borders of the system—that is, they provide a Eurocentric critique of Eurocentrism. The colonial epistemic difference is located some place else, not in the interiority of modernity defined by its imperial conflicts and self-critiqued from a postmodern perspective. On the contrary, the epistemic colonial difference emerges in the *exteriority* of the modern/colonial world, and in that particular form of exteriority that comprises the Chicano/as and Latino/as in United States a consequence of the national conflicts between Mexico and the United States, in 1848 and of the imperial conflicts between the United States and Spain in 1898. However, what is important to underline here is that the feminist challenges to modern epistemology are as follows: while postmodern feminists show the limits of "masculine epistemology" (Harding 1998), women of color and Third World feminism (Mohanty, Russo, and Torres 1991; Mohanty and Alexander 1997) show the limits also of "white epistemology," of which postmodern feminism critics remain prisoner (Harding 1998; Haraway 1997), as Moya's critique of Haraway suggests (Moya 1997). In Wallerstein's perception, the two challenges to the social sciences I mention here fall short in understanding the colonial difference. He perceives the gender critique to epistemology, not its racial component. In the case of Abdel-Malek, Wallerstein perceives a different notion of time beyond the limits of the world system, but he fails to see that Abdel-Malek's elaboration of the differences in the conceptualization of time is, indeed, ingrained in the colonial epistemic difference. *It is the colonial epistemic difference that calls for border thinking.*

II

"As a European, I am especially proud of two breakthroughs for which Europe is responsible, and which seem to be of decisive importance for the future: the formulation of the project of modern science in the seventeenth century, and the promulgation of the ideal of democracy. Europeans live at the intersection of at least two different systems of values—scientific rationality on one side, and collective behavior rationality on the other. This polarity imposed by historical evolution could not but lead to some stress which was to be felt in much European thought. It is of great importance, particularly at present, that we reach a better harmony between the different rationalities involved in sciences, democracy and civilization." So suggests Ilya Prigogine (1986).

If I were European, I would also be proud of *Radio Tarifa*, a musical ensemble from southern Spain whose great impact and creativity reside in the style in which the musicians articulate Spanish with Arabic music memories and stretch themselves from the fourteenth century to today, across the Mediterranean and across the Atlantic. They provide a powerful music whose power emanates from the quality of the musicians, of course, but also and perhaps mainly from the remapping of the colonial difference and transcending it through border thinking. This kind of cultural production is no less relevant for the future of planetary democratic diversity that will no longer rely on the values and credos of the local concept of "democracy" launched in eighteenth-century Europe. The "good" thinking on just social organizations coming from all social knowledges, past and present, South and North, East and West, are as important as the legacies of the European Enlightenment. The same can be said about science. The future of planetary knowledge requires transcending the colonial difference, the pride in the belief in the privilege of some geohistorical locations without looking at the historical conditions making them possible. Transcending the epistemological colonial difference, having in border thinking one way to pursue it, is of the essence once we understand that the splendors of Western sciences go together with its miseries. There is something beyond the dialectics of the Enlightenment that Walter Benjamin thought us to be proud of and that the other members of the Frankfurt School (Adorno, Horkheimmer) had difficulty in understanding. That "something" is a dimension of knowledge beyond the logic of science and the dialectic of the Enlightenment. In the case of Benjamin (but also of Adorno and Horkheimmer), it was the experience of the imperial (internal) difference as it was lived and endured by Jewish communities in the rearticulation of racial-religious differences in the sixteenth century, at the inception of Occidenalism as the imaginary of the modern/colonial world.

The link between knowledge and geohistorical locations was one of the main concerns of this book. As someone who grew up and was educated in Latin America, who had no choice but to internalize the fact that the Americas are a by-product of the modern/colonial world, I recognize, of course, the contribution of science. However, I cannot be proud of it in the same way that Prigogine is because I am not European. And that is another version of Chakrabarty's dilemma. Science, Prigogine is telling me, is not a human achievement but a European one. I suspect, however, that the question is not the distinction in the intelligence of European men who invented science, but the favorable conditions under which they did so. Such conditions were, in large measure, due to the emergence of the Americas in the colonial horizon of modernity, the forced labor of slaves and Amerindians that produced the gold and silver of the American mines and the cotton, sugar, and coffee from the Caribbean that made possible the economical takeoff of Europe and the conditions for intellectual production. I cannot celebrate Prigogine's European pride without thinking of the darker side of the Renaissance and the Enlightenment. But I am certainly proud of the achievement of the "human species" and world civilizations, from ancient to contemporary China; from ancient Mesoamerica and the Andes to contemporary Latin America; from modern to contemporary Europe; from the Muslim world south of the Mediterranean to the complex civilization of India. Regarding the ideals of democracy, I am concerned with the fact that the universal proclamation of democracy was blind to the local histories in which that very proclamation was taking place in relation to almost three hundred years of colonialism and the constitution of the modern/colonial world system. I am concerned, in general, about the legitimization of social truth that is not predicated on the responsibilities of those who made the predicament, but on some transcendental value that was supposed to be independent of those who invoked it. Democracy, we all know, was invoked by Pinochet to justify the military coup that dethroned Salvador Allende; was invoked by Stalin on the name of socialism; was constantly named by presidents Ronald Reagan and George Bush as the imponderable spirit that keeps Western civilization alive.

Blindness is not a feature that can be attributed to those living and making local histories engendering and enacting global designs as universal models. Perhaps one of the most salient features of the late eighteenth century in western Europe was the fact that it was projected from hegemonic local histories and embraced by subaltern ones as a model to be imitated. The confluence of the industrial revolution in England with the social revolution in France, together with the powerful philosophical contribution of Kant, Hegel, and Marx, became a desirable model for others, including raising nation-states (e.g., in the Americas), imperial states in decay (e.g., Spain), nations peripheral to the modern/colonial world (e.g., the North Atlantic world), and countries that joined in the standards of civilization at the end of the nineteenth (e.g., China and Japan). Spain is an interesting case for my argument. I would like to quote Leopoldo Zea's description of the situation of Spain at the turn of the eighteenth century vis-à-vis the global order and the interior conflict and borders of the modern/colonial world:

> The first half of the nineteenth century witnessed a constant struggle for liberalism in Spain, which, though repressed again and again, sought to change her into a modern nation. It was a version of liberalism perpetually battling the forces of theocratic Spain and the interests of Western Europe that were turning

Spain into a new economic colony for the profit of the West. The liberal struggled in vain to establish a national bourgeoisie, a middle class which, as in
Western Europe [e.g., France, England, Germany, Holland], would contribute
greatly to the new Spanish nation . . . .

What liberalism could no longer do was to carry out the necessary social, political, and economic reforms to transform Spain into a modern nation. In Spain,
as in Spanish America during the same period, old privileges remained in force
and prevented the establishment of a middle class that might have acted as a
springboard for the nation's progress. (Zea [1957] 1992, 129)

There is more to it, however, as Philip Silver (1998, 3–41) has shown in
his analysis of Spanish romanticism and intellectuals and their reaction to
Napoleon's invasion of Spain at the beginning of the nineteenth century.
The Spanish were caught in a double bind: they envisioned a modernization
of Spain following (and imitating) the northern (French and English)
model, but they could not of course endorse Napoleon's invasion. The decision to imitate and to bring Spain at the level of France was their decision,
not Napoleon's. Thus caught in between a foreign invasion and the theo-
cratic forces of Spain's past, Spanish intellectuals at the beginning of the
nineteenth century faced a different dilemma than Spanish American postcolonial intellectuals during the same period.

Esteban Echeverría, a postindependence ideologue in Argentina, bought
into the same idea and embraced "democracy" as defined in France. He did
not spend much time either in thinking about the colonial difference and
how it shaped the local histories of France in Europe and Argentina in Spanish America nor to the two hundred years of imperial conflicts in the North
Atlantic that preceded the French Revolution. Born and educated in Latin
America, I am concerned with the ideological presuppositions of Prigogine's remarks in which the colonial difference is once more reproduced,
the colonial side of modernity obscured, and the contribution of other local
histories around the planet ignored. Asians, Africans, and (Latin) Americans
shall not feel less proud that Prigogine for having made it this far in the
history of the universe, of life on earth. However, the imaginary of the mod-
ern/colonial world is such that Prigogine's remarks are made out of a "natural" belief and as a "natural" development of universal history. Cosmopolitanism cannot be achieved by insisting on continental pride forged by the
history of the modern/colonial world system. Nativism or regionalism from
the center is as pernicious as nativism or regionalism from the periphery.
Border thinking, as an intellectual and political project, calls attention to the
fact that achievements located in Europe (and not in Africa, Asia, or [Latin]
America) are a historical consequence of the formation and transformation
of the modern/colonial world. I shall not repeat here what crossed the Atlantic from east to west while the general belief was that civilization was

marching from west to east. Neither shall I mention again the slave trade, paradoxically following the same geographical direction as the spread of civilization, from East to West.

The epistemological potential of border thinking is to contribute to Dussel's call to move beyond Eurocentrism, recognizing the achievements and revealing the conditions for the geopolitics of knowledge in the modern/colonial world—recognizing and revealing the coloniality of power imbedded in the geopolitic of knowledge. As someone who was educated and lived in (Latin) America half of his present life span and relocated in (Anglo) America, after a three-year intermission in France, I am proud (echoing Prigogine) of the Haitian Revolution. I am proud because it showed the limits of liberal democracy a few years after its very promulgation and was locally based on the experiences of a "new" European order in which France, England, Holland, and Germany were displacing and replacing previous imperial orders. More recently, almost two hundred years after the Haitian Revolution and its "natural" failure (Trouillot 1995), the Zapatistas are again showing the limits of democracy in its regional eighteenth-century definition and recasting it based on the five hundred years of particular local histories in the Americas (Mignolo 1997d). "Democracy" was taken off the domain of global designs and reconverted to the needs of Chiapas's local history where indigenous and Western wisdom interact—where the colonial difference is being addressed and border thinking enacted. Government of the people, by the people, for the people has next to it today another dictum: "To rule and at the same time obeying" (Dussel 1995; Mignolo 1997d). If "democracy," as a word, is the place of encounter from Pinochet to the Zapatistas and to Prigogine, one should not waste time trying to define it by finding its universal (or perhaps transcendental) meaning. Instead, one could think of putting all the people and communities claiming democracy in a domain of interaction where social organization will be made out of the decisions and understandings of all of them. The management of democracy by those who hold power and the right interpretation of the word will not solve the problem of democratic societies held together by the persuasive language and seduction of arms. New ways of thinking are required that, transcending the colonial difference, could be built on the borders of competing cosmologies whose current articulation is due in no small part to the coloniality of power imbedded in the making of the modern/colonial world.

III

In my discussion I have talked about the differences between "Creoles" in continental South America and in the Caribbean. When I refer to South America, "indigenous" people are indeed both Amerindians and Creoles.

The very meaning of Creole implies a particular relation to the territory these people inhabit or inhabited. Amerindians are "natives" of the land, descending from Asian migrations through the Pacific before the encounter of Europeans crossing the Atlantic. It is this date, indeed the moment of the "discovery" of America, that gave Amerindians a particular reading of their being "native." The "discovery" was indeed crucial to redistribute and classify people and communities in their relation to the Americas and in the emerging modern/colonial world. "Creole" in South America applies only to "natives" of the land from Spanish or Portuguese descent, whereas in the Caribbean it applies both to people of European (British, French, Dutch) and to those from African descent. Consequently, "Crioulo" in Brazil has all the ambiguities of referring to people from both European and African descent. "Amerindians" applies instead to "native" people who inhabited the land when Spaniards and Portuguese arrived. So "native" is not a very meaningful category if it is not specified in its historical dimension. And here historical dimension implies the colonial difference and the coloniality of power.

An interesting tour of events is available in this single word, as well as a good map of the racial foundation of the modern/colonial world both in its interior (British/Spanish) and exterior borders (British/Spanish on the one hand and Amerindian and African slave on the other). First, "Creole" has been used to refer to "native" (in South America and the Caribbean) from European and African descent. Whether the "natives" in question implied "metissage/mestizaje" is another problem. The Mexican Revolution, in 1910, for example, adopted "mestizaje" as the national ideology operating on a significant oxymoron: it was mixture that became the emblem and the image of a homogeneous nation, an homogenous nation of mixed people, the purity of the impure, so to speak. Now "Creole" from European descent could be legally established by birth registration. The question of blood, of course, was more difficult to measure when "Creole" was linked to "mestizo" (mixture of European with Amerindian) or "mulatto" (mixture of European with African). However, blood proportion and skin pigmentation per se was not and is not still today the real issue. The point is that a discourse emerged in the imaginary of the modern/colonial world in which "Creole" was defined in relation to descent, blood, and skin pigmentation. The bottom line was that a group of people began to feel as "Americans" (in whatever region), to identify themselves and to claim their right to autonomy from European management and governance. In the Caribbean, however, French and English "Creole" referred to language in a way that did not hold water in Spanish. And once "Créolité" in language began to be extended to the realm of culture and knowledge, it took over the previous definition of Créolité/ Metissage based on biological configurations. The publication of *Éloge de la Créolité* (Bernabé et al. 1993) which I commented on chapter 5, was crucial in this respect for two reasons:

1. It extended "Créolité" beyond language and opened up the way to question epistemology. Although this latter aspect was not developed, the obvious question emerges when one considers that "culture" is readily accepted as "Creole" but "knowledge" has more difficulty to be accepted as such. "Knowledge," particularly academic knowledge, has to be pure, not mixed. And when "knowledge" is mixed (transdisciplinary), it is no longer considered "knowledge" but "culture."

2. It was an identification that could be assumed by people from European but not from African descent.

Equally interesting here is the difference between "Creole" in Bolivia, for instance, and in Martinique, or similar places. If "Creole" in Martinique applies to those people from French African descents, it is interesting to note that "Créolité" was proudly claimed by the Afro-Caribbean and not by people from French descent. In this regard, *Éloge de la Creolité* (with the limitations that Conde and James point out) is a major step in appropriating "Créolité" and making of it a place of celebration rather that the locus of subalternity enacted by the coloniality of power. The distinction is not without relevance historically. Henry Cristophe and Toussaint L'Overture, two heroes of the Haitian Revolution, were black Creole, while Sans Souci, the radical rebel, was African, presumably from the Congo (Rolph-Trouillot, 1995). Tupac Amaru and Tupac Katari, in Peru and Bolivia respectively, were identified as Amerindian. These distinctions are not being made to establish a code of privilege. Amerindians do not have more privilege than "Creoles" or Spaniards to inhabit where they inhabit. However, Amerindians *have equal rights* (of the people, of men and citizens, or, in the last version, human and indigenous rights; see Stavenhagen and Iturralde 1990), *and these rights have never been recognized, neither by Spaniards nor by Creoles*. The same could be said for the Caribbean, albeit the equivalent of Amerindians on the continent would be their symmetric opposite: people from African descent who, like Spaniards, French, or English, are "Creole" are at the opposite side of the spectrum. If, as I said, blood or skin pigmentation is not the issue, it is because the issue is the coloniality of power, establishing and naturalizing the colonial difference.

IV

I would like to move further into observations on deconstruction/decolonization that I have introduced in chapter 1, and to extend it to transdisciplinarity and the culture of transience, in the sense that Pulin K. Garg and Indira J. Parikh (1995) use the word: the problems involved in the transition of Indian society from agrarian-rural to technological-industrial. I would like to explore further the implications of border thinking

in the articulation of subaltern and hegemonic knowledges from the perspective of the subaltern. Transdisciplinarity and culture of transcience can
not be an adaptation of "traditional" knowledge to "modern" epistemology,
but a transcendence of the colonial difference implied in this distinction.
Border thinking could also be linked to the moment of disciplinary transience in which modern gnoseology is recast in terms of subaltern knowledges, from the perspective of subaltern knowledge. Some of the basic assumptions from which the culture-of-transience project emerges are the
following:

> Western theory which has been the only theory available for universalisation is
> definitely culture specific and grounded in the Judeo-Christian and Greco-
> Roman assumptions of man, collectivity and their relationship. They may have
> been internalized by educated groups of people but not by the masses; and any
> way they have not been introjected. Hence they have not yet become enlivened
> and energized by the psychic energy held in the cultural identity of India. (Garg
> 1986, 8)

The problems that prompt the culture of transience are revealing of both
the colonial difference and the coloniality of power. The question is how to
rearticulate the two ethoses that have been in contention, in India, since the
arrival of the British. The preamble of the Constitution of the Republic, Garg
points out, has been formulated on the cognitive internalization of Western
principles. Dysfunctional behavior has resulted from it and from the trust
of a culture of transience as if to find alternatives for the colonial difference
and the coloniality of power, which are at the root of unrest and violence in
India (as well as elsewhere and for the same reasons). Garg confronts these
conflicts with three possible options: two of them are pernicious; the third
one carries some hope. The first option, which produced economic growth
and a resurgence of Indian nationalism, was established in 1830 by Raja
Ram Mohan Roy. But it also opened up the doors for corruption and disen-
gagement, violence and problems of law and order, and "a whole host of
unethical practices in day-to-day transactions that operate unchecked"
(Garg 1986, 9). Pursuing this option will end up, according to Gark, in the
rise of military dictatorial regimes or in the rise of fundamentalism, which
could also lead to dictatorial regimes. The second option is to continue operating on the ethos of the West and believe that technology will take care
of all the problems. Garg opposes to this alternative the wide effects of any
"theory of borrowing," from the West or elsewhere, without some difficult
thinking about the conditions under which the borrowing is being implemented. Garg states that this position creates the condition for the rise of
military regimes and fundamentalist movements. The third option is the
culture of transience and its dynamics:

It involves a realistic review of the ethos we introject through our primary socialization. Like any ethos, the introjected ethos also has contents and processes. The assumptions and processes underlying the ethos tend to become masked by the ossified content, forms and rituals. These cannot be revived and deployed in the present. That would be the way of fundamentalism. We suggest that through a realistic review a separation of the content and the underlying processes is the first necessity. The identification of the basic assumption and processes of our own ethos can become the best anchor to formulate a new cultural identity relevant for the times as well as to evolve forms and processes which aim for dynamic and creative transactions between individual and our social systems. This option also involves going backward to go forward. Past is forever present in our introjected ethos. It is a heritage and source of dynamicity, but it is also a pathology and a source of immobility and degeneration. *The past ethos can be regenerative if we can decode the processes and use them to unleash the energy held in the cultural identity.* As an Indian, I believe that the third options is the only choice for us to survive as a self respecting society. (Garg 1986, 10)

I quote Garg in some details because his conclusion and project are very close to those expressed by Martín-Barbero. Barbero, a Spanish intellectual and longtime resident of Colombia since 1963, is a practitioner of cultural studies from a strong hegemony/subalternity perspective, owed to a reading of Gramsci and Benjamin grounded in Latin America history and current debates. Martín-Barbero, like Garg, is deeply concerned with producing knowledge and implementing it in public policy. Barbero, like Garg, sees the double bind of cultural identity, at the same time a potential for empowerment and also a legitimization of conservatism. Barbero, like Garg, reclaims the transformational potential of identity formation rather than a supplementary effort to preserve a mythical ideal of national essence or of indigenous purity. Martín-Barbero, unlike Garg, is thinking in and from Latin America where the "Creole" ethos dominated over the Amerindian, one, and both had to survive the project of modernity dealing, explicity or implicitly, with the colonial difference and the coloniality of power (Martín-Barbero [1986] 1997; 1993; 1998).

Thus, the emergence of concepts such as double critique and an other thinking, transculturation and Creolization, double counsciousness and new mestiza consciousness are not alien to the culture of transience (Garg and Parikh 1995). Consequently, I see decolonization imbedded in border thinking and transience epistemology as different ways of transcending the colonial difference. I see deconstruction, instead, as a critic of and from modern epistemology more concerned with the Western hegemonic constructions than with the colonial difference; and the colonial difference from the perspective of subaltern knowedges. Let me be more specific.

First, concerning deconstruction/decolonization, it is not a question of silence but also of silences at the first level of constructing "facts." The second level is beyond the archive and the translation of "facts" into the public imaginary. Postdam and Sans Souci, for instance, for several reasons will hardly be considered equal. The former involves Germany and Europe in the seventeenth century; black slaves and a Creole revolutionary in Haiti were not at the same level in the structure of the coloniality of power as the Great Prussian Empire (see Trouillot 1995). Thus, deconstruction within Western metaphysics needs to be decolonized from the silences of history. Decolonization needs to be deconstructed from the perspective of the coloniality of power. The logic of the conversation shall change, not just the terms.

Second, the question of the silence of history at various levels and Chakrabarty's dilemma needs to be emphasized. If history is a European kit as far as the content of the conversation is concerned, memory should become a practice of restitution that digs into the silences of the past transcending the disciplinary of history embedded in the colonial difference and the coloniality of power. From Hegel to Hayden White we find certainly a constant transformation of history as a Western discipline but not its decolonization, as Edouard Glissant has proposed (see chapters 1 and 5). Deconstructing "history" from inside "historiography" and "Western logocentrism" is without a doubt a necessary task. But decolonization of history is also a necessary and distinct one that cannot be reduced or attached to the former. In decolonization the transdisciplinary move is accompanied, unlike deconstruction, by a perspective from the external borders of the modern/colonial world where the colonial difference has been defined and maintained (see the final section in this chapter)—thus, the need to move beyond disciplines, beyond interdiscipline to knowledge as a transdisciplinary enterprise. Since disciplinarity in the social sciences and the humanities has been reconfigured in the nineteenth century in a new emerging national and colonial order (Wallerstein et al. 1995), decolonization cannot propose an adaptation of the disciplinary knowledge to the Third World (e.g., subaltern historiography). It is rather the move toward transdisciplinary practices (Dussel [1993] 1995; 1996a, 49–64) and the historicity of the border-knowing subjects (Fanon, Khatibi, Anzaldúa) that places decolonization as border thinking in parallel complementarity to deconstruction. I have been arguing for border thinking as one articulation of this double operation from the point of view of the colonial difference—the silenced perspective in the imaginary of the modern/colonial world system. It is worth noting here that Henri Lefebvre ([1974] 1991, 411–12; also Soja 1996, 26–53) has also used the concept of transdisciplinarity. The difference between Dussel and Lefebvre is the following. While Lefebvre used transdisciplinarity strictly as a transcendence of interdisciplinarity (which presupposes the disciplines), Dussel used it to refer to the external borders of the modern/colonial world where the colonial difference cleaned up all kinds of knowledge that will endanger the epistemological foundation of modernity. Dussel's transdisciplinarity implies a geopolitic of knowledge that Lefebvre himself recognized was out of his scope. He mentioned it several times in his superb analysis of *The Production of Space* (Lefebvre [1974] 1991), when he refered to Mesoamerican and Andean conceptualiztion of space, but he was not in a condition to think the colonial difference. In this line of reasoning, Trouillot's analysis of the three faces of Sans Souci is a bold articulation of events that do not respond to the rigid chronological and national grammar of Western historiography. Sans-Souci in Postdam is hardly chronologically and nationally related to Sans-Souci in Haiti. Trouillot (1995) shows their connections through the coloniality of power and knowledge and offers a good example of the promises of border thinking as decolonization of scholarship.

If we take as a reference point a definition of deconstruction offered by Derrida in the early moments of his influential work, deconstruction was conceived not as a science or a discipline but as critical position vis-à-vis scientific and disciplinary knowledge:

> One can say *a priori* that in every proposition or in every system of semiotic research . . . metaphysical presuppositions coexist with critical motifs. And this by the simple fact that up to a certain point they inhabit the same language. Doubtless, grammatology is less another science, a new discipline, charged with a new content or new domain, than the vigilant practices of this textual division. (Derrida [1972] 1981)

Grammatology is a vigilant practice spin on deconstruction that avoids neutralizing binary oppositions of metaphysics and simply "*residing* within the closed field of these oppositions thereby confirming it" ([1972] 1981, 41). And deconstruction as the space where grammatology spins is articulated in a "double séance," a double science (which is no longer science) or a double register:

> On the one hand, we must traverse a phase of *overturning*. To do justice to this necessity is to recognize that in a classical philosophical opposition we are not dealing with the peaceful coexistence of a *vis-à-vis*, but rather with a violent hierarchy. *One of the two terms governs the other (axiologically, logically, etc.), or has the upper hand.* To deconstruct the opposition, first of all, is to overturn the hierarchy at a given moment. To overlook this phase of overturning is to forget the conflictual and subordinating structure of opposition. (Derrida [1972] 1981, 43)

The second moment of the "double séance," after overturning the opposition and in order not to remain within the system overturned, is the moment of dissemination of the oppositions as they dissolve themselves without *ever constituting a third term* (1982, 43). Now, since colonial discourse established itself in the constant and charged construction of hierarchical oppositions, deconstructing colonial discourse is indeed a necessary task. There is, however, another related task that goes beyond the analysis and deconstruction of colonial discourse and the principle of Western metaphysics underlining it. I am referring here to the colonial difference, the intersection between Western metaphysics and the multiple non-Western principles governing modes of thinking of local histories that have been entering in contact and conflict with Western thoughts in the past five hundred years in the Americas, and in the past two hundred years in India from where Garg thinks and projects the culture of transience. The Sun and the Moon, in Amerindian categories of thought are not opposite, contrary, or contradictory; they are complementary. To extend deconstruction beyond Western metaphysics or to assume that there is nothing else than Western metaphysics will be a move similar to colonizing global designs under the belief of the pretense of the improvement of humanity if we can make them all like us. Grammatology and deconstruction have vis-à-vis the colonial experience the same limitations as Marxism vis-à-vis race and indigenous communities in the colonized world: the colonial difference is invisible to them. Decolonization should be thought of as complementary to deconstruction and border thinking, complementary to the "double séance" within the experience and sensibilities of the coloniality of power.

Double consciousness, double critique, an other tongue, an other thinking, new mestiza consciousness, Creolization, transculturation, and culture of transience become the needed categories to undo the subalternization of knowledge and to look for ways of thinking beyond the categories of Western thought from metaphysics to philosophy to science. The projects of Edward Said, Gayatri Spivak, and Homi Bhabha, in the past twenty years, have been instrumental for a critique of subalternization of knowledge. Said showed through Michel Foucault the construction of the Orient as a discursive formation; Bhabha described through Lacan the hybridity and the third space of colonial discourse; Spivak pushed the deconstruction of colonial discourse through Derrida. However, beyond these conceptual genealogies where the postcolonial emerges, piggybacking on postmodern (or poststructuralist) theories, there were also emerging in a parallel fashion similar manifestations of border thinking, which I have explored in this book, attached to particular *places* resulting from and produced by local modern/colonial histories. My own conceptualization, in this book, followed the move made by Said, Bhabha, and Spivak, but is based on the work of Wallerstein, an (Anglo) American sociologist rather than French philosophers or psychoanalysts. But I have also departed from Wallerstein by introducing the colonial difference and the coloniality of power and thus linking my work with that of Anibal Quijano in Peru and Enrique Dussel in Argentina and Mexico, both active since the late 1960s and early 1970s—about the same years that Wallerstein, Foucault, Derrida, and Lacan were producing their intellectual impact. One of the reasons, and not a trivial one, of my decision to follow Wallerstein and then move to Quijano and Dussel was my need to go beyond the eighteenth century and the Enlightenment, which is the reference and starting point of poststructuralist and early postcolonial theorizing. I needed the sixteenth century and the Renaissance, the emergence of the Americas in the colonial horizon of modernity, a local history out of which Quijano, Dussel, Anzaldúa, and myself (among many others, of course) are made. What I needed to argue for was a way of thinking in and from the borders of the colonial differences in the modern/colonial world: the borders between enacting and desiring global designs; the borders between transforming received global designs into local projects; the borders between subaltern and hegemonic knowledges rearticulated from the perspective of the subalterns.

Where is then border thinking located, in terms of disciplines? Philosophy, because I claimed gnoseology, epistemology, and hermeneutics? Sociology, because I located it in the external borders of the modern/colonial world? History, because my argument was built historically and from the perspective of coloniality? Anthropology, because I dealt with issues that have been the province of anthropology, which is the closer discipline to the colonial difference? Cultural studies, because it is none of the above? I would say that the transdisciplinary dimension of border thinking is cultural critique in the precise sense that Stuart Hall defines cultural studies, as transdisciplinary and trans-national: "In a sense, if there is anything to be learnt from British cultural studies, it's the insistence that cultural studies is always about the articulation—in different context of course—between culture and power. I am speaking in terms of the epistemological formation of the field, not in the sense of practicing cultural studies" (Hall 1992, 395).

V

There are indeed remarkable differences between Western civilization, Occidentalism, and modern/colonial world system. Western civilization is neither a synonym for Occidentalism, nor for modern/colonial world system. Western civlization is supposed to be something "grounded" in Greek history as is also Western metaphysics. This reading, implicit in the Renaissance, became explicit in the Enlightenment. Occidentalism is basically the master metaphor of colonial discourse since the sixteenth century and specifically in relation to the inclusion of the Americas as part and margin of the West. It is an ambiguous metaphor in the sense that from the sixteenth century up to the Enlightenment, America has had an ambiguous role in colonial discourse. On the one hand it was portrayed and conceived as the daughter and inheritor of Europe, thus its future. On the other, as daughter and inheritor, it occupied a subaltern position in the geopolitics of knowledge and in the coloniality of power: the Americas, from the point of view of European intellectuals and until post–World War II, was the subaltern same. There is certainly another parallel story here, which is the relocation of the Americas (Spanish and Anglo) after 1848 and 1898. But this process seemed to have been bypassed (perhaps with the exception of Tocqueville) by the European intelligentsia. The situation was further complicated by the fact that in the rearticulation of the geopolitics of colonial power, Amerindians and Afro-Americans, with all their diversity in the Americas, were left out of the picture of an updated Occidentalism.

Western civilization was not (could not have been) yet conceived as a cultural entity in the fifteenth century. There Christendom was located in something as ill-defined as Europe (Tawantinsuyu or Anahuac were ill-defined at the same time), the land of Western Christians (in a sense, the land of Japhet). On the other hand *it was precisely the imaginary of the modern/ colonial world that began to build on the idea of Western civilization without which there would not (could not) have been a modern/colonial world system.* Thus the imaginary of the modern/colonial world was the location for the grounding of the very idea of Western civilization. *I call Occidentalism, then, the Western version of Western civilization (its own self-description) ingrained in the imaginary of the modern/colonial world.* The idea of Western civilization, Western metaphysics, Western logocentrism, and the like is a consequence and necessity of the modern/colonial world as the modern/colonial world was articulated in the growing imaginary of Western civilization, and so on. It is indeed interesting to note that Derrida's *De la grammatologie* (1967) left blank the moment in which the very idea of Western civilization and Western metaphysics became the seeds of the overarching imaginary of the modern/colonial world system.

De la grammatologie (1967) has three exerges: one from ancient times and the writing of the people (*l'écriture du peuple* [EP]), the second from Rousseau, and the third from Hegel. There is nothing in between in this diagram of universal history from ancient Greece to modern France and Germany—nothing in between and nothing on the side, in the space of parallel geohistorical configurations, from the east to the northwest of the Mediterranean; from the Indian to the Pacific Ocean; from the Mediterranean to the Atlantic in the sixteenth century. Now, I am not suggesting that this frame shall be corrected in the name of the truth of universal history. I am just saying that, for Derrida, Rousseau and Hegel are the references of "modern" times, whereas for Quijano, Dussel, Marmon Silko, and myself, universal history has a different reference: the five hundred years summarized in Marmon Silko's historical map (see my introduction). This is one of the silenced, paralleled, and interconnected histories left on the side because of the blindness to the colonial difference.

And certainly there is more, much more. From the perspective of China and Japan there are other histories and variegated perspectives on the colonial difference. But the colonial difference is there, hiding most of the time the interaction of China and Japan with the modern/colonial (North Atlantic) world. There is also the history of Islam and the Arabic countries after the sixteenth century articulating a zone of violent conflicts. And, of course, it is not just the "history" I am talking about here. I am talking about "knowledges" hidden under the reproduction of Western civilization and Western metaphysics. All those stories are tangential to Western metaphysics; Western metaphysics is tangential to them. The coloniality of power and the colonial difference are what link them in problematic and conflictive ways. If they are outside of Western metaphysics, such a statement could only be meaningful from the hegemony of the coloniality of power, not from the local histories for which Western metaphysics is not a totality but a global design. It is precisely the coming into being of a historical and critical consciousness of both the global scope of Western metaphysics as an instrument of colonization (from religion to reason), and the knowledges subalternized by it, that brings to the foreground the awareness of the borders and of border thinking. There is nothing outside of totality, of course, but totality is always projected from a given local history. Therefore, there is nothing outside the totality of a given local history, other than other local histories perhaps producing either alternative totalities or an alternative to totality. A nonontological cosmology, as Amerindian's cosmologies illustrate from the sixteenth to the end of the twentieth century, is an alternative to Western ontological cosmology as the grounding of totality (be it Christian faith or secular reason). The interesting aspect of all of this is how such imaginary, which is part of the history of the modern/colonial world system itself, justified economic decisions, public policy designs and implementations, wars and other forms of control, exploitation, and the management of peoples.

VI

Between 1950 and 1970 an interesting discussion was taking place in Latin America and the Caribbean around Occidentalism and decolonization. Such a discussion began to fade away with the arrival, in the late 1960s of the French structuralist and poststructuralist boom. Saussure was "discovered" and became influential in anthropology (Lévi-Strauss), philosophy (Derrida), and psychoanalysis (Lacan). Saussure's linguistic system was questioned in the 1950s by Mihail Bajtine in the Soviet Union and by Ortega y Gasset in Spain in the name of dialogic interactions (Bajtine) and the speech of the people (Ortega y Gasset). Finally, the linguistic system was questioned and extended to discursive interactions and to discursive formations (Foucault). These transformations and debates were convincing everybody that modernization of scholarship meant jumping on the bandwagon of structuralism and poststructuralism. The works of Lyotard (1983) and Bourdieu (1982) were added to the list, introducing a more sociological dimension complementing the linguistic and discursive scope of the formers. The debate of previous years, in Latin America, on Occidentalism (O'Gorman 1958; Fernández Retamar [1974] 1975), dependency (Cardoso and Faletto 1979), decolonization (Fanon; [1959] 1967; 1961; Dussel 1973; Delich 1964; Fernández Pardo 1971), and national consciousness (Hernández Arregui 1973), became the symptom of a Third World intellectual community somewhat obsolete that needed to update itself by entering in the new and exciting modern intellectual debate. And exciting it certainly was.

Now, some twenty-five years after the fact one can look at the moment of intersection between the original debates, on the one hand, and then consider new perspectives on Occidentalism and decolonization and structuralism and poststructuralism, on the other. We can compare not in order to reverse the course of history and play the former against the latter but rather to listen again to those voices and concerns that were buried under "noble" intellectual global designs that were deconstructing Occidentalism from within and from the center of knowledge production, in one of the three major languages of modernity (French in this case). Subaltern knowledge production in the margin of the modern/colonial world was linked to subaltern languages, either previous colonial ones (Spanish, Portuguese) or those emerging from the colonial difference (French Créole, French from Martinique, or English from Barbados). In the case of continental Latin America and, more particularly, Spanish America, the margins were occupied by the "inteligencia Criolla" (the Creole—in the sense described earlier—intelligentsia) and the Amerindian intellectuals, less visible due to the work of internal colonialism. The Creole intelligentsia, next to Amerindian communities, suffered the consequences of a strong internal colonialism implanted by themselves (the Creole intelligentsia) in their building of the nation-state in connections with the new and emerging nineteenth-century colonialisms. My discussion of Roldolfo Kusch's critical explorations of Aymara's conceptual legacy is a particular case of these tensions within the margin itself. My discussion on the Caribbean concept of "Créolité" in chapter 6 brought out a similar tension between an ascending black Caribbean intellectuality after the 1950s (Lamming, Cesaire, Fanon), although ingrained in different local histories, the histories shaped by the strong contingent of

African slaves in the "new" continent. The interesting outcome of the comparison is to see a reversing situation in the Caribbean vis-à-vis continental Latin America.

Three examples will provide an ample spectrum of problems and debates between 1950 and 1970 related to knowledge and the coloniality of power I have been discussing in this book and may help in devising cultural politics connected to future research and teaching agendas. I obviate here the discussion of Mexican historian and philosopher Edmundo O'Gorman, which I have discussed elsewhere (Mignolo 1992a; 1993b), and concentrate on three examples from Argentina, a country I have not devoted much attention to and where it is common to think that, because the low percentage of Amerindian population and even less of black Americans, coloniality is not as relevant as is modernity. This is a sort of one-eyed vision, to honoring (and changing) well-known novelist and literary critic David Viñas, for his expression "los dos ojos del romanticismo" (romanticism's two eyes; Viñas 1982). Viñas analyzed postindependence ideology in Argentina (roughly from 1810 to 1850), and he claimed that Argentinian romantic poets and intellectuals had one eye directed toward Europe and the other toward (what they believed was) the authentic spirit of the country and of the America. This foundational dichotomy engendered one of the classic books in the intellectual history of Latin America, *Facundo: Civilization and Barbarism* (1845), by Domingo Faustino Sarmiento, who became president of Argentina for the period 1872–78, as I already mentioned in chapter 7. *Civilization and Barbarism* summarized and projected toward the future, the continental Latin American Creoles' vision of themselves, of their country, and of the subcontinent. This vision was rearticulated in the late nineteenth and early twentieth centuries by Euclides D'Acuña (González Echeverría 1990; see also chapter 3 in this book), a Brazilian essayist well versed in geography and in the current debates of the time prompted by the increasing influence of the "civilizing mission" ideology.

The intellectual debates in Argentina between 1860 (year of the "National Organization") and 1950 turned around the building of the nation-state. At the center of the debate were the present and the future of the Argentine economy at the intersection of two competing imperialism (England and the United States); the production and exportation of meat in the new global order; and the extension of the western frontiers and its consequences to satisfy imperial demands. Finally, the major issue related to the previous one was the large contingents of European immigrants generating a radical demographic transformation of the country between 1875 and 1914, entangled with building a "modern" Argentina in consonance with new imperial models of modernity and civilization. Populism became the pervasive state ideology in the country from 1930 to 1960 (Martín-Barbero [1986] 1997, part 3) and created the conditions for the military regimes from 1975 to 1982. After 1950, however, the question of Occident and of America emerged and complemented the energy devoted to Argentine history and identity. Such large issues were considered, at the time, an evasion of the real issues Argentinians had to face in order to decide on their future. In retrospect, one could speculate that the beginning of the cold war was being felt by prompting a rethinking of larger questions about Occidentalism and the location of the Americas in it. Then Bernardo Canal Feijóo (a historian and sociologist who up to that point had only written on Argentinian history) published what is today a surprising but forgotten book: *Confines de occidente. Notas para una socio-logia de la cultura americana* (1954) (Confines of the West: Notes toward a sociology of American culture), in which by *Americana* he meant Spanish American. At the "confines" of the West what we encounter in Canal Feijóo's argument is the historical tension, since the conquest, between Spaniards, Spanish American Creoles, and Amerindians. The distinction between *ser* and *estar* (that Kusch will later on exploit) was introduced by Canal Feijóo in this book, perhaps with a twist that Kusch was not able or willing to pursue. For Canal Feijóo *ser* (to be as existence) is what characterizes a given culture and a person's cultural belonging. *Estar* is transitory. Thus, his take on Latin Americans was that they *estan* where they *no son*. Translated into English it can be rendered in a sensical nonsense of: "they are where they are not."

Canal Feijóo's diagnosis is, of course, a diagnosis of the 1950s, a re-articulation of (Latin) American identification as a response to the new demands of modernization and development after World War II. Europe, more than the United States, was the reference point. Spain, seen from the middle of the twentieth century, was compared with France and England, the "Spanish" archetype with the "French" and the "English" ones. In spite of the suspicions that arguments based on archetype may awaken today, in the case of Canal Feijóo the archetype was the symptom of a larger issue: the imperial conflicts, the internal and external borders of the modern/colonial world. Canal Feijóo perceived in the English or French "men," as archetypes, a confidence in themselves that was not paralleled by the Spanish and Latin American archetypes. He perceived, indeed, a larger issue that cannot be explained through national differences but rather through imperial conflicts and the interior borders of the modern/colonial world system; by the long memories of each local history being rearticulated in the system. Canal Feijóo observed that Spain is less "Hellenistic" than France and England in the horizon of the already consolidated modern nations, and that Catholic Spain's interactions with the Islamic world and Jewish communities gave its people a more open approach to mixing with Amerindians and Afro-Americans in the Americas. In this argument he is indeed talking about local histories, about long memories and pointing toward differentiating England and France from Spain in the rearticulation of the modern/colonial world system. He is arguing, indeed, the rearticulation in the modern/colonial world system by the rising of new colonial powers. Finally, Canal Feijóo, insisting that the "discovery" of America was a meeting of West and East, echoed a sixteenth-century hypothesis advanced by Spanish Jesuit José de Acosta ([1590] 1962), recently rehearsed by Enrique Dussel (1998a), from the perspective of the 5,000-year world system (Gunder Frank and Gill 1993). Moving back in time, before the formation of the modern/colonial world system, allowed Dussel to correct the colonial imaginary on Amerindian people and history that was established by Spanish missionaries and men of letters in the sixteenth century. Canal Feijóo brought to the foreground the history of the Pacific, before the "discovery," and the migrations through the Bering Strait that formed the current Amerindian and Native American population from Labrador to Patagonia.

Canal Feijóo's statement proclaiming a "We Americans" was, indeed, a marginal and fractured voice of the Creole intellectuals in Spanish America. It was similar, although from the South and forty years ago, to Richard Rorty's (1998) current statement proclaiming a "We Americans," which is an inverted mirror image in relation to Canal Feijóo's. The difference is that the latter is louder than the former. And I am not comparing, of course, the individual intelligence of the two persons in question. I am referring to language, knowledge, and the coloniality of power imbedded in the imaginary modern world and to how the colonial difference is highlighted or blurred in each case.

The Creole Spanish American intellectuals fought to define their place in between what I have called elsewhere "saying out of places" (Mignolo 1995d). During the sixteenth century, Amerindians' and Spaniards' discourses were both out of place: the first because they had to articulate their sayings in front of people who disrupted their social organization and submitted them to their control. On the other hand, Spaniards' discourses in the New World were out of place because of two reasons. When they wrote Amerindian history they were writing about a past to which they do not belong, and they were also writing in a location for which their own local history was a remote story being told in another place, across the Atlantic. The Creole intelligentsia found its location between the two, saying out of place in asymmetric and complex relations of mutual knowledge and understanding, the Amerindian's and European Spanish's. Spaniards' saying became also out of place for different reasons. The Spanish legacies gave them their foundation, but it became the oppressive power from where they claimed independence. The Creole intelligentsia had to define itself at the intersection of the Amerindian voices, which were alien to them, and the Spanish voices, which became their identity in difference. Consequently, the Creole intelligentsia began to model itself, imitating and following the models of the new emerging powers: England and France.

Canal Feijóo came up with an illuminating formula to capture this dislocation, playing with the difference in Spanish language between *ser* and *estar*: (Latin) Americans "are not [*no son*] where they are [*donde ellos estan*]." Canal Feijóo's argument, in 1954, oscillated between an essentialist perspective on American being, and a historical perspective of the making of the Americas at the crossroads of imperial conflicts and previous erased memories (the immigrations from Asia forming the Amerindian population). In this tension, Canal Feijóo's description of Latin Americans as not able to be where they are was pronounced with a negative connotation. Today, it is possible to read Canal Feijóo's historical argument and forget the essentialist one, thus transforming nostalgia into celebration: "not being able to be [*ser*] where one is [*estar*]" becomes *the fundamental condition of border thinking.* Furthermore, the dislocation here in question is a dislocation of the colonial difference as experienced by the white/mestizo (e.g., no Amerindian, no Afro-American) Creole intelligentsia. To be in such a position in 1954, when Canal Feijóo published the book, had as one of its consequences a sense of inferiority because English and French "archetype men," for sure, *were able to be where ever they were.* The colonial difference was, so to speak, in their back, invisible to their experience. From 1999's perspective things have changed. *Not being able to be where one is is the promise of an epistemological potential and a cosmopolitan transnationalism that could overcome the limits and violent conditions generated by being always able to be where one belongs. I am where I think.*

VII

Shortly after Canal Feijóo wrote this book, sociology as a discipline was officially included in the curriculum of the Universidad Nacional de Buenos Aires as a graduate program. This symbolic introduction of the social sciences in Latin America displaced the force and the popularity of the essays as a discursive genre in the production of knowledge. "Scientific" analysis of history and society in and of Latin America in the social sciences replaced the "personal" analysis of history and society in the essays, a genre not attached to any discipline, freely moving between the social sciences, the humanities, and literature itself. A new space was created were the expert in the social sciences subalternized intellectual production outside of scientific norms. These epistemological requirements were part of modernization and development ideology. To become modern implied to become disciplined; knowledge was considered rigorous not because of the rigor of thinking but because of the rigors of disciplinary norms. To think well implied thinking according to disciplinary norms and rules. A new profile emerged: the profile of the intellectual expert in some of the domains of the social sciences. Dependency theory was perhaps the first intellectual production in Latin America in which experts trained in economy and sociology were at the same time intellectuals engaged in social and not only academic transformations.

But this was also the period of the emergence of a new kind of intellectual, the postcolonial intellectual à la Frantz Fanon. Thus, the coming out of the postcolonial intellectual in the second half of the twentieth century is considerably different from the counterpart in the early nineteenth century, à la Esteban Echeverría or Domingo Faustino Sarmiento, in Argentina, and Thomas Jefferson in the United States. In between them, and also in the second half of the twentieth century, the social sciences arrived in Latin America while revolution and decolonization arrived in India, Algeria, and Indochina. The margins or the confines of the West, in Canal Feijóo's expression—but the West nevertheless—had a different rhythm in their local histories. The legacies of the Creole intellectual of the early nineteenth century had to be adapted to match the concerns in the Third World that Latin America was experiencing after the Cuban Revolution. With the Cuban Revolution the scenario changed in three significant directions. On the one hand, a new form of colonialism without territorial possession, similar to that of the United States in logic but opposite in content, invaded the history of Latin America. On the other hand, it forced the rethinking of Russia and the Soviet Union in the making of the modern/colonial world system. Finally, it made possible to see the limits in Latin America of both Western Christian and liberal imperialism and the Soviet Union's socialist imperialism. And the limits revealed the colonial difference, which had been unseen and unthought by both (neo) liberals and (neo) Marxists. There was not an easy match, say, between the Marxist intellectuals supporting the Cuban Revolution and a position such as the one developed by Frantz Fanon. There was, obviously, a strong sense of solidarity, but an almost invisible, although very important, difference between the two: class as the basic concerns of the former (liberals and Marxists); race and the colonial difference entrenched in the modern/colonial world (and reemerging in the French/ Christian and Algeria/Muslim). But, above all, a rearticulation of "blackness," based on Fanon's experience in Martinique, not far from Cuba but far from Cuban Marxist intellectuals for whom the Afro-Cuban component it was not yet clearly processed, was a large blind spot. Here we confront once again, the blindness to the colonial difference.

In Argentina, Frantz Fanon was very influential among a group of intellectuals who were explicitly theorizing decolonization between 1966 and 1974, approximately. Fanon contributed to bust the movement of the Argentinian and Latin American new left. Its clear appearance could be placed with the creation of *Past and Present*, published by a group of young intellectuals (José Aricó, Oscar del Barco, Hector Smuchgler) of the Communist Party. The journal was published in Córdoba, not in Buenos Aires, and the first issue was released in 1963. There was, however, a clear distinction between the Fanonists and the Marxist new left. The latter were concerned with revolution and social classes; the former, with decolonization and racism. However, in Argentina itself, the Marxist new left carried the weight through the years of the "Dirty War" (1976–82) and in exile (José Aricó, Oscar del Barco, and Juan Carlos Portantiero, three of the major intellectual figures of the new left, were in Mexico during those years). The Fanonist new left did not have the strength to become a force next to Marxism and it is difficult to find articles or discussion about Fanon after 1976. The conclusions seem to be clear, although it shall be explored in more detail: dictatorship took the place of decolonization and implanted a brutal internal colonialism, introducing some fundamental changes in relation to the internal colonial situation described by Pablo González Casanova (1965) and Rodolfo Stavenhagen (1965): the "enemy" changed his face and the repression became more violent. The enemy was no longer classified by race (blacks, Jews, Amerindians) but by ideology (Communists) that revealed the new face of Western civilization. This figure of speech was pronounced quite frequently during the "Dirty War," in alliance with the support that the Argentinian military "junta" received from Washington. A paradoxical turn of events, indeed. Socialism and communism, which are clearly part of the Western ideology and part of Western metaphysics, were constructed as anti-Western projects by the liberal and neoliberal Western hegemony. In this paradoxical move, in which the colonial difference was once again suppressed, ethnic, gender, and generation struggles were united and homogenized under the ideological classificatory rubric of "communism." When someone was suspected of being a Communist (or any of its Argentinian versions), he was persecuted, put in prison, killed, or forced to exile.

The postcolonial question in Latin America shall be reframed in terms of post-Occidentalism and postdictatorship. This is one of the significant parallels and differences, between decolonization in Africa and Asia and in Latin America. For, decolonization in Argentina and in the Southern Cone did not have the Western state-national model as the point of arrival. As I showed in chapter 3, the period of nation building in Latin America was not after the consolidation of the nation-state in Europe but was constitutive of the project of modernity. The question is not whether nation-states were put in motion earlier in the Americas than in Europe (as Benedict Anderson [1983] 1991 argued) but the fact that nation-state building in the Americas was constitutive with the project of modernity. Decolonization, during the cold war, implied nation building as the point of arrival (Fanon 1961; [1964]

1988), with all the failures that are being recognized today (Béji 1982; Mamdani 1996). Decolonization in the early nineteenth century did not have the same take on nation building since the nation-state was not something already constituted in Europe, but something that was being made both in Europe and in Latin America. The enormous gap was, however, the colonial difference to which, once again, Anderson ([1983] 1991) was oblivious.

VIII

Once upon a time I was convinced that there is no such a thing as "inside and outside." I still hear today such a statement, in which I no longer believe. I am not saying, of course, that "there are" inside and outside, but that neither of such proposition holds water and that both are supported by the same epistemological presupposition: that a referential assertion can be made regarding the world and that assertions can be judged by their true referential value. I understand that the assertion "there is no such a thing like inside and outside" has another admonition. The question is not whether such a "thing" exists or doesn't exist. To say that "there is an inside and outside" is as absurd as to say that there is not. For who can tell us really which one is true beyond God? On the other hand, both propositions—as I just stated them—are supported in a very questionable principle: that it is possible to assert what really is or is not. What I do seriously believe is that what "is" is someone asserting what there "is." The undeniable fact is the assertion itself, whether or not the content of the assertion corresponds to what the assertion asserts. I do believe, consequently, that the glass is indeed half full as it is half empty.

However, there is another caution to the assertion that "there is no such a thing as inside and outside." What the proposition asserts is that we should eliminate dichotomies from our vocabulary. And in this principle I do believe, since colonial discourse was one of the most powerful strategies in the imaginary of the modern/colonial world system for producing dichotomies that justified the will to power. Historically, that is that. It is fine with me to assert that there is no inside and outside, out there in the world. It is fine for me to eliminate dichotomies, or at least to try. What is more difficult to achieve is forgetting or eliminating the historical dichotomies that colonial discourse and epistemology imposed upon the world by inventing colonial differences.

I am not so much interested here in a logical as I am in pursuing a historical argument. If you talk about interior and exterior borders (e.g., exteriority) in the modern/colonial world system, you are in some ways presupposing that there is indeed an outside and an inside. If you assert, furthermore, that

"Occident" is the overarching metaphor of the modern/colonial world imaginary, you are somewhat asserting that "Occident" defines the interior while you are also presupposing that there is an exterior, whatever that exterior may be. Of course, you can say that the "totality" is the sum of the interior and the exterior of the system and, therefore, there is no outside of the totality. That is fine, but it is historically dangerous and irrelevant. Historically, and in the modern/colonial world, the borders have been set by the coloniality of power versus colonial difference.

Historically, and in the frame of the modern/colonial world system, I hear today assertions equivalent to the logico metaphysical "there is no outside and inside." It so happens that such an assertion is pronounced by colleagues who are clearly placing themselves "inside" and, by so doing, being oblivious to the "outside." I have heard, on the other hand, colleagues (more clearly colleagues in some corner of the Third World) who do believe in the inside/outside distinctions. Now, one could explain this fact by saying that, it is unfortunate, but they are theoretically behind, underdeveloped, as they do not know yet that the last discovery in the humanities in the metropolitan research centers is that truly there is no such thing as inside and outside. It would be nice to have such an explanation, except that it counters the facts. Colleagues in the Third World asserting vehemently the distinction between inside and outside (which is made in the form of center and periphery, or center and margin, or First and Third World) are the ones who are most theoretically sophisticated and "developed." I also know colleagues in the Third World who will no doubt emphatically assert that there is no inside and outside. It may be that they are the less theoretically sophisticated and the most intellectually colonized, repeating and rehearsing dominant propositions coming from an academic avant-garde intelligentsia, and responding to local histories "interior" to the modern/colonial world.

Inside and outside, center and periphery are double metaphors that are more telling about the loci of enunciation than to the ontology of the world. There are and there aren't inside and outside, center and periphery. What really is is the saying of agents affirming or denying these oppositions within the coloniality of power, the subalternization of knowledge, and the colonial difference. The last horizon of border thinking is not only working toward a critique of colonial categories; it is also working toward redressing the subalternization of knowledges and the coloniality of power. It also points toward a new way of thinking in which dichotomies can be replaced by the complementarity of apparently contradictory terms. Border thinking could open up the doors to an other tongue, an other thinking, an other logic superseding the long history of the modern/colonial world, the coloniality of power, the subalternization of knowledges and the colonial difference.

Bibliography

Aarsleff, Hand. 1982. *From Locke to Saussure: Essays on the Study of Language and Intellectual History.* Minneapolis: University of Minnesota Press.

Abdel-Malek, Anouar. 1981. *Social Dialectics.* Vol. 1, *Civilizations and Social Theory.* London: Macmillan.

Abu-Lughod, Janet L. 1989. *Before European Hegemony: The World System, A.D. 1250–1350.* New York: Oxford University Press.

Adam, I., and H. Tifin, eds. 1990. *Past the Last Post: Theorizing Post-Colonialism and Post-Modernism.* Calgary, Alberta: University of Calgary Press.

Adams, Hazard. 1988. "Canons: Literary Criteria/Power Criteria." *Critical Inquiry* 14: 748–64.

Adorno, Rolena, and Walter D. Mignolo, eds. 1989. *Colonial Discourse.* Special issue *Dispositio/n* 36–38.

Adorno, Theodor W. [1966] 1995. *Negative Dialectics.* New York: Continuum.

Ahmad, Aijaz. 1987. "Jameson's Rhetoric of Otherness and the 'National Allegory.' " *Social Text* 16: 3–25.

———. 1992. *In Theory: Classes, Literatures, Nations.* London: Verso.

Ahmed, Akbar, and Ziauddin Sardar. 1990. *Islam, Globalization and Postmodernity.* New York: Routledge.

Alarcón, Norma. 1990. "The Theoretical Subject(s) of This Bridge Called My Back and Anglo-American Feminism." In *Making Face/Making Soul,* edited by Gloria Anzaldúa, 356–69. San Francisco: Aunt Lute Foundations Books.

———. 1994. "Conjugating Subjects: The Heteroglosia of Essence and Resistance." In *An Other Tongue: Nation and Ethnicity in the Linguistic Borderland,* edited by A. Arteaga, 125–38. Durham, N.C.: Duke University Press.

Al-Azmeh, Aziz. 1993. *Islams and Modernities.* London: Verso.

Albó, Xavier. 1994. "And from Kataristas to MNRistas? The Surprising and Bold Alliance between Aymaras and Neoliberals in Bolivia." In *Indigenous Peoples and Democracy in Latin America,* edited by D. L. Van Cott, 55–82. New York: St. Martin's Press.

———. 1995. "Our Identity Starting from Pluralism in the Base." In *The Postmodern Debate in Latin America,* edited by J. Beverley, J. Oviedo, and M. Aronna, 18–32. Durham, N.C.: Duke University Press.

Albó, X., and R. Barrios, eds. 1993. *Cultura y política.* Vol. 1, *Violencias encubiertas en Bolivia.* La Paz: CIPCA-Aruwiyiri.

Alcoff, Linda. 1995. "The Elimination of Experience in Feminist Theory." Paper presented at the Women Studies Symposium, Cornell University, February 3.

Amin, Samir. 1995a. "Introducción. Mundialización y acumulación capitalista." In *La nueva organización capitalista mundial vista desde el Sur,* vol. 1, *Mundialización y acumulación,* edited by S. Amin and P. González Casanova, 11–50. Barcelona: Anthropos.

———. 1995b. "El debate sobre la mundialización." In *La nueva organización capitalista mundial vista desde el Sur,* vol. 1, *Mundialización y acumulación,* edited by S. Amin and P. González Casanova, 367–90. Barcelona: Anthropos.

Amin, Samir. 1996. "Reflections on the International System." In *Beyond Cultural Imperialism: Globalization, Communication and the New International Order*, edited by P. Golding and P. Harris, 10–24. London: Sage.

Anand, R. P. 1966. "Attitude of the Asian-African Countries towards Certain Problems of International Law." *International Comparative Law Quarterly* 15: 55–75.

Anderson, Benedict. [1983] 1991. *Imagined Communities: Reflections on the Origin and Spread of Nationalism*. Rev. ed. London: Verso.

Angenot, Mard, Jean Bessiere, D. Fokkema, and E. Kushner, eds. 1989. *Théorie litteraire: Problèmes et perspectives*. Paris: PUF.

Anzaldúa, Gloria. 1987. *Borderlands/La frontera: The New Mestiza*. San Francisco: Spinsters/Aunt Lute.

Aparicio, Frances. 1996. "Whose Spanish, Whose Language, Whose Power? An Ethnographic Inquiry into Differential Bilingualism." Paper presented at the conference Relocation of Languages and Cultures, Duke University, May 10–12.

———. 1997. "On Sub-Versive Signifiers. Tropicalizing Languages in the United States." In *Tropicalizations: Transcultural Representations on Latinidad*, edited by F. Aparicio and S. Chávez-Silverman, 194–212. Hanover, N.H.: University Press of New England.

Apel, Karl-Otto. 1996. "Discourse Ethics before the Challenge of Liberation Philosophy." In *The Underside of Modernity: Apel, Rorty, Taylor and the Philosophy of Liberation*, edited by Enrique Dussel, 163–204. Translated and edited by Eduardo Mendieta. Atlantic Highlands, N.J.: Humanities Press.

Apffel-Marglin, F., and S. A. Marglin, eds. 1990. *Dominating Knowledge: Development, Culture and Resistance*. Oxford: Clarendon Press.

Appadurai, Arjun. 1996. *Modernity at Large: Cultural Dimensions of Globalization*. Minneapolis: University of Minnesota Press.

Appiah, Kwame Anthony. 1991. "Is the Post- in Postmodernism the Post- in Postcolonial?" *Critical Inquiry* 17: 336–57.

———. 1996. "Against National Culture." In *Text and Nation*, edited by P. C. Pfeiffer and L. Garcia-Moreno, 175–90. Columbia, S.C.: Camden House.

Ardao, Arturo. 1980. *América Latina y la Latinidad*. Mexico: UNAM.

———. 1993. *Génesis de la idea y el nombre de América Latina*. Caracas: Centro de Estudios "Romulo Gallegos."

Arendt, Hannah. [1948] 1968. *The Origins of Totalitarianism*. New York: Harcourt, Brace.

Arguedas, José Maria. 1962. *Tupac Amaru Kamaq Taytanchisman*. Lima: Ediciones Salqantay.

———. 1975. *Formación de una cultura nacional indoamericana*. Mexico: Siglo XXI.

Aricó, José. 1980. *Marx y América Latina*. Lima: Centro de Estudios para el Desarrollo y la Participación.

———. 1988. *La cola del diablo: itinerario de Gramsci en América Latina*. Buenos Aires: Nueva Sociedad.

Arnheim, Rudolf. 1988. *The Power of the Center: A Study of Composition in the Visual Arts*. Berkeley: University of California Press.

Arnold, James. 1995. "The Gendering of Créolité. The Erotics of Colonialism." In *Penser la créolité*, edited by M. Condé and M. Conttenet-Hage, 19–40. Paris: Editions Karthala.

Arrighi, Giovanni. 1994. *The Long Twentieth Century*. London: Verso.

———. 1998. "Capitalism and the Modern World-System: Rethinking the Nondebates of the 1970's." *Review* 21, no. 1: 113–39.

Arteaga, Alfred, ed. 1994. *An Other Tongue: Nation and Ethnicity in the Linguistic Borderlands*. Durham, N.C.: Duke University Press.

Asad, Talal. 1988. "The Concept of Cultural Translation in British Social Anthropology." In *Writing Culture: The Poetics and Politics of Ethnography*, edited by James Clifford and George E. Marcus, 141–64. Berkeley: University of California Press.

Azpurúa, Ramón, and José Felix Blanco. 1875–78. *Documentos para la historia del Libertador*. Caracas: Impr. de "La Opinión nacional."

Baker, Houston. 1988. "The Promised Body: Reflections on Canon in an Afro-American Context." *Poetics Today* 9, no. 2: 339–56.

Balibar, Etienne. 1985. *Spinoza et la politique*. Paris: Press Universitaires de France.

———. 1994. *Masses, Classes, Ideas: Studies on Politics and Philosophy before and after Marx*. Translated by J. Swenson. New York: Routledge.

Balibar, E., and I. Wallerstein. [1988] 1991. *Race, Nation, Class: Ambiguous Identities*. London: Verso.

Balutansky, K. M., and M. A. Sourieau. 1998. *Caribbean Creolization: Reflections on the Cultural Dynamics of Language, Literature and Identity*. Barbados: University Press of the West Indies.

Barker, F., P. Hulme, and M. Iversen, eds. 1994. *Colonial Discourse/Postcolonial Theory*. Manchester: Manchester University Press.

Barragán, Rossana. 1997. "The Spirit of Bolivian Modernity. Citizenship, Infamy and Patriarchal Hierarchy." *Economic and Political Weekly* 32, no. 30: 58–67.

Barrán, José Pedro. 1990. *Historia de la Sensibilidad en Uruguay*. Vol. 2, *El disciplinamiento, 1860–1920*. Montevideo: Facultad de Ciencias y Humanidades.

Bauzon, Leslie E. 1997. "Comments on the Borderless State of Indigenous Culture in the Process of Globalization." In *Globalization and Indigenous Culture*, 122–33. Tokyo: Institute for Japanese Culture and Classics.

Becker, Alton. 1991. "A Short Essay on Languaging." In *Research and Reflexivity*, edited by Frederick Steier, 226–34. London: Sage.

Behdad, Ali. 1994. *Belated Travelers: Orientalism in the Age of Colonial Dissolution*. Durham, N.C.: Duke University Press.

Béji, Héle. 1982. *Désenchantement national*. Paris: Maspéro.

———. 1997. *L'imposture culturelle*. Paris: Stock.

Benhabib, Seyla. 1986. *Critique, Norm and Utopia: A Study of the Foundations of Critical Theory*. New York: Columbia University Press.

Berger, Mark T. 1993. "Civilizing the South: U.S. Rise to Hegemony in the Americas and the Roots of 'Latin American Studies,' 1898–1945." *Bulletin of Latin American Research* 12, no. 1: 1–48.

———. 1995. *Under Northern Eyes: Latin American Studies and U.S. Hegemony in the Americas, 1898–1990*. Bloomington: Indiana University Press.

Bernabé, Jean, Patrick Chamoiseau, and Raphael Confiant. [1989] 1993. *Éloge de la Créolité/In Praise of Creoleness*. Paris: Gallimard.

Bernasconi, Robert. 1997. "African Philosophy's Challenge to Continental Philosophy." In *Postcolonial African Philosophy: A Critical Reader*, edited by C. E. Eze, 183–96. Oxford: Blackwell.

Beverley, J. 1996. "Sobre la situación actual de los estudios culturales." In *Asedios a la heterogeneidad cultural. Libro de homenaje a Antonio Cornejo Polar*, edited by J. A. Mazzotti and U. J. Zevallos Aguilar. Philadelphia: Asociación Internacional de Peruanistas.

Beverley, J., J. Oviedo, and M. Aronna, eds. 1995. *The Postmodern Debate in Latin America*. Durham, N.C.: Duke University Press.

Beuchot, Mauricio. 1981. *El problema de los universales*. Mexico: Universidad Autonoma de Mexico.

Bhabha, Homi. 1994. *The Location of Culture*. New York: Routledge.

Bilbao, Francisco. [1862] 1988. *La América en peligro*. Caracas: Biblioteca Ayacucho.

———. [1864] 1988. *El evangelio Americano*. Caracas: Biblioteca Ayacucho.

Bolívar, Simón. [1783–1830] 1985. *Doctrina del Libertador*. Caracas: Biblioteca Ayacucho.

Bonfil Batalla, Guillermo. 1982. *Etnodesarrollo y etnocidio*. Mexico: FLACSO.

Bonilla, F., E. Meléndez, R. Morales, M. de Angeles Tórres, eds. 1998. *U.S. Latinos, Latin Americans, and the Paradox of Interdependence*. Philadelphia: Temple University Press.

Boone, Elizabeth, and Walter D. Mignolo, eds. 1994. *Writing without Words: Alternative Literacies in Mesoamerica and the Andes*. Durham, N.C.: Duke University Press.

Bornholdt, Laura. 1944. "The Abbé de Pradt and the Monroe Doctrine." *Hispanic American Historical Review* 24: 201–21.

Bourdieu, Pierre. 1982. *Ce que parler veut dire: L'économie des échanges linguistiques*. Paris: Fayard.

———. 1991. *Language and Symbolic Power*. Edited by John B. Thompson. Cambridge: Polity/Blackwell.

———. 1992. "Thinking about Limits." In *Cultural Theory and Cultural Change*, edited by M. Featherstone. London: Sage.

———.1998a. "L'essence du néoliberalisme." *Le Monde Diplomatique*, no. 548: 3.

———. 1998b. *Contre-feux. Propos pour servir á la résistance contre l'invasion néolibéral*. Paris: Raison d'Agir.

Bouysse-Cassagne, T., O. Harris, T. Platt, and V. Cereceda. 1987. *Tres reflexiones sobre el pensamiento Andino*. La Paz: Hisbol.

Boyarin, J. 1996. *Thinking in Jewish*. Chicago: Chicago University Press.

Brathwaite, Edward Kamau. [1977] 1993. "La criollizacion en las Antillas de lengua inglesa." In *Fuentes de la cultura Latinoamericana*, edited by L. Zea, 3:251–72. Mexico: Fondo de Cultura Económica.

———. 1983. *Third World Poems*. Essex: Logman.

———. 1984. *History of the Voice: The Development of National Languages in Anglophone Caribbean Poetry*. London: New Bacon.

———. 1992. "Reading of His Poetry." Paper presented at the workshop The Inventions of Africa: Africa and the Literature of the Continent and the Diaspora. Center for Afroamerican and African Studies, University of Michigan, Ann Arbor, April 17.

Bruns, Gerald L. 1984. "Canon and Power in the Hebrew Scriptures." *Critical Inquiry* 10: 463–79.

Bull, H., and Watson, eds. 1984. *The Expansion of International Society*. New York: Oxford University Press.

Burgess, John William. 1890. *Political Science and Comparative Constitutional Law.* Boston: Ginn.

Calderón, H., and J. Saldívar, eds. 1991. *Criticism in the Borderlands: Studies in Chicano Literature, Culture, and Ideology.* Durham, N.C.: Duke University Press, 1991.

Calhoun, Craig. 1995a. *Critical Social Theory.* New York: Blackwell.

———. 1995b. *Critical Social Theory: Culture, History and the Challenge of Difference.* Cambridge: Cambridge University Press.

Canal Feijóo, Bernardo. 1954. *Confines de occidente. Notas para una sociología de la cultura americana.* Buenos Aires: Editorial Raigal.

Cándido, Antonio. 1995. *Essays on Literature and Society.* Translated, edited, and introduced by Howard S. Becker. Princeton, N.J.: Princeton University Press.

Capra, Fritjof. 1975. *The Tao of Physics: An Exploration of the Parallels between Modern Physics and Eastern Mysticism.* New York: Bantam Books.

Caputano Scarlato, Francisco, et al., eds. 1994. *O novo mapa do mundo. Globalização e espaço Latino-Americano.* São Paolo: Editora Hucitec.

Cardoso, Fernando Enrique. 1977. "The Consumption of Dependency Theory in the United States." *Latin American Research Review* 12, no. 3. Reprinted in *As idéias e seu lugar,* 125–50. Petropolis: Editora Vozes, 1993.

———. 1993. *As idéias e seu lugar.* Petropolis: Editorial Vozes.

Cardoso, Fernando Enrique, and E. Faletto. 1969. *Dependencia y desarrollo en América Latina. Ensayo de interpretación sociológica.* Mexico: Siglo XXI.

———. 1979. *Dependency and Development in Latin America.* Berkeley: University of California Press.

Cassirer, E. 1951. *The Philosophy of the Enlightenment.* Princeton: Princeton Uunversity Press.

Cassirer, E., P. O. Kristeller, and J. H. Randall Jr., eds. 1948. *The Renaissance Philosophy of Man.* Chicago: Chicago University Press.

Castro-Gómez, Santiago. 1996. *Crítica de la razón latinoamericana.* Barcelona: Puvill Libros.

Cerrón-Palomino, Rodolfo. 1989. "Language Policy in Peru: A Historial Overview." In *Bilingual Education and Language Planning in Indigenous Latin America,* edited by N. H. Hornberger, 11–33. Special issue *International Journal of the Sociology of Language* 77.

Céspedes del Castillo, Guillermo. 1985. *América hispánica (1492–1898).* Madrid: Labor.

Chakrabarty, Dipesh. 1992a. "Postcoloniality and the Artifice of History: Who Speaks for 'Indian' Pasts?" *Representations* 37: 1–26.

———. 1992b. "Provincializing Europe: Postcoloniality and the Critique of History." *Cultural Studies* 6, no. 3: 337–57.

———. 1993. "Marx after Marxism: History, Subalternity and Differene." *Meanjin* 52, no. 3, 421–34.

———. 1993. "Marx after Marxism: Subaltern Histories and the Question of Difference." *Polygraph* 6–7: 11–16.

Chambers, Ian, and Lidie Curti, eds. 1996. *The Post-Colonial Question.* New York: Routledge.

Chatterjee, Partha. 1986. *Nationalist Thought and the Colonial World.* Minneapolis: University of Minnesota Press.

Chatterjee, Partha. 1993. *The Nation and Its Fragments: Colonial and Postcolonial Histories*. Princeton: Princeton University Press.

———. 1997. "Talking about our Modernity in Two Languages." In *A Possible India: Essays in Political Criticism*, 263–85. New Delhi: Oxford.

Chen, Kuan-Hsing. 1992. "Voices from the Outside: Towards a New Internationalist Localism." *Cultural Studies* 6, no. 3: 476–84.

Chen, Xuaineu. 1995. *Occidentalism: A Theory of Counter-Discourse in Post-Mao China*. Oxford: Oxford University Press.

Choque, Roberto, Humberto Mamani, and Esteban Ticona, et al. 1992. *Educación indígena: ciudadanía o colonización?* Prologue by Victor Hugo-Cárdenas. La Paz, Bolivia: Aruwiyiri.

Churchill, Ward. 1992. "I am Indigenist." In *Struggle for the Land: A Land Rights Reader*. Monroe, Maine: Common Courage.

———. 1997. *A Little Matter of Genocide Holocaust and Denial in the Americas, 1492 to the Preseent*. San Francisco: City Lights Books.

Citarella, Lucía. 1989. "Problemas de educación y modelos de desarrollo: el caso de los criollos del Caribe." In *Pueblos indios, estados y educación*, edited by Luis Enrique López and Ruth Moya, 167–88. Lima: Proyecto EBI.

Cliff, Michelle. 1985. *The Land of Look Behind*. Ithaca, N.Y.: Firebrand Books.

Clifford, James. 1989. "Notes on Travel and Theory." *Inscriptions* 5: 177–88.

———. 1997. "Traveling Cultures." In *Routes: Travel and Translation in the Twentieth Century*, 17–46. Cambridge, Mass.: Harvard University Press.

Cline, Howard F. 1966. "The Latin American Studies Association: A Summary Survey with Appendix." *Latin American Research Review* 2, no.1: 57–79.

Coe, Michael D. 1992. *Breaking the Maya Code*. New York: Thames and Hudson.

Colmenares, Germán. 1987. *Las convenciones contra la cultura. Ensayos sobre la historiografía hispanoamericana del siglo XIX*. Bogotá: Tercer Mundo Editores.

Coltelli, Laura. 1990. *Winged Words: American Indian Writers Speak*. Lincoln: University of Nebraska Press.

Condé, Maryse. 1998. "*Créolité* without Creole Language?" In *Caribbean Creolization: Reflections on the Cultural Dyamics of Language, Literature and Identity*, edited by K. M. Balutansky and M. A. Sourieau, 101–9. Gainsville: University Press of Florida.

Condé, Maryse, and Cottenet-Hage, M., eds. 1995. *Penser la créolité*. Paris: Editions Karthala.

Conde, Roberto Cortés, and Ezequiel Gallo. 1967. *La formación de la Argentina moderna*. Buenos Aires: Paidos.

Constable, Olivia Remie, ed. 1997. *Medieval Iberia: Readings from Christian, Muslim and Jewish Sources*. Philadelphia: University of Pennsylvania Press.

Cornejo Polar, Antonio. 1989. *La formación de la tradición literaria en el Perú*. Lima: CEP.

———. 1994. *Escribir en el aire. Ensayo sobre la heterogeneidad socio-cultural en las literaturas andinas*. Lima: Editorial Horizonte.

Coronil, Fernando. 1995. "Transculturation and the Politics of Theory: Countering the Center, Cuban Counterpoint." Introduction to *Cuban Counterpoint*, by Fernando Ortíz. Durham, N.C.: Duke University Press.

————. 1996. "Beyond Occidentalism: Toward Nonimperial Geohistorical Categories." *Cultural Anthropology* 11, no. 1: 52–87.

————. 1997. *The Magical State: Nature, Money and Modernity in Venezuela*. Chicago: University of Chicago Press.

Coulmas, Florian. 1988. "What is a National Language Good For?" In *Forked Tongues: What Are National Languages Good For?*, edited by F. Coulmas, 1–25. Singapore: Karoma Publishers.

Cuming, Bruce. 1997. "Boundary Displacement: Area Studies and International Studies during and after the Cold War." *Bulletin of Concerned Asian Scholars* 29, no. 1: 6–26.

Curtius, Ernst-Robert. 1929. *L'idée de civilisation dans la conscience française*. Translated by Henri Jourdan. Paris: Publication de la Conciliation Internationale.

————. 1953. *European Literature and the Latin Middle Ages*. Translated by W. R. Trask. Princeton: Princeton University Press. Originally published as *Europaische Literatur un lateinisches Mittelalter*. Bern: A. Francke AG Verlag, 1948.

Cussen, Antonio. 1992. *Bello and Bolívar: Poetry and Politics in the Spanish American Revolution*. Cambridge: Cambridge University Press.

Das, Veena. 1989. "Subaltern as Perspective." *Subaltern Studies* 6: 310–24.

De Acosta, José. [1590] 1962. *Historia natural y moral de las Indias*. Mexico: Fondo de Cultura Económica.

De Ipola, Emilio. 1997. "Jose Aricó: pensar entre reflejos." In *Las cosas del creer. Creencia, lazo social y comunidad política*. Buenos Aires: Ariel.

Deleuze, Gilles, and Felix Guattari. [1987] 1996. *A Thousand Plateaus: Capitalism and Schizophrenia*. Translated by B. Massumi. Minneapolis: University of Minnesota Press.

Delich, Francisco. 1964. "La teoría de la revolución en Frantz Fanon." *Pasado y Presente* 4: 23–41.

Deloria, Vine, Jr. 1978. "Civilization and Isolation." *North American Review* 263, no. 1: 11–14.

————. 1990. "Vision and Community." In *Yearning to Breathe Free: Liberation Theologies in the United States*, edited by Mar Peter-Raoul et al., 71–79. New York: Orbis Books.

————. 1999. *For this Land: Writings on Religion in America*. New York: Routlege.

De Nebrija, Antonio. 1481. *Introductiones latinae*. Salamanca.

————. 1482. *Grámatica de la lengua castellana*. Salamanca.

————. 1517. *Reglas de orthografía en la lengua castellana*. Alcalá de Henares.

Depestre, René. [1969] 1993. "Problemas de la identidad del hombre negro en las literaturas antillanas." In *Fuentes de la cultura Latinoamericana*, edited by L. Zea, 1:231–41. Mexico: Fondo de Cultura Económica.

Derrida, Jacques. 1967. *De la grammatologie*. Paris: Minuit.

————. [1972] 1991. *Positions*. Translated by A. Bass. Chicago: University of Chicago Press.

————. 1992. *Points . . .* Edited by E. Weber. Translated by P. Kamuf et al. Standford, Calif.: Standford University Press.

————. 1996. *Le monolinguisme de l'autre*. Paris: Galilee.

————. 1998. *Monolingualism of the Other or the Prosthesis of Origin*. Translated by Patrick Mensah. Stanford, Calif.: Stanford University Press.

Desnoes, Edmundo. 1994. "Nacer en Español." In *An Other Tongue: Nation and Ethnicity in the Linguistic Borderlands*, edited by A. Arteaga. Durham, N.C.: Duke University Press.

De Vos, Jan. 1994. *Vivir en frontera. La experiencia de los Indios de Chiapas*. Mexico: Secretaría de Educación Pública.

Dirlik, Arif. 1994. "The Postcolonial Aura: Third World Criticism in the Age of Global Capitalism." *Critical Inquiry* 20, no. 2: 328–56.

Dissanayake, Wimal, and Mimi Nichter. 1987. "Native Sensibility and Literary Discourse." In *Discourse across Cultures: Strategies in World Englishes*, edited by Larry E. Smith, 114–22. New York: Prentice-Hall.

Djaït, Hichem. [1980] 1990. *Europa y el Islam*. Madrid: Libertarias/Prodhufi, S.A.

Dorfman, Ariel. 1998. *Heading South, Looking North: A Bilingual Journey*. New York: Farrar, Strauss and Giroux.

Du Bois, W.E.B. [1905] 1990. *The Souls of Black Folk*. New York: Vintage Books.

——. 1995. *A Reader*. Edited by D. Levering Lewis. New York: Henry Holt.

——. 1996. *On Race and Culture*. Edited by B. W. Bell, E. R. Grosholz, and J. B. Stewart. New York: Routledge.

Durand, Gilbert. 1969. "On the Disfiguration of the Image of Man in the West." *Eronos* 38: 45–93.

During, Simon. 1985. "Postmodernism or Postcolonialism." *Landfall* 155: 366–80.

Dussel, Enrique. [1973] 1976. *History and the Theology of Liberation: A Latin American Perspective*. Translated by J. Drury. New York: Orbis Books.

——. 1973. *Caminos de la liberacion latino-americana*. Vol. 1. Buenos Aires: Latinóamerica Libros.

——. [1974] 1985. *Philosophy of Liberation*. Translated by A. Martinez and Ch. Morkovsky. New York: Orbis Books.

——. 1975. *Liberación Latinoamericana y Emanuel Levinas*. Buenos Aires: Editorial Bonum.

——. 1985. *La producción teórica de Marx*. México: Siglo XXI.

——. 1988. *El capital: los Grundrisse (1857–1858)*. México: Siglo XXI.

——. 1990. *El último Marx (1863–1882) y la liberación latinoamericana*. México: Siglo XXI.

——. [1992] 1995. *The Invention of the Americas*. Translated by Michael D. Barber. New York: Continuum.

——. [1993] 1995. "Eurocentrism and Modernity." *Boundary* 2: 20–23. Reprinted in *The Postmodernism Debate in Latin America*, edited by J. Beverley, J. Oviedo, and M. Aronna, 65–76. Durham, N.C.: Duke University Press.

——, ed. 1994a. *Debate en torno a la ética del discurso de Apel. Diálogo filosófico Norte-Sur desde América Latina*. Mexico: Siglo XXI.

——. 1994b. *Historia de la filosofía y filosofía de la liberación*. Bogotá: Editorial Nueva América.

——. 1995. "Ethical Sense of the 1994 Maya Rebellion in Chiapas." *Journal of Hispano-Latino-Theology* 2–3: 41–56.

——, ed. 1996a. *The Underside of Modernity: Apel, Ricoeur, Rorty, Taylor and the Philosophy of Liberation*. Translated and edited by E. Mendieta. Atlantic Highlands, N.J.: Humanities Press.

———. 1996b. "World System, Politics, and the Economic of Liberation Philosophy." In *The Underside of Modernity: Apel, Rorty, Taylor and the Philosophy of Liberation*, translated and edited by Eduardo Mendieta, 213–39. Atlantic Highlands, N.J.: Humanities Press.

———. 1998a. "Beyond Eurocentrism: The World-System and the Limits of Modernity." In *The Cultures of Globalization*, edited by F. Jameson and M. Miyoshi, 3–30. Durham, N.C.: Duke University Press.

———. 1998b. *Etica de la liberación en la edad de la globalización y de la exclusión*. Mexico: Universidad Autonoma Metropolitana-Iztapalapa.

Duviols, Pierre. 1971. *La lutte contre les religions autochtones dans le Pérou colonial (L'extirpation de l'idolatrie entre 1532 et 1660)*. Paris: Institut Français d'Etudes Andines.

Elias, Norbert. [1937] 1982. *The Civilizing Process*. Vol. 1, *The History of Manners*. Translated by E. Jephcott. New York: Pantheon Books.

———. 1978. *The Civilizing Process*. Vol. 2, *State Formation and Civilization*. Translated by E. Jephcott. New York: Pantheon Books.

———. 1987. "The Retreat of Sociologists into the Present." *Theory, Culture and Society* 4, nos. 2–3:223–47.

———. 1998. *On Civilization, Power, and Knowledge: Selected Writings*. Edited with an introduction by Stephen Mennell and Johan Goudsblom. Chicago: University of Chicago Press.

Engels, Frederick, and Karl Marx. 1959. *On Colonialism*. Moscow: Progress Publishers.

Escobar, Arturo. 1995. *Encountering Development: The Making and Unmaking of the Third World*. Princeton: Princeton University Press.

———. 1997. "Cultural Politics and Biological Diversity: State, Capital, and Social Movements in the Pacific Coast of Colombia." In *The Politics of Culture in the Shadow of Capital*, edited by L. Lowe and D. Lloyd, 201–26. Durham, N.C.: Duke University Press.

Esteva, Gustavo. 1996. "Hosting the Otherness of the Other: The Case of the Green Revolution." In *Decolonizing Knowledge: From Development to Dialogue*, edited by F. Apffel-Marglin and S. A. Marglin, 185–248. Oxford: Clarendon Press.

Étienne, Bruno. 1987. *L'Islamisme Radical*. Paris: Hachette.

Eze, C. E., ed. 1997a. Post*colonial African Philosophy: A Critical Reader*. Oxford: Blackwell.

———. 1997b. "The Color of Reason: The Idea of 'Race' in Kant's Anthropology." In Post*colonial African Philosohpy: A Critical Reader*, edited by C. E. Eze, 103–40. Oxford: Blackwell.

———. 1997c. "Democracy or Consensus? A Response to Wiredu." In Post*colonial African Philosophy: A Critical Reader*, edited by C. E. Eze, 313–22. Oxford: Blackwell.

———. 1997d. "Toward a Critical Theory of Postcolonial African Identitities." In Post*colonial African Philosohpy: A Critical Reader*, edited by C. E. Eze, 339–46. Oxford: Blackwell.

EZLN. 1995a. *Documentos y Comunicados*. Vol. 1, *Prólogo de Antonio García León*. Vol. 2, *Cronica de Carlos Monsivais*. Mexico: Era.

EZLN. 1995b. *Shadows of Tender Fury:* The Letters and Communiques of Subcomandante Marcos and the Zapatista Army of National Liberation. Translated by Frank Bardacke, Leslie Lopez, and the Watsonville, California, Human Rights Committee. Introduction by John Ross. New York: Montly Review Press.

EZLN, CG. 1995. "Declaration of the Lacandon Jungle: Today We Say 'Enough.' " In *Shadows of Tender Fury:* The Letters and Communiques of Subcomandante Marcos and the Zapatista Army of National Liberation, translated by Frank Bardacke, Leslie Lopez, and the Watsonville, California, Human Rights Committee, introduction by John Ross, 51–54. New York: Monthly Review Press.

Fabian, Johannes. 1983. *Time and the Other: How Anthropology Makes Its Object.* New York: Columbia University Press.

Fanon, Frantz. [1952] 1967. *Black Skin, White Masks.* Translated by Charles Lam Markmann. New York: Grove Press.

———. [1959] 1967. *A Dying Colonialism.* Translated by H. Chevalier. New York: Grove Press.

———. 1961. *Les damnés de la terre.* Paris: Maspéro.

———. [1961] 1963. *The Wretched of the Earth.* Translated by C. Farrington. New York: Grove Weidenfeld.

———. [1964] 1988. *Toward the African Revolution.* Translated by H. Chevalier. New York: Grove Press.

Farías, Victor. 1987. *Heidegger et le nazisme.* Paris: Verdier.

Fernández Pardo, Carlos A. 1971. *Frantz Fanon.* Buenos Aires: Editorial Galerna.

Fernández Retamar, Roberto. [1973] 1989. *Caliban and Other Essays.* Translated by E. Baker. Minneapolis: University of Minnesota Press.

———. [1974] 1995. "Nuestra América y Occidente." In *Para el perfil definitivo del hombre,* 222–50. Cuba: Editorial Letras Cubanas.

———. 1981. *Para el perfil definitivo del hombre.* Ciudad de La Habana: Editorial Letras Cubanas.

Ferrater, Mora, José. [1944] 1969. *Diccionario de Filosofía.* Mexico D.F.: Editorial Atlante.

Ferré, Rosario. 1995. *The House in the Lagoon.* New York: Plume Book.

———. 1998. *Eccentric neighborhoods.* New York: Farrar, Straus, Giroux.

Fichte, Johann Gottlieb. [1808] 1922. *Addresses to the German Nation.* Translated by R. F. Jones and G. H. Turnbull. Chicago: Open Court Company.

Fishman, Joshua. 1996. "Perfecting the Perfect: Improving the Beloved Language." In *Text and Nation,* edited by P. C. Pfeiffer and L. Garcia-Moreno, 3–16. Columbia, S.C.: Camden House.

———. 1997. *In Praise of the Beloved Language: A Comparative View of Positive Ethnolinguistic Consciousness.* The Hague: Mouton de Gruyter.

Fishman, Joshua, and Avon Clevedon. 1989. *Language and Ethnicity in a Minority Sociolinguistic Perspective.* Philadelphia: Multilingual Matters.

Fiske, John. 1902a. *American Political Ideas Viewed from the Standpoint of Universal History.* Three lectures delivered at the Royal Institute of Great Britain in May 1880. New York: Harper & Brothers.

———. 1902b. *The Discovery of America with Some Account of Ancient America and the Spanish Conquest.* Boston: Houghton Mifflin.

Fontana, Joseph. 1994. *Europa ante el espejo.* Barcelona: Crítica.

Fornet, Ambrosio. 1997. "Soñar en cubano, escribir en inglés: una reflexión sobre la triada lengua-nación-literatura." *Temas* 10: 4–12.

Foucault, Michel. 1966. *Les mots et les choses: Une archeologie des sciences humaines.* Paris: Gallimard.

———. 1969. *L'archéologie du savoir.* Paris: Gallimard.

———. [1972–77] 1980. *Power/Knowledge.* Edited by C. Gordon. New York: Pantheon Books.

———. [1976] 1980. "Lecture One: 7 January 1976." In *Power/Knowledge: Selected Interviews and Other Writings, 1972–1977.* Edited by C. Gordon. New York: Pantheon Books.

Franco, Carlos. 1980. "Presentación." In *Marx y América Latina* by J. Arico, 9–36. Lima: Centro de Estudios para el Desarrollo y la Participación.

Frankenberg, Ruth, and Lata Mani. 1993. "Crosscurrents, Crosstalk: Race, 'Postcoloniality' and the Politics of Location." *Cultural Studies* 7, no. 2: 292–310.

Freire, Paulo. [1972] 1993. *Pedagogy of the Oppressed.* New York: Continuum.

Fukuyama, Francis. 1992. *The End of History and the Last Man.* New York: Avon Books.

García Canclini, Néstor. [1989] 1995. *Hybrid Cultures: Strategies for Entering and Leaving Modernity.* Translated by C. L. Chiappari and S. L. Lopez. Minneapolis: University of Minnesota Press.

———. 1995. *Consumidores y ciudadanos. Conflictos multiculturales de la globalización.* México: Grijalbo.

García Rodriguez, Gloria. 1996. *La esclavitud desde la esclavitud. La visión de los siervos.* México: Centro de Investigación Científica Ing Jorge L. Tamayo.

Garg, Pulin K. 1986. "Keynote Address." In *Proceedings of the International Conference on Transcience and Transitions in Organization,* vol. 1, *Corporate Culture in India: Perspectives of Chief Executives,* edited by I. K. Parikh, V. K. Garg, and P. Garg. New Delhi: ISISD.

Garg, Pulin K., and Indira J. Parikh. 1995. *Crossroads of Culture: A Study in the Culture of Transience.* New Delhi: Sage.

Garvin, P., ed. 1970. *Cognition: A Multiple View.* New York: Spartan Books.

Geertz, Clifford. 1973. "Thick Description: Toward an Interpretive Theory of Culture." In *The Interpretation of Culture,* 3–32. New York: Basic Books.

———. [1976] 1983. "Art as a Cultural System." *Modern Language Note* 91. Reprinted in *Local Knowledge,* 94–120. New York: Basic Books.

Gerbi, Antonello. [1955] 1982. *La naturaleza de las Indias Nuevas.* Mexico: Fondo de Cultura Económica.

Gerholm, Tomas. 1994, "Two Muslim Intellectuals in the Postmodern West: Akbar Ahamed and Ziauddin Sardar." In *Islam, Globalization and Postmodernity,* edited by A. S. Ahmed and H. Donnan, 190–212. New York: Routledge.

Giddens, Anthony. 1994. *Beyond Left and Right: The Future of Radical Politics.* Stanford, Calif.: Stanford University Press.

Gilroy, Paul. 1990–91. "It Ain't Where You're From, It's Where You're At: The Dialectics of Diasporic Identification." *Third Text* 13: 3–16.

———. 1993. *Black Atlantic: Modernity and Double Consciousness.* Cambridge, Mass.: Harvard University Press.

Glissant, Edouard. [1981] 1989. *Caribbean Discourse: Selected Essays.* Translated by J. M. Dash. Charlottesville: University Press of Virginia.

———. [1990] 1997. *Poetics of Relation.* Translated by Betsy Wing. Ann Arbor: University of Michigan Press.

———. 1998. "Le divers du monde est imprevisible." Keynote address at the conference Beyond Dichotomies. Stanford University, Stanford, Calif., May 8–10.

Gobineau, Arthur, comte de. [1853–55]. *Essai sur l'inegalité des races humaines.* Philadelphia: Lippincott, 1856. Reprinted as *The Moral and Intellectual Diversity of Races.* New York : Garland, 1984.

Gollnick, Brian. 1994. "Modernity and the Discourse of Allochronism in the Rain Forest of Chiapas." Paper presented at the conference The Wisdom of the Maya. University of Florida, Gainesville, March.

Gong, Gerrit W. 1984. *The Standard of 'Civilization' in International Society.* Oxford: Clarendon Press.

Gonzalbo Aizpurú, Pilar. 1990. *Historia de la educación en la época colonial. La educación de los criollos y la vida urbana.* Mexico: El Colegio de México.

González, Andrew. 1987. "Poetic Imperialism or Indigenous Creativity?: Philippine Literature in English." In *Discourse across Cultures: Strategies in World Englishes,* edited by Larry E. Smith, 141–56. New York: Prentice-Hall.

González Casanova, Pablo. 1965. "Internal Colonialism and National Development." *Studies in Comparative International Development* 1, no. 4: 27–37.

———. 1996. "El colonialismo global y la democracia." In *La nueva organización capitalista mundial vista desde el Sur,* vol. 2, *El estado y la política del Sur del Mundo,* edited by S. Amin and P. González Casanova, 11–144. Barcelona: Anthropos.

González Stephan, Beatriz. 1985. *Contribución al estudio de la historiografía literaria hispanoamericana.* Caracas: Biblioteca de la Academia Nacional de la Historia.

———. 1987. *La historiografía literaria del liéberalismo hispano-americano del Siglo XIX.* Cuba: Casa de las Americas.

Gorostiaga, Xabier. 1993. "Latin America in the New World Order." In *Global Visions: Beyond the New World Order,* edited by J. Brecher, J. Brown Childs, and J. Cutler, 67–86. Boston: South End Press.

Gramsci, Antonio. [1944] 1992. *Prison Notebooks.* Edited with introduction by Joseph A. Buttigieg, translated by Joseph A. Buttigieg and Antonio Callari. New York: Columbia University Press.

Greenfeld, Liah, and Michel Martin. 1988. *Center: Ideas and Institutions.* Chicago: University of Chicago Press.

Grillo, E. F. 1993. "La cosmovisión andina de siempre y la cosmología occidental moderna." In *Desarrollo o descolonización en los Andes?* Lima: Proyecto Andino de Tecnologías Campesinas (PRATEC).

Grosfoguel, Ramón. 1996. "From *Cepalismo* to Neoliberalism. A World-System Approach to Conceptual Shifts in Latin America." *Review* 19, no. 2: 131–54.

———. 1997a. "A TimeSpace Perspective on Development. Recasting Latin American Debates." *Review* 20, nos. 3–4: 465–540.

———. 1997b. "Migrations and Geopolitics in the Greater Antilles. From the Cold War to the Post-Cold War." *Review* 20, no. 1: 115–45.

———. 1998. Introduction to the Workshop on Historical Capitalism, Coloniality of Power and Transmodernity. Fernand Braudel Center for the Study of Economies,

Historical Systems, and Civilizations, State University of New York at Binghamton, December 5.

Gruzinski, Sérge. 1988. *La colonization de l'imaginaire*. Paris: Gallimard.

———. 1990. *La guerre des images. De Christophe Colomb a 'Blade Runner' (1492–2019)*. Paris: Fayard.

Guha, Ramachandra. 1996. "Two Phases of American Environmentalism: A Critical History." In *Decolonizing Knowledge: From Development to Dialogue*, edited by F. Apffeel-Marglin and S. A. Marglin, 110–41. Oxford: Clarendon Press.

Guja, Ranajit. 1988. "On Some Aspects of the Historiography of Colonial India." In *Selected Subaltern Studies*, edited by R. Guha and G. C. Spivak, 37–44. New York: Oxford University Press.

Guizot, M. François. [1828–30] 1868. *Histoire de la civilisation en Europe depuis la chute de l'Empire romain jusqu'à la révolution française*. Paris: Didier.

Gunder Frank A., and Barry K. Gills, eds. 1993. *The World System: Five Hundred Years or Five Thousand?* New York: Routledge.

Gyekye, Kwame. 1997. *Tradition and Modernity: Philosophical Reflections on the African Experience*. New York: Oxford University Press.

Habermas, Jürgen. [1968] 1971. *Knowledge and Human Interests*. Translated by J. Shapiro. New York: Beacon Press.

Hall, Stuart. 1991a. "The Local and the Global: Globalization and Ethnicity." In *Culture, Globalization and the World-System*, edited by A. D. King, 19–39. Binghamton, N.Y.: Art and Art History.

———. 1991b. "Old and New Identities, Old and New Ethnicities." In *Culture, Globalization and the World-System*, edited by A. D. King, 40–68. Binghamton, N.Y.: Art and Art History.

———. 1992. *Stuart Hall: Critical Dialogues in Cultural Studies*. Edited by D. Morley and K.-H. Chen. New York: Routledge.

Hannerz, Ulf. 1987a. "The World in Creolization." *Africa* 57: 546–59.

———. 1987b. "American Culture: Creolized, Creolizing." In *American Culture: Creolized, Creolizing and Other Lectures from NAAS Biennial Conference in Upsala, May 28–31*, edited by E. Asard. Upsala: Swedish Institute for North American Studies.

———. 1991. "Scenarios for Peripheral Cultures." In *Culture, Globalization and the World-System*, edited by A. D. King, 107–28. Binghamton, N.Y.: Art and History.

Haraway, Donna J. 1997. *ModestWitness@FemaleMan_Meets_OncoMouse: Feminism and Technoscience*. New York: Routledge.

Harding, Sandra. 1998. *Is Science Multicultural? Postcolonialism, Feminisms, and Epistemologies*. Bloomington: Indiana University Press.

Harvey, L. P. 1990. *Islamic Spain, 1250 to 1500*. Chicago: University of Chicago Press.

Hay, Denys. 1957. *Europe: The Emergence of an Idea*. Edinburgh: Edinburgh University Press.

Hayek, F. A. 1944. *The Road to Serfdom*. Chicago: University of Chicago Press.

Heath, Shirley Brice. 1972. *Telling Tongues: Language Policy in Mexico, Colony to Nation*. New York: Teachers College Press.

Hegel, G.W.F. 1955. *Lectures on the History of Philosophy*. Translated by E. S. Haldane and Frances H. Simson. New York: Humanities Press.

Hernández Arregui, J. J. 1973. *Qué es el ser nacional?* Buenos Aires: Plus Ultra.

Heidegger, Martin. [1951] 1977. "Building Dwelling Thinking." In *Basic Writings*, 319–68. New York: Harper and Row.

———. [1954] 1977. "What Calls for Thinking?" In *Basic Writings*, 319–68. New York: Harper and Row.

Hinkelammert, Franz J. 1996. *El mapa del emperador. Determinismo, caos, sujeto*. San Jose de Costa Rica: Departamento Ecumenico de Investigaciones.

Hinojosa, Rolando. 1986. *Claros varones de Belken/Fair Gentlemen of Belken County*. Tempe, Ariz.: Bilingual Press.

Hobsbawm, E. J. 1990. *Nations and Nationalism since 1780: Programme, Myth, Reality*. New York: Cambridge University Press.

Hoffner, Joseph. 1957. *La ética colonial española del siglo de oro*. Madrid: Ediciones Cultura Hispánica.

Horkheimer, Max. [1950] 1972. "Traditional and Critical Theory." In *Critical Theory*, 188–214. New York: Herder and Herder.

Horkheimer, Max, and T. W. Adorno. [1947] 1995. *Dialectic of Enlightenment*. New York: Continuum.

Horowitz, Donald L. 1985. *Ethnic Groups in Conflict*. Berkeley: University of California Press.

Hountonkji, Paulin J. [1992] 1988. "Recapturing." In *The Surreptitious Speech: Presence Africaine and the Politics of Otherness, 1947–1987*, edited by V. Y. Mudimbe. Chicago: University of Chicago Press.

Howland, D. R. 1996. *Borders of Chinese Civilization: Geography and History at Empire's End*. Durham, N.C.: Duke University Press.

Humboldt, Wilhelm von. [1836] 1988. *On Language: The Diversity of Human Languages-Structure and Its Influence on the Mental Development of Mankind*. New York: Cambridge University Press.

Huntington, Samuel P. 1993. "The Clash of Civilizations." *Foreign Affairs* 72, no. 3: 28, 48.

———. 1996. *The Clash of Civilizations and the Remaking of World Order*. New York: Simon and Schuster.

Husserl, Edmund. [1950] 1970. *The Crisis of European Sciences and Transcendental Phenomenology*. Translated by David Carr. Evanston, Ill.: Northwestern University Press.

Ianni, Octavio. 1995. *Teorias da globalizaçao*. Rio de Janeiro: Civilizacao Brasileira.

———. 1997. *A era do globalismo*. Rio de Janeiro: Civilizaçao Brasileira.

Ishay, Micheline, ed. 1997. *The Human Rights Reader*. New York: Routledge.

Jameson, Fredric. 1986. "Third-World Literature in the Era of Multinational Capitalism." *Social Text* 15: 65–88.

———. 1987. "A Brief Response." *Social Text* 16: 26–27.

———. 1991. *Postmodernism: Or the Logic of Late Capitalism*. Durham, N.C.: Duke University Press.

Jefferson, Thomas. [1774–1846]. 1998. *The Life and Selected Writings of Thomas Jefferson*. Edited with an introduction by A. Koch and W. Peden. New York: Modern Library.

Jensen, Lionel M. 1997. *Manufacturing Confucianism: Chinese Tradition and Universal Civilization*. Durham, N.C.: Duke University Press.

John, Mary E. 1996. *Discrepant Dislocations: Feminism, Theory and Postcolonial Histories*. Berkeley: University of California Press.

Jonas, Hans. 1958. *The Gnostic Religion: The Message of the Alien God and the Beginnings of Christianity*. New York: Beacon Press.

Kachru, Yamura. 1983. *The Other Tongue: English across Cultures*. New York: Prentice-Hall.

———. 1987. "Cross-Cultural Texts, Discourse Strategies and Discourse Interpretation." In *Discourse across Cultures: Strategies in World Englishes*, edited by Larry E. Smith, 87–100. New York: Prentice-Hall.

Kang, Liu, and Xiaobing Tang, eds. 1997. *Politics, Ideology, and Literary Discourse in Modern China: Theoretical Interventions and Cultural Critique*. Foreword by Fredric Jameson. Durham, N.C.: Duke University Press.

Kant, Immanuel. [1790] 1973. "What Is Enlightenment?" In *The Enlightenment: A Comprehensive Anthology*, edited by P. Gay, 383–90. New York: Simon and Schuster.

———. [1796–97] 1978. *Anthropology from a Pragmatic Point of View*. Translated by Victor L. Dowdell. Carbondale: Southern Illinois University Press.

Kaplan, Caren. 1996. *Questions of Travel: Postmodern Discourses of Displacements*. Durham, N.C.: Duke University Press.

Karttunen, Frances. 1982. "Nahuatl Literacy." In *The Inca and Aztec States: 1400–1800*, edited by G. A. Collier, R. Rosaldo and J. D. Wirth. New York: Academic Press.

Keping, Yu. 1994. "Culture and Modernity in Chinese Thought in the 1930's: Comments on Two Approaches to Modernization in China." Working Papers in Asian/Pacific Studies. Beijing and Durham, N.C.: Institute of Contemporary Marxism.

Khatibi, Abdelkebir. [1976] 1983. "L'orientalisme désorienté." In *Maghreb Pluriel*, 113–46. Paris: Denoel.

———. [1983] 1990. *Love in Two Languages*. Translated by Richard Horward. Minneapolis: University of Minnesota Press.

———. 1983. *Maghreb pluriel*. Paris: Denoel.

Kilminster, Richard. 1998. "Globalization as an Emergent Concept." In *The Limits of Globalization: Cases and Arguments*, edited by A. Scott, 257–83. London: Routledge.

Klor de Alva, J. Jorge. 1992. "Colonialism and Post Colonialism as (Latin) American Mirages." *Colonial Latin American Review* 1–2: 3–24.

———. 1995. "The Postcolonization of (Latin) American Experience: A Reconsideration of 'Colonialism,' 'Postcolonialism,' and 'Mestizaje.'" In *After Colonialism: Imperial Histories and Postcolonial Displacements*, edited by G. Prakash, 241–78. Princeton: Princeton University Press.

Kramer, Michael P. 1992. *Imagining Language in American: From the Revolution to the Civil War*. Princeton: Princeton University Press.

Krishna, Daya. 1988. "Comparative Philosophy: What It Is and What It Ought To Be." In *Interpreting across Boundaries: New Essays in Comparative Philosophy*, edited by G. Larson and E. Deutsch, 70–136. Princton: Princeton University Press.

Kristeller, Paul Oskar. 1965. *Renaissance Thought and the Arts*. Princeton: Princeton University Press.

Krupat, Arnold. 1983. "Native American Literature and the Canon." *Critical Inquiry* 10, no. 1: 145–72.

Kusch, Rodolfo. 1953. *La seducción de la barbarie. Análisis herético de un continente mestizo.* Buenos Aires: Fundación Ross.

———. 1963. *América profunda.* Buenos Aires: Hachette.

———. [1970] 1977. *El pensamiento indígena y popular en América.* Buenos Aires: Hachette.

———. 1976. *Geocultura del hombre americano.* Buenos Aires: Garcia Cambeiro.

———. 1978. *Esbozo de una antropología Americana.* Buenos Aires: Ediciones Castañeda.

Labov, William. 1972. *Language in the Inner City: Studies in the Black English Vernacular.* Philadelphia: University of Pennsylvania Press.

Laclau, Ernesto. 1996. *Emancipation(s).* London: Verso.

Lacoue-Labarthe, Philippe. 1990. *Heidegger, Art, and Politics: The Fiction of the Political.* Oxford: Blackwell.

Lambert, Richard D. 1990. "Blurring the Disciplinary Boundaries: Area Studies in United States." *American Behavioral Scientist* 33, no. 6: 712–32.

Lander, Edgardo. 1997. "Modernidad, Colonialidad y Postmodernidad." *Anuario Mariateguiano* 9, no. 9: 122–31.

———. 1998a. "Eurocentrism and Colonialism in Latin American Social Thought" In *Sociology in Latin America (Social Knowledge: Heritage, Challenges, Perspectives)*, edited by R. Briceño-León and H. R. Sonntag, 65–76. Proceedings of the Regional Conference of the International Association of Sociology, Venezuela, 1997.

———. 1998b. "Modernidad, colonialidad y posmodernidad" In *Democracias sin exclusiones ni excluidos*, edited by E. Sader, 83–98. Caracas: Nueva Sociedad.

Larui, A. 1974. *La crise des intellectuels arabes.* Paris: Maspero.

Lazzarato, Maurizio. 1996. "Immaterial Labor." In *Radical Thoughts in Italy: A Potential Politics*, edited by P. Virno and M. Hard, 132–46. Minneapolis: University of Minnesota Press.

Lee, Richard. 1996. "Structures of Knowledge." In *The Age of Transition: Trajectory of the World-System, 1945–2025*, 178–208. London: Zed Books.

Lefebvre, Henri. [1974] 1991. *The Production of Space.* Oxford: Blackwell.

Lewis, Bernard. 1996. *A Brief History of the Last 2,000 Years.* New York: Scribner.

Lewis, Martin W., and Karen E. Wigen. 1997. *The Myth of Continents: A Critique of Metageography.* Berkeley: University of California Press.

Lhumann, Niklas. 1990. *Essays on Self-Reference.* New York: Columbia University Press.

López, Milagros. 1994. "Post-Work Society." *Social Text* 34: 23–35.

López Segrera, Francisco, ed. 1997. *Los retos de la globalización. Ensayos en homenaje a Theotonio Dos Santos.* Caracas: UNESCO.

Lowe, Lisa. 1991. *Critical Terrains: French and British Orientalism.* Ithaca, N.Y.: Cornell University Press.

Lyotard, Jean François. 1983. *Le diffirend.* Paris : Editions de Minuit.

MacCormack, Sabine. 1991. *Religion in the Andes: Vision and Imagination in Early Colonial Peru.* Princeton: Princeton University Press.

Mahan, A. T. 1890. *Influence of Sea Power upon History, 1660–1783.* Boston: Little.

Makang, Jean-Marie. 1997. "Of the Good Use of Tradition: Keeping the Critical Perspective in African Philosophy." In *Postcolonial African Philosophy*, edited by C. E. Eze, 324–38. Oxford: Blackwell.

Malinowski, Bronislaw. 1943. "The Pan-African Problem of Culture Contact." *American Journal of Sociology* 48, no. 6: 649–65.

Mallon, Florencia. 1994. "The Promise and Dilemma of Subaltern Studies: Perspective from Latin American History." *American Historical Review* 99, no. 5, 1491–515.

———. 1995. *Peasant and Nation: The Making of Postcolonial Mexico and Peru*. Berkeley: University of California Press.

Mandani, Mahmood. 1996. *Citizen and Subject: Contemporary Africa and the Legacy of Late Colonialism*. Princeton: Princeton University Press.

Mannheim, Bruce. 1990. *The Language of the Incas since the European Invasion*. Austin: University of Texas Press.

Manning, Patrick. 1990. *Slavery and Africa Life: Occidental, Oriental, and Africa Slave Trades.* Cambridge: Cambridge University Press.

Mariátegui, José Carlos. [1924] 1991. *Textos Básicos*. Selección, prólogo y notas introductorias de Aníbal Quijano. Lima: Fondo de Cultura Económica.

Marmon Silko, Leslie. 1991. *Almanac of the Dead*. New York: Simon and Schuster.

Martín-Barbero, Jesús. [1986] 1997. *De los medios a las mediaciones. Comunicación, cultura y hegemonía*. México: Gustavo Gili.

———. 1993. *Pre-Textos. Conversaciones sobre la comunicación y sus contextos*. Cali: Universidad del Valle.

———. 1998. *Mapas nocturnos. Diálogos con la obra de Jesús Martín-Barbero*. Bogotá: Universidad Central.

Maturana, Umberto. 1970. "Neurophysiology of Cognition." In *Cognition: A Multiple View*, edited by P. Garvin, 3–23. New York: Spartan Books.

———. 1978. "Biology of Language: The Epistemology of Reality." In *Psychology and Biology of Language and Thought: Essays in Honor of Eric Lenneberg*, edited by G. A. Miller and Eric Lenneberg, 27–63. New York: Academic Press.

Maturana, Umberto, with Francisco Varela. 1984. *El árbol del conocimiento*. Santiago: Editorial Universitaria.

———. 1987. *The Tree of Knowledge: The Biological Roots of Human Understanding*. Boston: New Science Library.

McClintock, Anne. 1992. "The Angel of Progress: Pitfalls of the Term 'Postcolonial.' " *Social Text* 31–32: 84–98.

Meggers, Betty J. 1991. Introduction to *O Processo Civilizatorio. Etapas da Evoluçao Socio-Cultural*, by Darcy Ribeiro. Petropolis: Vozes.

Menchú, Rigoberta. 1984. *I, Rigoberta Menchú: An Indian Woman in Guatemala*. Translated by A. Wright. London: Verso. Originally published as *Me llamo Rigoberta Menchú y asi me nació la conciencia*. Barcelona: Editorial Argos Vergara, 1983.

Mennell, Stephen. 1990. "The Globalization of Human Society as a Very Long-Term Social Process: Elias's Theory." In *Global Culture: Nationalism, Globalization and Modernity*, edited by M. Featherstone, 359–72. London: Sage.

Messick, Brinkley. 1997. "Genealogies of Reading and the Scholarly Cultures of Islam." In *Cultures of Scholarship*, edited by S. C. Humphreys, 387–412. Comparative Studies in Society and History Book Series. Ann Arbor: University of Michigan Press.

Mignolo, Walter D. 1978. *Elementos para una teoría del texto literario*. Barcelona: Critica-Grijalbo.

Mignolo, Walter D. 1981. "El metatexo historiográfico y la historiografía indiana."
Modern Language Notes 96: 358–402.

———. 1982. "Cartas, crónicas y relaciones del descubrimiento y de la conquista."
In *Historia de la literatura Hispanoamericana. Epoca Colonial*, edited by Luis Iñigo
Madrigal, 57–125. Madrid: Cátedra.

———. 1983. "Comprensión hermenéutica y comprensión teórica." *Revista de literatura* 94: 1–35.

———. 1986. *Teoría del texto e interpretación de textos*. Mexico: UNAM.

———. 1989a. "Literacy and Colonization: The New World Experience." In *Hispanic Studies*, edited by R. Jara and N. Spadaccini, 51–96. Minneapolis: University of
Minnesota Press.

———. 1989b. "Teorías literarias o de la literatura? Qué son y para qué sirven?" In
Teorias literarias en la actualidad, edited by G. Reyes, 7–46. Madrid: Arcos.

———. 1991. "(Re)modeling the Letter: Literacy and Literature at the Intersection
of Semiotics and Literary Studies." In *On Semiotic Modeling*, edited by M. Anderson
et. al., 357–95. The Hague: Mouton.

———. 1992a. "Semiosis colonial: la dialéctica entre representaciones fracturadas y
hermenéuticas pluritópicas." *Foro Hispánico. Revista de los Paises Bajos* 4: 11–28.

———. 1992b. "Nebrija in the New World: The Question of the Letter, the Colonization of Amerindian Languages, and the Discontinuity of the Classical Tradition."
L'Homme 122–24: 185–209.

———. 1992c. "On the Colonization of Amerindian Languages and Memories: Renaissance Theories of Writing and the Discontinuity of the Classical Tradition."
Comparative Studies in Society and History 34, no. 2: 301–35.

———. 1992d. "The Darker Side of the Renaissance: Colonization and the Discontinuity of the Classical Tradition." *Renaissance Quarterly* 45, no. 4: 808–28.

———. 1993a. "Colonial and Postcolonial Discourse: Cultural Critique or Academic
Colonialism?" *Latin American Research Review* 28, no. 3: 120–34.

———. 1993b. "Misunderstanding and Colonization: The Reconfiguration of Memory and Space." *SAQ* 92, no. 2: 212–60.

———. 1994. "Are Subaltern Studies Postmodern or Postcolonial?: The Politics and
Sensibilities of Geocultural Locations." *Dispositio/n* 19, no. 46: 45–53.

———. 1995a. *The Darker Side of the Renaissance: Literacy, Territoriality and Colonization*. Ann Arbor: University of Michigan Press.

———. 1995b. "Afterword, Human Understanding and (Latin) American Interests:
The Politics and Sensibilities of Geocultural Locations." *Poetics Today* 16, no. 1:
171–214.

———. 1995c. "Occidentalización, imperialismo, globalización: herencias coloniales y teorías postcoloniales." *Revista Iberoamericana* 61, nos. 170–71: 26–39.

———. 1995d. "Decires fuera de lugar: sujetos dicentes, roles sociales y formas de
inscripción." *Revista de crítica literaria latinoamericana* 11: 9–32.

———. 1996a. "La razón postcolonial. Herencias coloniales y teorías postcoloniales." *Gragoata* 1: 7–30.

———. 1996b. "Herencias coloniales y teorías postcoloniales." In *Cultura y Tercer
Mundo*, edited by B. Gonzalez, 1: 99–136. Caracas: Nueva Sociedad.

————. 1996c. "Postoccidentalismo: las epistemologias fronterizas y el dilema de los estudios (latinoamericanos) de areas." *Revista Iberoamericana* 62, nos. 176–77: 679–96.

————. 1996d. "Linguistic Maps, Literary Geographies, Cultural Landscapes." *Modern Language Quarterly* 57, no. 2: 181–96. Special Issue *The Places of History: Regionalism Revisited in Latin America*.

————. 1997a. "Espacios geográficos y localizaciones espistemológicas o la ratio entre la localización geográfica y la subalternización de conocimientos." *Disenso* 3: 1–18.

————. 1997b. "Gnosis, Colonialism and Cultures of Scholarship." In *Cultures of Scholarship*, edited by S. C. Humphreys, 311–38. Comparative Studies in Society and History Book Series. Ann Arbor: University of Michigan Press.

————. 1997c. "La razón postcolonial: herencias coloniales y teorías postcoloniales." In *Postmodernidad y Postcolonialidad. Breves reflexiones sobre Latinoamérica*, edited by Alfonso de Toro, 51–70. Leipzig: Veurvert-Iberoamericana.

————. 1997d. "The Zapatistas's Theoretical Revolution: Its Epistemic, Ethic and Historical Consequences." Keynote address to the thirty-first annual CEMERS conference *Comparative Colonialisms: Preindustrial Colonial Intersections in Global Perspectives*, October 31–November 1.

————. 1998. "Globalization, Civilization Processes, and the Relocation of Languages and Cultures." In *The Cultures of Globalization*, edited by F. Jameson and M. Miyoshi, 32–54. Durham, N.C.: Duke University Press.

————. Forthcoming. "The Larger Picture and the Historical Argument: Hispanics/Latinos/as (and Latino Studies) in the Colonial Horizon of Modernity." Paper presented at the conference Ethnic Identity, Culture and Group Rights. A Discussion across the Disciplines on the Situation of Hispanics/Latinos in the U.S. University of Buffalo, Samuel P. Capen Chair in Philosophy Symposia, November 14.

Mignolo, Walter D., and Freya Schiwy. Forthcoming. "Translation/Transculturation and the Colonial Difference." *Conference Proceedings*, Carlos Rincón, ed., Berlin: Free University.

Miller, G. A., and Eric Lenneberg, eds. 1978. *Psychology and Biology of Language and Thought: Essays in Honor of Eric Lenneberg*. New York: Academic Press.

Minh-ha, Trinh T. 1989. *Women, Native, Other: Writing Postcoloniality and Feminism*. Bloomington: Indiana University Press.

Mires, Fernando. 1991. *El discurso de la Indianidad. La cuestión indígena en América Latina*. Quito: Ediciones Abya-Yala.

Mohanty, Chandra Talpade. 1988. "Under Western Eyes: Feminist Scholarship and Colonial Discourse." *Feminist Review* 30: 65–68.

Mohanty, Chandra Talpade, and M. J. Alexander, eds. 1997. *Feminist Genealogies, Colonial Legacies, Democratic Futures*. Bloomington: Indiana University Press.

Monthanty, T., A. Russo, and L. Torres, eds. 1991. *Third World Women and the Politics of Feminism*. Bloomington: Indiana University Press.

Moraga, Cherrie. 1993. *The Last Generation: Prose and Poetry*. Boston: South End Press.

Morin, Edgar. 1987. *Penser l'Europe*. Paris: Gallimard.

Morse, Richard. [1964] 1989. "On Grooming Latin Americanists." In *New World Soundings: Culture and Ideology in the Americas*, 169–200. Baltimore: John Hopkins University Press.

Moya, Paula. 1997. "Postmodernism, 'Realism,' and the Politics of Identity: Cherrie Moraga and Chicana Feminism." In *Feminist Genealogies, Colonial Legacies, Democratic Futures*, edited by Chandra Talpade Mohanty and M. J. Alexander, 125–50. New York: Routledge.

Mudimbe, V. Y. 1988. *The Invention of Africa: Gnosis, Philosophy and the Order of Knowledge*. Bloomington: Indiana University Press.

Murra, J. V., and R. Adorno, eds. 1980. *El primer nueva corónica y buen gobierno por Felipe Guaman Poma de Ayala [Waman Puma]*. Translation and textual analysis by Jorge L. Urioste. Mexico: Siglo XXI.

Najita, Tetsuo. 1974. *Japan: The Intellectual Foundations of Modern Japanese Politics*. Chicago: University of Chicago Press.

Nancy, Jean-Luc. 1994. "Cut Throat Sun." In *Other Tongue: Nation and Ethnicity in the Linguistic Borderland*, edited by A. Arteaga, 113–24. Durham, N.C.: Duke University Press.

Nandy, Ashis. 1995. *The Savage Freud and Other Essays on Possible and Retrievable Selves*. Princeton: Princeton University Press.

Netanyahu, B. 1995. *The Origins of the Inquisition in Fifteenth Century Spain*. New York: Ramdom House.

Oboler, Suzanne. 1997. " 'So Far from God, so Close to the United States.' The Roots of Hispanic Homogenization." In *Challenging Fronteras: Structuring Latina and Latino Lives in the U.S.*, edited by M. Romero, Pierrette Hondagneu-Sotelo, and Vilma Ortiz, 31–54. New York: Routledge.

O'Gorman. Edmundo. [1958]. *La invención de América. El universalismo en la cultura de occidente*. México: Fondo de Cultura Económica.

———. 1961. *The Invention of America*. Bloomington: Indiana University Press.

Ortega y Gasset, José. 1954 "The Difficulties of Reading." Translated by Clarence E. Parmenter. *Diogenes* 28: 1–17.

Ortiz, Fernando. [1906] 1995. *Los negros brujos*. La Habana,: Editorial de Ciencias Sociales.

———. [1916] 1996. *Los negros esclavos*. La Habana: Editorial de Ciencias Sociales.

———. [1940] 1995. *Cuban Counterpoint: Tobacco and Sugar.* Durham, N.C.: Duke University Press.

Ortiz, Renato. [1994]1997. *Mundialización y cultura*. Translated Elsa Noya. Buenos Aires: Alianza Editorial.

Osorio Romero, Ignacio. 1990. *La ensénanza del latín a los Indios*. México: Universidad Autónoma.

Osterhammel, Jurgen. 1997. *Colonialism: A Theoretical Overview*. Kingston: Ian Randle Publisher; Princeton: Markus Wiener Publishers.

Outlaw, Lucius. 1997. "African 'Philosophy': Deconstructive and Reconstructive Challenges." In *Contemporary Philosophy: A New Survey*, vol. 5, *African Philosophy*, edited by G. Floistad, 9–44. Dordrecht: Nijhoff.

Pagden, Anthony. 1982. *The Fall of Natural Man: The American Indian and the Origins of Comparative Ethnology*. London: Cambridge University Press.

———. 1996. " 'Americanism' from Modernity to Post-Modernity." In *E Nouveau Monde/Mondes Nouveaux. L' experience americaine*, edited by S. Gruzinski and N. Wachtel, 611–22. Paris: Ecole des Hautes Etudes en Sciences Sociales.

Pérez-Firmat, Gustavo. 1995. *Next Year in Cuba: A Cubano's Coming-of-Age in America*. New York: Anchor Book.

Pizarro, Ana, ed. 1985. Introduction to *La literatura latinoamericana como proceso*, 13–67. Buenos Aires: Centro Editor de América Latina.

Pletsch, Carl E. 1981. "The Three Worlds, or the Division of Social Scientific Labor, circa 1950–1975." *Comparative Studies in Society and History* 23, no. 4: 565–90.

Poblete, Juan E. 1997. "Leer la disciplina y disciplinar la lectura literatura, discurso y legitimidad en Chile 1829–1925." Ph.D. diss., Duke University.

Portantiero, Juan Carlos. 1977. *Los usos de Gramsci*. Mexico: Siglo XXI.

Prakash, Gyan. 1990. "Writing Post-Orientalist Histories of the Third World: Perspectives from Indian Historiography." *Comparative Studies in Society and History* 32, no. 2: 383–408.

———. 1994. "Subaltern Studies as Postcolonial Criticism." *American Historical Review* 99, no. 5: 1475–90.

Prigogine, Ilya. 1986. "Science, Civilization and Democracy: Values, Systems, Structures and Affinities." *Futures* 18, no. 4: 493–507.

Quijano, Anibal. 1981. *Introduccion a Mariategui*. Mexico: Ediciones Era.

———. 1992. "Colonialidad y modernidad-racionalidad." In *Los Conquistadores*, edited by H. Bonilla, 437–47. Bogota: Tercer Mundo.

———. [1993] 1995. "Modernity, Identity, and Utopia in Latin America." In *The Postmodernism Debate in Latin America*, edited by J. Beverley, M. Aronna, and J. Oviedo, 202–16. Durham, N.C.: Duke University Press.

———. 1997. "Colonialidad del poder, cultura y conocimiento en América Latina." *Anuario Mariateguiano* 9, no. 9: 113–21.

———. 1998. "The Colonial Nature of Power and Latin America's Cultural Experience." In *Sociology in Latin America (Social Knowledge: Heritage, Challenges, Perspectives)*, edited by R. Briceño-Leon and H. R. Sonntag, 27–38. Proceedings of the Regional Conference of the International Association of Sociology. Venezuela.

Quijano, Anibal, and Immanuel Wallerstein. 1992. "Americanity as a Concept, or the Americas in the Modern World-Sytem." *ISSA1*, no. 134: 549–47.

Rabasa, Jose. 1997. "Of Zapatismo: Reflections on the Folkloric and the Impossible in a Subaltern Insurrection." In *Politics and Culture in the Shadow of Capital*, edited by L. Lowe and D. Lloyd, 399–431. Durham, N.C.: Duke University Press.

Radhakrishnan, R. 1993. "Postcoloniality and the Boundaries of Identity." *Callaloo* 16, no. 4: 750–71.

Rafael, Vicente. 1984. *Contracting Colonialism: Translation and Christian Conversion in Tagalog Society under Early Spanish Rule*. Ithaca, N.Y.: Cornell University Press.

Rama, Angel. 1982. *Tranculturación narrativa en América Latina*. Mexico, D.F.: Siglo Veintiuno.

———. [1965] 1993. "Aportación original de una comarca del Tercer Mundo: Latinoamérica." In *Fuentes de la cultura Latinoamericana*, edited by L. Zea, 3:59–67. Mexico: Fondo de Cultura Economica.

Ramos, Demetrio, et al. 1984. *La ética en la conquista de América*. Madrid: Consejo Superior de Investigaciones Cientificas.

Ramos, Julio. 1989. *Desencuentros de la modernidad en América Latina. Literatura y Política en el siglo XIX*. Mexico: Fondo de Cultura Económica.

Rangel, Carlos. [1982] 1986. *Third World Ideology and Western Reality*. Translated by the author with the assistance of V. Tismaneanu, R. van Roy, and M. H. Contreras. New Brunswick, N.J.: Transaction Books.

Rappaport, Joanne. [1990] 1998. *The Politics of Memory: Native Historical Interpretation in the Colombian Andes*. Durham, N.C.: Duke University Press.

Readings, Bill. 1996. *The University in Ruins*. Cambridge, Mass.: Harvard University Press.

Reinaga, Fausto. 1967. *La 'inteligentsia' del cholaje Boliviano*. Bolivia: Partido Indio de Bolivia.

———. 1969. *La revolución india*. Bolivia: Cooperativa de Artes Gráficas.

———. 1974. *América India y Occidente*. Bolivia: Partido Indio de Bolivia.

———. 1978. *Indianidad*. Bolivia: Litografías e Imprentas Unidas.

Renan, Ernst. 1863. *Histoire générale et systèm comparés des languessémitiques*. Paris: L'Impremerie Imperiale.

Rengifo Vásquez, Grimaldo. 1991. "Desaprender la modernidad para aprender lo andino. La tecnología y sus efectos en el desarrollo rural." *Revista Unitas* 4: 32–42.

———. 1998a. "The Ayllu." In *The Spirit of Regeneration: Andean Culture Confronting Western Notions of Development*, edited by F. Apffel-Marglin and PRATEC, 89–123. London: Zed Books.

———. 1998b. "Education in the Modern West and in Andean Culture." In *The Spirit of Regeneration: Andean Culture Confronting Western Notions of Development*, edited by F. Apffel-Marglin and PRATEC, 172–92. London: Zed Books.

Reyes, Garciela, ed. 1989. *Las teorías literarias en la actualidad*. Madrid: Anaya.

Ribeiro, Darcy. 1968. *Las América y la civilización. Proceso de formación y causas del desarrollo desigual de los pueblos americanos*. Caracas: Biblioteca Ayacucho.

———. [1969] 1978. *O Processo Civilizatorio. Etapas da Evoluçao Socio-Cultural*. Petropolis: Editora Vozes.

Ribeiro, Darcy, and Mercio Gomes. 1996. "Ethnicity and Civilization." In *First Nations-Pueblos Originarios*, 41–52. Occasional Papers of the Indigenous Research Center of the Americas 1. University of California at Davis.

Richard, Nelly. 1987–88. "Postmodernism and Periphery." *Third Text* 2: 6–12.

———. 1995. "Cultural Peripheries: Latin America and Postmodrnist De-Centering." In *Posmodernism Debate in Latin America*, edited by J. Beverley et al., 217–22. Durham, N.C.: Duke University Press.

Rivera Cusicanqui, Silvia. 1984. *Oprimidos pero no vencidos: Luchas del campesinado aymara y qhechwa de Bolivia, 1990–1980*. La Paz: CSUTCB.

———. 1990. "Liberal Democracy and Ayllu Democracy in Bolivia: The Case of Northern Potosi." *Journal of Development Studies* 5: 97–121.

———. 1992. "Sendas y senderos de la ciencia social Andina." *Autodeterminación: Análisis histórico político y teoría social* 10: 83–108.

———. 1993. "La raíz: colonizadores y colonizados." In *Violencias encubiertas en Bolivia*, vol. 1, *Cultura y Política*, edited by X. Albó et al. La Paz: CIPCA-Aruwiyiri.

———. 1996. "Los desafíos para una demoracia etnica en los albores del tercer milenio." In *Ser mujer indígena, chola o birlocha en la Bolivia postcolonial de los años 90*, edited by S. Rivera Cusicanqui, 17–86. Bolivia: Ministerio de Desarollo Humano.

———. 1997. "La noción de 'derecho' O las paradojas de la modernidad postcolonial: indigenas y mujeres en Bolivia." *Temas Sociales* 19: 27–52.

Rivera Cusicanqui, Silvia, and Rossana Barragan, eds. 1997. *Debates post-coloniales: una introducción a los estudios de la subalternidad*. La Paz: Sephis/Aruwiyri.

Robertson, Roland. 1992. "Civilization and Civilizing Process: Elias, Globalization and Analytic Synthesis. In *Cultural Theory and Cultural Change*, edited by M. Featherstone, 211–28. London: Sage.

Roig, Arturo A. 1993. *Rostro y filosofía de América Latina*. Mendoza: Universidad Nacional de Cuyo.

Rojas de Ferro, Cristina. 1995. "The 'Will to Civilization' and Its Encounter with Laissez-Faire." *Review of International Political Economy* 2, no. 1, 150–73.

Rojas Mix, Miguel. 1992. *Los cien nombres de América*. Barcelona: Editorial Lumen.

Romero, M., P. Hondagneu-Sotelo, V. Ortiz, eds. 1997. *Challenging Fronteras: Structuring Latina and Latino Lives in the U.S.* New York: Routledge.

Rorty, Richard. 1979. *Philosophy and the Mirror of Nature*. Princeton: Princeton University Press.

———. 1982. *The Consequences of Pragmatism*. Minneapolis: University of Minnesota Press.

———. 1998. *Achiving Our Country: Leftist Thought in Twentieth-Century America*. Cambridge, Mass.: Harvard University Press.

Said, Edward. 1978. *Orientalism*. New York: Vintage Books.

———. 1983. "Traveling Theory." In *The World, the Text and the Critic*, 226–47. Cambridge, Mass.: Harvard University Press.

———. 1993. *Culture and Imperialism*. New York: Knopf.

Salazar Bondy, A. 1966. *La cultura de la dependencia*. Lima: Instituto de Estudios Peruanos.

———. 1969. *Existe una filosofía de nuestra América?* México: Siglo XXI.

Saldívar, José. 1992. *The Dialectics of Our America*. Durham, N.C.: Duke University Press.

———. 1997. *Border Matters: Remapping American Cultural Studies*. Berkeley: University of California Press.

Saldívar, José, and H. Calderón, eds. *Criticism in the Borderlands: Studies in Chicano Literature, Culture and Ideology*. Durham, N.C.: Duke University Press.

Sandoval, Ciro A. 1998. Introduction to *José María Arguedas: Reconsiderations for Latin American Cultural Studies*, edited by Ciro A. Sandoval and Sandra M. Boschetto-Sandoval, xxi–xlii. Athens: Ohio University Center for International Studies.

Santiago-Vallés, Kelvin A. 1994. *"Subject People" and Colonial Discourses: Economic Transformation and Social Disorder in Puerto Rico, 1898–1947*. Albany, N.Y.: State University of New York Press.

Santos, Milton, et al., eds. 1994a. *Globalizaçao e Espaçio-Latino Americano*. São Paulo: Editora Hucitec.

———, eds. 1994b. *Territorio, Gobalizaçao e Fragmentaçao*. São Paulo: Editora Hucitec.

Sardar, Zia, Ashis Nandy, and Merryl Wyn Davies. 1993. *The Barbaric Others: A Manifesto of Western Racism.* London: Pluto Press.

Sardar, Ziauddin. 1987. *The Future of Muslim Civilization.* London: Muansell Publishing.

Scharlau, B., and M. Münzel. 1987. *Quelcay: Mündliche Kultur und Schrifttradition bei Indianern Lateinamerikas.* Frankfurt am Main: Campus Verlag.

Schwarz, Roberto. 1992. *Misplaced Ideas: Essays on Brazilian Culture.* Edited with an introduction by John Gledson. London: Verso, 1992.

Seed, Patricia. 1991. "Colonial and Postcolonial Discourse." *Latin American Research Review* 26, no. 3: 181–200.

Sekyi-Out, Ato. 1996. *Fanon's Dialectic of Experience.* Cambridge, Mass.: Harvard University Press.

Serequeberhan, Tsenay. 1994. *The Hermeneutics of African Philosophy: Horizon and Discourse.* New York: Routledge.

———. 1997. "The Critique of Eurocentrism and the Practice of African Philosophy." In *Postcolonial African Philosophy: A Critical Reader,* edited by C. E. Eze, 141–61. Oxford: Blackwell.

Shiva, Vandana, ed. 1994. *Biodiversity Conservation: Whose Resource? Whose Knowledge?* New Delhi: Indian National Trust for Art and Cultural Heritage.

Shiva, V., and M. Mies, eds. 1993. *Ecofeminism.* New Delhi: Kaly for Women.

Shohat, Ella. 1992. "Notes on the 'Post-Colonial.'" *Social Text* 31–32: 114–40.

Sicroff, Albert A. 1960. *Les controverses des statut de "pureté de sang" en Espagne du xve au xviie siècle.* Paris: Didier.

Skutnabb-Kangas, Tove, and Robert Phillipson, eds. 1995. *Linguistic Human Rights: Overcoming Linguistic Discrimination.* The Hague: Mouton.

Slotkin, Richard. 1973. *Regeneration through Violence: The Mythology of the American Frontier, 1600–1860.* Middletown, Conn.: Wesleyan University Press.

———. 1985. *The Fatal Environment: The Myth of the Frontier in the Age of Industrialization, 1800–1890.* Middletown, Conn.: Wesleyan University Press.

Smith, Larry E., ed. 1987. *Discourse across Cultures: Strategies in World Englishes.* New York: Prentice-Hall.

Snow, C. P. 1959. *The Two Cultures and the Scientific Revolution.* Rede lecture. New York: Cambridge University Press.

Soja, Edward W. 1996. *Thirdspace: Journeys to Los Angeles and Other Real-and-Imagined Places.* Oxford: Blackwell.

Sonntag, Heinz Rudolf. [1969] 1978. "Epilogo a ediçao alema." In *O Processo Civilizatorio. Etapas da Evoluçao Socio-Cultural,* edited by Darcy Ribeiro, 216. Petropolis: Editora Vozes.

Spengler, Oswald. [1926–28] 1950. *The Decline of the West.* Translated with notes by Charles Francis Atkinson. New York: Knopf.

Stavenhagen, Rodolfo. 1965. "Classes, Colonialism and Acculturation." *Studies in Comparative International Development* 1, no. 7: 53–77.

———. 1990. *The Ethnic Question: Conflict, Development, and Human Rights.* Tokyo: United Nations University.

Stavenhagen, Rodolfo, and Diego Iturralde, eds. 1990. *Entre la ley y la costumbre. El derecho consuetudinario indígena en America Latina.* México: Instituto Indigenista Interamericano/Instituto Interamericano de Derechos Humanos.

Stephanson, Anders. 1995. *Manifest Destiny: American Expansion and the Empire of Right*. New York: Hill and Wang.

Subcomandante Marcos. 1997a. *El Sueño Zapatista. Entrevistas con el Subcomandante Marcos, el Mayor Moisés y el comandante Tacho, del Ejército Zapatista de Liberación Nacional*. Edited by Yvon Le Bot. México: Plaza & Janes.

———. 1997b. La quatrième guerre mondiale. *Le Monde Diplomatique* (August).

Suleri, Sara. 1992a. *The Rhetoric of English India*. Chicago: Chicago University Press.

———. 1992b. "Woman Skin Deep: Feminism and the Postcolonial Condition." *Critical Inquiry* 18: 756–69.

Tanaka, Stefan. 1993. *Japan's Orient: Rendering Pasts into History*. Berkeley: University of California Press.

———. 1997. "Security in Asia Pacific: Power Politics in the Frontier of New Medievalism." Lecture presented at Duke University, October 1997. Mimeographed.

Tandeter, Enrique. 1976. "Sobre el análisis de la dominación colonial." *Desarrollo Económico* 16, no. 61: 151–60.

Taylor, Charles. 1985. *Human Agency and Language: Philosophical Papers, 1*. Cambridge: Cambridge University Press.

———. 1989. *Sources of the Self: The Making of Modern Identity*. Cambridge, Mass.: Harvard University Press.

Tempels, Placide. 1945. *La philosophie bantoue*. Elisabethville: Lovania.

Thiong'o, Ngugiwa. 1981. *Decolonizing the Mind: The Politics of Language in African Literature*. London: James Currey.

Toulmin, Stephen. 1971. *Human Understanding*. Princeton: Princeton University Press.

Tourain, Alain. 1992. "Beyond Social Movements?" In *Cultural Theory and Cultural Change*, edited by M. Featherstone, 125–45. London: Sage.

Trouillot, Michel-Rolph. 1995. *Silencing the Past: Power and the Production of History*. Boston: Beacon Press.

———. 1998. "Global Flows, Open Cultures." Paper presented at the conference Beyond Dichotomies. Stanford University, Stanford, Calif., May 8–10.

Tu Wei-ming. 1985. *Confucian Thoughts: Selfhood as Creative Transformation*. Albany: State University of New York.

UNESCO. 1998. *Universal Declaration of Linguistic Rights*. Translated by B. Krayenbuhl and I. Gusi. Barcelona: Institut d'Edicions de la Diputaci'o de Barcelona.

Valcárcel, Carlos Daniel. 1947. *La rebelión de Túpac Amaru [por] Daniel Valcárcel*. México: Fondo de Cultura Económica.

Valcárcel, Carlos Daniel, and L. D. Flórez, eds. 1981. *La revolución de los Túpac Amaru: antología*. Lima: Comisión Nacional del Bicentenario de la Rebelión Emancipadora de Túpac Amaru.

Valla, Lorenzo. [1442?] 1952. "In sex libros elegantiarum praefatio." In *Prosatori Latini del Quattrocento*, edited by E. Garin. Milan: Mondadori.

Van Cott, Donna Lee. 1994. *Indigenous Peoples and Democracy in Latin America: Inter-American Dialogue*. New York: St. Martin's Press.

Varese, Stefano, 1996a. "Parroquialismo y globalización. Las etnicidades indígenas ante el tercer milenio." In *Pueblos indios, soberanía y globalismo*, 15–30. Quito: Biblioteca Abya-Yala.

Varese, Stefano. ed. 1996b. *Pueblos indios, soberania y globalismo.* Quite: Biblioteca Abya-Yala.

Viñas, David. 1982. *Indios, ejército y frontera.* Mexico: Siglo Veintiuno Editores.

Viswanathan, Gauri. 1989. *Masks of Conquest.* New York: Columbia University Press.

Vives, Luis. [1533?] 1964. *De tradendis disciplines.* London: Rowman and Littlefield.

Von der Walde, Erna. 1997. "Limpia, fija y da esplendor: el letrado y la letra en Colmbia a fines del siglo xix." *Revista Iberoamericana,* 178–79: 71–86. Special issue *Siglo XIX: Fundación y fronteras de la ciudadania.*

Wallerstein, Immanuel. 1974. *The Modern World-System: Capitalist Agriculture and the Origins of the European World-Economy in the Sixteenth Century.* New York: Academic Press.

———. 1980. *The Modern World-System II: Mercantilism and the Consolidation of the European World-Economy, 1600–1750.* London: Academic Press.

———. 1987. "World-Systems Analysis." In *Social Theory Today,* edited by A. Giddens and J. H. Turner, 309–24. Cambridge: Polity Press.

———. 1989. *The Modern World-System III: The Second Era of Great Expansion of the Capitalist World-Economy, 1730–1840s.* London: Academic Press.

———. 1990. "Culture as the Ideological Battleground of the Modern World System." In *Global Culture: Nationalism, Globalization and Modernity.,* edited by M. Featherstone, 31–56. London: Sage.

———. 1991a. *Geopolitics and Geoculture: Essays on the Changing World-System.* Cambridge: Cambridge University Press.

———. 1991b. "Marx, Marxism-Leninism, and Socialist Experiences in the Modern World System." In *Geopolitics and Geoculture: Essays on the Changing World-System,* 87–94. Cambridge: Cambridge University Press.

———. 1992. "The West, Capitalism and the Modern World-System." *Review* 14, no. 4: 561–620.

———. 1995a. "World-Systems Analysis: The Second Phase." In *Unthinking Social Sciences: The Limits of Nineteenth-Century Paradigms,* 266–72. New York: Polity Press.

———. 1995b. "The Insurmountable Contradictions of Liberalism: Human Rights and the Rights of Peoples in the Geoculture of the Modern World-System." In *Nations, Identities, Cultures,* edited by Valentin Mudimbe, 1161–78. Special issue *SAQ* 94, no. 4.

———. 1996. "Open the Social Sciences." *ITEMS,* Social Science Research Council, 50, no.1: 1–7.

———. 1997. "Eurocentrism and Its Avatars: The Dilemmas of Social Science." *New Left Review* 226: 93–107.

———. 1998a. "The Heritage of Sociology, The Promise of Social Science." Presidential address. XIVth World Congress of Sociology, Montreal, July 26, 1998.

———. 1998b. "The Rise and Future Demise of World-Systems Analysis." *Review* 21, no. 1: 103–12.

Wallerstein, I., C. Juma, E. Fox Keller, J. Kocka, D. Lecourt, V. Y. Mudimbe, K. Mushakoji, I. Prigogine, P. J. Taylor, M.-R.Trouillot. 1996. *Open the Social Sciences.* Report of the Gulbenkian Commission on the Restructuring of the Social Sciences. Stanford, Calif.: Stanford University Press.

Wang, Jing. 1997. *High Culture Fever: Politics, Aesthetics, and Ideology in Deng's China*. Berkeley: University of California Press.

Weber, Max. [1904] 1992. *The Protestant Ethics and the Spirit of Capitalism*. Edited by Anthony Guiddens. New York: Routledge.

West, Cornel. 1989. *The American Evasion of Philosophy: A Genealogy of Pragmatism*. Madison: University of Wisconsin Press.

———. 1993. *Keeping Faith: Philosophy and Race in America*. New York: Routledge.

Whitaker, Arthur P. 1954. *The Western Hemisphere Idea: Its Rise and Decline*. Ithaca, N.Y.: Cornell University Press.

White, Lynn, Jr., ed. 1956. *Frontiers of Knowledge in the Study of Man*. New York: Harper and Brothers.

Williams, P., and L. Chrisman, eds. 1994. *Colonial Discourse and Post-Colonial Theory*. New York: Columbia University Press.

Wing, Betsy. 1997. "Translator Introduction and Glossary." In *Poetics of Relation*, edited by E. Glissant. Ann Arbor: University of Michigan Press.

Wiredu, Kwasi. 1997. "Democracy and Consensus in African Traditional Politics: A Plea for a Non-Party Politiy." In *Postcolonial African Philosophy*, edited by C. E. Eze, 303–12. Oxford: Blackwell.

Wolf, Eric R. 1982. *Europe and the People without History*. Berkeley: University of California Press.

Woodhull, Winifred. 1993. *Transfigurations of the Maghreb: Feminism, Decolonization and Literatures*. Minneapolis: University of Minnesota Press.

Woolf, Leonard. 1928. *Imperialism and Civilization*. New York: Harcourt, Brace.

The World Almanac and Book of Facts. 1967. New York: Press Publishing.

Wright, Richard. 1993. *Conversations with Richard Wright*. Edited by Keneth Kinnamon and Michel Fabre. Jackson: University Press of Mississippi.

Young, Robert J. C. 1995. *Colonial Desire: Hibridity in Theory, Culture and Race*. New York: Routledge.

Zea, Leopoldo. [1957] 1992. *The Role of the Americas in History*. Edited with an introduction by A. A. Oliver. Translated by Sonja Karsen. Westfield: Rowman and Littlefield.

———. 1958. *América en la historia*. México: Fondo de Cultura Económica.

———. 1988. *Discurso desde la marginación y la barbarie*. Barcelona: Anthropos.

PRINCETON STUDIES IN
CULTURE/POWER/HISTORY

High Religion: A Cultural and Political History of Sherpa Buddhism
by *Sherry B. Ortner*

A Place in History: Social and Monumental Time in a Cretan Town
by *Michael Herzfeld*

The Textual Condition by *Jerome J. McGann*

Regulating the Social: The Welfare State and Local Politics in Imperial Germany
by *George Steinmetz*

Hanging without a Rope: Narrative Experience in Colonial and
Postcolonial Karoland by *Mary Margaret Steedly*

Modern Greek Lessons: A Primer in Historical Constructivism
by *James Faubion*

The Nation and Its Fragments: Colonial and Postcolonial Histories
by *Partha Chatterjee*

Culture/Power/History: A Reader in Contemporary Social Theory
edited by *Nicholas B. Dirks, Geoff Eley, and Sherry B. Ortner*

After Colonialism: Imperial Histories and Postcolonial Displacements
edited by *Gyan Prakash*

Encountering Development: The Making and Unmaking of the Third World
by *Arturo Escobar*

Social Bodies: Science, Reproduction, and Italian Modernity
by *David G. Horn*

Revisioning History: Film and the Construction of a New Past
edited by *Robert A. Rosenstone*

The History of Everyday Life: Reconstructing Historical Experiences and
Ways of Life edited by *Alf Lüdtke*

The Savage Freud and Other Essays on Possible and Retrievable Selves
by Ashis Nandy

Children and the Politics of Culture *edited by Sharon Stephens*

Intimacy and Exclusion: Religious Politics in Pre-Revolutionary Baden
by Dagmar Herzog

What Was Socialism, and What Comes Next? *by Katherine Verdery*

Citizen and Subject: Contemporary Africa and the Legacy of Late Colonialism
by Mahmood Mamdani

Colonialism and Its Forms of Knowledge: The British in India *by Bernard S. Cohn*

Charred Lullabies: Chapters in an Anthropography of Violence
by E. Valentine Daniel

Theft of an Idol: Text and Context in the Representation of Collective Violence
by Paul R. Brass

Essays on the Anthropology of Reason *by Paul Rabinow*

Vision, Race, and Modernity: A Visual Economy of the Andean Image World
by Deborah Poole

Children in Moral Danger and the Problem of Government in
Third Republic France *by Sylvia Schafer*

Settling Accounts: Violence, Justice, and Accountability in Postsocialist Europe
by John Borneman

From Duty to Desire: Remaking Families in a Spanish Village
by Jane Fishburne Collier

Black Corona: Race and the Politics of Place in an Urban Community
by Steven Gregory

Welfare, Modernity, and the Weimar State, 1919–1933 *by Young-Sun Hong*

Remaking Women: Feminism and Modernity in the Middle East
edited by Lila Abu-Lughod

Spiritual Interrogations: Culture, Gender, and Community in Early
African American Women's Writing *by Katherine Clay Bassard*

Refashioning Futures: Criticism after Postcoloniality
by David Scott

Colonizing Hawaii: The Cultural Power of Law
by Sally Engle Merry

Local Histories/Global Designs:
Coloniality, Subaltern Knowledges, and Border Thinking
by Walter D. Mignolo